T0073118

"The case for the updated review of project management body of knowledge is well made. Such an update is particularly timely with the emergence of new technologies (like blockchain) and the new skills required to successfully deliver projects with distributed organisations and teams. Professionals from all facets of project management will find this book useful and it should give them new perspectives to thrive in their chosen profession."

Laszlo Peter
Partner, Head of Blockchain Services Asia Pacific
CEO KPMG Origins

"This book provides the latest insights on the effective management of information technology (IT) projects. It illustrates the theory and practice of IT project management using real-world examples and case studies. This book is a valuable addition to the syllabus of any undergraduate or postgraduate course on information technology project management."

Professor Mike Kagioglou
Dean, and PVC Global Development (UK & Europe)
School of Engineering Design & Built Environment
Western Sydney University

"This book is a timely support of the new revolution, labelled as Industry 5.0 in Europe or Society 5.0 in Japan, where the respect to the limits of the planet is equally positioned to human wellbeing. IT fabric enables both and IT project management is decisive for the success."

Professor Simeon Simoff
Dean of Computer, Data and Mathematical Sciences |
Professor of Information Technology
School of Computer, Data and Mathematical Sciences
Western Sydney University

Domain-Specific Bodies of Knowledge in
Project Management – **Volume 2**

Managing Information Technology Projects

Building a Body of Knowledge in IT Project Management

Domain-Specific Bodies of Knowledge in Project Management

Print ISSN: 2811-0889
Online ISSN: 2811-0897

Series Editor: Mohan M Kumaraswamy
 (The University of Hong Kong, Hong Kong)

Published:

Vol. 2 *Managing Information Technology Projects:*
  Building a Body of Knowledge in IT Project Management
  edited by Srinath Perera (Western Sydney University, Australia) and
  Robert Eadie (Ulster University, UK)

Vol. 1 *Building a Body of Knowledge in Construction Project Delivery,*
  Procurement and Contracting
  edited by Giovanni C Migliaccio (University of Washington, USA)
  and Pramen P Shrestha (University of Nevada Las Vegas, USA)

Domain-Specific Bodies of Knowledge in
Project Management – **Volume 2**

Editor-in-Chief: Mohan M Kumaraswamy
The University of Hong Kong, Hong Kong
The University of Moratuwa, Sri Lanka

Managing Information Technology Projects

Building a Body of Knowledge in
IT Project Management

Editors

Srinath Perera
Western Sydney University, Australia

Robert Eadie
Ulster University, UK

World Scientific

NEW JERSEY • LONDON • SINGAPORE • BEIJING • SHANGHAI • HONG KONG • TAIPEI • CHENNAI • TOKYO

Published by

World Scientific Publishing Co. Pte. Ltd.

5 Toh Tuck Link, Singapore 596224

USA office: 27 Warren Street, Suite 401-402, Hackensack, NJ 07601

UK office: 57 Shelton Street, Covent Garden, London WC2H 9HE

Library of Congress Cataloging-in-Publication Data
Names: Perera, Srinath, editor.
Title: Managing information technology projects : building a body of knowledge in
 it project management / editors Srinath Perera, Western Sydney University, Australia,
 Robert Eadie, Ulster University, UK ; editor-in-chief Mohan M. Kumaraswamy,
 The University of Hong Kong, Hong Kong.
Description: Hackensack, NJ : World Scientific, [2023] | Series: Domain-specific bodies of
 knowledge in project management ; volume 2 | Includes bibliographical references.
Identifiers: LCCN 2022048806 | ISBN 9789811240577 (hardcover) |
 ISBN 9789811240584 (ebook for institutions) | ISBN 9789811240591 (ebook for individuals)
Subjects: LCSH: Project management. | Information technology--Management.
Classification: LCC HD69.P75 M327 2023 | DDC 658.4/04--dc23/eng/20221125
LC record available at https://lccn.loc.gov/2022048806

British Library Cataloguing-in-Publication Data
A catalogue record for this book is available from the British Library.

For any available supplementary material, please visit
https://www.worldscientific.com/worldscibooks/10.1142/12377#t=suppl

Desk Editor: Nicole Ong

Typeset by Stallion Press
Email: enquiries@stallionpress.com

About the Editors

Srinath Perera is the Chair Professor of Built Environment and Construction Management, and the founding Director of the Centre for Smart Modern Construction (c4SMC) at Western Sydney University. He joined WSU in June 2016 after serving as a Professor of Construction Economics at Northumbria University, Newcastle, in the UK. He is a Board member and the chair of the Future leaders' committee of the International Council for Research and Innovation in Building and Construction (CIB, www.cibworld.org).

He is a Fellow of the Royal Society of New South Wales (FRSN) and also a Fellow of the Australian Institute of Building (AIB). He is a Chartered Surveyor and a member of the Royal Institution of Chartered Surveyors (RICS), the Australian Institute of Quantity Surveyors (AIQS) and the Australian Institute of Project Management (AIPM). He has over 30 years of experience in academia and industry and has worked as a consultant Quantity Surveyor and Project Manager in the construction industry.

Professor Perera is a pioneer in the field of construction informatics integrating AI technologies into construction and project management. He co-authored a research monograph, "Advances in Construction ICT and e-Business" (2017) and two internationally recognised textbooks "Cost Studies of Buildings" (2015) and "Contractual Procedures in the Construction Industry" (2017) published by Routledge. He has authored over 250 peer-reviewed publications and his current research leads work in the areas of Blockchain and IoT applications in construction, BIM,

Digital Twin, offsite construction, construction business models and construction performance leading to Industry 4.0.

He recently published the Digitalisation of Construction report, indicating the status and future directions of digitalisation of the NSW construction industry. https://www.nsw.gov.au/building-commissioner/how-digital-ready-construction-industry. His current research focuses on blockchain applications in construction and project management, BIM, offsite construction, sustainability and carbon management, construction business models and construction performance leading to Industry 4.0.

Robert Eadie is an Academic Lead for Civil Engineering at Ulster University and a MSc Civil and Infrastructure Engineering Course Director. He is responsible for putting together the first Civil Engineering Apprenticeship to Master's Degree Level in the United Kingdom.

He obtained a PhD related to e-procurement in construction and his research focuses on BIM, e-procurement, digital photography and photogrammetry in construction, project management and pedagogy. As a fellow of Engineers Ireland, he was the Chair of the Northern Region from 2017–2019. Currently, he fulfils the role of immediate past Chair and represents them on the Professional College of Construction Industry Group for Northern Ireland (CIGNI). He holds position in multiple Institutions as: Chartered Committee Member, Fellow of the Chartered Institution of Highways and Transportation in Northern Ireland and a member of the Association for Project Management. Since 2012, he was voted to represent Northern Ireland as the treasurer for the Association of Civil Engineering Departments. He has over eighty peer-reviewed academic publications.

About the Contributors

Samisa Abeysinghe MSc BSc Eng
Institution: Aivnya Foundation
Email: samisa.abeysinghe@gmail.com

Samisa Abeysinghe is a seasoned software engineering leader with over 20 years of experience managing large-scale delivery teams, product management, customer success, and software delivery excellence. He has a proven track record of driving product innovation and delivering successful software products to market. Samisa is passionate about people development and career growth and has a talent for mentoring and coaching team members to reach their full potential. He is a strong leader and effective communicator who can build and lead high-performing teams. Additionally, he has a deep understanding of the software development lifecycle and can drive software delivery excellence throughout the organization.

Kolitha Dassanayake MBA PMP
Email: kolithd@gmail.com

Kolitha Dassanayake is an IT Project/Program manager with over three decades of experience in the successful delivery of large strategic projects and programs in Cloud Enablement, ERP Implementation, Business Intelligence and Data and Analytics. They have delivered across a broad range of domains such as Airlines, Superannuation, Telecommunication, Banking, Insurance and Australian Public Sectors. A variety of Waterfall and Agile project management methodologies was used to deliver these for well-known global and Australian tier 1 organizations, including Emirates Airlines, Hewlett Packard, Telstra, Cbus Super, Virgin Australian Airline, Melbourne Airport, Victoria Education and Training, Victoria Supreme Court, Parks Victoria, National Bank of Australia, and Medibank Private.

Dr Chris D'Souza PhD
Institution: Western Sydney University, Australia
Email: c.d'souza@westernsydney.edu.au

Chris D'Souza (PhD) is an experienced academic. He has taught at Australian and international universities in the Engineering and IS/IT/CSc stream for over 30 years. He did his Bachelor of Electrical Engineering and Master of Information Systems from India and his PhD from Western Sydney University, Australia. In his PhD thesis, he designed and developed an auto-generation tool to help Business Analysts (BAs) develop fully functional applications from requirements specified via wireframes to eliminate communication errors between BAs and developers and to reduce project timelines. He has also worked as a Software Engineer managing projects on web hosting systems.

Professor Temitope Egbelakin PhD MSc (PM) MSc Arch
Institution: University of Newcastle, Australia
Email: t.Egbelakin@newcastle.edu.au

Professor Temitope Egbelakin is a world-class researcher in disaster resilience, project management and sustainable developments. Her research focuses on enabling the resilience of the built environment, communities, and organisations, by creating pathways to improve the resilience and sustainability of buildings and communities at the national and international scales. Temi has led the development and implementation of numerous innovative projects in her areas of expertise. She has published over 100 peer-reviewed publications. The impacts and relevance of her research outcomes are evident through policy interventions, collaborative industry engagements, international collaborations and the uptake and application of her scholarly works.

Professor Athula Ginige PhD
Institution: Western Sydney University, Australia
Email: a.ginige@westernsydney.edu.au

Athula Ginige (PhD) is a highly experienced professor of Information Technology at Western Sydney University in Australia. He is known for his deep thinking, problem-solving abilities, and ability to work effectively across multiple disciplines. He is a pioneer in establishing Web Engineering as a discipline and researching meta-design paradigms. He has developed many large IT systems for businesses and the agriculture sector using meta-design and complementary IT project management approaches to suit emerging system architectural patterns. These tools have been effective in helping organizations to optimize their IT systems and achieve their goals.

Roshana Goonewardene MSc PMP MSP SCM
Email: rsgoonewardene@gmail.com

Roshana Goonewardene (MSc) is a seasoned Project Management professional with deep experience delivering multi-million-dollar enterprise-wide technology and business transformation programs that realise strategic, commercial and customer-centric outcomes. Agile, PMP, MSP and Prince II qualified, Roshana has successfully led complex application development, data analytics, systems integration, and IT infrastructure programs within complex and rapidly changing environments. He has strength in establishing PMO and governance frameworks that are aligned with strategic intent across diverse sectors such as Retail, FMCG, Financial Services, Insurance and Consulting.

Geetha Gopal MSc (Oxon) PMP EMBA BE
Institution: Panasonic Asia Pacific
Email: geetha.gopal.mmpm18@said.oxford.edu

Geetha, a PMI Future 50 awardee, is an accomplished senior management professional based in Singapore. She holds a masters degree from Oxford, specialising in Major Programme Management. She is currently heading Infrastructure Projects Delivery and Digital Transformation for Panasonic Asia Pacific. Previously, she worked on emerging technologies for the

Automotive giant, Daimler. She is a passionate public speaker who speaks on various topics like digital transformation, trends in technology, IT infrastructure, project management, Diversity, Equity, and Inclusion (DEI), and self-development, to name a few.

Dr Steffen Heinig PhD PGCert FHEA MSc

Institution: Liverpool John Moores University, UK
Email: s.Heinig@ljmu.ac.uk

Dr Steffen Heinig oversees the property section as a principal lecturer at Liverpool John Moores University. Having a solid real estate background, both practically and academically, he teaches Real Estate Investment and Management. His research interests lie in the field of Sentiment Analysis and Housing. Besides his academic experience, Steffen has worked in the German real estate industry for some time. He led and participated in different IT projects during his years as a Senior Data Scientist for a national real estate investor. This experience has helped him to understand the differences between traditional and modern project management approaches.

Madhawa Herath BSc (Eng) Hons MBA CEng PMP CLSSGB MIEEE

Institution: Sri Lanka Institute of Information Technology
Email: madhawa.h@sliit.lk

Madhawa is a Doctoral Researcher at the Faculty of Engineering, Sri Lanka Institute of Information Technology (SLIIT), and his PhD research is focused on the use of Artificial Intelligence and Deep Learning for the conservation of domestic energy use. Madhawa has served several multinational companies in the capacity of Head of Projects and Head of Corporate Solutions counting more than 17 years of experience in industry and academia. Currently, he is a Senior Lecturer at SLIIT and also serving the industry as a project management consultant. Madhawa is the founder of Globel Eye International (Private) Limited and edXcope online institute.

Manmeet Kaur PMP CPPD P3O
Institution: Transport for NSW (previously Western Sydney University)
Email: mkaur13@hotmail.com

Successful track record in leading and managing strategic and transformation programs and projects in a broad range of industries including ICT, Transport, Higher Education, Health and Financial Services. Manmeet's leadership and consultative style is underpinned by extensive experience working collaboratively alongside a diverse range of stakeholders to help deliver a positive impact for customers and communities. Very proficient in implementing PMO best practices and contemporary methods to enhance an organisation's agility and capabilities to successfully perform in a rapidly changing, dynamic and complex environment. Manmeet is passionate about sharing her knowledge and skills to empower others to succeed.

Associate Professor Malik Khalfan PhD
Institution: RMIT University, Australia. Khalifa University, Abu Dhabi.
Email: malik.khalfan@rmit.edu.au

Malik Khalfan is an Associate Professor with more than 20 years of research, teaching, consultancy, agile practice, and construction industry experience by working in the UK, Hong Kong, Vietnam, Pakistan, Australia, Singapore, and the UAE. He has published more than 150 papers in refereed journals and conference proceedings. He has ScrumMaster-certified qualifications from Scrum Alliance, Scaled Agile and Disciplined Agile. He is one of the leading researchers in the area of Circular Economy within Australian and UAE construction industries.

Professor Mohan Kumaraswamy DSc PhD MSc Construction Management BSc Eng
CEng FICE FIESL FCIOB FHKIE FHKICM MASCE MIEAus APEC Eng IntPE(Aus) MCIArb
Institution: Honorary Professor, The University of Hong Kong, Hong Kong; Honorary Professor, University of Moratuwa, Sri Lanka
Email: mohan@hku.hk

Mohan worked on designs, construction, project management and led World Bank and UNDP funded consultancies before joining academia. He was at the University of Hong Kong for 21 years from 1992. He now advises on research and development and co-supervises PhD research in Hong Kong and Sri Lanka. Mohan is also an Adjudicator and Arbitrator. Having been active in professional institutions in Sri Lanka and Hong Kong, he is active in industry-link bodies e.g., CIB Working Commission on PPP. Mohan is Editor-in-Chief of the BEPAM journal and also of this Book Series on Domain-Specific Bodies of Knowledge in Project Management.

Professor Tayyab Maqsood PhD
Institution: RMIT University, Australia
Email: tayyab.maqsood@rmit.edu.au

Tayyab Maqsood received his PhD in the area of Project Management from RMIT University in 2006 specialising in Knowledge Management, Organisational Learning and Innovation. He is a recognised expert in this area and has widely published and presented internationally. He has used his knowledge and experience to solve issues about supply chain management and knowledge management in the construction industry in Australia.

Eng. Samudaya Nanayakkara PhD (Eng.) MSc (CS) BSc Eng. (Hons) BIT CEng (Computer)
Institution: University of Moratuwa, Sri Lanka
Email: samudaya@uom.lk

Eng. Samudaya Nanayakkara is currently serving as a Senior Lecturer at the University of Moratuwa, Sri Lanka. He completed his PhD in 2022 at

Western Sydney University, Australia. He gained his Master of Computer Science and BSc Engineering (Honours) degrees from the University of Moratuwa and a Bachelor of Information Technology degree from the University of Colombo. He obtained his Chartered Engineer status for computer discipline in 2012. He has contributed to over 30 large-scale IT projects. Recognizing his contribution to the Engineering profession, research and academia, he was bestowed with several national and international awards, including the Young Chartered Engineer Award 2013.

Ananth Natarajan BSME MSME MBA MSc (Oxon) PE (Professional Engineer) PMP CEng (Chartered Engineer, IMechE)
Institution: cybereum
Email: ananth.natarajan@cybereum.io

Ananth is an experienced project manager on complex global EPC projects with over 20 years of experience in R&D, product development, systems engineering, and project management. He holds patents in offshore wind and blockchain technology. He holds BEng & MS degrees in Mechanical Engineering, an MBA from IESE, and an MSc in Major Programme Management from the University of Oxford. He is a professional engineer (PE), project management professional (PMP), and Chartered Engineer (CEng). He is currently engaged in building cybereum, a project governance platform that incorporates blockchain technology for collective planning and AI/ML for forecasting and risk management.

Pearl Li Ng MEng
Institution: RMIT University, Australia
Email: s3817516@student.rmit.edu.au

Pearl Li Ng is a digital transformation specialist with eight years of industry experience in top-tier consulting firms. She has a successful track record of helping her clients drive sustainable change through emerging technologies. She is currently pursuing her PhD at RMIT University, with her research interests centring around agile management and construction management. She holds a Master of Engineering and Business from the University of Melbourne.

Dr Olabode E. Ogunmakinde PhD
Institution: Bond University, Gold Coast, Australia
Email: bogunmak@bond.edu.au

Olabode Ogunmakinde is a construction/project management researcher in his early career. In 2019, he received his PhD from the University of Newcastle, Australia. Olabode has published several papers in prestigious journals, and his work has been widely cited by other researchers in his field. He has also received research grants and awards, including Bond University's VC ECR Award in 2022. In addition to his research, Olabode is an enthusiastic teacher and mentor to undergraduate and graduate students, actively working to inspire the next generation of construction/project managers.

Dr Omoleye Ojuri PhD MPhil BSc FHEA
Institution: Liverpool John Moores University, UK
Email: o.b.ojuri@ljmu.ac.uk

Omoleye Ojuri is Senior Lecturer in Quantity Surveying at Liverpool John Moores University and a Fellow of the Higher Education Academy. She studied for her PhD at the University College London's Bartlett School of Construction and Project Management where she developed a framework on social value creation from stakeholder engagement in the construction projects. Omoleye has published several articles in the area of construction cost, transaction cost and more recently in social value creation in construction projects. She is interested in contributing to the development of infrastructure projects to deliver society support "placemaking" and well-being, not purely for economic profit.

John Pereira BSc IT (Hons)
Institution: Rentman B.V.
Email: john@jnx.me

John Pereira is a technology enthusiast who is passionate about his work and all forms of technology. With over 15 years in the technology space, his area of expertise lies in API and large-scale web application development, and its related constellation of technologies and processes. His sporadic writing can be found at http://randomcoding.com.

Prasad Perera MBA (PM) BSc (CS) BIT
Institution: Western Sydney University, Australia
Email: prasad.perera@westernsydney.edu.au

Prasad is a Doctoral Researcher at the Centre for Smart Modern Construction (c4SMC), School of Engineering, Design and Built Environment, Western Sydney University. His PhD research is focused on the use of Artificial Intelligence and Deep Learning for Construction Compliance.

Prasad has served the industry for 15 years and his academic engagements include serving as a visiting lecturer for universities in Sri Lanka, UK, Australia, Thailand, and Malaysia. He started his career as a software engineer and has served and contributed as a capacity-building consultant and a project manager in many notable projects in diverse business domains funded by international donor agencies.

Ian Sharpe FAIPM CPPD ChPP IPMA-A 4-DM PMP
Institution: Bydand Consulting
Contact: https://www.linkedin.com/in/isharpe/

Ian is an internationally respected leader in the Project Management Industry and has worked with a range of global organisations on their critical initiatives — including establishing and maturing global practices, frameworks and capability on project, program and portfolio management. He has over 23 years of experience in helping clients deliver real value from their key investments across multiple sectors including Utilities, Mining, Government, Aerospace and Astronautics, Security and Education.

In 2020 he was awarded a medal for Services to the Community and Project Management, from His Excellency General the Honourable David Hurley C DSC (Retd), Governor-General of the Commonwealth of Australia.

Peter Tow M Econ BE Env DipPM FIEAust CPEng NPER FAIPM CPPD
Institution: Western Sydney University, Australia
Email: peter.tow@gmail.com

Peter is an experienced executive leader with over 20 years of engineering and project management experience. Peter has studied engineering, economics, and project management, and has worked across a range of industries, including infrastructure, transport, construction, oil & gas, mining, and the higher education sector. Peter has established and led numerous PMOs and has led major strategic and digital transformation programs of work from planning through to delivery. Peter is highly versatile with global experience in countries such as UAE, Oman, Chile, Brunei, Afghanistan, and Pakistan.

G. Thilini Weerasuriya BSc MIT (Special)
Institution: Western Sydney University, Australia
Email: t.weerasuriya@westernsydney.edu.au

Thilini Weerasuriya is a Doctoral Research Candidate at the Centre for Smart Modern Construction (c4SMC), Western Sydney University. Her PhD research aims to develop a blockchain-based framework to ensure compliance in the built environment through trusted and traceable certification of the quality and progress of construction work and its related payments. Thilini graduated with First Class Honours in the B.Sc. (Special) Degree in Management and Information Technology from the University of Kelaniya, Sri Lanka. She served as a Lecturer (Probationary) at the Faculty of Information Technology, University of Moratuwa, Sri Lanka prior to joining Western Sydney University.

Dr Indrajit Wijegunaratne BSc (Hons) Essex, MSc PhD (London)
Email: injiwije@gmail.com

Inji Wijegunaratne has over 30 years of experience in IT with consulting and systems integration houses such as Unisys, Deloitte, IBM, Capgemini, and Infosys in the UK and Australia. He specialises in enterprise architecture and IT architecture management and has experience across several large IT and business transformation programs. He anchored Blockchain in the Australian New Zealand region for two and a half years for a large system integrator and currently advises a Blockchain company on business and operation modelling for Blockchain systems. He holds Masters' and Doctoral degrees from the University of London. He has published several papers on enterprise architecture and has co-authored a book entitled "Enterprise Architecture for Business Success".

Foreword

It gives me a great pleasure to write a foreword to this book on Managing Information Technology Projects. This book is extremely topical and timely. Information Technology (IT) is an indispensable component of the world today, continuously supporting and influencing human activities. Effective project management is essential to deliver IT projects that meet their defined scope, on time, and within budget. The unique and fast-evolving nature of IT presents numerous challenges, which IT project managers should understand, identify, and mitigate. However, the IT industry has a comparatively high level of unsuccessful projects.

This book presents a body of knowledge on IT Project Management to enhance the successful delivery of projects. The book examines the project lifecycle and compares IT project management methodologies. It provides guidance on the selection of appropriate processes by a review of software delivery life cycle models. The book gives an outlook on roles and responsibilities of IT project team members and stakeholders, including a case study on stakeholder management within a complex project. The critical elements of the iron triangle are examined in chapters dedicated to time and cost management, quality management, and risk management. The book also contains an analysis of case studies of large IT projects to distinguish their success and failure factors, present a capability framework for large IT projects, and draw lessons from the construction industry for areas of improvement. New software for IT project schedule, cost, and quality management are reviewed within the book and criteria to select the most appropriate software are presented. Finally, the book identifies the impact of new technologies on project management and envisions the future of IT project management. Therefore this book is highly recommended for IT project management practitioners of all levels of experience, from students to seasoned experts, to acquire new and valuable knowledge on the state-of-the-art of IT project management.

Professor Ghassan Aouad
Chancellor of Abu Dhabi University in the United Arab Emirates
Former President of Applied Science University, Bahrain
Past President of the Chartered Institute of Building (CIOB)

Contents

https://doi.org/10.1142/9789811240584_0001

Chapter 1

Managing IT Projects: The Case for Consolidating and Developing a Body of Knowledge

Srinath Perera*, Robert Eadie[†,¶], Mohan Kumaraswamy[‡,‖],
Samudaya Nanayakkara[§,**], and G. Thilini Weerasuriya[*,††]

Centre for Smart Modern Construction,
Western Sydney University, Locked Bag 1797, Penrith,
New South Wales 2751, Australia
[†]*Ulster University, School of the Built Environment,*
Belfast Campus, Northern Ireland
[‡]*Department of Civil Engineering,*
The University of Hong Kong, Hong Kong
srinath.perera@westernsydney.edu.au
[§]*University of Moratuwa, Sri Lanka*
[¶]*r.eadie@ulster.ac.uk*
[‖]*mohan@hku.hk*
[**]*samudaya@uom.lk*
[††]*t.weerasuriya@westernsydney.edu.au*

1

1. Background

Effective and efficient Project Management (PM) is vital to delivering successful Information Technology (IT) projects. This requires a sound knowledge of management processes that deliver successful projects. Historically, IT projects have a reputation for higher failure rates, resulting in billions of dollars of financial losses. Like any other project, IT projects do follow the typical project lifecycle and need to be executed as projects. But the particular context and special nature of these projects must be carefully factored in by a successful IT project manager. IT projects are often special because these deal with technologies often with a short shelf life, cut across many and seemingly unknown or unanticipated stakeholders, have multiple dependencies on other projects, and are often rapidly executed with a vague initial scope. It is, therefore, important and timely to develop a body of knowledge on IT PM that would help project managers to understand and improve their present practices. This book aims to initiate the development of this special body of knowledge in IT PM, also learning from relevant experiences from other sectors, such as construction, where PM is well established and successfully practised.

This book is designed to be of value to practitioners at all levels of IT PM, e.g., elevating the knowledge of novices' current best practice levels, while providing pointers to experienced practitioners on areas for potential improvement, based on a wider array of lessons learned. Needless to say, the book will also provide students, researchers and other academics with important insights into how best to appreciate and apply, as well as to adapt and develop relevant principles of PM in IT project scenarios.

2. Defining the discipline of IT PM

PM safeguards the success of the project by systemising the process and therefore increasing the project's added value. IT PM is different from general PM in more developed disciplines due to many systematic procedures, which were already developed with IT in mind, being little used. The organisation's governance criteria, IT business process transformation, business system change, IT system change, IT system integration and the IT infrastructure itself are all parts of IT PM that need to be carefully managed to deliver the best value for the client.

PM is all about creation or change and project managers are the change managers of the industry. To achieve this, the Iron Triangle of Time, Cost and Scope is put into practice. Each of these elements is maximised to achieve the best value for management.

The resources that are managed have similarities and differences in IT compared to other disciplines. For example, staff time and staff costs are similar, but the scope of the projects are very different. Plant and materials are applicable to construction in terms of resources, but IT differs. In terms of plant, the processing power, and capacities of the computer being worked on in IT PM could be counted as analogous. However, there is little by way of similarity in terms of scope.

IT PM differs internally between the manufacturing element and the programming elements. For example, in the manufacturing of IT systems, the PM element is to ensure mass production of the system with minimum unit cost and maximum output. However, the software element is normally a service on a unique program. This is similar to construction where the projects are all unique. However, it differs a lot in terms of location, as construction projects are built on site and this changes for each project. Plans and specifications differ between the two industries.

IT PM programming and system redesign differ from manufacturing as well in terms of personnel changes. Software projects tend to be awarded through a tendering process at short notice, meaning planning lead in time is limited and volumes of workload vary greater over short spaces of time. These changes have major impacts on Human Resource planning. Team sizes and turnover are impacted by the tender process.

This is further exacerbated in other industries such as construction. The flexibility in IT, logging in remotely and allowing access through the internet is in complete contrast to construction. Construction, with its variety of locations, tends to depend on a transient workforce and to service one-off sites in different locations. This leads to travel expenses and different phases of a project having a different workforce, whereas in IT, those who take a project on normally see it through to completion.

All these issues cause different IT PM issues. Therefore, embedding continuous improvement into the processes, as described within this book is vital to project success. Frameworks such as PRINCE, the Critical Path method and others ensure project success is enabled. However, as shown throughout this book, much of IT works on an *ad hoc* basis, which unfortunately has resulted in cost and time overruns.

Compared to many sectors, the IT industry can be categorised as one with a high percentage of unsuccessful projects. The time, cost and scope performance of IT projects clearly illustrate the level of unsuccessfulness. According to the Panorama Consulting Solutions (2020) report, 47% of enterprise system projects were time overrun, and 38% were cost overrun. Projects which overran cost had around 66% budget overrun issues. According to the report, benefits realisation was less than 70%. According to these three parameters, the level of project success in the IT sector can be gauged.

The common reasons behind IT project failures include no clear, finalised scope for the project; frequent changes in project scope; budgeting and scheduling mainly depend on expert opinions; scarcity of methodologies to estimate time and cost; comparatively challenging to manage the quality of work produced by individuals; largely intangible outcomes for IT projects; and the client or end users cannot assess the finished product until the end of the project. Novel software development methodologies such as Agile approaches attempt to mitigate some of these challenges. However, either traditional software approaches such as Waterfall, V-model, Spiral model, and Fish model or Agile approaches such as Scrum, Extreme Programming (XP), Rapid-Application Development (RAD), and Feature-Driven Development (FDD) could not successfully solve these issues completely.

However, most IT PM methodologies mainly focus on the software development life cycle management and focus less on well-established PM knowledge bases such as the Project Management Body of Knowledge (PMBOK). Therefore, this book focuses on harvesting PM knowledge from well-established methods and other industries and enhancing the Body of Knowledge of IT Projects.

3. Framework and building blocks of the body of knowledge on managing IT projects

Section 1 quite rightly and neatly conveys the rationale for this book, along with its 'Background'. To place the book in context, it is useful to step back to the underlying rationale for the 'Book Series' itself, hence in a way to the 'Background to the Background'. To convey this succinctly, one can do no better than draw on the essence of what is conveyed in the introduction to the book series on *Domain-Specific Bodies of Knowledge in Project Management* (Ofori, 2021): "The science and art of Project Management in many specific domains, such as Public Private Partnership (PPP), have moved beyond generic principles and practices. It is therefore timely to capture and consolidate specialist bodies of project management knowledge that have proliferated and grown in hitherto unstructured modes within specific domains, such as those of megaproject management, project management in developing countries, and the management of Information and Communication Technology (ICT) projects."

As also conveyed: "Each book in this series aims to identify and focus on current and emerging issues in a particular domain by developing insightful and proactive ways forward. In the long term, this would enable the development and deployment of a domain-centred, if not domain-focused Body of Knowledge that is more directly applicable to the context and priorities of that domain, making it more effective and efficient. These domain-focused frameworks, building blocks, guides and toolkits, together with the adapted core common knowledge components, would help focus the minds and therefore the approaches of Project Management researchers and practitioners, enabling them to formulate optimal domain-specific strategies ..."

An overview of the structure and contents of this book on *Managing Information Technology Projects* as presented in the following section shows that such a well-focused framework and building blocks have clearly been provided to inform and inspire cutting-edge researchers and leading-edge practitioners in IT PM. Valuable examples of guides, tips and tools have also been provided in specific sub-areas. It is expected that these would accelerate and empower the growth of knowledge, including of widely, if not universally, acceptable core principles and best practices in this increasingly vital domain. Indeed, the IT domain, along with its almost synonymous 'digital' ecosystem, has expanded exponentially to help deal with 'new normal' imperatives such as working from home, virtual conferencing and online transactions with necessary security provisions. What seemed sorely needed is to capture, consolidate and build on the emerging knowledge. This is what this book aspires to achieve and you, our readers, are invited to let us know if the book's aspirations were achieved, e.g., to help in generating more good ideas and even better innovations, which in turn lead to breakthrough solutions and more successful IT projects.

4. Structure of the book

The book is structured into four distinct parts in addition to the Introduction and Conclusion chapters. These are as follows:

(1) PM Methodologies for IT Projects
(2) IT PM Teams and Stakeholders
(3) Critical Managerial Elements in the Iron Triangle
(4) New and Innovative Technologies and Software for Improved PM

Part 1 provides an understanding of PM methodologies, examines the context of IT projects, and compares and contrasts traditional and agile approaches to the management of IT projects (Chapters 2–4).

Building the correct team for IT projects is vital to the success of the project and considered essential for project leaders. Part 2 elaborates on the roles and responsibilities of IT project stakeholders, IT project teams, and especially IT project managers to ensure project success (Chapters 5–7). It also presents a case study to illustrate the approaches, challenges, and stakeholder involvement in delivering an IT project (Chapter 8).

Part 3 delves into a project from the perspective of the Iron Triangle, sometimes known as the Triple Constraint of Time, Cost and Quality. Project time and cost management, quality management, risk management are covered in depth within Part 3 (Chapters 9–11). Furthermore, critical factors affecting the success or failure of large IT projects are analysed through multiple case studies, while also drawing lessons from PM in the construction sector as a more mature industry (Chapters 12 and 13).

Lastly, Part 4 discusses various software available for IT PM in terms of schedule, cost, and quality (Chapters 14 and 15). It further provides insight into the future developments of IT PM (Chapter 16).

The chapters in the book are briefly introduced in the following paragraphs.

Chapter 1 introduces the concepts in the book by defining PM and the discipline of IT PM and illustrates the difference between IT projects and other types of projects. It also contextualises the book in the global series on *Domain-Specific Bodies of Knowledge in Project Management* (Ofori, 2021).

Chapter 2 discusses the PM body of knowledge including the project life cycle, project hierarchy and organisational structures, and knowledge areas. It also presents the principles of several prevalent PM methodologies along with a comparison of the methodologies.

Chapter 3 defines and describes IT projects, highlights the evolution of IT PM, examines project constraints and successful approaches for IT evolution. It also looks into procurement methodologies, financing approaches for IT projects, and new trends related to data and IT operations.

Chapter 4 showcases the management approaches of IT projects with a focus on software development projects. Software delivery life cycle models such as the waterfall, spiral, scrum, extreme programming, and hybrid models are reviewed with an aim to guide the selection of the correct processes to effectively manage IT projects. The chapter provides an analysis of the advantages, disadvantages, and criteria for the adoption of each of the models.

Chapter 5 discusses the various stakeholders in an IT project and examines the roles and responsibilities of these stakeholders within different software development methodologies.

Chapter 6 presents the duties, skills, and expected qualifications of different IT project team members in traditional and agile working environments. It also provides an analysis of the current annual income for the roles in different countries.

Chapter 7 highlights the role of the IT project manager in ensuring the successful delivery of IT projects. It further describes the success and failure factors of IT projects and key performance indicators to measure the effectiveness of IT PM.

Chapter 8 is dedicated to a real-world case study on the delivery of an enterprise service management project. It brings to light the challenges related to stakeholder management in a complex project and the approaches and capabilities to successfully fulfil the requirements of the project.

Chapter 9 examines concepts and issues related to time and cost management of IT projects, including various models for estimation and measurement of project performance.

Chapter 10 delves into the theory and practice of IT project quality management by providing definitions, models, standards, and measures for IT project quality. The business impact and cost of quality management and related issues and challenges are discussed in the chapter. It also provides an overview of roles and tools for quality management.

Chapter 11 discusses the risk factors in IT projects and the need for risk management. It reviews risk management methodologies, approaches, and tools, and proposes best practices and recommendations for risk management.

Chapter 12 analyses 10 case studies of large IT projects to identify factors that influence their success or failure. The chapter then proposes a generalised capability framework to be used in the planning stage of large IT projects.

Chapter 13 compares and contrasts the success and failure factors described in the previous chapter with equivalent programs of work in the construction industry. It draws lessons from construction to propose areas for improvement for large IT projects.

Chapter 14 reviews prevalent software applications used for project schedule and cost management. The key features which would influence the selection of the software are presented in the chapter along with a comparison of the software applications.

Chapter 15 examines a large selection of software applications for IT project quality management. It introduces the supporting technologies, features, and limitations of tools for process, structural, and functional quality management. It also presents the quality management processes applicable to the various phases of the software development life cycle.

Chapter 16 highlights the evolution of IT PM, IT systems, and applications, and recommends a futuristic IT PM framework that evolves as technology advances.

Chapter 17 concludes the book by analysing the key themes discussed within the chapters and presenting the developments in IT PM. It presents the impact of technologies on PM and a vision for the future of IT PM.

References

Ofori, G. (2021). Domain-Specific Bodies Of Knowledge In Project Management. In *Building a Body of Knowledge in Project Management in Developing Countries*. Singapore: World Scientific Publishing Co. Pte. Ltd. Available at: https://www.worldscientific.com/series/dsbkpm (Accessed 16 December 2021).

Panorama Consulting Solutions. (2020). The 2020 ERP Report. Greenwood Village, USA.

Chapter 2

Overview of Generic Project Management Methodologies, Frameworks, and Standards

Madhawa Herath*,‡ and Prasad Perera†,§

*Sri Lanka Institute of Information Technology, Sri Lanka
†Centre for Smart Modern Construction,
Western Sydney University, Australia
‡madhawa.h@sliit.lk
§perera.prasad@gmail.com

A guide to 'Project Management' has been presented with the aim of providing a firm guarantee regarding the on-time delivery of projects, allowing an individual to achieve all the specifications within a scheduled budget plan. Using proper methodology reduces risks because it guides the management team along with life cycle phases pertaining to maintenance. Managers often prefer a specific project methodology or framework and face resistance and difficulties in managing different projects or other projects with a framework. This is due to a lack of awareness of the similarity between their preferences and the new required methodology. Use this knowledge wisely by gaining an understanding of the different dynamics of methods of project management for managers and their organizations, combining different power components or knowing the similarities with competitors to enhance their overall performance. All types of project methodologies can be divided into traditional and modern approaches. Hence, various approaches that can be used in different types of project management are presented.

1. Introduction

To ensure the smooth functioning of the organization, it is necessary to administrate different types of projects which hand over extensible deliverables. Considering the usability of projects, the management of a project is necessary to achieve deliverables with processes applied, knowledge, and skills. This process is defined as project management (Project Management Institute, 2018). A generic overview of project management is that it consists of regular stages such as planning, executing, monitoring, and closing. But, with evolving methodologies, these steps can be changed without removing them. Different types of project management methodologies are used by organizations when managing a project by ensuring a reduction in the scope-creep or exceeding the budget and estimated time. These processes can be further divided into ten knowledge areas for guaranteeing the successful management of the project.

In this chapter, some common project management frameworks and methodologies that are defined in PMBOK are discussed along with detailed justifications regarding methodologies and frameworks as well as the relationship between them (Visual Paradigm, 2021).

2. Project management framework vs methodology

Almost all organizations have different achievements to be completed with specific aims, which fall under the purview of the project, and these projects have a series of processes that can be produced, depending on the inputs and some processes.

It is necessary to achieve project purposes and objectives by planning and organizing allocated resources. This is known as project management.

Without proper management of the project, various difficulties might be presented, such as overrunning the budget, having an elastic scope or delay in the time scope and limited resources, or not enough resource forecasting. Considering the framework and methodologies, proper project management methodologies and frameworks provide a highly competitive ecosystem for rapid changes that may arise due to external and internal environment (Kissflow Inc, 2021).

2.1. *Project management framework*

The project management framework can be justified as a list of tasks and processes which are used to give direction and structure. This involves helping organizations to notice or report the phases of each project from start to end. Projects can be guided by frameworks to achieve specific targets by providing more flexible conditions. The project management framework provides a concise and non-specific infrastructure to achieve outstanding project goals. The project management framework can be divided into three components: control cycles with management and monitoring functions, tools for providing a structured framework, and project life cycle, which defines the milestones or aims.

2.2. *Project management methodology*

Project management methodologies are justified as the terms and rules which are used to manage the projects by proceeding in stages through well defined processes. This provides a more detailed road map regarding the stages and processes which are used to conclude the projects successfully. This normally consists of a list of processes, principles, activities, and other specific deliverables.

By using these project management methodologies, team members can systematically plan, implement, deliver, and maintain the project until

Table 1. Comparison between project management framework and methodology.

Framework	Methodology
Mostly used by experts.	Beginners can also use this.
Includes related tools and procedures.	Does not include any practice or tool.
Gives comprehensive overview regarding implementation of rules and guidelines.	Provides strict rules and activities to successfully complete a project.
Allows changes and is adaptable.	Methodology is prescriptive and cannot change with the scenario.
It can be tough to implement performance metrics.	Describes all guidelines and practices in more detail at a micro level.

it is successful. Table 1 compares the project management framework and methodology.

3. Introduction to PMBOK

PMBOK stands for Project Management Body of Knowledge, and it consists of processes, practices, and guidelines which contain project management standards.

Companies will be able to standardize these practices among each department according to the specific needs as well as defend from project failures through the use of this framework. PMBOK provides an industrial framework that incorporates the best practices in project management.

The PMBOK Guide is a book with comprehensive instructions containing basic standards, guidelines, and terminology to help industry professionals manage various projects. The book has separated project management processes into five PMBOK process groups, which can be incorporated into the project scheme of your choice. The PMBOK framework consists of five process groups in its life cycle, ten knowledge areas, and 47 project management (PM) processes.

3.1. *Project life cycle*

Figure 1 illustrates the different phases in a project life cycle.

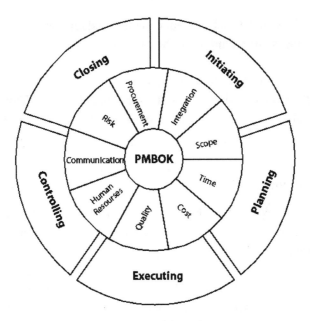

Figure 1.   Project life cycle.

3.1.1. *Initiating*

The initial process stage is inclusive of all the processes, key activities, and critical skills which define the start of a project. The preparation for all licenses, permits, and start-up work orders for starting the project activities and effective and logical progress defines the stage for the ultimate success at all project stages. Normally, the tasks that should be performed in the initiating stage include the following:

- Identification and planning of the vision of what is to be accomplished, and identification of scope of the project.
- Paying attention to the strategic objectives of the organization, i.e., whether the project is properly aligned with a well-planned goal or objective.

3.1.2. *Planning*

This action stage addresses a broader scope for all project objectives and aspirations, and prepares the project infrastructure required to achieve those objectives in a timely manner, within budget constraints. The following key tasks are including in the planning stage:

- Establishing the full scope of the project.
- Developing project documents at a more detailed level. This is termed progressive expansion, which is an active and more detailed design process.

3.1.3. *Executing*

This stage involves guiding the team in adhering to the timeline expectations and managing teams effectively while reaching benchmarks.

This stage involves the following tasks:

- Team-building exercises can be used to develop close-knit teams.
- Project Management involves not only managing communications but also management of stakeholder engagement, further guaranteeing project and product quality.
- For procurement related activities, the team assists in attempting to enter into an agreement with a merchant.

3.1.4. *Monitoring and controlling*

Making change orders, discussing remaining budget concerns, and reducing unexpected conditions affecting a team's capability to reach the start-up project goals can be defined as a part of the core skills and competencies in the monitoring stage. This includes the following tasks:

- Identifying areas that require planning and initiating consistent changes.
- Continuous monitoring where the project follows a predefined plan where the variances can be traced through the actual values in order to take relevant corrective decisions and actions.

3.1.5. *Closing*

The final defined process stages are not essentially easy to implement. Further, not doing so could result in the team possibly never achieving the complete outcomes of their highly strategic project objectives. This stage has the following aims:

- This stage formally closes the project, getting client withdrawal and acceptance.
- The project manager should formally close the project by documenting, conducting a lesson study session, making final payments, concluding contracts, and releasing the team after a celebration.
- Lessons learned and the other key experiences gained should be centrally conserved for use as inputs for future projects in order to prevent the wheel from being redesigned.

3.2. *Project hierarchy and organizational structures*

The organizational structure is a system that governs the hierarchy of people, their activities, workflow, and the reporting system. It can be defined as the enterprise that drives how an organization conducts its operations. A well-defined structure can understand its potential and can achieve required objectives in an optimal manner. The type of structure depends on governance style, leadership style, workflow, hierarchy, and many more factors. The PMBOK Guide defines eight organizational structures, which can be described as given below (Twproject Staff, 2019).

3.2.1. *Organic or simple organization*

This is the modest organizational structure which could be composed only of one employee, such as a freelancer. The role of the project manager is partly covered by the entrepreneur or professional.

3.2.2. *Functional or centralized organization*

This structure is more commonly used. Here, employees with the same skill sets are grouped together, and the organization is divided into various departments. This is the formation in which the staff is structured in divisions and departments.

3.2.3. *Multi-divisional organization*

Here, each division consists of human resources with different skill sets related to the same product or service, and those divisions have the resources needed to undertake the task autonomously.

3.2.4. *Matrix organization*

This organization structure is a mixture of functional organization and project-oriented organization. There are two main structures called vertical and horizontal, where employees can be part of a functional group and also work on a project. A matrix organization consists of the following three types.

1. **Strong matrix** — Strong organizations are similar to project-oriented organizations where the project manager is given more power and a full-time team.
2. **Weak matrix** — Weak matrix organizations are similar to functional structures. Therefore, the project manager may have less authority, minimum budget control, and often controls a part-time project team.
3. **Balanced matrix** — Balanced matrix organizations combine the qualities of both strong and weak matrix types. In this case, the project manager is given mid-level authority including a part-time team, and the budget is managed by the project manager.

3.2.5. *Project-oriented (hybrid or composite) organization*

This organizational structure takes on all the jobs as a project. In this case, the project manager is given full authority to complete the project, has a full-time role, budget control, and a full-time team.

3.2.6. *Virtual organization*

This structure is also known as virtual work environment. It permits the organization to work coherently. In a virtual structure, the organization maintains its core business and outsources the rest of the process. The project manager has less central authority and has mixed authority over the budget.

3.2.7. *Hybrid*

A hybrid organization is an amalgamation of the abovementioned structure types. Depending on the structure, the level of responsibility, authority, and other factors can be varied.

3.2.8. *Project Management Office (PMO)*

The PMO is also a combination of organizational structures; however, in this case, the project manager is given the highest authority, controls the budget, and has a team.

3.3. *Ten knowledge areas of PMBOK*

When considering the PMBOK (**P**roject **M**anagement **B**ody of **K**nowledge), it contains terms and guidelines for the management of projects, which are published and managed by the Project management institute (PMI). Those knowledge areas mainly involve five different aspects known as **Process groups** of project management (PMBOK Guide, 2001). They can be described as follows:

- **Project initiation** — The starting stage of the project identifies the main stakeholders of the project and creates a project initializing report, which is referred to throughout the following phases.
- **Project planning** — The second stage involves implementing the infrastructure of the project. Here, managers create the project plan, the scope of the project, work breakdown structure (WBS), etc.
- **Project execution** — The third stage involves executing the project as per the planned data in the planning stage. Project deliverables are

developed at this stage based on allocated time scope, resources, etc., by going through the ten knowledge areas.

- **Project monitoring and controlling** — The fourth stage involves the actual progress, the planned progress, and resources.
- **Project closing** — This final stage of the process group has some sub-processes such as completing the project records, delivering the project, and acknowledging the project management procedure.

With respect to the project process groups mentioned above, the ten knowledge areas are detailed below.

3.3.1. *Project integration management*

Here, the project management plan is created, and it is used to shift the initiation stage to the planning stage by providing details regarding the project direction, project data, resources, etc. Then, the progress of the project can be tracked during the monitoring and controlling stage. Project integration management ends with the project closing phase where the handing over the project is also included in the processes.

3.3.2. *Project scope management*

This knowledge area is mainly focused on implementing the scope of the project. The scope also helps to execute and achieve project goals. Here, the scope management is planned, and requirements of the project are gathered and analyzed by defining goals and making diagrams. Then, the scope needs to be validated and controlled.

3.3.3. *Project schedule management*

This mainly focuses on managing the time frames for the project. This includes the planning of the schedule. Then, activities must be defined for the successful completion of the project by using the work breakdown structure. Afterward, the schedule must be estimated by considering the resources, requirements, and skills of team members. Finally, the monitoring and controlling stage is implemented, which falls under the process groups.

3.3.4. *Project cost management*

First, it is necessary to make a cost management plan by considering budgets, change control criteria, and procedures. Then, an estimation of the cost for each task of the project should be performed. The cost should be monitored by going through the monitoring and controlling phase, and a budget should be generated at the conclusion of this by ensuring the actual expenses coincide with the estimated cost.

3.3.5. *Project quality management*

First, quality management should be planned by considering details of the quality of products or services.

Then, the quality of the project should be managed and monitored by ensuring the quality of the product and its attributes along with the end customer expectations. Only then can it be handed over as a good-quality product or service to customers.

3.3.6. *Project resource management*

It is necessary to plan resources by adding project roles concerning project scope, budget, and deliverables. Then, one can estimate the resource quantity for each necessary activity and identify the right resource for a specific activity. One can then assign estimated resources for the project, and the project can be executed. Finally, resources are monitored and managed to ensure the deliverance of products or services on deadlines.

3.3.7. *Project communications management*

First, communication needs to be planned with regard to the updates of the progress of processes, stakeholder requirements, project changes, etc.

Then, communications should be managed. These are planned previously during the implementation and execution of the project.

3.3.8. *Project risk management*

One first needs to create a risk management plan by categorizing potential risks which might arise in the internal and external environment and then prioritizing those risks by taking into account impacts. Finally, one needs to identify risks and analyze them by qualitative and quantitative risk analysis methods.

3.3.9. *Project procurement management*

It is necessary to first plan procurement management by considering outside procurement. Then, one needs to conduct procurement by creating work statements, terms of reference, etc., after deliverables are created.

3.3.10. *Project stakeholder management*

This knowledge area involves identifying possible stakeholders who can be a part of the project done by the organization. First, it is essential to identify the stakeholders with their designated roles in the project with relevant to the stakeholder management knowledge area. Monitoring and controlling stakeholder engagement is crucial for the successful delivery of project objectives.

4. PRINCE2 methodology

4.1. *Introduction*

PRINCE2 (PRoject IN Controlled Environments) is a well-known process-based project management methodology. PRINCE was initially developed by the Central Computers and Telecommunication Agency (CCTA) and is currently a part of the Office of Government Commerce (OGC). PRINCE was based on PROMPT (Project, Organization, Management, and Planning Technique), which is a well-recognized project management methodology. This generic approach, which addresses common project management questions, can be used for various types of projects. It also adapts a project into defined steps, making it logical and organized, to give better control over resources and risks. This process-based approach focuses on business justification and on creating a solid organizational structure. It consists of seven principles, themes, and processes and can be tailored to meet the unique requirements of a project (AXELOS, 2020).

4.2. *Principles*

The PRINCE2 methodology is based on seven core principles. These principles are the fundamental concepts of the methodology upon which everything else is built:

- **Continued Business Justification**: A reasonable justification is required for a project to be continued/managed further. If not, it should be closed.
- **Learn from experience**: Project members should be able to repeat the good habits and avoid the mistakes from their previous project experiences. Lessons learnt must be documented for future use.
- **Define rules and responsibilities**: The project team should have a well-defined organizational structure, and each individual should be clear about their roles and responsibilities.
- **Manage by stage**: The entire project must be divided into management stages, which should be well planned, monitored, and controlled. Go or no-go decisions are taken at stage boundaries.
- **Manage by exception**: Every project consists of six project objectives, and each of them is given a specific tolerance. Meetings between the project board and project manager are held only when the tolerance level is exceeded.
- **Focus on product**: The stakeholders of the project should understand and agree on the nature of the product to avoid misunderstanding.

- **Tailoring**: PRINCE2 accepts the uniqueness of the project, thereby allowing customization without deviating from the standard PRINCE2 methodology (Office of Government Commerce, 2002).

4.3. *Themes*

Themes are based on the principles and implemented during the processes, which require continuous attention.

- **Business Case**: A business case consists of the justifications of the project, cost–benefit analysis, a list of defined roles and responsibilities, and a benefits review.
- **Organization**: An organization defines the organizational structure and delegating roles and responsibilities to the individuals.
- **Quality**: The project manager checks if the product meets the requirements and is 'fit for purpose'.
- **Plans**: A plan defines the steps required for strategic planning and smooth product delivery.
- **Risk**: Risks help identify and prepare for any foreseeable issues to increase the probability of project success.
- **Change**: PRINCE2 accepts that change is inevitable and has a changing theme to assess and approve necessary changes. The change authority oversees the assessment and approval of the proposed changes.
- **Progress**: Progress evaluates the performance of the project by comparing it with the initial plan. PRINCE2 controlling and monitoring techniques are used if any deviation is observed.

4.4. *Processes*

PRINCE2 processes are where the principles and themes are implemented. Processes also determine the decision-maker during different stages of the project.

- **Starting a project**: This determines the feasibility of the project. Members are assigned roles and an initial stage plan, and a project brief is set up.

- **Initiating a project**: The customer will be briefed about the project, and the manager will prepare a project initiation document (PID) which will be approved by the project board.
- **Directing a project**: Key decisions are taken at critical phases of the project. Major plans are approved and resources are allocated.
- **Controlling a stage**: One must focus on monitoring, controlling, keeping senior management informed about the progress, and taking action if a deviation is observed.
- **Manage product delivery**: The team manager should control, monitor, and deliver the expected product and update the project manager at regular intervals. The expectation and tolerances are clearly defined in the project.
- **Manage stage boundaries**: The current situation is assessed by the project board, which approves further plans while acknowledging the risks.
- **Close a project**: The product is handed over to the customer on the agreed terms. The necessary documentation is done, and the project is officially finished. Figure 2 shows the integration of different processes in PRINCE2.

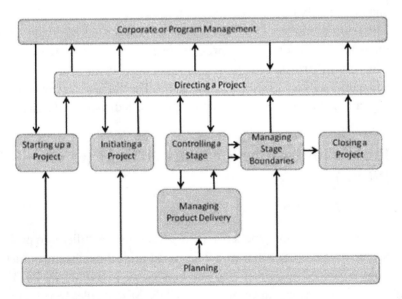

Figure 2.   Flow diagram of the processes in PRINCE2.

4.5. *Tailoring*

PRINCE2 acknowledges that projects are unique; thereby, the techniques can be customized according to the project without losing the core idea.

4.6. *Roles and responsibilities*

In PRINCE2, all project members are accordingly assigned roles and responsibilities.

- **The customer**: A project board member who pays for the project and is entitled to make key decisions.
- **The user**: Individuals who will be using the deliverables of the project or are affected by the project. Quite often, the customer is the user himself.
- **The supplier**: Professionals whose knowledge and skills are needed to execute the project.
- **The project manager**: The person who manages the project and keeps the project on track with the initial plan.
- **The project team**: A set of team members who take part in the project and do the bulk of the tasks required.
- **The team manager**: Leads the project team, oversees the activities of the team, and reports on the progress back to the project manager.
- **The administrator**: The person who supports the project team with adequate facilities to execute their plans. He/she also arranges meetings and manages all documentation work (Hedeman *et al.*, 2012).

5. Project Integrating Sustainable Management — PRiSM

5.1. *Introduction*

It has become a common practice to incorporate sustainability into project management. PRiSM is a new principle-based project management methodology developed by Green Project Management (GPM) in 2013. It embeds project management with the UN's Sustainable Development

Goals (SDG), which provide new tools to approach projects more sustainably while expanding the profit. GPM's PRiSM model is fundamentally based on the 5P Standard for Sustainability in Project Management (People, Profit, Product, Planet and Process). PRiSM extends beyond the typical project life cycle as it considers post-project impacts while planning. PRiSM is primarily used in large-scale construction projects including real estate and infrastructure, where environmental impacts are of alarming concern. PRiSM consists of four important phases and principles (Panneerselvam and Senthilkumar, 2010).

5.2. *Phases of PRiSM*

PRiSM has four phases, and these phases commence before a project and are continued after the project completion. To identify, define, control, and close various activities of the project, these phases are all interconnected.

- **Pre-project/Initiation phase**: The project's feasibility is determined considering the 5P standards. A business case is produced consisting of the justification and a sustainable approach.
- **Planning phase**: Project planning takes place according to the scope of the project.
- **Executing and controlling phase**: Planned activities are controlled and monitored according to the project plan. Corrective actions are implemented when the progress deviates from the initial plan.
- **Closure phase and reviews**: The project is completed, and the products are delivered. Project review and necessary documentation take place even after the project completion to record lessons learnt that could be useful for future reference. Figure 3 shows how the different phases of PRiSM are interconnected.

5.3. *Principles of PRiSM*

PRiSM's success depends on organizational interconnectivity. Thus, it is important to understand the principles of PRiSM before implementing them throughout the organization.

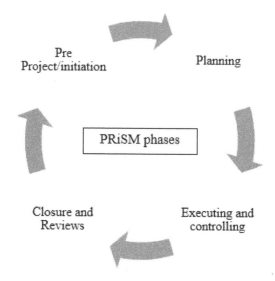

Figure 3.   The cyclic nature of PRiSM phases.

- **Commitment and Accountability**: Appreciate the need for a healthy, clean, and safe environment, fair remuneration, equal opportunities, ethical acquisition, and obedience to all necessary laws.
- **Ethics and Decision-making**: Align organizational ethics and decision-making with identification, reduction, and prevention of short-term and long-term negative impacts to the environment.
- **Integration and Transparency**: Appreciate interdependency among economic development, social integrity, and environmental protection in all aspects of project management.
- **Development of Resources**: Have a holistic approach toward resource utilization and usage of technology.
- **Social and Ecological Equity**: Use demographic dynamics to critically evaluate human vulnerability considering population centers and ecological sensitivity of the environment.
- **Economic Prosperity**: Establish financial strategies considering the needs of current and future stakeholders.

6. Critical Path Method (CPM)

6.1. *Introduction*

This concept focuses on finding the task dependencies, creating the network diagram, and determining the critical path.

This scheduling technique was introduced by Morgan R. Walker of DuPont and James E. Kelley of Remington Rand in the late 1950s. Progress is evaluated based on the Earn Value Management (EVM) principle. CPM provides a conceptual framework to define the early start, early finish, late start, and late finish dates for each task. A critical path in a project is a set of tasks dependent on each other with no float between the tasks and the path that contains only the critical activities. Conventionally, this path has the longest duration, which is equal to the duration of the project. A project can have one or more critical paths. Critical Path Management allows multitasking with small tolerance at the end of each task (Lockyer and Gordon, 1991).

6.2. *Steps to create the critical path method*

Six key steps are defined in the critical path method that are conventionally followed to determine the critical path (Thornley, 2013):

- Step 1 — Break down the project and specify each task.
- Step 2 — Establish dependencies between the different tasks of the project.
- Step 3 — Once the sequencing is sorted out, draw the network diagram.
- Step 4 — Estimate the task duration using available data or experience.
- Step 5 — Identify the critical path.
- Step 6 — Show progress upon task completion.

7. Critical Chain Method (CCM)

7.1. *Introduction*

Critical chain management was developed on the bases of methods and algorithms which are derivatives of the Theory of Constraints. The initial concepts of CCM were introduced in 1997 in Eliyahu M. Goldratt's book, *Critical Chain*. Dr. Eliyahu M. Goldratt evaluated the list of causes for project failure. This includes overestimation, lack of time transfer, path convergence, and multitasking. Dr. Eliyahu addressed these issues and introduced a new scheduling method called the Critical Chain Method based upon his Theory of Constraints. CCM goes a step further from CPM by accounting for any foreseeable risks and modifies the critical path while maintaining buffers to accommodate limited resources. This gives rise to a resource-constrained critical path. If there are no constraints, CCM will be identical to CPM. Tasks are not deadline based. However, the team members are encouraged to complete the task as soon as possible. Team members are not allowed to multitask when working on critical path activities. Generally, a pessimistic schedule is followed, considering the risks involved. However, in CCM, project members are supposed to work toward an optimistic duration. Buffers are added at the end of the paths, and their purpose is to provide a contingency for duration or resources if required. If any task is behind schedule, buffers can be utilized with the approval of the project manager. The rate of buffer consumption is used to determine project progress (Vanhoucke, 2012).

Thus, this approach is different from the Earn Value Management (EVM) technique used for progress evaluation. Buffers can be categorized into the following:

- **Project buffer** — Used for critical chain activities and is available upon approval from the project manager.
- **Feeding buffer** — Used for non-critical activities to avoid delays due to path convergence.
- **Resource buffer** — Used when excess resources are required.

Buffers are utilized, but in a more controlled and efficient manner than in CPM. Project members are not penalized for not meeting deadlines; however, they are encouraged to use the buffer more wisely.

The critical chain should be the primary focus for the project manager throughout the project. CCM is an effective approach in the manufacturing industry (Leach, 2014).

7.2. *Steps to implement the Critical Chain Method*

Implementing the Critical Chain Method is identical to implementing the Critical Path Method, but additional steps are involved due to resource constraints (Blokdyk, 2020).

- Step 1 — Generate the Work Breakdown Structure (WBS).
- Step 2 — Identify task dependencies between the lists of activities.
- Step 3 — Estimate optimistic time duration. Allocate only 50% of the time estimation obtained (if task A takes six days, allocate only three days).
- Step 4 — Construct a schedule using the late finish method starting from the date of delivery.
- Step 5 — Manage resources according to the WBS.
- Step 6 — Identify the critical chain.
- Step 7 — Rearrange activities to explore the possibility of shorter schedules.
- Step 8 — Add the project buffer at the end of the critical chain.
- Step 9 — Add a feeding buffer to the non-critical chain activities.

Example: Company A must come up with new software for their client. Table 2 shows the list of activities and the duration taken for each activity. Figures 4 and 5 illustrate the network diagrams for CPM and CCM, respectively (Goldratt, 2017).

Table 2.   Details of activities for a software development project.

Activity	Predecessors	Duration for CPM (Days)	Duration for CCM (Days)
A — Determine pricing model	–	14	7
B — Implement pricing changes	A	2	1
C — Write base code for features	–	14	7
D — Beta test feature	C	4	2

(Continued)

Table 2.   (*Continued*)

Activity	Predecessors	Duration for CPM (Days)	Duration for CCM (Days)
E — Release feature to all users	B, D and H	4	2
F — Write tutorials	–	6	3
G — Copyedit tutorials	F	6	3
H — Publish tutorials	G	2	1

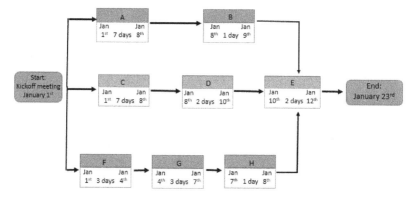

Figure 4.   Network diagram for critical path method.

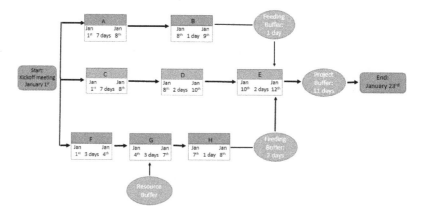

Figure 5.   Network diagram for critical chain method.

8. Agile methodology

Normally, agile is not a traditional project management methodology. It is a collection of principles and guidelines to implement a project similar to a software project. The agile methodology performs incremental processes along with the iteration, which is known as going through the same steps concurrently while moving forward. The principles of the agile methodology are focused on four different aspects as follows:

- Interaction of teams over agile tools and processes.
- Software that works throughout extensive documentations.
- Customers' cooperation through negotiation of contracts.
- Responding to changes by following plans.

The agile methodology can be adapted to all situations by changing its procedures and processes, and it helps maintain good communication within the project team members and other stakeholders such as clients and vendors of the project. Because of the adaptability of the agile methodology, it can be used in a dynamic project environment in the same manner as projects having a considerable scope. Agile projects are performed by a series of tasks that optimize the project development life cycle. The agile project management life cycle moves along the steps such as planning, executing, evaluating, and the closure of the project by handing over the deliverables.

First, one needs to find out the requirements of the project and break them down into smaller parts. Next, one can arrange them according to prioritization and importance as suggested by the team members (Association for Project Management).

The execution of the project is based on the prioritization of the requirement and by collaborating with team members the requirements are further refined. This process makes the project deliverables to create optimum business value and client satisfaction.

9. Scrum methodology

Scrum is one of the frameworks in the agile methodology, which follows several processes and techniques, and consists of scrum teams connected with roles, events, artifacts, and rules.

In the scrum methodology, prearranged proceedings are used to generate uniformity. The proceedings and the events are timeboxed, and each event has a maximum duration. A major component of Scrum is a sprint, which contains a maximum timebox of two to four weeks within which to release the created incremented product. After completing one sprint, a new spirit begins immediately, and sprint planning, daily scrums, development work, Sprint review, and Sprint retrospective follow after each sprint.

Scrum has major cross-functional team roles, namely, scrum master, product owner, and the team. The scrum master is the keeper of scrum processes, reducing obstacles and facilitating meetings. The product owner increases the value of the product by working with the team, managing major project data that have been provided to the stakeholders using scrum artifacts, and being aware of the project development details such as the components under development, the activities completed, and the activities being planned.

- **Product Backlog**: This is the complete list of required features, including the enhancements and fixes that produce the changes to be made to the product in forthcoming releases.
- **Sprint Backlog**: This is the collection of selected product backlog items for each sprint. It delivers the product with developed product goals as an incremented release.

10. Adaptive Project Framework (APF)

10.1. *Introduction*

In today's fast-paced world, the goals and objectives of a particular project are continuously changing. The conventional project management approach is no longer ideal due to multiple factors. Project managers need new methodologies to cope with this environment with a more responsive project team. The Adaptive Project Framework (APF) is an increasingly popular approach adopted by project managers to tackle constant change with an adaptive and iterative planning framework. Wysocki (2010) introduced the APF methodology in his book, *Adaptive Project Framework:*

Managing Complexity in the Face of Uncertainty. Wysocki explains the application of APF compared to the usual methodologies by using a real-world example. He says that a cook will implement a conventional methodology where he who focuses on the recipe closely produces an outcome, whereas a chef will implement APF where he has the knowledge of the recipe and experience to improvise during uncertainty. This is a systematic and structured approach that allows a project team to quickly adjust to the changing goals, priorities, schedule, conditions, etc., by learning to accept changes, adapt, and learn from them. This method follows the just-in-time planning approach and considers the client as an integral part of the project (Wysocki, 2010).

The framework allows continuous balance between staff, process, and technology. APF consists of six principles and five phases.

10.2. *Principles of APF*

As the client is the focus of the project, he/she can change the direction of the project as per his/her requirements. This approach has been embodied in the six core principles of APF as follows:

1. **Client-focused**: The client is the key decision-maker and will receive the support of the project team.
2. **Client-driven**: The client is engaged throughout the project to produce desired deliverables.
3. **Incremental deliverables early and often**: Deliverables are provided early and often as the cycles are short in APF. This allows the client to quickly learn how his decisions impact the outcome.
4. **Continuous questioning and introspection**: This highlights openness and honesty between the client and the development team for best possible outcomes.
5. **Change is progress**: Change is considered a rather good indicator of the health of the project. The frequency of the cycles should be high at the start and should reduce with time.
6. **Do not speculate on the future**: This eliminates unnecessary investment in non-value-adding elements of the project.

10.3. *Phases of APF*

The APF approach is divided into five main phases which allow optimum cost and time utilization for a given cycle (Wysocki, 2013):

1. **Defining the scope of the project**: Customer requirements are defined, and Conditions of Satisfaction (CoS) are produced and approved by the client. This document is used for strategic planning and project evaluation. A Project Overview Statement (POS) summarizes the CoS, achievements and how they will be approached, a list of risks and potential obstacles, and the prediction of success. Furthermore, a list of functional requirements, Work Breakdown Structure (WBS), and the scope triangle are produced during this phase.

2. **Cycle plan**: This consists of sub-projects or project cycles that should give one or more deliverables. Task dependencies are defined and given to project members along with a suitable deadline.

3. **Cycle build**: The cycle is monitored throughout this phase until the deadline. Any pending work, problems, and improvements are reconsidered and reprioritized in the next cycle.

4. **Client checkpoint**: This is an important phase of the project where the client reviews the quality of the deliverables in a particular cycle. Any corrections or improvements are added to the next iteration, and the process repeats until the objective is achieved.

5. **Final review**: Upon completion, the stakeholders will evaluate the success of the project and verify whether the client requirements are satisfied. Necessary documentation is done for future reference. Figure 6 illustrates the connection between the phases of APF.

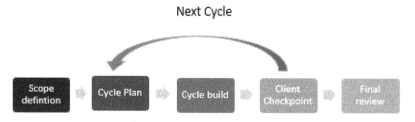

Figure 6.   Process flow of phases in Adaptive Project Framework.

10.4. *Types of APF*

The Adaptive Project Framework can be approached in two ways:

1. **Active**: The best possible strategy is decided with a series of experiments and should be flexible enough to be reversed if necessary.
2. **Passive**: Passive APF is where the project manager uses his experience from the previous iterations to encounter potential uncertainties.

11. CCM AND CPM comparison

Table 3 distinguishes the key differences between CCM and CPM.

12. Comparison between different methodologies

Table 4 shows the comparison between the different types of methodologies discussed in this chapter.

Table 3. Comparison between CCM and CPM.

CCM	CPM
Multitasking is avoided.	Multitasking is possible.
Buffer is a Critical Chain phenomenon.	Float is a Critical Path phenomenon.
The project schedule does not include buffer.	The project schedule includes floats.
Delayed start of non-critical activities.	Early start of non-critical activities.
The project is completed before the deadline.	The project is completed on time or gets delayed a bit.

Table 4. Advantages, disadvantages, and application of different project management methodologies.

Methodology	Advantages	Disadvantages	Application
PRINCE2	Not field-specific. Widely practiced project language. Flexible decision points	Significant documentation is required in case of a change.	Generic approach.

(Continued)

Table 4. (*Continued*)

Methodology	Advantages	Disadvantages	Application
	An early forecast of possible problems. Enhanced communication. Greater customer satisfaction.	Processes have heavy documentation. Inadequate guidance on risk management. Does not elaborate on interpersonal skills.	
PRiSM	Enhanced sociability and sustainability of the project. Eco-friendly option. Reduction of non-renewable resource dependency.	Provides only long-term benefits. Entire organization's commitment is required.	For eco-friendly projects such as construction projects.
CCM	Visual representation of resource availability. Faster project completion. Optimize resource utilization. Prevents misuse of float time. More realistic schedules can be created. Better forecast of project progress.	Unsuitable for small projects with quick turnarounds.	Generic approach.
CPM	Visual representation of project progress. Gives adequate time to complete a task. Tracks critical activities. Helps in optimal resource allocation. Helps in resource prioritization.	Only suitable for projects with minimum uncertainties. Resource constraints not considered in project schedule.	For projects where resource allocation is less flexible.

Table 4. (*Continued*)

Methodology	Advantages	Disadvantages	Application
Agile	On-time Project Completion and optimized resource utilization. Further Iterative and Incremental methodology assures the desired outcomes of the Projects.	Poor planning and documentation can lead to unrealistic Project goals. Fragmentation of the scope and minimal planning can be a hindrance.	For strictly time-bound and scope-bound Projects.
SCRUM	Developed on the basis of Agile Concept. Highly flexible and optimized Project goals. Timely delivery and creation of highest level of business value is focused when delivering Project outcomes.	Segmentation of the scope of the project can lead to confusion among team members due to tight time-bound schedules.	For strictly time-bound and scope-bound Projects.
APF	Faster project completion due to less non-value-adding work. Less expensive. Early indications of project termination. High-quality product delivery.	Excess flexibility for client. Original outcome may not be achieved. Limited authority for the project manager. Budget and time overruns are possible. Lack of documentation due to rapid pace.	For flexible projects such as software projects.

13. Conclusion

Project methodologies can be selected and implemented depending on the characteristics of the project. Most of these methodologies share common ideas and principles. For instance, PRINCE2 focuses on the delivery of the product, but some of its elements are identical to other methodologies.

For example, the themes are closely associated with Knowledge areas in PMBOK, and the processes are extremely similar to process groups in PMBOK. PRINCE2 is a widely practiced project management methodology. However, a thorough understanding of the elements in the methodology is required to obtain maximum benefits out of it.

With a growing need to be socially responsible, companies try to come up with eco-friendly strategies that also provide the necessary benefits in the long run. The PRiSM approach is applicable to common project management methodologies like PRINCE2 and agile. However, to reap maximum benefits from PRiSM, all levels of the organization should be willing to accept and follow the principles of the method.

CCM is an enhancement of CPM where the resource constraints are considered when developing a project schedule. It allows the members to work toward an optimistic time frame, thereby eliminating the misuse of excess time. This approach saves a lot of valuable time compared to the conventional CPM approach.

The agile methodology is an Iterative and Incremental methodology focusing on timely delivery and scope agility. The scope of the project is segmented throughout the tightly controlled timeline. The prime motive of introducing the agile methodology was to address the dynamic nature of scopes of modern projects.

The basis of the agile methodology was enhanced by several researchers, and Scrum is an approach specifically developed for time-bound, scope-bound projects. It focuses on delivering maximum business values through project outcomes via each iteration called a 'Sprint'. It is extremely productive for projects if the objectives are clearly set. Further, the selection of objectives to be achieved would be prioritized based on the business value generated.

APF is an agile approach to the constantly changing project environments. It is a just-in-time concept, and the involvement of the client is significant compared to other methodologies. APF is not a universal approach, but if the project consists of a flexible environment such as the IT industry, this would be a go-to solution.

References

Association for Project Management. What is Agile Project Management? [Online]. (2020). Association for Project Management. Available at: https://www.apm.org.uk/resources/find-a-resource/agile-project-management (Accessed 11 August 2021).

AXELOS. (2020). Effective Project Management: Why the PRINCE2 Method is More Relevant than Ever White Paper [Online]. AXELOS. Available at: https://www.axelos.com/case-studies-and-white-papers/effective-project-management-prince2-more-relevant (Accessed 11 August 2021).

Blokdyk, G. (2020). *Critical Chain Project Management a Complete Guide.* Aspley: Emereo Publishing.

Goldratt, E. M. (2017). *Critical Chain: A Business Novel.* Routledge: Netherlands.

Hedeman, B., Van Heemst, G. V. and Fredriksz, H. (2012). *Project Management Based on PRINCE2® 2009 Edition.* Van Haren.

Kissflow Inc. (2021). 7 Best Project Management Methodologies, Frameworks and Techniques Explained [Online]. Kissflow Inc. Available at: https://kissflow.com/project/project-management-methodologies-and-frameworks (Accessed 14 August 2021).

Leach, L. P. (2014). *Critical Chain Project Management.* Artech House: Boston, USA.

Lockyer, K. G. and Gordon, J. (1991). *Critical Path Analysis and Other Project Network Techniques.* Beekman Books Incorporated.

Office of Government Commerce. (2002). *Managing Successful Projects with PRINCE2.* Great Britain: The Stationery Office.

Panneerselvam, R. and Senthilkumar, P. (2010). *Project Management.* New Delhi: PHI Learning.

PMBOK Guide. (2001). A New Approach to PMBOK Guide 2000 [Online]. Available at: https://ricardo-vargas.com/articles/pmbokguide2000/ (Accessed 12 August 2021).

Project Management Institute. (2018). *Guide to the Project Management Body of Knowledge.* Project Management Institute.

Thornley, G. (2013). *Critical Path Analysis in Practice: Collected Papers on Project Control.* Routledge: England, UK.

Twproject Staff. (2019). Project Organizational Structures in Project Management [Online]. Italy: Twproject. Available at: https://twproject.com/blog/project-organizational-structures-project-management/ (Accessed 11 August 2021).

Vanhoucke, M. (2012). *Project Management with Dynamic Scheduling*. Springer: Berlin, Germany.

Visual Paradigm. (2021). What is PMBOK in Project Management? [Online]. Visual Paradigm. Available at: https://www.visual-paradigm.com/guide/pmbok/what-is-pmbok/ (Accessed 14 August 2021).

Wysocki, R. K. (2010). *Adaptive Project Framework: Managing Complexity in the Face of Uncertainty*. Addison-Wesley Professional: Boston, USA.

Wysocki, R. K. (2013). *Effective Software Project Management*. John Wiley & Sons: New Jersey, USA.

Chapter 3

Context, Priorities, Constraints, and Trends in Information Technology Projects

Geetha Gopal

University of Oxford, Oxford, UK
geetha.gopal.mmpm18@said.oxford.edu

Information Technology (IT) is no longer a support function. IT has progressed significantly to be at the helm of change and business growth. Organizations which align their business models with right technologies and processes realize maximum benefits. As the recent years have seen heavy investments through IT projects, it is imperative for IT project managers to understand the impact of their work beyond their scope. This chapter delves into the context in which IT projects function, elaborates on their evolution around business needs, illustrates the constraints that define success or failure of projects, and reviews the approaches used in handling them. The influencing factors of recent trends in IT projects including Digital Transformation, Artificial Intelligence (AI), Automation, Managed Services, and Cloud Computing are reviewed. The key considerations in IT procurement, and how project financing, sponsorship, and governance are shaping IT projects, are explained. The concerns related to data and their mitigation options are emphasized. As operational consideration is critical to long-term success of IT projects, the approaches for simplification and smooth transition from projects to operations are reviewed. In summary, this chapter gives a big picture of the IT landscape and the broader mindset needed to drive change through IT projects.

1. Introduction

Humans have always been fascinated by the sense of achievement of specific goals. Projects have shaped the world since time immemorial, and their legacy lives on. The Egyptian pharaohs built extraordinary pyramids that still stand the test of time. The steam-fed train system carried men and materials from one point to another at speeds unheard. The first human in space. The worldwide web which provided a way to access information over the Internet. There is no shortage of such inspiring projects worldwide. These achievements are outcomes of exceptional project leaders who had specific goals and worked tirelessly with their teams to realize them.

Project organizations are temporary structures of people who pursue specific goals and disband when their goals are achieved. Though projects have been delivered successfully for thousands of years, the 20th Century saw the standardization of project management, as more scholars and practitioners began promoting its importance. The Project Management Institute explains projects as 'defined beginning and end in time, and therefore defined scope and resources' and project management as 'the application of knowledge, skills, tools, and techniques to project activities to meet the project requirements'. PMI's PMBOK® Guide categorizes the project management process into initiating, planning, executing, monitoring, controlling, and closing. The Association for Project Management defines project management as 'the application of processes, methods, skills, knowledge, and experience to achieve specific project objectives according to the project acceptance criteria within agreed parameters'. Other popular project management standards have similar definitions too.

1.1. *Introduction to Information Technology (IT) projects*

There are discussions on whether IT is an industry or a sector. While the industry is a specific group of companies with similar functions and services, a sector denotes a broader segment of the economy comprising other industries and groups.

- The Global Industry Classification Standard (GICS) has classified IT as a sector with three industry groups: Software & Services, Technology Hardware & Equipment, and Semiconductors & Semiconductor Equipment.
- The Industrial Classification Benchmark (ICB) categorizes Technology as an industry with two super-sectors: Software & Computer Services; Technology Hardware & Equipment.

The shift from IT as an industry to IT as a sector has been gradual over the years. Among the established sectors in GICS and ICB, it is interesting to note that IT/Digital Technology is emerging as the operational backbone for other sectors. IT has integrated across the spectrum from small and medium businesses to conglomerates to government organizations to education to voluntary organizations, empowering them to meet their evolving business needs. Microsoft, Apple, Amazon, and Alphabet, to name a few, have achieved the US$500 billion status, and seven out of the top ten companies by market value in 2020 were such tech giants.

As organizations invest more in technology projects to meet their strategic goals, they inadvertently tie their functioning and sustainability to the outcome of these projects. Technology-related service exports have doubled in the last decade, reaching US$536 billion in 2017. Traditional IT categories like hardware, software, and telco will garner new revenue streams for organizations which are expected to be routed to topics like Artificial Intelligence (AI), Internet of Things (IoT), Blockchain, Cyber security, and Augmented/Virtual/Mixed Reality. Though IT's impact on business and the economy is phenomenal, its projects suffer from poor performance. Studies by Flyvbjerg and Budzier (2011) demonstrate that IT projects are costly, risky, and inadequate on benefits. On average, they are 45% over budget, 56% under-delivered, and 7% over time. In the Public sector, 18% of IT projects were over 25% above budget (Budzier and Flyvbjerg, 2012). When one out of every five multi-million-dollar public sector IT projects overruns, its impact on the economy tends to be severe.

2. Understanding the context

A diverse and well-prioritized project portfolio facilitates organizations to be competitive and sustainable. In a portfolio, project classification is based on variables like cost, duration, size, risk, and complexities, which are backed by practical tools and extensive literature. First, it is important to understand that the dynamic nature of IT challenges the completeness of standard project classification and demands its evolution. Second, the diversity of projects based on scope and end goals are to be understood for prioritization. Third, the team and roles needed in a healthy project portfolio are to be considered, because the right resources must be assigned to the right projects for desired results.

2.1. *Classification of IT projects*

An IT project classified as small due to its team size and costs would likely be categorized as a lower-priority project. This lower category project could be groundbreaking for the organization in cyber security or innovation. There is a risk of underprioritizing such projects among higher-value or more complex ones in a portfolio. Thus, IT projects need six additional classification factors as shown in Table 1: strategic relevance, business value, innovation, cyber security, technological uncertainty, and customer experience.

- Strategy and project management have great potential when tied together. The strategic alignment of projects by project managers is often overlooked (Artto and Dietrich, 2007) and so is the case in a project portfolio (Crawford *et al.*, 2006). Strategic relevance is thus recommended as the foremost consideration in prioritization. For example, a cloud-based user experience project following a cloud-first strategy is higher in relevance for prioritization, when compared to a

Table 1. Additional project classifiers.

Type	Classifier	Small	Medium	Large
Traditional	Cost	<$100,000	$100,000–$500,000	>$500,000
	Duration	<3months	3–18 months	>18 months
	Size	<10 pax	10–20 pax	>20 pax
	Risk	low	medium	high
	Complexities	low	medium	high
Futuristic	Strategic relevance	low	medium	high
	Business value	low	medium	high
	Innovation	low	medium	high
	Cyber security	low	medium	high/critical
	Technological uncertainty	low	medium	high
	Customer experience	low	medium	high

legacy system fix. An experimental data intelligence project is higher in strategic relevance following a data monetization strategy.

- The second consideration is business value. Projects must be clear of the business value they are expected to create. Understanding the tangible business value of projects must begin well in the early stages. Once the expected business value is identified as measurable outcomes, it becomes easy to classify the project.

- Innovation is another factor in classification due to its importance for businesses in staying relevant. Innovation is a top priority for 75% of organizations in their COVID-19 pandemic recovery journey, and the most innovative organizations bounced back faster (BCG, 2021). Innovation goals and actions do not match in many lower-performing organizations. Understanding and measuring the level of innovation in every project undertaken is a good place to start.

- In common practice, cyber security is classified under risk, but that comes with a hindsight of blanketing the various technical aspects under a common factor. The context of cyber security varies on a case-by-case basis, as it depends on many factors like data sensitivity, robustness, process controls, and legal and organizational regulations.

In a portfolio, the specific cyber security factors must be identified, their individual criticality assessed, and the overall cyber security classification must be defined for projects.

- Technological uncertainty is a highly recommended classification factor in academia, ranging from low-tech to super-high-tech (Raz *et al.*, 2002; Shenhar and Holzmann, 2017). As business functioning is tied with technology, considering technological uncertainties is vital. When evaluated against strategic relevance, organizations can decide on their approaches on high uncertainty projects. The greater the level of uncertainty and stakes involved, the greater the need for review and appropriate prioritization. Lesser ones offer scalability. However, they are not spared from failures and need relevant assessments throughout.

- Finally, customer or user experience is a factor that is not classified at the portfolio level. The more organizations go closer to customers, and expect their projects to bring real value, the higher the need for understanding the expectations. With this understanding comes the opportunity to cater projects to customer need, and thereby trust and growth.

Since the context, considerations, and impact will vary across organizations, the decision of what low, medium, and high constitute is best left up to the individual organizations and portfolios. The above additional classification factors will aid organizations in identifying dependencies and help in navigating their projects toward intended outcomes.

2.2. *Diversity in IT projects*

The next context to understand in IT is the assortment of scope areas. The type of IT projects is ever-growing; a selective list of common ones based on their technical scope is indicated from 1–21 in Table 2.

Wheelwright and Clark (2007) sought to map development projects, which is still relevant in today's diverse IT climate. Figure 1 is an adaptation of Wheelwright and Clark's plan, which demonstrates how the above project types could be mapped into a portfolio. Such a classification system will provide support in estimating resources against capacity,

Table 2. Common IT projects based on scope.

Scope areas	1–7	8–14	15–21
	1. Network infrastructure	8. Migrations, Upgrades	15. Hardware systems
	2. Applications, Software	9. Product development	16. Big Data, Storage
	3. Middleware	10. User Experience	17. Data Science, Visualization, Automation
	4. Cyber security	11. Compliance, Governance	18. Data-centers
	5. Cloud Computing	12. Office Infrastructure	19. Operational Changes
	6. Digital Transformation	13. Vendor Management	20. Blockchain, IoT
	7. AI/ML	14. Service Excellence	21. Systems, Process Integrations

deciding on the desired mix of initiatives, and executing them. The clarity this visualization brings is a good starting point to prioritize any typical IT portfolio.

2.3. *The IT project team*

An IT project team is diverse. Be it waterfall or agile, a wide variety of roles and skills are needed for projects to be successful. Though the project manager (PM) is accountable for the outcome of the project, understanding the different pieces of an IT team puzzle and ensuring all the components are secured are crucial to project success.

• A typical waterfall project team will include a sponsor, PM, PMO, technical leads, working members, and identified user group. Sponsorship comes from stakeholders, like investors, clients, department, or business leaders, who could be individuals or groups. The PM is expected to be technically inclined though the technical leads

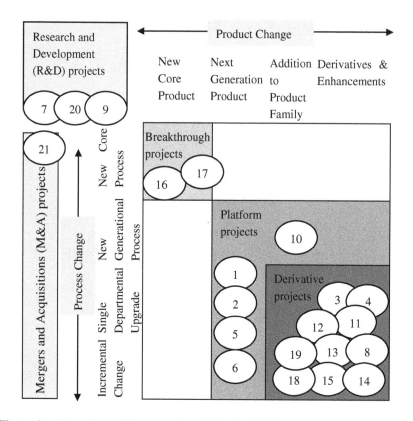

Figure 1. Adaptation of Wheelwright and Clark's (2007) Aggregate Project Plan with common IT project types from Table 2.

are responsible for the individual work packages. A PMO is usually assigned for larger projects, while for smaller projects, the PM oversees this role. As technical leads are often bound by functional hierarchy, PMs often engage with functional tower leaders for resourcing and escalations. The working members could be internal or external. Due to the increasing use of outsourcing and partnering models in IT, PMs must identify such external resources and their dependencies. A user group from the business or end-user side plays a crucial role in requirements, user acceptance testing, and providing valuable feedback. Technical towers also include members from operations who will take over the project post-go-live and hyper-care.

- In agile projects, the roles are slightly more evolved, feedback driven, and flexible. A typical Scrum team has a Scrum Master, a Product Owner, and a pool of Developers. With no hierarchies, the team works on common product goals. The Scrum Master ensures the efficiency of the team and work, while the Product Owner manages and prioritizes the product backlog. The developers work on specific targets for each iteration or sprint. End users are a crucial group of stakeholders for agile teams for both testing and user feedback.

While the nature of IT projects transforms, focusing on these three core areas will help projectized organizations in adapting to ongoing advances in technology and business expectations.

3. IT project management evolution

IT projects have come a long way from Charles Babbage's Difference Engine that calculated astronomical tables, and Harvard's 5-ton Mark 1, which aided the world war. As more players entered the software and hardware segments, IT became more affordable, optimized, and standardized. Outsourcing and service orientation made IT more manageable. The recent trends of automation and intelligence capabilities and the race for digitalization across all industries have put IT at the center stage of transformation. Advancements in technologies like Robotic Process Automation (RPA), AI, and self-services will offload much of IT's manual work. As per the latest predictions (Edlich *et al.*, 2021), AI is expected to create up to $15.4 trillion in value annually. Automation in the areas of business processes and digital services will be further expedited. While organizations target the low-hanging fruits to get themselves on the automation and AI track, traditional IT services will continue to be the backbone and revenue generator.

3.1. *From software projects to service orientation*

Software projects dealt with the development of specific software that was targeted to address business and user requirements. Several software organizations specialized in designing, developing, testing, and managing such customized software and frameworks. They were expensive, often caused integration issues, and were prone to a high rate of failure. This made the undertaking organizations seek options for transferring accountability. The result was managed services which streamlined costs and aligned outcomes based on agreed service levels. Managed services worked well on areas like specialized software, mature requirements, or operational scope, while standalone software applications became increasingly irrelevant. In today's context, managed services have increased organizational collaborations, interconnecting various systems and thereby generating more projects in Big Data, Cloud Computing, IoT, Containerization, DevOps, and Digital Transformation. When implemented successfully, managed services can reduce IT costs by 25% to 45% and increase operational efficiency from 45% to 65% in the next five years, according to Mordor (2021).

The aerospace industry where some of the world's costliest software issues have happened demonstrates this shift distinctly. The Mariner 1 Spacecraft, which cost $18 million in 1960 value, was wiped off in under 5 mins of takeoff. The reason was a software bug that went unnoticed during development and testing. The lunar probe Clementine that was lost in space was an experimentation of off-the-shelf commercial software. Though these lessons helped NASA greatly, new complexities were always uncovered. Since the early 2000s, NASA has changed its program model from building to managed services and has entered contractual partnerships with private companies. Instead of procuring specific skills, this approach shifts the role of NASA from integrator to consumer of managed services like Commercial Orbital Transportation, Resupply, Gateway Logistics, and Crew Development. The most recent contract with SpaceX's Starship at $2.9 billion is for a holistic service of taking NASA astronauts from the lunar orbit to the moon's surface. This trend of increasing managed services is not limited to the aerospace industry but across the IT spectrum.

3.2. *From projects to products*

Waterfall and agile are two common project management methodologies which have their specific benefits and relevance in today's project landscape. While Waterfall is a phased approach, Agile is an iterative and incremental one. Building a new data center, digitizing a complex business process, and phasing out a legacy system are some examples where traditional waterfall approaches are still used successfully. Agile methodologies like scrum are popular in developments where products are built iteratively with user feedback, through continuous releases. Capabilities like DevOps/Continuous Integration/Continuous Delivery (CI/CD) have strengthened the transition from phased projects to iterative products. It is interesting to see how agile-only projects are increasingly successful (Rigby *et al.*, 2016). Product management encompasses agile and DevOps principles, which helps plan, build, test, deploy, and upgrade applications, modules, and functionalities. Best implemented as a fully automated process, it simplifies testing and deployment in isolated environments. Alerting mechanisms proactively indicate areas of code failure. User testing, which is a crucial element in software development, is also simplified when it is integrated with the CI/CD flow. Apart from regression tests, CI/CD can help automate almost any type of test. Such technical advancements in agile development, the ability to deliver business value iteratively, and the transparency make the product approach to projects more lucrative than ever.

3.3. *From business goals to business continuity*

A PwC (2019) study found that 73% of CEOs expected at least one major crisis that would push organizations to tough limits in three years. But, the unexpected COVID-19 pandemic escalated within a few months and disrupted the functioning and stability of organizations beyond imagination. Twilio (2020) notes that the pandemic has expedited digital transformation by 5.3 years. With crisis came opportunities and organizations that adapted their business models swiftly could thrive in the new reality. While business goals set for 2020 became irrelevant in the pandemic, companies that had invested in proactive programs saw unprecedented growth. The connected employee and end-user empowerment tools by companies like Microsoft and Zoom proved to be well rewarding. Microsoft's Teams grew from 20 million to 115 million daily active users by the end of 2020. The pandemic also proved that investments in programs like digitized logistics, self-services, virtual engagements, e-commerce, and process automation gave rewards beyond their intended business goals. ServiceNow, the IT service management company that believed in cloud-based automation of infrastructure technologies, is a relevant example. Its business model had strategically and proactively aligned R&D programs with sales. With a market share of over 40% and retention rate of 97%, in 2018, ServiceNow went on to top the list of Future 50 companies in 2020. It is interesting to note that organizations like Airbnb, which were thriving, were plunged into record lows within a quarter into the pandemic. This is because such organizations had fewer programs on business continuity and alternate streams of revenue. They were heavily invested in vertical growth. As economies ease out of the pandemic and transition back to pre-COVID-19 functioning, organizations will continue to embark on programs to sustain their revenue streams while harmonizing pre-pandemic processes with lessons learned from the pandemic.

4. Project constraints

Project constraints are boundaries for the project to ensure progress, quality, and desired success. They are restrictions that demonstrate the health of the project and guide in decision-making. However, they are not enough in avoiding project failures. Even with such agreed restrictions, these major initiatives are so powerful that they persist beyond economic rationality, forcing one to spend 'good money after bad', leading to non-bailable situations (Staw and Ross, 1987; Flyvbjerg, 2009). As the scale and impact of projects grow, so is the need for additional constraints and customized parameters.

4.1. *Common constraints*

Project management practice lived in the false belief that projects were successful if the scope, time, and costs were met (Kerzner and Saladis, 2009). Commonly called the triple constraints, scope, time, and cost formed the Iron triangle, which evaluated the performance of projects and their managers. Academics have discussed in detail the constraints, causes, and potential measures to avoid project failures. Prof. Flyvbjerg (2013) from Oxford, who has led megaproject research across three decades, demonstrates the Iron Law of Projects which is 'over time, over budget, over and over again'. Nobel laureate Daniel Kahneman and his colleague Amos Tversky, who take a behavioral science approach, find cognitive biases and lack of distributional view as the reasons for decisions and failure (Kahneman and Tversky, 2013). When considering constraints, planners must include performance of similar projects or a reference class to mitigate estimation errors (Kahneman, 2011). Application of Reference class (Flyvbjerg, 2007) on project constraints has been demonstrated successfully by studies in transportation (Flyvbjerg *et al.*, 2004), IT (Budzier and Flyvbjerg, 2011), and hydroelectric dams (Awojobi and Jenkins, 2016).

4.2. *Challengers of constraints*

While it is good practice to be in control of the triple constraints, that is not a holistic measure for project success. Many projects which were regarded as successful since they met the triple constraints were flawed in the eyes of the stakeholders. This is because the factors that mattered were not measured or reported. In recent times, the most typical and grim example is the Boeing 737-MAX. It was a cost-effective and fast-track program that saw an influx of business orders and was hailed as a commercial success for Boeing. Shortly after the planned deliveries, malfunctions were reported on multiple airlines across the world which led to the immediate grounding of its entire fleet of 400 aircraft. While investigations are still in progress, project cost constraints and internal pressures seem to have worked for the project but not for the product. This brings up the question of how to ensure the comprehensive success of projects. Apart from time and cost, the third constraint recommended by academics is benefits. Projects must identify and measure their value, scope, and capability by integrating quantifiable benefits with projects. Constraints like value delivery, relationships, and risks are also equally important. While it is tough to recommend one fixed approach to project success, project criteria must be agreed upon with stakeholders on a case-by-case basis and driven accordingly (Wateridge, 1998). There is also the need for an integrated approach which means several factors are required for success, adding fitness and future-ready as project constraints (Silvius and Schipper, 2016). Satisfaction is another crucial criterion that projects must uphold. The power of communication in ensuring project satisfaction is often underestimated. Formal communication plans are formed only for a small fragment of projects. Poorly handled communication or total lack of it has counterproductive outcomes. On the other hand, well-managed communication will increase the morale of the team, confidence of key stakeholders, create transparency across many levels, and contribute to the overall success of the project.

5. Successful approaches for IT evolution

As the distinction between business and technology thins, organizations are driven toward projects like digital transformation, data monetization, self-service, and software-as-a-service. However, most new-technology product developments are known to fail (Taylor, 2010). Their hurdles arise from business complexities, legacy, security, data concerns, and cost constraints. At the root of such challenges lies great potential.

5.1. *Evolving business needs and complexities*

Organizations that seize the potential of technology to meet their evolving business needs have seen exponential growth and power within their respective domains. For example, Amazon, which started as an online book house, branched out into technical services at the start of the cloud computing era. Within a decade, it churned out unprecedented profits because it had seized the growth potential that came with the business opportunity. As of 2020, AWS leads the $130 billion Cloud Market, helping elite clients like NASA and CIA embark on data-intensive projects. Such tremendous opportunities can only be sustained by providing consistent and adequate quality of service. Studies have attributed project failure to complexities like technological, organizational, structural, dynamic, uncertainty, and socio-political characteristics. There is no traditional approach to eliminate such diverse complexities. Awareness, understanding, and handling them closely, on a case-by-case basis, will help manage them and reduce project impact.

5.2. *Legacy systems*

Critical systems tend to get functionally deep rooted; this worsens when other systems and business processes get intertwined with them. In many cases, these legacy systems have the power to disrupt the business; hence, they are fiercely guarded, and fought over to be retained. Projects aiming to uproot such legacy systems are met with challenges and solid displeasure from functional teams. Legacy systems affect projects in at least 40% of organizations. On the other hand, companies with no legacy systems tend to have smoother projects. Smaller and younger companies have lesser dependencies on legacy systems, whereas with larger and older organizations, the chances of legacy-related issues for projects are higher. Elimination of legacy systems and business processes must be dealt with more favorably to increase project success.

5.3. *Security and privacy*

Security is considered as one of the riskiest characteristics in IT projects. Organizations are constantly at an increased risk of ill-intentioned security incidents from causes like software bugs, system vulnerabilities, malware, and phishing. Cyber security threats have increased greatly in recent years. As the world grappled with the pandemic in 2020, malware increased by 358% and ransomware by 435% compared to 2019 (Deep Instinct, 2020). A data breach, on average, sets back an organization by $3.86 million. Capital One suffered a breach that compromised 100 million US and 6 million Canadian users' data. LifeLabs compromised the personal data of 15 million users and is consequently facing a $1 billion lawsuit. Equifax faced an unprecedented data breach of about 148 million customers, which set them back by ~$1.2 billion in compensations (Deep Instinct, 2019). There are not enough proactive projects in IT security; most projects are reactive in nature. Since security breaches are costly, cyber security projects are valuable investments for organizations. A healthy IT project portfolio must include at least 30% security projects.

5.4. *Data orientation*

Data-driven projects have grown in significance. Data's role in decision-making is further strengthened by technologies like AI/ML. Corporate organizations embark on projects to manage, visualize, make decisions with, automate processes with, and monetize their data. Government and non-profit organizations are investing in AI projects to combat causes like climate change, world hunger, and illiteracy. The UN Global Pulse program aims to use Big Data and AI to achieve their humanitarian and peace goals. The World Bank backs 60+ digital/data projects in developing and underdeveloped economies. Projects can consider data management through two approaches: data defense and data offense (DalleMule and Davenport, 2017). Data defense focuses on minimizing risks, regulatory compliance, and data-driven analytics to manage threats, while data offense focuses on business goals and other identified criteria for success. While maximizing data utilization and driving project goals with data, IT projects must thoroughly consider the impact of compliance or data-related risks, and plan for their mitigation.

5.5. *Cost reduction expectations*

IT is often the go-to place for CEOs to meet their organizational cost reduction exercises. Conditions like market performance, unforeseen legal claims or penalties, and changing shareholder expectations are some reasons for organizations to reconsider their operating costs. Such specific targets leave the management with not much choice. Cost reduction initiatives require changes to existing systems and environments, leading to unnecessary technical issues disrupting operational stability. Thus, IT projects have the additional responsibility to build lean, secure systems which deliver maximum business value at minimum costs. Domain-level peer reviews and outside views from other organizations or similar methods will help in cost-effective planning and offer resilience during these exercises.

6. Procurement methodologies

Procurement covers a wide range of activities, ranging from purchasing of goods and services, supply management, contractual agreements, and specific strategic partnerships to legal adherence arrangements. A keen supporter of innovation and the outsourcing model, IT projects are special. In addition to standard benefits like cost control, quality, risk, and supplier management, evolving project procurement goals also include innovation, collaboration, green measures, and business resilience. As engineering is catching up with technology and concept-to-market happens at a fast pace, companies that secure strong collaborative networks have a competitive edge over their rivals. Companies can no longer think of a traditional buyer–seller arrangement of a one-time transaction but should prioritize a continuous partnership process. For example, Microsoft boosts its Partner Network with various benefits, discounts, and facilitates customer success through data analytics. This in turn helps the organization expand and engage better with customers. Google also offers similar partner programs to encourage innovation and user engagement while increasing its footprint.

6.1. *Importance of right procurement approaches in project management*

Procurement is one of the key components which defines the smooth flow of a project to success. If a project's procurement is not managed well, it means at least 50% of the overall project is inappropriately managed (Nissen, 2009). The first step in setting up a project contract would be to decide the type of procurement approach and methodology that is ideal for the project. Several factors influence this decision: scope, value and nature of project, skill sets needed, location, expected schedules, readiness, sponsorship, financing, and confidentiality, to name a few. Being a crucial decision, the project procurement approach is best aligned with the organization's strategy in this decision-making process. Strategic alignment helps projects to leverage existing partnerships, forge new alliances, increase project visibility, and secure senior management support. However, the influence of existing partnerships in the procurement decision is high. A known partner is convenient. This puts the projects in a risk of strategic partnerships overriding more capable providers. Hence, there should be a healthy balance between project needs and organizational preferences. Unclear scope, high-level requirements, and generic specifications lead to ambiguous interpretations by the procurement teams and suppliers. This is a critical cause of project delays and failure. Thus, even before the procurement approaches are decided, it is imperative for the project team to finalize, elaborate, and elucidate the scope, requirements, and deliverables. Legal, social, and ethical aspects are increasingly important in projects and for organizations, and compliance to procurement terms must be abided by legally. Any disputes must be pursued until a mutual agreement is secured. When project disputes are left unresolved, they can disrupt operations and potentially tarnish the organization's reputation. A procurement grievance could be blown out of proportion with the influence of social media. Most common issues arise from non-compliance with Service Level Agreements, Intellectual Property Rights, security and data breaches, accountability, and ownership. As a mitigation measure, the United Nations (2019) recommends evaluating pre-contractual agreements and risk assessments to its member states while pursuing technologies like cloud computing. With a specific emphasis on data localization, their guidelines recommend understanding interoperability, statistics on security incidents, compliance with technical standards, licenses, exit strategies, and insurance policies. This proactive mindset is much needed in IT procurement.

6.2. *Emerging procurement approaches*

The commonly practiced IT procurement approaches include multi-supplier quotations, request for proposals, invitation to bids, and in specific scenarios, competition waivers. The existing supplier base, strategic alliances, and legacy dependencies are some of the factors that drive these traditional procurement practices. While this continues to yield stable results, organizations are adopting innovative approaches to manage growing business needs. Two approaches are gaining popularity in recent IT project management: agility and partnerships. These approaches do not aim to replace traditional measures but complement and strengthen them wherever possible.

6.2.1. *Agility*

Agile procurement and lean procurement are two practices that aim to increase speed of delivery and reduce inefficiencies.

- Agile procurement is an additional layer of procurement to increase speed of deliverables and iteratively enhance procurement outcomes. Agile procurement is very useful in large projects as a cross-functional setup. With a team of functional and technical stakeholders who offer guidance in their respective areas, agile procurement increases the accuracy of the requirements, goals, and understanding of gaps. As the traditional procurement of a megaproject could span many months and even years, including an agile approach into the duration of the procurement will yield tangible, measurable results quickly and iteratively. Other advantages are continual negotiations, increased transparency, eliminating bottlenecks, resolved ambiguities, and increased collaboration.
- Lean procurement helps to reduce waste in the procurement process. Projects struggle with organizational procurement processes which are cumbersome and outdated. Inefficient processes will waste time, increase costs, increase layers of dependencies, and diminish the value addition of procurement to projects. Automation through RPA

is an effective approach to introduce lean by identifying cross-functional overlaps, streamlining procurement practices across the project, and thereby increasing productivity. The challenge in implementing lean is felt greatly from external factors like supplier environment, legal and ethical restrictions, and regulatory and compliance requirements, and it is not possible to eliminate all inadequacies. A good documentation of the project boundaries is useful to track these limitations and align as opportunities arise.

6.2.2. *Partnerships and outsourcing*

Public Private Partnerships (PPPs) are ideal for megaprojects, allowing the public and private sectors to collaborate, build, and operate. Originally intended for construction projects, PPPs have been expanded and adapted to all sectors. In IT projects, owing to the high demand for outsourcing, a similar model of partnership is common between project organizations and suppliers. Outsourcing is popular as it is cheaper and less accountable than running the services in-house. The $3.2 billion Daimler–Infosys global partnership, the $1.5 billion Vanguard–Infosys contract, the $2.25 billion Nielson–TCS partnership, and the $1.6 billion IBM–Lloyds deal are some recent high-value strategic initiatives based on this model. The ownership of the project and service lies with the project organization whereas the accountability lies with the main supplier. Such large ventures often follow a complicated partner-of-partner engagement model with a heavy reliance on many levels of subcontractors to fulfill the project and service obligations. The advantages are access to state-of-the-art technologies at low costs, higher innovation, scalability, and managed security. The disadvantages are lack of control, data privacy, high cost for termination, and a complicated model for resolving extreme cases.

6.3. *IT procurement best practices*

General procurement best practices include being stringent with the procurement process, controlling the critical path, including procurement specialists to project teams when needed, being flexible and efficient, benchmarking, managing technological growth, and handling software procurements with caution (Nissen, 2009). While these are effective, the increasingly business-oriented and outcome-oriented IT world needs the following additional project procurement heuristics:

- Involve early in contractual arrangements,
- Enforce detailed and stringent RFPs/tenders,
- Evaluate options to meet business needs,
- Include legal, social, and ethical considerations,
- Include sustainability goals.

The value chain that IT creates for other industries increases the demand for IT-related goods and procurement of services. High availability and lower failure tolerance from business push IT to increase digital resources like larger data centers, fleets of IoT sensors, digital twins for real-time monitoring, and sourcing from multiple providers to meet these demands. In the drive to meet sustainability goals from the business, IT projects must be mindful of their footprint and keep a check on the sustainability of their resources. For example, almost 0.6 million barrels of oil products per day were avoided by the electric vehicle industry. On the other hand, manufacturers like Tesla harvest and store tonnes of real-time data from electric vehicles. This shows their big data capabilities and the enormity of their data processing infrastructure which will have relevant environmental implications. The complex system of environmental goals and the impact of the undertaken projects must be facilitated by procurement.

Many business opportunities do not mature into projects, and it is not feasible to assign a project manager to general procurement negotiations. But, including project professionals in potential business discussions results in positive outcomes. The level of collaboration, perks, penalties, and flexibility needed must be agreed upon and made enforceable. With the hybrid work model, project teams in the future will include bigger virtual teams. Procurement must consider the implications and dependencies of the virtual workforce, from both internal and external parties, in the new reality.

7. Financing

Projects backed by corporate vision and driven by organizational strategy find better management support. Such projects also find the necessary financing support. The recent IT trends indicate a strong role of the sponsor and the innovative financing options available for project teams. Traditional funding, venture capitals (VC), and project finance are the three financing options that are commonly observed in recent IT projects.

7.1. *Financing approaches in latest IT projects*

Sponsorship is crucial for projects in terms of direction and funding. The lack of sponsor support led to project failures in one out of three cases of failed projects. Meanwhile, active project sponsorship is regarded as the highest factor for project success. In large and functional organizations, the sponsor is most likely the department or business unit head that finances the project. In small organizations and self-funded start-ups, the project sponsor and manager are often the same person. In megaprojects and public–private partnerships, sponsorship is held by multiple parties, either individuals with directorial roles or an organization. Apart from being accountable for the overall project's financial viability, the sponsor is also the due diligence agent who represents the financial interests of the undertaking organization. Be it traditional funding, VCs, or project financing, as indicated in Figure 2, the options are chosen based on various factors like scale, funding requirement, and complexity, and sponsorship is a crucial decision.

7.1.1. *Traditional funding*

Traditional funding includes self-financing and debt financing commonly practiced by all types of organizations. Self-financing refers to in-house budgets for the project or portfolio. The project finance control is executed either by the finance department or project controller, depending on the organization's structure, processes, and scale of the project. In such cases, the funds must be approved from the internal budget for the project's entire duration; the actual allocation will be handled yearly if the project

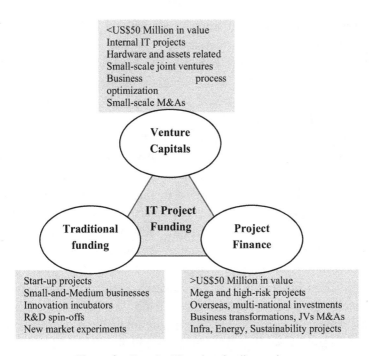

Figure 2.   Popular IT project funding options.

spans more than a year. Debt financing refers to the loans from lending organizations that are to be repaid in installments within an agreed duration. Commonly approved for values lesser than $50 million, both self-financing and debt financing sponsor organizations must have financial resources and a risk appetite. In joint ventures, the project investment and risks are shared between the parties. Traditional funding is ideal for projects with quick return of investment and immediate benefits. In many cases like security projects, the benefits are non-tangible but could save the organization from potential financial and legal risks. A 3–5-year ROI is a common acceptance criterion observed in higher-value self/debt-funded projects, and this varies depending on organizational goals.

7.1.2. *Venture capital*

Venture Capital (VC) is the aid that start-ups and small or medium business (SMB) organizations secure from investors. This is a crucial lifeline for aspirants to fulfill their funding needs without hefty guarantees that debt financing banks seek. Increasingly popular in the recent years, between 2019 and 2020, the monthly VC funding approvals recorded $18–40 billion. January 2021 saw the highest monthly recorded VC funding ever at ~$40 billion. VC project sponsorship has made garage start-up projects into billion-dollar giants. Google's first $100,000 came from Sun Microsystem's Andy Bechtolsheim in 1998, and in the next one year, Google raised $25 million from VC firms. Andy's $100,000 stake grew to a value of $1.7 billion in two decades; the rest, as they say, is history. The right VC partnerships are important for funding, branding, and growth. As in Google's case, investment interests from acclaimed VCs add credibility to start-ups and SMBs, bringing in more investments, attachments with other big banners and growth. There are different stages of VC funding and organizations can choose the appropriate type of VCs for their project initiatives. Seed funding is ideal for research, early-stage ideas, product, or service development projects. The start-up stage is ideal for a mature business plan with a goal to convert a minimum viable product into a full-fledged product or service. The first/subsequent stage is an option for supporting commercially viable solutions, and will require heavier investments and preferably more investors. The expansion stage is ideal for mass production, to meet growing demands and commercially proven ventures. The bridge stage is apt for taking the next step toward going public and is useful especially in M&A projects.

7.1.3. *Project finance*

The third category of financing that is gaining importance is project finance or project bonds and is popular in megaprojects. Project bonds allow investors to fund projects safely through listed and tradable securities, offering good repayment terms and fixed interest rates (Credit Agricole, 2018). The cash flow generated by the project is used to repay financial debts and equities. Being more flexible than loans from banks in terms of financial guarantee and risk acceptance, they are ideal for projects greater than $50 Million in value. The Global Project Bond Market has tripled in the last decade and, by 2018, was at $64 billion mainly in the energy and infrastructure sectors. Project bonds are a promising option for large IT projects. As business-driven IT demands an expansive IT infrastructure footprint, energy efficiency initiatives, and environmental requirements, the total cost of operation of recent IT builds are valued at billions of dollars. Project bonds are a secure and proactive way to undertake such high-value IT projects and are expected to gain traction in the post-pandemic recovery phase.

8. Data is the new oil

Data are increasingly gaining importance in all industries, with IT leading the generation and utilization. In the IT project context, data refer to the performance indicators, the referential information on constraints, and the data handled by its systems. Be it program selection, investment planning, or performance evaluation, data play a significant part in making informed decisions. Irrespective of the project category, value, or phase, data culture is essential for making the right decisions (Frame and Chen, 2018). National governments are embracing data from projects into their decision-making process for new initiatives. South Korea has cut program approval from 97% to 50% since 2005, which has reduced overruns drastically. Singapore scrutinizes programs using data through a Gateway Process and controls project health in the public sector. As early warning signals for the program's key objectives, data will support proactive management (The Stationary Office, 2011).

8.1. *Data generated from IT projects*

Data are both the fuel and by-product in technology projects. The legal, geographical, regulatory, and social implications of data must be understood and managed. Accountability, ownership, protection obligations, and safety measures are to be evaluated, documented, and agreed upon with the relevant stakeholders at the initiation of a project. Any deviation must be immediately and appropriately addressed.

8.1.1. *Custodianship and ownership*

In IT projects, the Business or end user is the owner of the data, while IT is seen as the custodian who is responsible for processing, integrating, managing, securing, and protecting the data. Risk assessment on data must be integrated into the project, with vital warning signs to be placed to raise attention proactively. Risk acceptance is a mandatory procedure that project teams must enforce for handling deviations.

8.1.2. *Data protection*

The EU has enforced the Global Data Protection Regulation (GDPR) to protect member states' data. Similar laws have been implemented across the world, with millions of dollars in fines for offenders. Legal considerations and geographical regulations must be understood before handling data. The sensitivity of the subject and its huge impact make the handling of protected data critical. Data protection is the responsibility of every member of the team. It is a continuous process that is closely tied to due diligence and proactiveness. It is imperative for project teams to question the type of data gathered vs. needed, and whether it is rightfully gained and consistent (Pritchard, 2018).

8.1.3. *Data classification and relevance*

Data must be classified for confidentiality, appropriately documented, always agreed upon with relevant stakeholders, and complied with. Any deviations must be addressed immediately and appropriately. As vast amounts of data are gathered and stored, data retention policies must be adhered to. Data must be regularly housekept and unnecessary data must be deleted securely. This will reduce the scale and impact in case of security incidents.

9. Operations empowerment

Projects and operations in IT are often at loggerheads with each other. Resolving conflicts between these two parties is a regular engagement for senior management. A possible reason is that operations teams are often not involved in early project planning discussions when the scope, design, and timelines are being finalized. Once a project is handed over to operations, issues become the responsibility of the operations teams. Any changes needed by the systems or applications must go through the change acceptance process. While it is customary to allow teething time, frequent change requests and issues after implementation indicate project quality issues. Thus, it is essential to include Operations as a work package in all IT projects. Involving operational stakeholders throughout the project will allow them to understand and guide the project teams on operational considerations.

9.1. *Role of operations in project perception*

Another commonly observed issue in IT project implementations is technical complexities which could surface at crucial times, like just before the go-live. When such critical gaps are uncovered, fast-track firefighting often leads to burnout of project and operational teams due to lack of reaction time. In cases where all the technical requirements are not implemented properly, projects face severe hyper-care or post-go-live issues. Inadequate setup could trigger failures, sometimes with drastic consequences that jeopardize the organization's business, reputation, and overall economic stability. For example, the IT system of London Heathrow's Terminal 5 faced a mega-scale baggage handling disruption a few days after going live. While thousands of passengers were affected by missing baggage, the operational employees had to struggle with the damage. British Airways suffered severe losses with millions of pounds of claims from passengers and, consequently, a wipeout of some of its stock value due to the negative coverage. This demonstrates that projects and operations must complement each other for organizational stability.

9.2. *Smooth transition from projects to operations*

Operational dependencies could be eased by driving projects from a change management perspective. Project teams must identify and incorporate streamlined processes that will eliminate and avoid unnecessary operational tasks. This will reduce the operational burden and create efficiency in operations. In large, traditional projects, incorporating change management practices like Prosci's ADKAR (Hiatt, 2006) will increase awareness, desire, knowledge, and ability of end users and, with necessary reinforcement, the knowledge can be made sustainable. This will gain user acceptance, empower them to handle the product or tools effectively, and reduce the operations load from mundane and repetitive queries. This issue can be reduced in agile projects using the earlier discussed CI/CD and user-feedback-driven processes.

9.3. *Need for long-term success factor measurement*

Project KPIs must include long-term success factors in addition to the traditional measures. The performance of projects over time operationally is a crucial factor to be measured and evaluated. The project team may have been disbanded and reassigned when the project is over, but the performance over time is important from an organizational project portfolio and a customer satisfaction perspective. Project lessons learned must include operational handover and post-hand-over issues as well. Post-go-live KPIs are to be reported with performance results periodically. PMOs and sponsors must review the performance of these KPIs over time and use the findings to optimize their projects and operations.

10. Summary

IT projects function in a dynamic environment and they continue to evolve around business strategies. Today's success does not guarantee tomorrow's profits as technology sees more dynamism than any other sector. The quality of its outcomes will assess projects over time.

References

Artto, K. A. and Dietrich, P. H. (2007). Strategic business management through multiple projects, In Morris, P. W. G. and Pinto, J. K. (eds.) *The Wiley Guide to Project Program & Portfolio Management*, New Jersey: John Wiley & Sons Inc. (pp. 1–33).

Awojobi, O. and Jenkins, G. P. (2016). Managing the cost overrun risks of hydro-electric dams: An application of reference class forecasting techniques, *Renewable Sustainable Energy Rev.*, 63, 19–32.

BCG. (2021). Most Innovative Companies 2021: Overcoming the Innovation Readiness Gap, Boston Consulting Group: United States.

Budzier, A. and Flyvbjerg, B. (2012). Overspend? Late? Failure? What the data say about IT project risk in the public sector, In Commonwealth Secretariat (eds.) *Commonwealth Governance Handbook 2012/13*, Democracy, Development, and Public Administration: United Kingdom. (pp. 145–157).

Crawford, L., Hobbs, B. and Turner, J. R. (2006). Aligning capability with strategy: Categorizing projects to do the right projects and to do them right, *Proj. Manage. J.*, 37(2), 38–50.

Credit Agricole. (2018). *Project Bond Fundamentals 2018*, Credit Agricole Corporate and Investment Bank: United States.

DalleMule, L. and Davenport, T. H. (2017). What's your data strategy, *Harvard Business Review*, 95(3), 112–121.

Deep Instinct. (2020). *Cyber Threat Landscape Report*, Deep Instinct Ltd: United States.

Deep Instinct. (2019). *Cyber Threat Landscape Report*, Deep Instinct Ltd: United States.

Edlich, A., Phalin, G., Jogani, R. and Kaniyar, S. (2021). *Driving Impact at Scale from Automation and AI*, McKinsey & Company: United States.

Frame, J. D. and Chen, Y. (2018). *Why Data Analytics in Project Management?* Auerbach Publications: New York. (pp. 7–22).

Flyvbjerg, B., Glenting, C. and Rønnest, A. (2004). *Procedures for Dealing with Optimism Bias in Transport Planning*, London: The British Department for Transport, Guidance Document.

Flyvbjerg, B. (2008). Curbing optimism bias and strategic misrepresentation in planning: Reference class forecasting in practice, *Eur. Plann. Stud.*, 16(1), 3–21.

Flyvbjerg, B. (2009). Survival of the unfittest: Why the worst infrastructure gets built — and what we can do about it, *Oxford Rev. Econ. Policy*, 25(3), 344–367.

Flyvbjerg, B. and Budzier, A. (2011). Why your IT project might be riskier than you think, *Harvard Bus. Rev.*, 89(9), 23–25.

Flyvbjerg, B. (2013). Over budget, over time, over and over again: Managing major projects, In Morris, P., Pinto, J. and Söderlund, J. (eds.) *The Oxford Handbook of Project Management*, Oxford: Oxford University Press (pp. 321–344).

Hiatt, J. (2006). ADKAR: A model for change in business, government, and our community, Prosci.

Kahneman, D. (2011). *Thinking, Fast and Slow*, Macmillan: New York.

Kahneman, D. and Tversky, A. (2013). Prospect theory: An analysis of decision under risk, In *Handbook of the fundamentals of financial decision making: Part I* (pp. 99–127).

Kerzner, H. and Saladis, F. P. (2011). *Value-driven Project Management* (Vol. 1), John Wiley & Sons: Hoboken, New Jersey.

Mordor (2021). Managed Services Market – Growth, Trends, COVID-19 Impact, and Forecasts (2021–2026), Mordor Intelligence.

Nissen, M. E. (2009). Procurement: Process overview and emerging project management techniques, In *The Wiley Guide to Project Technology, Supply Chain & Procurement Management* (pp. 247–257).

Pritchard, C. (2018). Data analytics risk: Lost in translation? In Spalek, S. (ed.) *Data Analytics in Project Management,* Auerbach Publications: New York. (pp. 23–41).

PwC. (2019). *PwC 22nd Global CEO Survey – ASEAN Findings: CEOs' Curbed Confidence Spells Caution*, Singapore: PwC.

Raz, T., Shenhar, A. J. and Dvir, D. (2002). Risk management, project success, and technological uncertainty, *R&D Manage.*, 32(2), 101–109.

Rigby, D. K., Sutherland, J. and Takeuchi, H. (2016). Embracing agile, *Harvard Bus. Rev.*, 94(5), 40–50.

Shenhar, A. and Holzmann, V. (2017). The three secrets of megaproject success: Clear strategic vision, total alignment, and adapting to complexity, *Proj. Manage. J.*, 48(6), 29–46.

Silvius, A. G. and Schipper, R. (2016). Exploring the relationship between sustainability and project success-conceptual model and expected relationships, *SciKA-Assoc. Promot. Dissemination Sci. Knowledge*, 4(3), 5–22.

Staw, B. M. and Ross, J. (1987). Behavior in escalation situations: Antecedents, prototypes, and solutions, *Res. Org. Behav.*, 9, 39–78.

Taylor, A. (2010). The next generation: Technology adoption and integration through internal competition in new product development, *Org. Sci.*, 21(1), 23–41.

The Stationary Office. (2011). *Managing Successful Programmes*, London: The Stationery Office, UK.

The United Nations. (2019). Notes on the main issues of cloud computing contract, United Nations Commission on International Trade Law.

Twilio. (2020). COVID-19 digital engagement report, Twilio Inc.

Wateridge, J. (1998). How can IS/IT projects be measured for success? *Int. J. Proj. Manage.*, 16(1), 59–63.

Wheelwright, S. C. and Clark, K. B. (2007). *Leading Product Development: The Senior Manager's Guide to Creating and Shaping the Enterprise*, Simon and Schuster: New York.

Chapter 4

Traditional and Agile Software Development Project Management Methodologies

Pearl Li Ng,* Malik Khalfan[†] and Tayyab Maqsood[‡]

*s3817516@student.rmit.edu.au,
[†]malik.khalfan@rmit.edu.au,
[‡]tayyab.maqsood@rmit.edu.au

This chapter focuses on the management approaches of information technology (IT) projects and how they fit into the context, priorities, and constraints of IT projects. The increased competition and velocity of change have encouraged software companies to utilize sound project management techniques to release new technology to the market quickly. New-school thinking recognizes that each IT project is unique and that there are no one-size-fits-all management solutions. This recognition was especially true for IT projects in which the technology evolves over time. A project environment that supports flexibility and proactively responds to change is crucial to improve value delivery. This chapter describes the interaction between project management and software development processes. It provides an overview of the different software delivery life cycle (SDLC) models such as waterfall, agile, scrum, v-model, and spiral. The core principles of advanced project management approaches are discussed and compared with generic project management methods. Managing a meaningful IT project requires an understanding of the organizational and technological environment. The main emphasis is to provide a primer on how these life cycle models work and how to select the techniques to manage IT projects effectively. Selecting the right processes also helps the team to meet the needs of the stakeholders within a specified time frame and budget.

1. Introduction

The information technology (IT) industry is always growing, evolving, and changing. The IT field is very broad with many commonly seen terminologies such as 'systems development', 'application development', and 'software development' being classified under the umbrella of IT.

Despite the increase in number of IT projects throughout the years, studies have also shown that many of these projects were unsuccessful. The two largest reasons for failure were attributed to managerial (65%) and technical issues (35%) (McManus, 2003). Increased competition and velocity of change have encouraged organizations to utilize sound project management techniques to overcome managerial and technical issues, as well as to release new technology to the market quickly.

Various project management methodologies were developed throughout the years and it is not unusual for these methodologies to be modified from time to time to be more effective. The selection of an appropriate IT project management methodology will influence the success of a project. Projects are said to have higher success rates if a project management methodology is applied (Sauer *et al.*, 2007). Essentially, selection of a methodology is the first step of an IT project, which will define how the team will work.

In the following sections, we are going to review several management approaches of IT projects. This chapter also describes the interaction between the project management process and the software development process. It provides an overview of the different software delivery life cycle (SDLC) models such as waterfall, agile, scrum, v-model, and spiral. The main emphasis is to provide a primer on how these life cycle models work and how to select the processes for managing IT projects effectively to meet the needs of the stakeholders within a specified time frame and budget.

2. Software Development Life Cycle (SDLC)

SDLC is a framework that describes the different phases involved in developing and maintaining software. Given the various types of IT projects that have emerged in the last few decades, different types of SDLC models have been employed with varying degrees of success.

2.1. *Processes for IT projects*

A generic SDLC is made up of six stages, as illustrated in Figure 1. It is common for the SDLC to be illustrated as a loop diagram. This is because most software applications typically undergo several development phases corresponding to its creation and subsequent upgrades. It is also important to note that these stages may not be sequential.

The subsequent paragraphs describe the objectives of each of these phases and examples of activities that can be actioned to realize these objectives.

The first phase of a generic SDLC is requirements gathering and analysis. The objectives of this phase are to do the following:

- Gain a clearer picture of what is expected from the system.
- Identify the potential opportunities and issues.
- Define the various technical approaches that can be undertaken to develop the system or software with minimum risks.

To achieve these objectives, a series of activities needs to be performed such as conducting a feasibility study, as well as gathering and

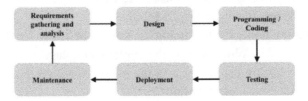

Figure 1.   Generic software development life cycle.

analyzing requirements. Other key activities that are conducted at this stage involve developing the quality assurance (QA) and data requirements.

The second phase is the design phase where the team defines the solution to be developed. The main objectives of this phase are to translate business requirements into specific technical requirements and to design a system or software that satisfies the defined requirements. For high-risk projects, a cyber security consultant may also be involved to perform a security risk assessment. As a result of all these activities, the two main deliverables or outputs are high-level design and low-level design documents. The high-level design document covers the overall system design. On the other hand, the low-level design document is a detailed version of the high-level design document and encompasses the complete details of the interface.

The third phase is the programming or coding phase where the team creates the system or software. The objectives of this stage are to do the following:

- Build the system or software with all the components implemented.
- Ensure the program is error free and can be executed efficiently.
- Translate the system or software design into source code and system components.

Once the code is developed, it will be tested to ensure it works according to the agreed quality requirements. Depending on the agreed quality requirements, the QA analyst or tester will test the functionality by performing a series of structured tests such as unit testing. The rise in cyber security threats also prompts the needs for security testing in modern technology. To facilitate the testing activities, a test plan and test scripts are usually prepared. Following these, a test report will be generated that documents the test results, bugs, and fixes.

With testing done, the technology is said to be ready for the users to access and use. The objectives of the deployment stage are to bring the technology to life by deploying it in the production environment to support the intended business functions.

The final phase in an SDLC process is the operation and maintenance (O&M) phase. The objectives of this stage are to do the following:

- Ensure the technology continues to meet the user needs and aligns with the business priorities.
- Perform consistent maintenance and upgrade.

While the maintenance phase appears to be the last phase of the SDLC, it does not imply the end of the life cycle. Depending on the user's needs and resource availability, the technology may reenter the requirements gathering phase if more features are to be added to the technology. Occasionally, the business may decide to shut down or terminate a technology due to, e.g., it not being financially viable to maintain. If termination takes place, the team will need to ensure the data are retrieved securely for preservation.

2.2. *IT project management approaches versus generic PM approaches*

While project management is applied in various industries, its application is different in these industries. According to Sommerville (2003), modern IT projects are exposed to three types of challenges:

1. **The Heterogeneity Challenge**: The new technology needs to be flexible to operate on and integrate with multiple hardware and software platforms.
2. **The Delivery Challenge**: The new technology needs to be developed quickly and be functional within a short period of time in response to rapidly evolving global business needs.
3. **The Trust Challenge**: This new technology, especially defense and medical technology that is mission and/or life critical, needs to be of high quality and should conforms to the security requirements.

Other factors that may contribute to the complexity of IT projects include the following:

- Selecting suitable software architecture patterns.
- Managing assumptions and unclear expectations.
- Managing remote teams.
- Dealing with interdependent integrations, hardware types, rapid technology upgrades, and version changes throughout the project.

Given the multifaceted challenges in an IT project, an IT project management function is crucial to ensure that the wide range of technology and management tasks are in alignment and well managed.

3. Traditional approaches

3.1. *Waterfall model*

The waterfall model is a linear and sequential model where the SDLC phases are cascaded into each other in a steady downward direction. With the waterfall model, the development of the next phase starts only when the previous phase is complete, as illustrated in Figure 2.

The key phases of the waterfall model are as follows:

- **Requirement gathering and analysis**: Detailed requirements are gathered from key stakeholders and documented in the requirement specification document.

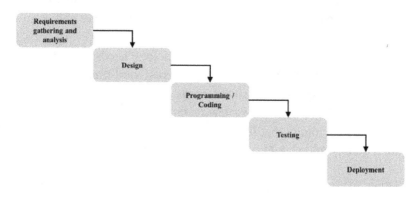

Figure 2.　Phases in a waterfall model.

- **Design**: Overall structure and technical details are defined.
- **Programming/coding**: The technology is built and integrated with other components as required.
- **Testing**: The technology is tested, fixed, and verified to ensure that it is working as per the specifications.
- **Deployment**: The technology is made available to the end users.

The waterfall model is a document-intensive process as all the activities and outcomes need to be clearly documented. The advantages and disadvantages of the waterfall model are listed in Table 1.

Table 2 highlights the scenarios where the waterfall method is suitable to use and where it should be avoided.

Table 1. Advantages and disadvantages of the waterfall model.

Advantages	Disadvantages
• Easy to understand and manage through departmentalization and control.	• Late changes in requirements will lead to a high cost.
• Allows for efficient knowledge transfer through well-defined and well-documented deliverables.	• Difficult to measure progress because the technology will only be available late in the life cycle.
• Clear timeline and milestones with specific review process.	• Unable to identify problems early because integration is done at the later stage.
• Results in better quality due to comprehensive test cases.	• Lacks provision for reflection or revision.

Table 2. Use cases for a waterfall model.

Adopt when...	Avoid when...
• The definition of the software/system/product is stable.	• The technology involves complex, object-oriented programming.
• The requirements are clear and precisely documented at the early stage.	• The requirements are not stable and have high possibility of changing.
• The technology stack is understood, predefined, and not dynamic.	
• The resources with required skills and expertise are available.	

3.2. V-Model

The V-model is also known as the verification and validation model. In this model, the verification and validation phases take place concurrently, as illustrated in Figure 3. This means that each phase is planned in parallel and the development and testing go hand in hand. The phases are as described:

- **Requirements and acceptance testing**: Requirements are gathered and analyzed based on the user's needs. At this phase, acceptance tests are designed to ensure that the system is functional in the live environment using real data. Acceptance test takes place after all other tests (unit, integration, and system) are completed.
- **System design and system testing**: All technical components such as the data layers and business logics are outlined based on the requirements gathered. System tests, mainly performance and regression tests, are created to be used after integration testing.
- **Architecture design and integration testing**: Specifications are designed to understand the relationship between different components. Integration tests are also developed at this stage to ensure that

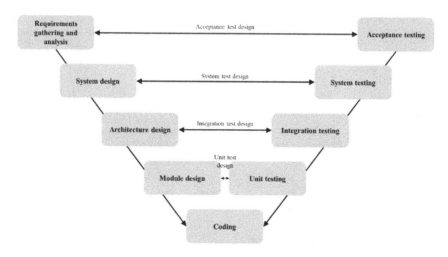

Figure 3.   Phases in a V-model.

the system or technology is functional when all components, including third-party components, are integrated. Integration test happens after unit testing.

- **Module design and unit testing**: This phase involves the detailed specifications of the technology such as the models, components, interfaces, coded business logic, and others. The unit tests are prepared and will be executed post coding to eliminate all the potential bugs and issues within the codebase.
- **Coding**: The actual coding takes place where the designs and specifications are translated into a coded, functional technology.

Table 3 lists the benefits and setbacks of the V-model, while Table 4 lists criteria for when the V-model should be adopted.

Table 3. Advantages and disadvantages of the V-model.

Advantages	Disadvantages
• Easy to control and manage because every stage has strict, defined results. • Results in better quality due to comprehensive systematics and disciplined testing. • Early detection of issues as testing and verification take place in the early stages.	• Late changes in requirements will lead to a high cost. • Lacks provision for reflection or revision. • Lacks flexibility.

Table 4. Use cases for a V-model.

Adopt when...	Avoid when...
• The requirements are clear and precisely documented at the start. • The technology stack is understood, predefined, and not dynamic. • The size of the project is small. • Skilled or qualified testers are available throughout the project. • Accurate testing is required.	• The project is likely to span a long period of time.

3.3. *Spiral model*

The spiral model is a risk-driven process model that utilizes a combination of iterative and prototype approaches in design and development activities. It is cyclical and extends upon the linear model, as shown in Figure 4. It primarily consists of four quadrants: planning, risk analysis, engineering, and evaluation. Each quadrant brings value to the development and skipping a quadrant implies that the team is making one or more assumptions, thus putting the project at risk.

A brief description of each phase or quadrant is given as follows:

- **Plan and determine objectives**: The objectives of the development are defined and the requirements for that iteration are gathered.
- **Analyze and resolve risks**: Risks associated with that iteration are identified and resolved or mitigated.
- **Develop and test**: The technology, along with the required features, is designed, developed, tested, and deployed. A proof of concept (PoC) or a working product is expected to be produced.
- **Evaluate and plan the next iteration**: After the technology is deployed and reviewed by the users, feedback is received. The feedback will be used to identify potential improvements and used as inputs for the planning of the subsequent phase.

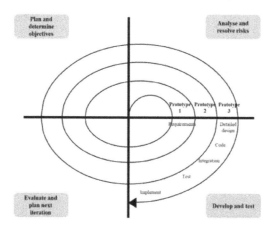

Figure 4.   Phases in a spiral model.

Table 5. Advantages and disadvantages of the spiral model.

Advantages	Disadvantages
• Better risk management as risk analysis is done extensively in every iteration. • Emphasizes learning on experience where knowledge gained during early iterations is used to inform subsequent iterations. • Progress is visible as the stakeholders can see the prototype early. • More control toward all phases of development. • The development process is documented to facilitate knowledge transfer. • The model supports scalability for more features or functionalities to be added at relatively late stages.	• Risk of running it in an indefinite loop. • Involves complex management, excessive documentation, and potentially high costs due to many intermediate stages. • Involves a lot of resources especially the technical knowledge during risk assessment.

Table 6. Use cases for a spiral model.

Adopt when...	Avoid when...
• The requirements are complex and require continuous clarification. • The project involves medium or high risk and risk evaluation is important. • Skilled professionals are available to manage risks and change requests. • The users are available to provide feedback during each release. • The project involves many exploration tasks, potentially due to unfamiliar domain or unproven technical approaches.	• The project has low risk. This model may be too effort intensive and expensive.

Table 5 describes the pros and cons when using the spiral model, while Table 6 lists the scenarios in which the spiral model is suitable to be used.

3.4. *Unified Software Development Process*

The Unified Software Development Process (USDP) is a component-based process. It is made up of multiple software components,

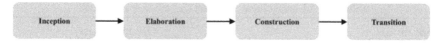

Figure 5.   Phases in an USDP model.

interconnected via well-defined interfaces. Use cases help to define the goals and the work required during each iteration, and the architecture serves as a structure to execute the work required.

USDP primarily consists of four phases, as shown in Figure 5. While the USDP is iterative, these phases often take place in a linear way.

- **Inception**: A feasibility study and a business case are developed. Requirements are captured in the form of use cases and a project scope is defined based on the use cases.
- **Elaboration**: System requirements are defined, along with the creation of use case diagrams, conceptual diagrams, and class diagrams. Other elements such as interface design and data management design are elaborated.
- **Construction**: The technology is built based on the diagrams developed in the previous phase.
- **Transition**: The technology is delivered to the customers and their feedback is incorporated from improvements.

The four phases are supported by workflows, tools, and processes. Examples of workflows are project management, configuration, and change management. Table 7 lists the benefits and pitfalls when applying the USDP model in an IT project, while Table 8 lists the use cases for this model.

3.5. *Fish model*

The fish model is a methodology in which the verification and validation are performed in parallel by separate teams in each phase of the model, as shown in Figure 6.

Table 7. Advantages and disadvantages of the USDP model.

Advantages	Disadvantages
• Emphasizes complete and accurate documentation. • Focuses on mitigating risks through risk-based development. • Minimizes problems associated with late integration as integration happens throughout the development. • Supports functional, behavioral, and structural modeling of the problem domain and system at all levels from problem domain to objects, and logical to physical. • Allows for traceability through seamless transformation of use cases to sequence diagrams. • Addresses customizability. • Utilizes rich modeling language (UML).	• It is a complex process. • High possibility for model inconsistency. • Any changes will result in a restart of the development process. • Less customer involvement.

Table 8. Use cases for an USDP model.

Adopt when...	Avoid when...
• The project is large and risky. • Fast development of high-quality software is needed. • The team is familiar with use-case-based development. • Experts or professionals are available to manage and assign activities to project participants.	• The organization, project, or team is small due to the challenge associated with task distribution and implementation.

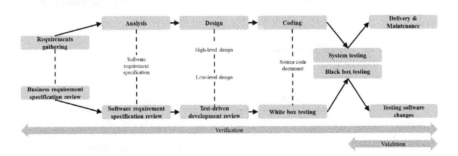

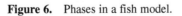

Figure 6. Phases in a fish model.

All phases of the SDLC are represented in the fish model. The phases are as follows:

- **Requirements gathering**: The information about what to build is identified. A business requirement specification (BRS) is created to document this information.
- **Analysis**: The business requirements are converted into technical requirements. These technical requirements are documented in the software requirement specification (SRS).
- **Design**: The low-level and high-level design documents are produced to document the working models such as the architecture, and cross-system interactions.
- **Coding**: Coding is executed, and the code is documented in the Source Code Document (SCD).
- **Testing**: Various types of testing (such as acceptance testing) are conducted to verify that the technology is working as expected.
- **Delivery and maintenance**: Once the technology is tested and has no defects, the technology is made available to the end users. Any issues reported will be fixed based on the agreed approach between the technology provider and the business sponsors.

Table 9 contains the pros and cons when using the spiral model, while Table 10 lists scenarios in which the spiral model is suitable to be used.

Table 9.   Advantages and disadvantages of the fish model.

Advantages	Disadvantages
• The parallel arrangement of validation and verification enhances the quality of the technology. • Complete documentations are available to facilitate knowledge transfer.	• The process is time consuming and can be costly.

Table 10.   Use cases for a fish model.

Adopt when...	Avoid when...
• The project is complex. • The project has high security requirements.	• The size of the project is small.

4. Agile approaches

The agile approaches have revolutionized the ways of working in the IT sector. Developed in 2001, the agile manifesto highlights the differences between agile and traditional project management methods in four aspects:

1. Customer collaboration versus contract negotiation.
2. Individuals and interaction versus process and tools.
3. Responding to change versus following a structured plan.
4. Working solutions versus comprehensive documentation.

Ultimately, agile adopts a combination of iterative and incremental models and focuses on adaptation to change and customer satisfaction. While there are multiple agile project management frameworks that have been developed in recent years, the overarching approach is similar. With agile project management, the team breaks down a large project into smaller, incremental builds that will be executed in an iterative manner. The team will allocate a small time frame (also known as timeboxes) to deliver a specific set of features. Each iteration serves as an opportunity to showcase the tool to the customers, gather their feedback, and incorporate the necessary enhancements in the next cycle of development.

4.1. *Scrum*

The Scrum framework is a lightweight agile framework that utilizes an iterative, incremental approach to develop adaptive solutions for complex problems. The Scrum framework consists of working solutions (also known as artifacts) and key activities (also known as rituals or ceremonies) that the team can adopt to facilitate the delivery process. In Scrum, the term 'Product' is used to describe the technology, system, or software that the team will be developing. Figure 7 shows how the Scrum process works.

The key Scrum activities are a sprint, a sprint planning meeting, a sprint review, and a sprint retrospective:

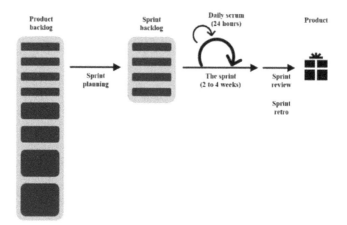

Figure 7.   Activities in a Scrum model.

- **The sprint**: The sprint is a short, fixed period when a Scrum team works to complete a set amount of work to complete an increment.
- **Sprint planning**: The sprint planning meeting is held at the start of each sprint for the team to identify how the product could increase value and what can be done within the selected time frame.
- **Daily Scrum**: The daily scrum session is held daily for 15 minutes. The development team will gather to inspect progress, communicate, and ensure they are tracking toward the sprint goals.
- **Sprint review retrospective**: The sprint review is held at the end of each sprint for the team to present the product increment to the stakeholders and gather their feedback.
- **Sprint retrospective**: The team reflects on how to improve their ways of working to be more effective.

The common Scrum artifacts are as follows:

- **Product backlog**: An emergent, ordered list of features and work that need to be completed within a project.
- **Sprint backlog**: A list of features and work that need to be completed within a sprint iteration.

Table 11. Advantages and disadvantages of the Scrum model.

Advantages	Disadvantages
• A semi-prescriptive framework and helps to remove ambiguities. • Motivates team members and stakeholders and provides job satisfaction through quick releases. • Provides greater customer satisfaction and returns due to the ability to respond and adapt to new demand and customer requests. • Enables team collaboration through daily scrum. • Reduces development cost as customers are consulted regularly.	• Knowledge transfer to new team member is challenging due to the lack of documentation. • High dependency on team members' dedication and teamwork. Lack of cooperation among team members may yield negative outcomes.

Table 12. Use cases for the Scrum model.

Adopt when...	Avoid when...
• The development team is versatile and open to change.	• The environment is rigid and it is challenging for the team to collaborate.

While Scrum is an effective method in managing technology projects, it may work well or otherwise depending on the situation. Table 11 presents the advantages and disadvantages of Scrum. Table 12 provides suggestions on when Scrum can be effectively deployed.

4.2. Extreme Programming (XP)

Extreme Programming (XP) is another lightweight agile methodology used by small-to-medium-sized teams in software development. The sprints in XP are often shorter than that of Scrum. XP has strong emphasis on an evolutionary design process. Its development stages are releases, iteration, and implementation (as shown in Figure 8):

• **Releases**: The customers identify the most valuable features.

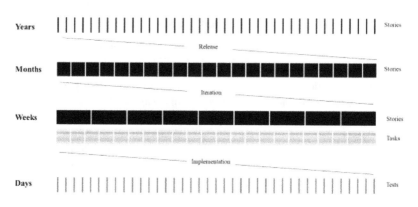

Figure 8.   Phases in an XP model.

- **Iteration**: The customers and the team select the most valuable stories in the release.
- **Implementation**: The team translates the stories into smaller tasks and writes a set of test cases for each task. Each team member will work with a partner to run the test cases and improve the design.

Pair programming is one of the main XP practices. With pair programming, two members work on the same machine concurrently. This practice encourages the team members to hold each other accountable, clarify ideas, and brainstorm refinements. This practice helps to improve quality and solve problems.

Table 13 shows the advantages and disadvantages of XP practices. Table 14 suggests when XP practices are suitable to be used.

4.3. *Feature-driven Development (FDD)*

The feature-driven development (FDD) is a methodology where progress is measured based on the features developed. A feature is a distinguishing characteristic of a software item such as performance that delivers value to the customer or user. FDD is feature-centric. The planning process, project schedule, and workflow are designed based on the features that need to be developed. The overall technology is built progressively and

Table 13. Advantages and disadvantages of the XP model.

Advantages	Disadvantages
• The framework can be applied by a team of any size but needs to be adapted for larger teams. • Enables the team to adapt to rapidly changing requirements. • Allows for early concrete and ongoing feedback throughout the short duration. • Enables the project plan to evolve quickly through incremental planning. • Delivers quickly via continuous integration and deployment. • Encourages open communication and visibility among the project team.	• Does not take into account future possibilities. • Does not include project management activities. • Less emphasis on design. • Constant changes are difficult to be documented properly and thus lead to a lack of documentation.

Table 14. Use cases for XP practices.

Adopt when...	Avoid when...
• The requirements or functionalities are subject to regular changes. • The team is able to work closely with the customers or users. • Skilled resources, i.e., testers, are available to create automated tests. • Rules are there to monitor social issues associated with pair programming.	• The customers are far away from the development team. • The team members are separated geographically

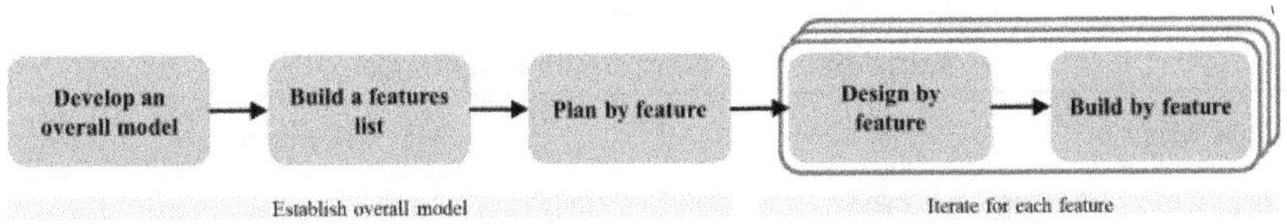

Develop an overall model → Build a features list → Plan by feature → Design by feature → Build by feature

Establish overall model   Iterate for each feature

Figure 9. Phases in an FDD model.

each feature is planned, designed, and built individually before merging into the overall product, system, or software. There are five main stages in an FDD project as illustrated in Figure 9.

The major stages of the FDD are as follows:

- **Develop an overall model**: An FDD project starts with identifying the project vision, scope, context, target audience, and the overall user experience and user interface.
- **Build a features list**: This phase involves identifying the key features. For a complex feature, the team may break it down to smaller features to reduce the risk and allow for quicker turnaround.
- **Plan by feature**: The team will determine the order of the features to be built and provide a reasonable estimate to complete the feature considering the potential risks, dependencies, and obstacles.
- **Design by feature**: The team members design, inspect, and refine each feature. A design review is conducted at this phase.
- **Build by feature**: The team members build the feature(s) assigned to them and test the prototype. If the team is satisfied with the feature, the team will add it to the main build and deliver the completed main build to the customers.

Table 15 lists the benefits and setbacks when applying the FDD model in an IT project. Table 16 lists when the FDD model should be adopted.

Table 15. Advantages and disadvantages of the FDD model.

Advantages	Disadvantages
• Encourages large teams to develop the system with continuous success. • Leverages predefined development standards.	• Ineffective knowledge transfer due to lack of documentation. • Has high dependency on lead developers or programmers.

Table 16. Use cases for an FDD model.

Adopt when...	Avoid when...
• It is a large, long-term project. • The project involves ongoing changes and features are added in a regular, predictable fashion. • The project or team size is growing and scalability is important. • There is a solid architecture which each iteration can be built on.	• The size of the project is small. • The project involves older systems where there are no overall models to define it.

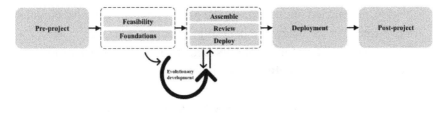

Figure 10.   Phases in a DSDM model.

4.4. *Dynamic Systems Development Method (DSDM)*

The Dynamic Systems Development Method (DSDM) focuses on the full project life cycle. It is an extension of Rapid Application Development (RAD) with additional governance and structure. The development of business cases is crucial in DSDM to ensure that the technology is delivering real business values. DSDM is made up of multiple stages, as illustrated in Figure 10.

The multiple phases are as follows:

- **Pre-project**: The team defines the objectives of the project clearly.
- **Feasibility**: The team examines the feasibility and viability of the technology, technically and commercially. A delivery timeline is prepared along with a high-level risk assessment.
- **Foundation**: The requirements are refined to provide a better understanding of the scope. The quality standards are also defined.
- **Evolutionary development**: At this stage, key practices such as iterative development, timeboxing, and MoSCoW[1] prioritization are applied together with modeling and facilitated workshops. The team creates solution increments by iteratively exploring and refining the requirements.
- **Deployment**: The goal of this stage is to prepare the technology for operational use. Three main activities, i.e., assemble, review, and

---

[1]A form of prioritization that classifies objectives as 'must have', 'should have', 'could have', and 'will not have this time'.

deploy, are carried out to achieve the goal. The team will also conduct a retrospective to review the overall project performance.

- **Post-project**: The team monitors and measures to what extent the expected business benefits are achieved.

Table 17 shows the pros and cons when applying the DSDM model in an IT project. Table 18 contains scenarios in which the DSDM model can be adopted.

4.5. *The Open Unified Process (OpenUP)*

OpenUP is a variation of the Unified Software Development Process which combines the Unified Process with Agile methods. OpenUP is easy to manage and execute as it involves a minimal set of practices and ceremonies. Figure 11 shows the project phases of OpenUP.

Table 17. Advantages and disadvantages of the DSDM model.

Advantages	Disadvantages
• Delivers basic features rapidly. • Encourages communication between developers and end users. • The process balances flexibility and reliability for on-time delivery.	• Requires large management involvement and overhead. • Can be costly and may be perceived as a disruptive change in organization culture. • The framework inhibits creativity.

Table 18. Use cases for a DSDM model.

Adopt when...	Avoid when...
• The organization or the project team values predictability and consistency. • There is a strict budget.	• The organization is at a start-up phase. • The organization is small.

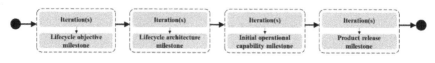

Figure 11. Phases in an OpenUP model.

The project life cycle of OpenUP comprises four phases (Kontchakov 2010):

1. **Inception**: The project team gains an understanding of the scope of the project and identifies the high-level architecture.
2. **Elaboration**: The project team validates the use cases and architecture. The technical risks are identified and addressed.
3. **Construction**: The team builds the technology including the design, programming, and testing.
4. **Transition**: The technology is released to the users. The team will also reflect on the performance and identify opportunities to improve the process and technology.

Each of the phases ends with a measurable milestone followed by a go or no-go decision by the project team. As OpenUP advocates for iterative development, this life cycle can be applied iteratively, i.e., the activities throughout the life cycle can be applied as many times as needed. Table 19 describes the advantages and disadvantages when adopting the OpenUP model. Table 20 demonstrates when the OpenUP model can be used effectively.

Table 19.   Advantages and disadvantages of the OpenUP model.

Advantages	Disadvantages
• The framework is open source and can be used by at no cost. • The framework is extensible and expandable. Additional materials can be added to the basic model and third-party practices can be integrated as necessary. • Project management elements are included as part of the process. • The process is lightweight and tool agnostic and can be adapted to different project types.	• The framework can be complex and less organized given that each iteration can be of different lengths with different amounts of work done from each discipline.

Table 20.   Use cases for an OpenUP model.

Adopt when...	Avoid when...
• The project size is small, i.e., around 3 to 6 people per team. • The project is of short duration, i.e., between 3 to 6 months.	• End-of-phase milestone checkpoints may impact progress. • The project team is large. • The project is complex.

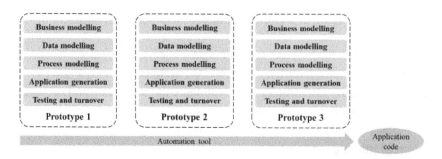

Figure 12. Phases in an RAD model.

4.6. *Rapid application Development (RAD)*

Rapid application development (RAD) focuses on developing the technology, getting feedback from customers, and improving the technology using the feedback in a short span of time. Without any specific initial planning, the team builds the prototype and tests the solutions rapidly. The RAD approach encompasses five phases: business modeling, data modeling, process modeling, application generation, and testing and turnover. The phases are shown in Figure 12.

The five phases are as follows:

1. **Business modeling**: The team identifies the source and flow of information between various business functions.
2. **Data modeling**: The information collected is refined into a set of data objects that are important to the business. The team identifies the attributes of each object and the relationship between them.
3. **Process modeling**: Using the data model created, the data object is transformed to achieve the information flow required for a business function. The transformation includes processing description of editing, deleting, or retrieving a data object.
4. **Application generation**: The data and process models are converted into prototypes using automated tools. The team will reuse existing program components where possible or create new reusable components (Nautiyal, Tiwari, Dimri and Bahuguna 2012).
5. **Testing and turnover**: The new components are tested at this phase. As RAD focuses on reuse, many components are tested during previous interactions, thus reducing the overall testing time.

Table 21. Advantages and disadvantages of the RAD model.

Advantages	Disadvantages
• The framework encourages the reusability of components. • The short development and iteration duration allows quick initial reviews by users and stakeholders. • Early integration takes place, thus reducing integration issues.	• The cost of modeling and automated code generation is significantly high. • The building of the components can be challenging if the technology is not modularized properly. • It is complex to manage as the project phases are not well defined.

Table 22. Use cases for an RAD model.

Adopt when…	Avoid when…
• The technology needs to be developed quickly, i.e., 2 to 3 months. • The technology can be modularized to be delivered in an incremental manner and within 2 to 3 months. • The designers are available for modeling. • Automated tools are available for code generation.	• The technical risks are high. • The project has a low-cost margin. • Resources with strong technical or modeling skills are not available. • The project is a large-scale infrastructure project and may involve large, distributed information systems such as corporate-wide databases.

Table 21 presents the advantages and disadvantages of the RAD model, and Table 22 suggests situations where the RAD is suitable to be used.

RAD is a model that requires strong collaboration among highly skilled resources. Care needs to be taken when used on large but scalable projects, which require sufficient resources to create adequate number of RAD teams.

4.7. *Traditional versus agile approaches*

Broadly speaking, the two prevalent methodologies in IT project management are traditional and agile, each with its respective strengths and weaknesses. The traditional method follows a linear approach which requires detailed planning and complete forecast. On the other hand, the agile

Table 23.   Characteristics of traditional and agile approaches.

Traditional	Agile
Adopts a predictive life cycle where scope, time, and costs are determined at the start of the project.	Adopts an adaptive life cycle where the scope is defined before the start of an iteration.
A plan-driven approach that does not expect changes. Any changes are carefully managed.	A change-driven approach where the team expects changes and accepts the changes.
Phases are structured in a linear sequential manner. Each phase depends on the deliverables of the previous phase.	Composed of short incremental deliveries called 'sprints'.
Focuses on documentations.	Focuses on prototypes, working solutions, and planning, e.g., sprint planning.
Customers or end users are involved at the start and the end of the project.	Customers are involved throughout the project.

Table 24.   Advantages and disadvantages of the traditional model.

Advantages of traditional model	Disadvantages of traditional model
• Agreed deliverables at the start of the project will facilitate the planning and design process. • Easy to measure progress and costs. • Defined roles and responsibilities. • Facilitates knowledge transfer through detailed documentation. • The structure and end goals are clear to the project team and stakeholders.	• Finalizing the requirements at the early stages can be costly. • The rigid structure does not encourage changes to be made midway through the project. • The process to manage changes adds effort and risk which may slow down the project, leading to a delay. • The stakeholders can only see the solution at the end of the project. • Limited customer engagement.

method focuses on adapting to changing requirements dynamically. Table 23 summarizes the characteristics of these two approaches.

Table 24 presents the advantages and disadvantages of the traditional model, while Table 25 presents those of the agile model.

Table 26 provides suggestions on when the traditional or agile approaches are suitable to be used.

Table 25. Advantages and disadvantages of the agile model.

Advantages of agile model	Disadvantages of agile model
• Provides the flexibility to adapt and accept changes as required. • Increases customer satisfaction due to strong focus on customers. • Promotes efficient communication among team members. • Working solutions are released quickly and improved in subsequent iterations. • Customers or end users are involved at all stages of development. • Emphasizes continuous improvement where lessons learned are applied in the next iteration.	• Requires regular customer involvement and feedback, which may not be realistic if the customers have other priorities. • Customers or stakeholders may not be comfortable with uncertainties around scope and timeline. • Changes in priority may lead to additional sprints and cost increase. • Requires ongoing planning to manage and prioritize the backlog. • A strict sprint timebox may lead to solutions that are incomplete or with reduced scope.

Table 26. Use cases for traditional and agile approaches.

Adopt traditional approaches when…	Adopt agile approaches when…
• The project carries significant risks, e.g., a flawed medical system that may lead to the loss of life. • The project is exposed to strict government-imposed regulations. • There are defined requirements and the environment is stable. • The team is distributed.	• The project calls for innovative, state-of-the-art solutions. • The requirements are unknown or subject to changes. • The project or business environment is familiar with agile. • The customers are available to provide timely feedback.

5. IT project management today: Reconceptualizing project environments

5.1. *Hybrid model*

The traditional and agile approaches have their respective merits and drawbacks. However, organizations are also looking at using a hybrid approach to project management. A hybrid approach is a combination of traditional and agile approaches, often customized to the needs of an organization or a project. The motivation to adopt a hybrid approach is to achieve the best of both worlds. The agile approach encourages adaptation to change while the traditional approach has a rigid, disciplined structure to manage contractual constraints and regulatory requirements. Some of the key considerations when adopting a hybrid approach include the culture of the organization and team, the technology domain, the organization structure, and the type of project *inter alia*. When adopting a hybrid approach, the team needs to have a clearly defined process to minimize confusion.

5.2. Agile for large-scale projects

The agile approaches are designed mainly for small teams. However, in recent years, the agile approaches are increasingly used at scale. In this section, four common agile scale-up frameworks are discussed, namely, Scaled Agile Framework 5.0 (SAFe 5.0), Scrum of Scrum (SoS), Large Scale Scrum (LeSS), and Disciplined Agile (DA).

The SAFe 5.0 framework is the most used agile scale-up framework that combines agile and lean practices. To accommodate the various levels of scale, there are four configurations in SAFe: Essential SAFe, Large Solution SAFe, Portfolio SAFe, and Full SAFe. Scaling practices within SAFe 5.0 include portfolio backlog and architecture epics that integrate with principal agile practices. SAFe 5.0 is said to be suitable when the project team participants are well versed in the use of portfolio management tools. The pros and cons of SAFe 5.0 are listed in Table 27.

Table 27. Advantages and disadvantages of SAFe 5.0.

Advantages of SAFe 5.0	Disadvantages of SAFe 5.0
• Helps cross-functional teams to collaborate more effectively. • Helps organizations to achieve greater transparency. • Aligns all aspects of a project to the broader business goals. • Facilitates the transition to an agile framework as it has a highly prescriptive structure.	• May not serve the purpose of agile given the prescriptive nature of the framework. • Requires upfront planning, process definition, and sufficient training for the framework to be effective. • Takes more of a top-down approach rather than a team-based approach.

Table 28. Advantages and disadvantages of the SoS model.

Advantages of SoS	Disadvantages of SoS
• Reduces communication overhead that can emerge when scaling project. • Allows teams to discuss their work, focusing on areas of overlap and integration.	• Daily meetings may be required as the team gets larger, leading to productivity loss and fatigue. • Ambassadors may make decisions on behalf of the team, thus reducing the impact of a self-organizing team.

Another framework to scaling agile is known as the Scrum of scrum (SoS), or meta-scrum. It is made up of multiple virtual teams delivering an integrated, potentially shippable product at the end of every sprint. SoS is suitable to be used when there is a balance of skills across the teams. The advantages and disadvantages of the SoS framework are presented in Table 28.

The Large-Scale Scrum (LeSS) framework is a lightweight framework that focuses on mindset, values, and principles without introducing too many processes and roles. The LeSS framework is centered on the 'One-team Scrum' approach, which entails the following traits:

• One single product backlog as there is only one product.
• One Definition of Done for all teams.
• One Product Owner with many complete, cross-functional teams.

The LeSS framework is suitable to be used when the organization and the leadership team are open to change, restructuring, and experimentation. The team will also need to be familiar with Scrum practices. For this framework to be effective, the team needs to be aligned on the definition of Done and the definition of Potentially Shippable Product Increment. Table 29 shows the advantages and disadvantages of the SoS framework.

Disciplined Agile (DA) is a hybrid process that extends Scrum to address the full delivery life cycle. It encompasses the proven strategies from many agile methods. Not only does DA enable teams or organizations to design their ways of working but DA also takes a goal-driven approach and provides guidance through process-related decisions. DA also considers the business and operation functions that underpin these

Table 29.   Advantages and disadvantages of the LeSS framework.

Advantages of LeSS	Disadvantages of LeSS
• Narrows the gap between the business and technical by having only one definition of Done and Potentially Shippable Product. • Provides the team with clarity. • Low cost of implementation for teams who are already using Scrum.	• Harder to implement for teams who have other frameworks and methodologies in place. • The idea of having one product owner may increase the responsibilities and workload of the Product Owner.

Table 30.   Advantages and disadvantages of the DA framework.

Advantages of Disciplined Agile	Disadvantages of Disciplined Agile
• Combines the best elements from various proven methodologies. • Provides the teams with freedom to adapt and customize the processes according to their needs. • Can be integrated with the capability maturity models.	• Requires upfront investment on training and guidance to implement it.

stages and life cycles such as program management. DA is suitable when an organization wants to remain flexible and define its own scaled agile framework while preserving existing processes. Table 30 shows the pros and cons of adopting Disciplined Agile.

5.3. *Integrated Project Management (IPM)*

While integrated project management is not an agile approach, it is often a crucial function in managing large-scale projects. IPM includes the processes and activities to identify and coordinate the various processes and project management activities. For IT projects, IPM involves three key areas, business management, IT management, and project management:

1. **Business management**: The role of IPM is to make sure that the IT investments are linked or driven by the goals and strategies of the business.

2. **Project management**: IPM is responsible for ensuring that the project teams adhere to IT PMO, processes, tools, and techniques. The IPM team members control the delivery timeline and resources to achieve the project goals.

3. **IT Management**: IPM ensures that the solution delivered is well integrated or compatible with other technology within the organization.

The overarching goal of IPM is to provide a holistic approach to manage an IT project. For IPM to be successful, individuals within the function need to have strong knowledge of cross-organization resource management to increase alignment between the project team and the different functions. Having IPM improves internal collaboration, increases innovativeness, and drives efficiency.

5.4. *DevOps*

DevOps aims to bring the software development (Dev) and IT Operations (Ops) teams together through a combination of cultural philosophies, practices, and tools. Historically, these teams operated in silos, leading to ineffective delivery. Through the implementation of DevOps, these teams use technology stacks and tools to automate manual processes. Examples of DevOps best practices are continuous integration, continuous delivery, microservices, as well as monitoring and logging. These practices help the organization deliver faster, more reliable updates to their customers.

5.5. *Model comparison*

As seen in the previous sections, there are many frameworks and methods in managing an IT project. Prior to selecting a framework, it is important for the team to understand the team dynamics and the stakeholders involved. The team should also understand the advantages and disadvantages of the different methods. Other selection parameters include requirements stability, skills and knowledge of the team, and familiarity with

Table 31.   Comparison between various traditional approaches.

	Waterfall	**V-model**	**Spiral model**	**USDP**	**Fish model**
Flexibility	Low	Low	Low	Low	Low
Complexity	Low	Low	Medium	Medium	High
User involvement	Low	Low	Medium	Medium	Low
Large team suitability	High	High	Medium	Medium	High
Speed to market	Low	Low	Low	Low	Low

Table 32.   Comparison between various agile approaches.

	Scrum	**XP**	**FDD**	**DSDM**	**Open-UP**	**RAD**
Flexibility	High	Medium	Low	High	Medium	High
Complexity	Medium	Medium	Medium	Medium	Medium	Medium
User involvement	High	Medium	Medium	High	Medium	Medium
Large team suitability	Low	Low	Low	Low	Low	Low
Speed to market	High	High	Medium	Medium	Medium	High

Table 33.   Comparison between various scaled agile approaches.

	SAFe	**SoS**	**LeSS**	**DAD**
Complexity	High	Medium	Medium	High
Ease of adoption	High	High	Medium	Low

technology and domain. Tables 31–33 provide a comparison between various traditional, agile and scaled agile approaches, respectively.

6. Summary

Managing a meaningful IT project can be challenging from time to time. It requires the team to understand the organizational and technological environment when selecting the right approach or framework. The frameworks introduced in this chapter possess respective merits and drawbacks and can be adapted to suit the needs of the teams, projects, or organizations. Selecting the right methodology allows the team to manage the IT project effectively within a specified time frame and budget, thereby achieving the goals of the project and the organization.

References

Australian Institute of Project Management. (n.d.). The Future of Project Management: Global Outlook (2019). https://www.aipm.com.au/resources/reports/future-of-project-management.

Bainey, K. R. (2004). Integrated IT project management framework: A model-centric approach to managing multiple IT projects. Paper presented at PMI® Global Congress 2004 — North America, Anaheim, CA. Newtown Square, PA: Project Management Institute.

Balduino, R. (n.d.). Introduction to OpenUP (Open Unified Process). https://www.eclipse.org/epf/general/OpenUP.pdf.

Beck, K. (1999). Embracing change with extreme programming, *Computer*, 32(10), 70–77.

Bourgeois, D. and Bourgeois, D. T. (2014). Chapter 10: Information Systems Development. https://bus206.pressbooks.com/chapter/chapter-10-information-systems-development/.

Burgan, S. C. and Burgan, D. S. (2014). One size does not fit all: Choosing the right project approach. Paper presented at PMI® Global Congress 2014 — North America, Phoenix, AZ. Newtown Square, PA: Project Management Institute.

Craddock, A., Richards, K., Tudor, D., Roberts, B. and Godwin, J. (2012). The DSDM® Agile Project Framework for Scrum. *DSDM Consortium*. https://cdn.ymaws.com/www.agilebusiness.org/resource/resmgr/documents/whitepaper/the_dsdm_agile_project_frame.pdf.

Cossentino, M., Hilaire, V., Molesini, A. and Seidita, V. (eds.) (2014). *Handbook on Agent-Oriented Design Processes*, Springer Berlin Heidelberg: Germany.

Department of Premier and Cabinet (Vic) (n.d.). End-to-end Project Delivery Framework. https://www.vic.gov.au/sites/default/files/2019-08/PM-GUIDE-03-End-to-End-Project-Delivery-Framework.pdf.

Eclipse Process Framework Composer (n.d.). OpenUP. http://www.utm.mx/~caff/doc/OpenUPWeb/index.htm.

Fitzgibbons, L. (2019). Feature-driven development (FDD). Agile Software Development. https://searchsoftwarequality.techtarget.com/definition/feature-driven-development.

Garton, C. and McCulloch, E. (2012). *Fundamentals of Technology Project Management*, MC Press Online, LLC.

Hassani, R., El Bouzekri El Idrissi, Y. and Abouabdellah, A. (2018). January. Digital project management in the era of digital transformation: Hybrid method. In *Proceedings of the 2018 International Conference on Software Engineering and Information Management* (pp. 98–103).

Jacobson, I., Booch, G. and Rumbaugh, J. (1999). The Unified Process, *IEEE Software*. https://people.eecs.ku.edu/~saiedian/810/Readings/rup-unified-process.pdf.

Keller, A., Rössle, A., Sheik, R., Thell, H. and Westmark, F. (2019). *Issues with Scrum-of-scrums: Investigating Factors of Failure Compared to Daily Stand-Up*, Göteborg, Sverige: Chalmers University of Technology.

Kontchakov, R. (2010). Information Systems Concepts Unified Process. http://www.dcs.bbk.ac.uk/~roman/isc/slides/isc5c.pdf.

McManus, J. (2003). *Risk Management in Software Projects*, Burlington, MA: Elsevier Publishing.

Nautiyal, L., Tiwari, U. K., Dimri, S. C. and Bahuguna, S. (2012). Elite: A new component-based software development model, *Int. J. Comput. Technol. Appl.*, 3(1), 119–124.

Sauer, C., Gemino, A. and Reich, B. H. (2007). The impact of size and volatility on IT project performance, *Commun. ACM*, 50(11), 79–84. doi: 10.1145/1297797.1297801.

Schwaber, K. and Sutherland, J. (2011). The scrum guide, *Scrum Alliance*, 21, 19.

Shivakumar, S. K. (2018). *Complete Guide to Digital Project Management*, Apress: Berkely, CA, United States.

Sommer, A. F., Dukovska-Popovska, I. and Steger-Jensen, K. (2014). Barriers towards integrated product development — Challenges from a holistic project management perspective, *Int. J. Proj. Manage.*, 32(6), 970–982.

Sommerville, I. (2003). Software Engineering, 6th edition, Pearson Education, India.

Tutorialspoint (2019). SDLC Tutorial. https://www.tutorialspoint.com/sdlc/index.htm.

Chapter 5

IT Project Stakeholders and Responsibilities in Different Software Development Methodologies

Steffen Heinig

Senior Lecturer, School of Civil Engineering and Built Environment, Cherie Booth Building, Byrom St, Liverpool, L3 3AF, UK
s.heinig@ljmu.ac.uk

This chapter will define the different categories and roles of stakeholders and what their genuine interest is. As there is a wide range of stakeholders, each party follows their demands and expectations. While some only have indirect power over the project, others can influence the outcome more severely. Management and clients are mainly driven by time and money concerns. In contrast, the developers also want to realize and fulfill themselves over the project's cause. Therefore, each stakeholder is analyzed, focusing on her powers and her influence on the project outcome.

This chapter provides an overview of different management models that have been used in the past. The chapter looks at traditional models, which have their origin in other sectors outside of the IT sector. While the Waterfall Model has been successfully used in manufacturing, it brings several disadvantages, which have brought criticism to the model and have led to the creation of alternatives. This chapter will discuss traditional models (i.e., Waterfall, V-Model, and Spiral models) and Agile, Scrum, and Kanban.

1. Introduction

According to Smith (2000), stakeholders are defined as individuals and organizations involved in a project, who are interested in its outcome. On a project sphere, there are usually internal and external stakeholders. While the internal stakeholders have a genuine interest in the project's positive outcome, the external stakeholders might negatively influence the project. A stakeholder is further described as a party that will mobilize available resources to influence the project's execution and outcome in line with their interest.

Some projects run over a long period, and during the project cycle, the interests of the various stakeholders may change. It is essential for the project's overall outcome to know who the stakeholders are and their interest in it. Since each stakeholder has a certain amount of power to influence the progress and outcome, the project manager needs to identify all the stakeholders in the long run. The manager needs to clarify the initial requirements and the interest of each participating party.

In this sense, requirements can be technical and non-technical. As technical requirements are usually planned and described in different documents, the non-technical details are subjective and change during the life cycle or once a stakeholder changes. Relatively stable requirements include the team members' general need to know the project goals and their roles during the process. Financial sponsors are interested in the effective spending of their resources. It is, therefore, understandable that they wish to be regularly updated on the progress of the project. Smith (2000) defines their main requirement in the functionality of the product. Figure 1[1] illustrates the typical project stakeholders.

While IT projects differ in many aspects from other projects, the underlying definitions of stakeholders and their roles can be applied

---

[1] ISO 21500:2012(E), Project Stakeholders, p. 7.

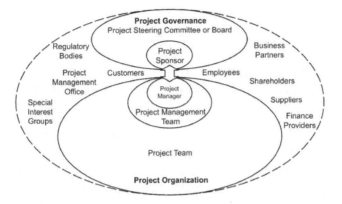

Figure 1.   Project stakeholders.

universally. In this chapter, the general stakeholders are defined. Based on the distinction made, these will be grouped and analyzed as internal and external. As software teams work in different environments and follow different strategies, the roles of stakeholders in software development methodologies differ slightly.

As the last decade has seen an unprecedented development of cooperation between companies that develop software and traditionally organized firms, two different working styles meet (Mirakyan and Golomejic, 2019). While classical companies follow either a hierarchical or flat structure, many start-ups organize themselves in decentralized, team-specific structures. These structural differences can cause tensions during the life cycle of the project. This chapter will discuss Agile, Scrum, Kanban, and other working styles and how different stakeholders can emerge next to traditional approaches.

1.1. *Stakeholder definition*

Stakeholders can be defined in different ways. The International Organization of Standardization defined stakeholders in the Guidance on Project Management (ISO21500). Here, stakeholders are either individuals or organizations that have a genuine interest in the outcome of a project.

Similarly, the Project Management Institute defines a stakeholder as follows:

an individual, group, or organisation, who may affect, be affected by, or perceive itself to be affected by a decision, activity, or outcome of a project.

(PMBOK guide, 2017, p. 577).

Sperry and Jetter (2019) follow this definition and generalize that stakeholders are all parties who have a stake in the project. It is worth mentioning that this interest does not have to align with the project's targeted goal. Some stakeholders might disagree with the project and want to influence its progress or outcome unfavorably. Every influence needs a certain amount of resources in order to be effective. Depending on the type of stakeholder, this influence or power might differ. Influence is a function of how much the outcome of the project will impact each party. As all stakeholders have their objectives, clashes with other participants are likely to occur. Smith (2000) rightfully states that forgetting just one influential stakeholder can ruin the project.

It is one of the primary duties of a Project Manager at the beginning of the project to identify stakeholders and define their requirements and interests. This is where the differentiation between internal and external stakeholders becomes essential. However, the Project Manager can only control external stakeholders in a limited way. Therefore, they bear a potential risk to the project.

Smith (2000) or Davis (2016) defines five traditional stakeholder groups: the project manager, the client, the owner, the user, and the project team. Some definitions describe the owner as also the financial sponsor. However, it becomes apparent that this list mainly includes internal stakeholders. Expanding this list to external stakeholders comes with difficulties, as only some may be known at the start of the project. Others remain unknown beyond the completion of it. As the project manager might not be able to identify all of them right away, it is necessary to consider potential new players in the long run.

This entire process is also known as Stakeholder Management. It includes an initial stakeholder analysis and the ongoing management of these. Depending on the roles and the responsibilities of the project, each stakeholder will need a different care level.

1.2. *Roles of stakeholders in an IT project*

As established in the previous section, stakeholders get involved in the project because of their interest in its outcome. While the outer sphere of the project is difficult to plot, the inner side can be planned. It is, therefore, possible for the project manager to define and communicate the roles and responsibilities of the participating parties. The ISO21500:2012(E) emphasizes this step and clarifies that this depends on the underlying organization and the project's goals.

An IT project aims to develop some software or improve existing company structures, which run under the current system inefficiently. In simplified terms, the project goal tries to achieve an outcome in a destined time frame by employing resources.

The general five stakeholders' roles and responsibilities have been discussed in the academic literature to some extent. Starting with the project manager, who has the project's overall responsibility, it is understandable that he or she also bears substantial power in control of the project. One of the prominent roles is project governance. As the project lead, the involvement in the technical implementation is outside of his duties. There is only a limited amount of understanding needed on this side of the project. His tasks involve creating the work plan, the allocation of all available resources, and risk management. Besides this, standard management tasks must be exercised, such as scope change control, milestones monitoring, and project status communication. As the leading internal stakeholder, he also manages people and conflicts throughout the project. The project manager needs to communicate regularly with the project sponsor. As they both have a positive mutual interest in the project's outcome, they govern the project together. This oversight is needed to align the project with stakeholders' objectives. Besides, both parties benefit from this structure which helps them make decisions or deal with situations where they may not be aligned. Coming back to the initial point of stakeholder analysis and management, according to Smith (2000), these tools help to discover expectations inside and outside the project environment. His role mandates the project manager to understand the attributes, interrelationships, and interfaces between project advocates and opponents. The PMBOK Guide further describes the additional tasks and responsibilities of the project manager. Section 3 will provide some additional insight into the different tasks of the project manager. The reader can find a detailed discussion about the project manager in Chapter 7.

The second stakeholder is the owner or financial sponsor. Crawford and Brett (2001) point out that the sponsor's role and responsibilities are not always clear. It further depends on various aspects within the organization. The need for upper management support toward the project comes from project management's general use of the broader economy. As more projects are run simultaneously, not all project managers can be hierarchical above the team members. Therefore, support from the upper management team is needed (Crawford and Brett, 2001). It is worth pointing out that not all projects have or require a specific sponsor, especially in projects where the project is delivered as some service to a third party. In these cases, the project team and the customer, who might act as the sponsor, are bound by a contract. Sponsors are therefore more often found in internal projects. Too and Weaver (2014) argue that a sponsor in an internal project links the project team and the executive management board. This means that the sponsor's responsibilities can be found in higher management tasks, such as the definition of business requirements. All activities of the sponsor are aligned with the company's interests (Hall *et al.*, 2003). As the sponsor is close to the company's management board, he shares the project's governance with the project manager. Taking an external perspective, he may pay more attention to the clients' side, which means that he monitors the business environment and draws the business benefits, which arise through the project (Bryde, 2008). Wright (1997) and Crawford *et al.* (2008) emphasize that the sponsor's support function is more important for internal projects. This helps the project manager concentrate on the main tasks. Helm and Remington (2005) clearly state that the likelihood of the sponsors' direct interference with the project manager's duties could cause lasting issues. The sponsor has been identified as the project's primary success factor if implemented by the company's management board. A new trend is that corporations actively look for people who can be held accountable if projects fail, meaning that the Project Sponsor has become the main link between the corporation and its project (Crawford *et al.*, 2008). The Association of Project Management (APM) defines the role of the Project Sponsor as 'part of the governance board of any project, programme or portfolio.' It states further that 'the sponsor is accountable for ensuring that the work is governed effectively and delivers the objectives that meet identified needs.' (APM. org, 2021).

The next group of project participants is the project team. These are the members who develop the product. It is not true that they have no say in the project direction or outcome, as they are actively involved. Therefore, it is important from a project manager's point of view to create a team that can work together and find solutions to the task. The literature has discussed various angles in Teamwork, as this style of problem-solving is used in many organizations. Throughout a project, members might come in to solve specific tasks only and leave the project once the tasks are completed. Other members might stay for the entirety of the project. Therefore, the nature of a project member could be both internal and external (i.e., consultant). This can make the mix of individuals complicated, as incoming members can cause tensions with the existing team. Team member roles can vary according to each project. Some may contribute to the overall project objectives, work out individual deliverables, or be hired based due to their expertise. Alternatively, their tasks may be centered on the client, where they work with the end user to establish business needs. Other aspects, and that is true for most IT projects, include the documentation of their work.

Teamwork has become an essential aspect of humans working together. Therefore, it is not surprising that the literature has developed different takes on it. As Teamwork is also performed outside of the project management realm, influences can be found from various disciplines. Lupuleac *et al.* (2012) referred to the difficulty of finding a balanced team. Referring to the work of Belbin (2012), each team can consist of up to nine different roles. Some team members may take more than one role, depending on their preferences. Belbin (2012) stated that teams with a sub-optimal mix of team members suffer when it comes to efficiency. The project manager must create a balanced team that incorporates all different roles.

Belbin (2012) identified nine identified roles: Plant, Resource Investigator, Coordinator, Shaper, Monitor Evaluator, Teamworker, Implementer, Completer/Finisher, and Specialist. Each of these roles comes with a different set of skills and responsibilities that can help to solve the task at hand. For instance, the Plant is described as a creative and imaginary thinker who can solve complex problems. At the same time, these individuals may have difficulties communicating appropriately since they are preoccupied with what they are doing. Quite to the contrary, the Resource Investigator is an outgoing individual who is enthusiastic and establishes new contacts. Unfortunately, their interest diminishes after some time. The Coordinator is an ideal people's person. He can identify the strengths and weaknesses of the team members and is, therefore, able to delegate tasks effectively. Some may take this skill offensively, as they assume that the coordinator delegates his share as well.

The Shaper, on the other hand, is described as a hard-working individual who can overcome obstacles. His behavior is likely to be offensive, as he can be provocative in his behavior. The Monitor Evaluator is an excellent evaluator and judges all available options. With this relatively sober attitude, he is unable to motivate others and can be identified as critical. The Teamworker tries to avoid conflicts as she is merely interested in a harmonic work environment. She is willing to cooperate with other members as much as needed to push the project forward. The Implementer is a hard-working individual that gets the work done. This group of team members is efficient in the way they work. However, due to the strict orientation on the work plan, they can also be inflexible when new tasks need to be solved right away. The Finisher can be seen as the last member who has her hands on the project. She is seen as a perfectionist and might never be done with the work. At the same time, she refuses to delegate as, in her view, she is the only one who can complete the task to her expectations. The last role in a team, according to Belbin (2012), is the specialist. While IT projects have many repetitive tasks, the last few decades have seen an increase in specialized work elements. These individuals come into the teams just for a narrow task and are likely to leave after completion. It can be seen that each individual carries some essential qualities to the project. However, it is also challenging to get the optimal mixture.

While the previous groups can be clustered as internal stakeholders, the clients or users are most likely external stakeholders. Many companies in the last few decades have identified the lack of internal innovation through IT. Therefore, companies have hired or created internal IT departments. They are sometimes seen as internal service providers. The customer can still be seen as an external stakeholder to some extent.

Nevertheless, the customer is relatively vital to the project's success as his final verdict decides the positivity and usefulness of the project. Irrelevant to their affiliation, customers are likely to have similar roles in projects. Initially, they provide information about their demands and requests. They are further an active partner in critical phases of the project, as the outcome needs to meet their expectations. Their say has a significant impact on the project deliverables.

According to Jergeas *et al.* (2000), judgment is one of the more distinct roles of the stakeholders, which is slightly more accurate for the external ones. Each project will be measured against the stakeholders' expectations. That again underlines the need for stakeholder management by the project manager.

2. External stakeholders

As defined in the previous chapter, many projects are negotiating interests among different groups of stakeholders. External stakeholders are defined as those affected or perceived to be affected by the project (Amadi *et al.*, 2018).

This chapter will present a shortlist of possible external stakeholders and what their expectations might be. Again, IT projects differ from other projects because IT solutions are created for an external customer in an arrangement where expertise remains with the project team. Contrary to a construction project, many people currently lack a deeper understanding of programming or the IT structure. This could lead to tension, as expectations of the customer may remain unrealistic.

Nevertheless, the last few years have seen an increase in demand for the consideration of the interest of external stakeholders. By adopting project-style work in many companies as an internal or external service, hierarchies were evaded. Therefore, external stakeholders have moved into the center of interest (Harrison and John, 1996).

2.1. *Possible stakeholders*

The reader should note that there is no finite answer to the totality of possible stakeholders. As each project, be it in construction or IT, has its impact and influence, the number of stakeholders is likely to change. Vogwell (2003) points out that external stakeholders for publicly funded projects can be easily identified. However, their number can increase significantly depending on the impact of the project. External stakeholders of privately funded projects are usually smaller in number. The only stakeholder that is constant might be the customer or client. Even when the client belongs to the same company or organization, he can be counted as external, relying on the project team's expertise.

Generalizing at this point, the broader sphere of stakeholders can include the following: *the Local Authorities, Governmental Authorities, Providers, Service users, Customers or Users, Suppliers, Funders, Quality assessors, Special interest groups, General Public and the Media* (Vogwell, 2003; Cleland, 1999; Olander and Atkin, 2010; Ezeabasili *et al.*, 2015). While each category seems manageable, the number of individuals involved can be challenging to be managed. Projects are initially more flexible, as the goals and deliveries are not 100% agreed upon, which means that the project manager and the team can react to the opinions of the external stakeholders.

2.2. *Expectations*

Looking at some of the mentioned categories, it is a good idea to illustrate their expectations. These have been discussed in the academic literature. Chan and Oppong (2017) analyzed the expectations of external stakeholders from a construction point of view. Projects in the built environment are usually centered on the creation of properties. As this creates a visible product, more people are likely to be affected. Lukes (2005) summarizes that external parties' expectations can be demands, reasons, needs, and values.

One can broaden this list with more project-related terms such as interest in the project outcome, the evaluation of project requirements, benefits, and design principles (Zhang and El-Gohary, 2016). Others used a broader, more encompassing view. Here, socio-cultural, economic, and political aspects are considered (Li *et al.*, 2012; Chinyio and Akintoye, 2008). Olander and Landin (2005) also point out that different social, educational, or political profiles influence the views and expectations of the external stakeholders.

Chan and Oppong (2017) provide a comprehensive list of expectations of different external stakeholders. While many of these are directly related to the project's construction site, others such as efficient use of resources can be applied to other project types.

Another influencing factor based on the expectations of the external stakeholders is defined through their nature. Parties such as local or governmental authorities have a much stronger influence or power on the project. These expectations need to be considered at any point. Others may control money, labor, or essential materials. These resources can influence the success of the project significantly. Beyond that, external partners may express their expectations during the planning phase of the project. In many cases, they may also control knowledge, which is essential for the project's development (Friedman and Miles, 2006). Karlsen (2006) emphasizes that controlling these resources provides the most significant leverage for the external stakeholders.

If external stakeholders are not appropriately managed, they may interfere negatively with the project. Jergeas *et al.* (2000) state that stakeholders could become dissatisfied with the project outcome. They may interrupt the project, which causes the budget to be endangered. Alternatively, they do not support the project from the start. In the worst case, this could create a lasting negative influence on the relationships.

The client or customer can be described as a hybrid role. Depending on the view taken, this stakeholder can be found on the internal or external side. Nevertheless, this is probably the most influential role in the project sphere. The client also represents the end user, and if the final product is not in line with the expectations, then the project could be described as having failed. In many instances, the method used can influence the success of the project. While traditional approaches have many project-related advantages, the lack of client involvement and the inability to change projects at a later stage have led to newer forms.

3. Internal stakeholders

The side of the internal stakeholders is the side which can be controlled and significantly influenced by the owner and project manager. The project's success depends on the team members, the upper management level, and the available resources. However, internal stakeholders are assumed to have an intrinsic motivation to create a successful project; each of the participating parties has its expectations. Given their roles, they may have more power and influence on the outcome or the specific deliverables. As pointed out in the previous section, some team members only participate in the project for a short period.

This chapter will illustrate a range of different internal stakeholders and what kind of expectations they may have. The chapter will try to give an overview of different roles during the project. Primarily, software developing projects have brought new work styles to the broader economy. Since each work style has a different set of roles, a summary is provided regarding the underlying methodology.

The following list does not claim to be complete. As pointed out above, the possible stakeholder differs from project to project. Lopes and Mañas (2013, p. 165) state that stakeholders are 'numerous and sometimes difficult to identify'.

Ali *et al.* (2019) did provide an overview of potential internal stakeholders in an IT project. The authors mention the 'project team, the project management office, the Executive Team, Business Analyst and Architect and Designer.'

The *Project Team* is the group of people developing the application. According to Maritato (2013), the usual members are the project manager, the analyst, the developer, the system architect, network engineers, User Acceptance Tester, and the quality analyst. They must understand the business and technical requirements. It is their role to ensure that all business requirements are met.

The members of the *Project Management Office (PMO)* have a rather administrative role. They monitor the project's progress and make sure that the budget remains in line with the expectations. It is advised that there is constant communication between the team and the management office to tackle unforeseen issues early. Other people extend the role of the department beyond the running project. Here, the PMO must ensure management standards in the entire institution. The main goal is the upkeep of productivity. A good structure ensures transparency, and members of the different teams know what is expected from them. The PMO relies on different instruments to guide the teams and to realize the maximum outcome for the company they are working for. So, for instance, through Strategic Planning and Governance, they define project criteria. Here, regular management duties such as aligning business goals come into play. Due to their far-reaching experience, they can provide Best Practices examples and models. This is mainly achieved through their documentation and the possible Project Archives. As with everything in life, the management style of the PMO can differ. Usually, three types are known: Supportive, Controlling, and Directive. Each of these has their advantages and disadvantages. The best method will depend on the underlying nature of the project.

Depending on the structure and to whom the project is delivered, the management board can gain additional control by using an Executive Team. The sponsor usually assigns a senior manager who has the authority to assign resources and enforce decisions.

The *Business Analyst* specializes in identifying 'technical, functional and non-functional requirements' (Ali *et al.*, 2019, p. 9). Other tasks include the collection of data and the appropriate documentation. Business Analysts are in a hybrid role where they communicate between the technical team and the operational team. Supporting the project manager, the analyst coordinates among the stakeholders by looking at all necessary business requirements.

The *Architect and the Designer* are specific members of the project team. They provide the internal structure to the project team. They are further responsible for delivering aspects of the project's architecture on the developing side.

3.1. *Traditional approaches*

Project management has been around for many years. Therefore, it is not surprising that different methods have been developed. Through many iterations, some methods have been identified as more valuable and efficient. More traditional approaches include the Waterfall Model, the V-Model, and the Spiral Model. However, these models have shortcomings when it comes to IT projects. This is why there has been a shift toward more adaptive styles such as Agile, Scrum, and Kanban in last decade.

3.1.1. *Waterfall model*

According to McCormick (2012), Waterfall Models were formally introduced by Winston Royce in 1970. Royce's Whitepaper included the general structure and argued for a high degree of documentation (Royce, 1970). Waterfall Models are part of the Software development life cycle (SDLC) methodology. Attributed models mainly deal with the design, the build, and the maintenance of information (Bassil, 2012). These models have been used in the manufacturing industry before — early software development projects in the manufacturing industry in the 70s already used these models.

A Waterfall Model is a project-specific structure that is sequential and linear (Balaji and Murugaiyan, 2012). Another way of describing it is by using the word hierarchical. The structure is intended to provide a high level of control and quality. Each phase of the project starts only after the previous phase has been completed.

An obvious shortcoming of this is that the project length is maximized as there is no overlap between the different phases. In addition, controls and checks are of great importance, as the management of Waterfall Models does not allow them to go back to the previous phase of the project. Altering elements of the project would require a restart on phase one.

Reminding the reader that this kind of project management has its roots in other sectors such as manufacturing may help one understand the importance of this strict structure. If one imagines a car's manufacturing, it becomes apparent that the team can only install doors once the frame has been modeled. Another aspect that comes into play with this project model is that the project's planning needs much more time. All possible aspects and issues need to be considered up front. The project team will be unable to provide input during the project. This puts more emphasis on planning, documentation, and communication. Team members need to be briefed before they participate.

Due to the high level of documentation, transparency is ensured. In other words, there is always a complete understanding of all aspects of the project. Team members can refer to the manuals and can, therefore, easily be replaced. On the other hand, new team members have short training periods, as they only need to read the existing manual. From a management perspective, the most significant advantage is that these projects can showcase progress since each phase ends with a solid result.

Furthermore, assuming that all potential issues had been anticipated early on, Waterfall projects save money and time. Thinking about the project structure, it becomes apparent that not all project team members will be needed for the entire life cycle. Therefore, the project budget can be relieved from unnecessary wage costs. In addition, the parent institution can work even more efficiently, as specialists can participate in many projects in shorter periods.

Let us suppose that the planned project is likely to have constant changes as the client might not specify requirements. In that case, Waterfall projects are not the way forward, and an Agile working style can be a better option. According to Balaji and Murugaiyan (2012), one of the main issues that arises through the strict structure is that the test team members get paid without much work — depending on the size of the institution. Nevertheless, it is very likely, that the project experiences a reset in a late stage. Many teams keep the testers outside of the leading project loop, and their input only comes in at a late phase of the project.

Based on these issues, the Project Sponsor should work closely with the Project Manager right from the start (Helm and Remington, 2005) to ensure that the project can run smoothly. The sponsor may like to demand regular meetings and updates to avoid unnecessary delays in the project.

3.1.2. *V-Model*

While some aspects of the Waterfall Model seem counterintuitive, the model is still prevalent. However, many of the above-presented disadvantages have led to the development of new alternative models. The V-Model has mainly been introduced through the issue of concentrated testing at the end of the project. As this is likely to generate issues and reset the entire project, the V-Model incorporates a strong focus on testing the proposed code. Therefore, the name of the model makes sense, the *Verification and Validation Model* (Balaji and Murugaiyan, 2012).

According to Childs (2013), the German Government developed the model to tackle complex problems. Unlike the previous model, the structure has become loosened. There is no prevention of additional testing during the project. Instead, it is the opposite, as verification of the previous phase is done right away before proceeding forward. This makes the model sequential. The V-Model again follows the SDLC methodology.

In general, the different phases are similar to the Waterfall Model. The phases can change depending on the underlying project or the definition in place. For instance, Childs (2013) defines the following five phases: *(1) Requirement Analysis, (2) Functional Specification, (3) High-Level Design, (4) Detailed Design/program specification, and (5) Implement/ Code.*

However, Fowler (2014) only states four overall phases: *(1) Requirements, (2) Analysis and architecture, (3) Design, and (4) Coding, prototyping, and engineering modeling.* At this stage, the model has two sides, one on each of the arms of the 'V'. The verification happens in the middle at each phase, through the testing on the right-hand side of the structure. Phase one is matched with Acceptance tests and the Analysis and the architecture phase is verified through an Integration test.

While many advantages of the model mirror those of the Waterfall Model, especially the consideration of the tester early on, it must be seen as a benefit. In such an environment, the developers and testers work in parallel and closely together. This creates a range of minor loops, ensuring high quality and a low level of issues. Testers are usually involved in the requirement phase already, which provides an additional perspective.

At the same time, constant backtesting can potentially become an issue. In the event of new or changed requirements, the V-Model is not flexible enough. In contrast, technical aspects can be improved; the entire document needs to be adjusted. In an unstable environment, this may lead to an extreme workload. Balaji and Murugaiyan (2012) state that short-term projects may need to apply a different model due to excessive documentation and other resources. Fowler (2014) further adds that similar to the earlier criticism of the Waterfall Model, the project's requirements are completed in the initial stage. According to the author, this approach is unrealistic for most projects.

3.1.3. *Spiral Model*

The Spiral Model is another modification of the two aforementioned models. As another representative of the SDLC models, it combines sequential and prototype-focused approaches. This setup is suited for managing large projects (Boehm, 1988).

The project follows a cycle of various iterations or spirals. Each spiral is defined by different activities, which result in a small prototype illustrating some aspects of the overall product. This process is then repeated multiple times until the entire project is completed.

Usually, there are four phases. Similar to the previous models, each project starts with a *(1) Planning Phase*, followed by *(2) Risk Analysis*, *(3) Engineering, and (4) Evaluation*. Different tasks are performed in each spiral, and there is a specific set of expected deliverables.

In the planning phase, all requirements are collected, and a feasibility study is created. The expected output is a finalized document, including a complete list of all requirements. The second phase is mainly concerned with drafting the necessary steps and identifying potential risks. A document with all findings is produced. The document reveals what steps are intended to tackle these risks. The actual development and testing are done during phase three. Again, the phase concludes with the final code as well as a detailed documentation of the product. Possible test cases and test results could be included as well. The final stage of the project is reached when the customer provides their opinion and tests the product. If necessary, additional features are implemented.

As mentioned, a Spiral model is best suited for large-scale projects, where software is created and handled strategically. Other ideal environments are where the software needs a high level of risk assessment or the project requirements constantly change. Nevertheless, the model allows the fast development of software. Another advantage is that control over all phases is given. Spiral models can also be seen as a toolbox that allows additional modules throughout the project. The downside, especially during the risk analysis, is that it usually requires a high level of expertise early on in the project. There is further risk of an infinite ongoing project.

3.2. *Agile*

The traditional models showed a range of shortcomings, especially in the project's sequential progress. Not being able to iterate one element of the project during its course is seen as one of the significant issues. According to McComick (2012), other models such as the Agile Model for software development evolved in the 1990s. Developers identified that many software projects required a more flexible approach outside traditional structures with their segmented and bureaucratic approaches.

The 'Agile' method went back to research by Edmonds in 1974. Scrum, for instance, is another representative of this model category and was introduced in 1995. The Agile movement declared a so-called 'Agile Manifesto' in 2001, which included the rules for agile software development (McCormick, 2012). Therefore, teams or 'followers' of Agile structures understand it as a philosophy — an alternative and rejection to the Waterfall Model.

The goal of the project shifts from the focus on the launch to the product itself. Developers start immediately and create a prototype or a 'minimum viable product'. This will then be developed further, with new information coming in from the users. The PMBOK (2017) also states that agile teams start creating the product and spend less time defining the scope.

Tasks are discussed with the entire team, and they are prioritized during the meetings. The phase where team members start working on these is called a 'Sprint'. A subgroup of the team works together in order to create a solution. This process runs in multiple iterations until all issues are solved. The most significant advantage of this is that the project team remains flexible and can respond to emerging requirements from the client.

Other advantages are that the Sprints allow a strategic prioritization. The project manager can allocate more resources to essential tasks if needed (Balaji and Murugaiyan, 2012). In addition, the process does not hinder productivity. Developers can engage deeply with their tasks and try to find insightful solutions. This helps the team to do what they are best at. Bureaucracy is lowered to a minimum level. Besides, Agile projects are relatively customer friendly, as they can deliver constant helpful software.

On the downside, agile models may work better in small-scale projects, as it becomes challenging to identify progress in large-scale environments. Since the structure is kept loose and the requirements and tasks are only identified, concrete planning can hardly be done.

3.3. *Scrum*

Scrum also belongs to the group of lightweight frameworks. It combines several advantages of the previous models. It is highly flexible in solving the issues, addressing new requirements, and allowing team members to work in an ideal working atmosphere. The most significant difference from other models is the focus on value. The Scrum team tries to create the best product possible. In other words, Scrum is a framework to address complex adaptive problems (Scrum.org, 2021).

Individuals who wish to know more about the framework are referred to the Scrum Guide, a composite of accountabilities, events, artifacts, and the rules that bind them together. Scrum teams also work in sprints.

Scrum was formally introduced by Jeff Sutherland and Ken Schwaber in 1995. The idea of Scrum was already used before but not formalized until then. Their work finally led to the Agile Manifesto in 2001, which is now widely used as a good starting point.

This framework is also different from other project management approaches because Scrum comes with its unique vocabulary and a different composite of internal stakeholders. The team consists of a Product Owner, a Scrum Master, and Developers. The project is run by a Scrum Master, who is different from a project manager. The Scrum Master tries to communicate the values of Scrum and wants to create an environment that is optimal.

A typical project runs in multiple iterations. The Product Owner orders a solution to a complex task, which is organized in a Product Backlog. The backlog is like a long shopping list of requirements. The Scrum Master uses each requirement for the sprints and breaks them down into an Increment of values for the Developers.

Each project starts with a Sprint meeting from a developer's perspective, where the tasks are discussed and distributed. During a sprint, which runs for several days, the team members meet for up to 15 minutes daily in a stand-up or daily scrum meeting to discuss the current process. Each Sprint is organized by the Sprint Backlog, which is intended to answer the Why, the What, and the How. Contrary to more hierarchical approaches, this backlog is developed by the developers themselves. This allows them to work on tasks that fit their strengths. Many teams add a Scrum Board here to visualize the steps currently in process. At the end of the Sprint, the requirement taken from the Project Backlog should be completed.

Unlike other management styles, the project stakeholders, in this case, the client, are invited to review the Sprint outcome. These meetings are called Review Meetings. Adjustments and recommendations are then used for the next Sprint. This allows a development close to the expectations of the client. At the end of the project, the team will meet one more time in the Retrospective. The team can exchange thoughts and comments on the process and the issues. This will help the team to make improvements for the next project.

3.4. *Kanban*

Kanban can be seen as another evolution of the previous models. While Scrum has already changed the focus to the values of the product, it still comes with some strings, such as structured sprints. However, as Scrum has been established as a philosophical approach to project management and not necessarily as a strict framework, project teams may incorporate both models simultaneously. Alternatively, they switch from Scrum to Kanban based on the requirements of the project.

The word Kanban comes from Japanese and stands for 'Visual signal'. Moreover, this is essentially the primary motivation behind the model. The project team tries to visualize the work as much as possible to achieve a good flow. Flow stands for efficiency and is mainly achieved through the limitation in the work progress. In addition, there is a stronger emphasis on reducing the time it takes to move a project from start to finish (Anderson, 2010).

Contrary to Scrum, teams utilize Kanban boards, which help to improve efficiency continuously. The underlying idea, though, is the same. The entire project is clustered into smaller work items, where a card represents each task. These cards are then moved through the Kanban board from the 'To do' section to the 'Done' section once completed. Therefore, Kanban is also described as a pull model. The usual structure of the cards comes with a title, the description of the task, and who is responsible for it.

While developing software mainly comes with virtual products, many people miss a visual confirmation of the work they have performed. So, for instance, a carpenter would see the chair at the end of the day. However, many software developers may only work on smaller items of the overall project. Therefore, both Scrum and Kanban bring the advantage of providing visual feedback.

One of the other advantages of Kanban comes through the limitation of work in progress. As there is only a certain amount of work completed at a specific time during the project, teams do not get overloaded. It also allows them to concentrate on the tasks without rushing through them fully — another way of improving quality. In addition, this helps to identify potential bottlenecks, which may block the workflow.

3.5. *Other*

The above-presented theories or frameworks are by far not the only ones. Over the years, different approaches have been developed and applied. Significantly, software development projects have changed the working approaches and have introduced alternative models.

The following are some other models:

3.5.1. *Crystal Clear*

This method was developed in the early 1990s by Alistair Cockburn. The main idea is centered on communication and the people within the team. Contrary to other models, it is not implementable as a working model as such. However, it is intended to provide ideas of how to adjust standing models. Seven main properties illustrate the critical aspects of communication and Teamwork. Many of the original ideas have been included in the Agile Manifesto.

3.5.2. *Extreme Programming*

Extreme Programming belongs to the Agile working models. The main goal is to produce high-level software by ensuring a higher quality of life for the development team. These models best work in dynamic environments. Similar to the Crystal Clear model, more emphasis is placed on communication in the team. A central idea, which has not been mentioned in the standard models, is the benefit of locating the team in a shared space. People work on different tasks; they can passively consume information, which helps them improve their work and the project outcome.

3.5.3. *Adaptive Software Development*

Adaptive Software Development is mainly used as a flexible model. The team pays much attention to the current environment the project is in. As another alternative to the Waterfall Model, the strict sequential structure is replaced by speculations, collaboration, *and learning*. While the speculation targets the planning phase, with the underlying assumption that the shareholders may be wrong or ill informed during the initial phase, the team tries to clarify inputs as much as possible. The collaboration part mainly tries to distribute the workload in the team evenly. Each iteration is used to learn more about the project, and new information is used to improve efficiency.

3.6. *Summary*

Both traditional and more modern forms of methodologies have their advantages and disadvantages in the way they work. Each project may need some specific adjustments to run as efficiently as possible. Research has discussed these differences. For instance, Patil (2019) looked at both types and identified that the sequential model structure of traditional models causes issues in a changing environment. Significantly, the client has less power in later stages, as sequential projects are based on lesser engagement. The earliest point for new customer input is the testing phase, which can be, in many cases, too late. In addition, excluding the client from the entire process can lead to a product that does not match the client's expectations, as he will only see a ready-made prototype. These issues do not occur in agile projects, as the client is involved in numerous stages throughout the project. Therefore, the client should make himself aware of these differences. In traditional models, more work needs to be done up front to ensure that the project matches the client's needs. Given the increased use of IT projects, cultural differences need to be considered as well. Brennan (2008) speaks of a potential cultural gap between the business and the IT side, which can cause tensions. Common issues are misunderstandings of goals or the inability to communicate effectively.

Given this, many corporations have created Project Sponsor roles that effectively represent the client side. They are a senior management role, in charge of resources and the strategic direction of the project. Research has shown that projects without such a role are more likely to fail. Steyn (2019) refers to statistics by the PMI, which states that a good and efficient sponsor is one of the main drivers of success. At the same time, roughly 40% of projects do not have exclusive sponsors (PMI, 2018).

4. IT packaging and outsourcing issues

Due to the adoption of IT applications in many industries and the hopes many businesses attach to the fourth industrial revolution, the last few years saw increased IT jobs. While many companies offered IT solutions to external companies in the last few decades, a new trend has become visible.

More and more companies have started to hire developers and run their own IT departments. Unlike the traditional jobs of internal IT people, who mainly dealt with broken hardware or installing new software, companies have started to develop customized software.

This brings about many advantages, such as shorter communication time and more power and influence over the final project. As the company hires the team, their intrinsic motivation is likely to produce a high-quality product.

This does not mean that outsourcing is not a common way forward anymore. Many companies may only have ad-hoc or current needs for software solutions. As these would not justify adding unnecessary employees to their payroll, the company may hire them temporarily.

5. Summary

As shown, for a successful project, it is necessary to identify all stakeholders. There is a difference between internal and external stakeholders, and the latter group especially might be hard to identify fully. It has been shown that depending on the scale of the project, the stakeholder list can be relatively vast. From a Project Manager's point of view, it is ideal to have a solid understanding of their powers and the potential influence on their success.

The internal group of stakeholders is similarly essential. While it is assumed that all work toward a positive outcome of the project, potential risks can arise if contradicting views exist. People may feel threatened in the way they work. Many projects are linked to change in processes. Therefore, it is essential to keep that in mind, as humans are creatures of habit. As pointed out, the Project Manager needs to establish a culture of communication inward and outward.

Various management styles exist and can help the team to create good products. While traditional approaches have been developed in other sectors such as the manufacturing industry, modern management models, such as the Agile models, have evolved due to IT-driven projects. Given the mentioned advantages and disadvantages of the Waterfall Model, these new models live from a more flexible and value-driven approach. The team, communication, and the value of the product are more important than the deadline. However, it is essential to note that the nature of the underlying project should dictate the model. Many software development projects do not have a complete set of requirements before the start of the project. Since new requirements may come throughout the project, more flexibility is needed.

References

Ali, A., Abdalla, S., Christian, R., Kumar, A., Javeed, G. and Shireesha Muthaluru, M. (2019). How Stakeholder Engagement Affects IT Projects. Available at: Research Gate, https://www.researchgate.net/publication/336144892. (Accessed 11 April 2021).

Amadi, C., Carrillo, P. and Tuuli, M. (2018). Stakeholder management in PPP projects: External stakeholders' perspective. Built Environment Project and Asset Management.

Anderson, D. J. (2010). *Kanban: Successful Evolutionary Change for Your Technology Business*. Blue Hole Press: Sequim Washington.

APM.org, Association of Project Management. (2021). What is Project Sponsorship? — Definition. Available at: https://www.apm.org.uk/resources/what-is-project-management/what-is-sponsorship/. (Accessed 3 August 2021).

Balaji, S. and Murugaiyan, M. S. (2012). Waterfall vs. V-Model vs. Agile: A comparative study on SDLC, *Int. J. Inf. Technol. Bus. Manage.*, 2(1), 26–30.

Bassil, Y. (2012). A simulation model for the waterfall software development life cycle. arXiv preprint arXiv:1205.6904.

Belbin, R. M. (2012). *Team Roles at Work*, Routledge: Oxford UK.

Boehm, B. W. (1988). A spiral model of software development and enhancement, *Computer*, 21(5), 61–72.

Brennan, O. (2008). Client and IT engagement in software development: A disconnect of mindsets.

Bryde, D. (2008). Perceptions of the impact of project sponsorship practices on project success, *Int. J. Proj. Manage.*, 26(8), 800–809.

Chan, A. P. and Oppong, G. D. (2017). Managing the expectations of external stakeholders in construction projects, Engineering, Construction and Architectural Management.

Childs, P. R. N. (2013). *Mechanical Design Engineering Handbook*, Butterworth-Heinemann: Oxford UK.

Chinyio, E. A. and Akintoye, A. (2008). Practical approaches for engaging stakeholders: Findings from the UK, *Constr. Manage. Econ.*, 26(6), 591–599.

Cleland, D. I. (1999). *Project Management — Strategic Design and Implementation*, 3rd ed., New York, NY: McGraw-Hill.

Crawford, L. and Brett, C. (2001). Exploring the role of the project sponsor. In *Proceedings of the PMI New Zealand Annual Conference*. PMINZ Wellington New Zealand.

Crawford, L., Cooke-Davies, T., Hobbs, B., Labuschagne, L., Remington, K. and Chen, P. (2008). Governance and support in the sponsoring of projects and programs, *Proj. Manage. J.*, 39(1_suppl), S43–S55.

Davis, K. (2017). An empirical investigation into different stakeholder groups perception of project success, *Int. J. Proj. Manage.*, 35(4), 604–617.

Ezeabasili, A. C. C., U-Dominic, C. M. and Okoro, B. U. (2015). Contentious issues on poor stakeholder management in some major road construction projects in Anambra State, Nigeria, *Civil Environ. Res.*, 7(2), 120–129.

Fowler, K. (ed.) (2014). *Developing and Managing Embedded Systems and Products: Methods, Techniques, Tools, Processes, and Teamwork*. Elsevier: London.

Friedman, A. L. and Miles, S. (2006). *Stakeholders: Theory and Practice*, Oxford University Press on Demand: Oxford.

Hall, M., Holt, R. and Purchase, D. (2003). Project sponsors under New Public Management: Lessons from the frontline, *Int. J. Proj. Manage.*, 21(7), 495–502.

Harrison, J. S. and St. John, C. H. (1996). Managing and partnering with external stakeholders, *Acad. Manage. Perspect.*, 10(2), 46–60.

Helm, J. and Remington, K. (2005). Effective project sponsorship an evaluation of the role of the executive sponsor in complex infrastructure projects by senior project managers, *Proj. Manage. J.*, 36(3), 51–61.

Jergeas, G. F., Williamson, E., Skulmoski, G. J. and Thomas, J. L. (2000). Stakeholder management on construction projects. AACE International Transactions, p. P12A.

Karlsen, J. T. (2002). Project stakeholder management, *Eng. Manage. J.*, 14(4), 19–24.

Li, T. H., Ng, S. T. and Skitmore, M. (2012). Conflict or consensus: An investigation of stakeholder concerns during the participation process of major infrastructure and construction projects in Hong Kong, *Habitat Int.*, 36(2), 333–342.

Lopes, L. and Mañas, A. V. (2013). Delays in it projects due to failures in the stakeholders management, *Future Stud. Res. J.*, 5(2), 155–186.

Lukes, S. (2005). Power and the battle for hearts and minds, *Millennium*, 33(3), 477–493.

McCormick, M. (2012). Waterfall vs. Agile methodology. MPCS, N/A.

Mirakyan, A. and Golomejic, R. D. V. (2019). Managing internal and external stakeholders in startup projects. Economic and Social Development: Book of Proceedings, pp. 309–316.

Olander, S. (2003). *External Stakeholder Management in the Construction Process*, Department of Building and Construction, Lund Institute of Technology, University.

Patil, A. V. (2019). Comparative analysis between sequential and iterative project management approaches, *Interfaces*, 6(07), 3035–3040.

PMBOK. (2017). A guide to the project management body of knowledge (PMBOK guide). *Project Management Body of Knowledge*, 6th ed. Newtown Square, PA: Project Management Institute. 6 September. p. 577. ISBN 978-1-62825-184-5.

PMI, Project Management Institute. (2018). *2018 Pulse of the Profession*. Philadelphia, PA: Project Management Institute.

Royce, W. W. (1970). Reprint in 1987, March. Managing the development of large software systems: Concepts and techniques. In Proceedings of the 9th International Conference on Software Engineering (pp. 328–338).

Smith, L. W. (2000). Stakeholder analysis: A pivotal practice of successful projects. Paper presented at Project Management Institute Annual Seminars & Symposium, Houston, TX. Newtown Square, PA: Project Management Institute.

Sperry, R. C. and Jetter, A. J. (2019). A systems approach to project stakeholder management: Fuzzy cognitive map modeling, *Proj. Manage. J.*, 50(6), 699–715.

Steyn, J. W. (2019). The elusive project sponsor. Available at: http://www.ownerteamconsult.com/the-elusive-project-sponsor/. (Accessed 03 August 2021).

Too, E. G. and Weaver, P. (2014). The management of project management: A conceptual framework for project governance, *Int. J. Proj. Manage.*, 32(8), 1382–1394.

Vogwell, D. (2003). Stakeholder management. Paper presented at PMI® Global Congress 2003 — EMEA, The Hague, South Holland, The Netherlands. Newtown Square, PA: Project Management Institute.

Wright, J. N. (1997). Time and budget: The twin imperatives of a project sponsor, *Int. J. Proj. Manage.*, 15(3), 181–186.

Zhang, L. and El-Gohary, N. M. (2016). Discovering stakeholder values for axiology-based value analysis of building projects, *J. Constr. Eng. Manage.*, 142(4), 04015095.

https://doi.org/10.1142/9789811240584_0006

Chapter 6

IT Project Teams

Steffen Heinig

Senior Lecturer, School of Civil Engineering and Built Environment, Cherie Booth Building, Byrom St, Liverpool L3 3AF, UK
s.heinig@ljmu.ac.uk

In this chapter, a range of roles and responsibilities within the project is presented. The focus is on the different stakeholders within the IT project team, external and internal. The presented list is by no means complete, but some of the most relevant roles are included. Each role is discussed around the required skills and expectations during the project.

Due to the change in the last few decades, expectations have shifted with agile working styles. Roles such as the Project Manager or the Software Architect have been influenced massively. At the same time, the Business Analyst is affected and can become an even more vital partner for agile teams.

Other roles, such as the design or quality assurance team, are highly relevant. However, they are highly skilled and, in many cases, covered by only one or two employees. This makes the role challenging, as their input is kept to a minimum, and apparent issues may only be addressed at the end of the project.

This chapter makes use of current job advertisements to illustrate what kind of skills and qualifications employers expect. Alongside this, the current annual income for these roles in different countries is presented.

1. Introduction

This chapter discusses different stakeholders involved in an IT project. Due to the methodological change in the last few decades, traditional roles have changed significantly in agile environments. Nevertheless, some of the presumed dead roles, such as the Project Manager, still exist. Agile work environments have taken the philosophical stand to oppose the classical position. Other roles, such as the Business Analyst, are somewhat flexible and help an agile team to work closely toward the solution of the requirements.

This chapter will discuss the roles of the *Project Manager, the Functional and the Operational Manager, the Business Analyst, the Subject Matter Expert, the Quality Assurance Manager, the Change Manager, the Software Architect, the Quality Assurance Engineer, the Database Administrator, the Software Engineer/Developer,* and *the Design Team.*

Since many of these roles are highly sought after, the chapter presents expected skills and requirements from the industry and a potential salary range for different countries in 2021.

A total of seven countries are used as a reference for the average annual salary. Six of the reported countries belong to the G7 states. Due to language barriers, Japan was omitted, and Australia was added. This is intended to provide an overview of salaries for the same roles in different world regions.

Many roles exist outside of educational paths and are learned on the job or through many years of experience.

2. Roles in traditional software development

Different stakeholders and a project team usually create a software product. The increased demand for software solutions in many industries requires an efficient organization of teams. At the same time, an increase in efficiency requires more specification and different highly skilled positions.

According to the Cambridge Dictionary (2021), a role is described in two ways. It is linked to a person's specific function, either in public as an actor or as a company member. However, it is also described by the expectations which are attached to it. This definition includes duties and responsibilities and considers the understanding of that role by the directly or indirectly affected society. The definition needed for this chapter links to our approach to dividing labor into smaller pieces. A software development project is an excellent example of this. As described in the previous chapter, a project is a construct of different stakeholders who, in the best case, share beliefs about the goal they want to achieve. The inner circle of stakeholders, the people who work on the project, is selected because of their skills. This probably defines, to some extent, their roles during the project.

2.1. *Project Manager*

The Project Manager (PM) is probably the best-known role in a project environment. One of the reasons for this is that he represents the project both internally and externally. Sommerville, Craig, and Hendry (2010, Title) describe the role of the PM as 'all things to all people'. The authors argue that the PM is responsible for delivering the project within the set time, budget, and quality requirements. This includes a technical and a managerial sphere. A manager is also required to lead a team. Therefore, interpersonal skills are essential.

Since the role of the PM is significant for the outcome of the project, a PM should educate himself constantly (Edum-Fotwe and McCaffer, 2000). At the same time, many researchers (Barber, 2004; Fryer, 2004; Jha and Iyer, 2006; Pant and Baroudi, 2008; and Shehu and Akintoye, 2008) have identified that the skill level of a PM is correlated with his age and the experiences gained in the past.

Among others, the duties of a PM include planning, organization, directing and developing staff (Fryer, 2004), forecasting, and communication (Griffith and Watson, 2004). These are classical management tasks. Other duties include the evaluation of potential risks as well as stakeholder management.

Due to the range of duties, the PM may hire a specific PM team that carries out some of his ordinary tasks so that he can concentrate on other aspects of his role.

Another way of clustering the tasks in the PM role can be done by looking at the different phases of a project. The phases are Initiating, Planning, Executing, Monitoring, and Closing. A wide range of responsibilities is again expected within each of these, such as stakeholder identification, cost planning, planning and identifying quality requirements, team building, and time management tasks (Alexander, 2019).

Becoming a PM is not a career path (Carbone and Gholston, 2004). Darrell, Baccarini, and Love (2010) showed that individuals are mainly selected because they have technical or managerial skills. However, many do lack the skills needed for project delivery.

2.1.1. *Project Manager in agile working environments*

The classical project management approach has reached its boundaries in software development projects. Many projects are now based on the Scrum or Kanban methodologies. They are more flexible, less hierarchical (Pettersen, 1991), and self-organized. Teams can take decisions independently regarding the distribution of workloads (Fowler and Highsmith, 2001; Cockburn and Highsmith, 2001). Shastri *et al.* (2021) point out that the role is regularly found, although it is not envisioned in any agile project approach. Therefore, this is an apparent disconnect between theory and practice. The PM tasks are assumed to be covered by the Scrum Master or the Product Owner (Drury-Grogan and O'Dwyer, 2013).

Scrum has introduced two new functions to the project world, the Scrum Master and the Product Owner. The first one is essentially responsible for the team functionality and how obstacles can be overcome. The second role mainly deals with the customer and envisions the product (Schwaber and Beedle, 2002).

2.1.2. *Job market requirements and salary perspectives*

This section looks at the current job market for IT Project Managers. The reported skills expected by the industry are from 2021. At the same time, the salaries quoted are the average salary for the US, the British, the German, the Australian, the Italian, the French, and the Canadian job markets. Other countries and regions may have different salary levels. The countries were selected based on the size of their economies. All but Australia count as G7 countries and provide a global overview.

One of the main factors influencing the salary grade is his or her level of experience. The difference in the salary grades can be significant.

Job market requirements
According to Glassdoor.co.uk (2021), IT project manager job advertisements have mainly required the following skills. Individuals are expected to *lead a cross-functional team to achieve project requirements, deadlines and schedules.* They are further expected to *Identify and resolve project issues.* Other tasks include the *preparation of project status reports* and the *coordination of change requests.*

As the PM is the representative of the project team, an applicant is expected to *lead the team in meeting client expectations and project deliverables.* At the end of the project, the PM is expected to '*Conduct post-project evaluations*' (Glassdoor.co.uk, 2021).

While these tasks are similar to the above-identified skills, the website further summarizes the different qualifications previously mentioned. These include the 'PMP[1] certification; An IT certification such as CISM,[2] CISSP;[3] Experience as CISO[4] or CSO;[5] Proven experience managing a team; Experience using Slack, Asana and Basecamp to manage workflow; Expert level in Microsoft Office applications, including Project; Excellent written and oral communication skills; and the Willingness to travel for extended periods' (Glassdoor.co.uk, 2021).

It is, therefore, fair to say that the skills discussed in the research and the industry do match. However, a PM career by accident is unlikely, as many companies require qualifications, such as the PMP certificate.

---

[1] Project Management Professional.

[2] Certified Information Security Manager.

[3] Certified Information Systems Security Professional.

[4] Chief information security officer.

[5] Chief Security officer.

Table 1. Average annual income — IT Project Manager (in national currency).

IT project manager	Min	Average annual salary	Max	Number of recorded salaries
Canada	$46,000	$91,000	$128,000	448
France	34,000 €	46,328 €	67,000 €	115
Italy	29,000 €	43,667 €	60,000 €	65
United States	$72,000	$102,013	$145,000	6,537
United Kingdom	£34,000	£52,343	£80,000	1,016
Germany	50,300 €	58,400 €	69,400 €	–
Australia	$64,000	$106,000	$148,000	–

Salaries[6]

Looking at the potential average annual salaries (see Table 1) for the position as an IT Project Manager, it can be said that the income seems attractive. As pointed out, the salary is strongly correlated to the number of years a PM has worked in the field.

2.2. *Functional Manager*

Depending on the project and the organization in the company, some departments may share responsibility for the product. If this is the case, projects benefit through a responsible Functional Manager (FM) appointment. The FM oversees the budget and the resources of the different business units (Rose, 2017). According to the PMBOK Guide, an FM is a person with management authority over an organizational unit within a company. They may, therefore, assign projects to the team they supervise. In addition, they evaluate the individual team members concerning progress and growth (Rose, 2017). Sometimes, they set career goals and try to motivate team members to reach those. As the role of the FM is of a

---

[6]For this analysis, the website Glassdoor was used. Here, current and former employees can review a company. They can further submit their salaries so that individuals can get a reference point. An alternative was used in cases where no salaries are recorded for the specific role, such as Stepstone.de (2021).

supporting nature to the PM, they regularly exchange information and assess the current progress (Muhoro, 2019).

2.2.1. *Functional Manager in agile working environments*

The transformation to an agile working style comes with some uncertainty for the traditional roles. In these environments, many people take on different cross-departmental or cross-functional tasks. If the organization relies on functional teams, it can be difficult for the manager to cover all necessary tasks. The possible work overload would hinder the person from being as efficient as possible. In traditional projects, this further creates a bottleneck issue, where the information stops flowing.

In an agile environment, teams work not only on a single part of the project. However, they are responsible for the product as such. This collaborative approach enables the team to work much more efficiently. The focus from one technical aspect is shifted to the product. The team becomes the product owner and is held responsible for the success.

This new environment demands that the functional manager focuses on one aspect of his previous skillset. Transferring his knowledge to a broader sphere of cross-functional teams would make him still relevant. Another task might be the organization of cross-functional teams, as this can be challenging in parts (Lung, 2019).

Veeraraaghavan (2018), on the other hand, takes the position that the FM can become an excellent addition to the new roles in Scrum or Kanban working teams. The separation of functions can help to increase efficiency. Relying on the FM would help the team to reach their deliverables through his guidance. Nevertheless, delegating power to one individual with regard to the organization of the team contradicts the main idea of self-organized teams.

2.3. *Operational Manager*

Another management level that can be utilized during a project is the role of the Operational Manager (OM). Similar to the FM, the role depends on the size of the enterprise and the project. In some cases, both roles are impersonated by the same person. As these are management roles, a certain level of experience and responsibility is needed. The main difference between the two roles, however, lies in the hierarchical level. While the FM is responsible for a specific business unit, the OM allocates resources on an organizational level. This differentiation has its roots in the different levels of management strategy. In order to accomplish the overall company's objectives, the OM needs to develop a specific strategy based on a thorough evaluation of the resources available. In essence, the PM is appointed by the OM or receives operational boundaries (Muhoro, 2019).

Responsibilities of the OM include the coordination and management of different departments, the review of financial (i.e., statements and budgets) aspects linked to the departments, and improvement of efficiency and productivity to achieve a higher return. Other tasks involve the constant production review, which is likely to happen in coordination with other departments, such as quality assurance. Like all management roles, communication internally and externally is also essential (Muhoro, 2019).

2.4. *Business Analyst*

A Business Analyst (BA) can work as part of the client company or the service provider. If he works for the client, he is involved before the project has started. The BA gathers information and investigates where potential improvements in the IT environment can be made.

A BA can also approach companies and offer improvements in their productivity through new software solutions. This makes sense if the company is specialized in a specific industry such as real estate or automotives. A working blueprint can then be used and applied to other customers.

The BA understands the IT side of things and can interpret the needs of businesses. This makes him a relevant individual, as many established companies cannot understand how software teams work. Pratt and White (2019) correctly state that they are responsible for bridging the IT world and the business gap.

The role is defined by the International Institute of Business Analysts (IIBA) as an agent of change. The Business Analyst aims to improve efficiency through a disciplined approach by managing this change. The role is sometimes hidden in other titles as well, such as 'as a business system analyst, system analyst, requirements engineer, process analyst, product manager, product owner, enterprise analyst, business architect, management consultant, business intelligence analyst, data scientist, and more' (IIBA, n/a, paragraph 3).

The BA also works across many departments within an organization. His involvement can be different depending on the aimed achievement. Sometimes, they just point out issues and potential productivity improvements and, sometimes, they are responsible for the entire project. In the best case, the BA leads to cost savings due to the identification of new business fields.

Shah (2017) clarifies that the BA works during a typical Waterfall project in all phases. The duties include 'understanding enterprise problems and goals; Analyzing needs and solutions; Devising strategies; Driving change, and Facilitating stakeholder collaboration' (Shah, 2017, p. 9).

2.4.1. *Business Analyst in agile working environments*

Due to its hybrid nature, the BA can easily adjust when new work environments, such as *agile,* are introduced. This seems especially easy when one considers software development as a service. The BA with knowledge about both industries is either hired to identify weaknesses or pitches a potential improvement.

In agile environments, the duties are spread among multiple team members (Georgio, 2012). The BA may remain responsible for the strategic direction. However, the decisions are not based on his input, as the team will collectively discuss all aspects.

In new working styles, the BA works closely with the Scrum Master, where his input can be used to write user stories. If the user story entered a sprint cycle, the BA could act as a tester to verify the proposed solution for the task.

It seems that agile projects benefit from considering a BA, as the quality improvement of the user stories will ultimately achieve a higher quality and usability of the product.

2.4.2. *Process Analyst*

The Process Analyst (PA) works closely with the client and the Business Analyst. His main work is done at the beginning of the project when the service provider or the project team evaluates the business case. He models the use case by considering the different actors and the 'normal processes'. The role is also described as a Business Designer.

Other duties include the management of the relationship to the stakeholders, documentation, as well as process review. Part of this is the evaluation of possible cost savings through business improvements (Rose, 2017).

Sonteya and Seymour (2012) had earlier criticized the absence of a more comprehensive understanding of the required skills and competencies needed. The demand for Business Process Analysts (BPA) did not match with the understanding of their role. Next to the modeling part, their duties include many tasks performed initially by the Business Analyst (Antonucci and Goeke, 2011). The authors state that the BPA role emerges from the BA's role, as more specific skills where needed.

2.4.3. *Job market requirements and salary perspectives*

The role does include many of the aspects mentioned above. However, like other roles, the BA is not a clear-cut career path. It is a position; many will develop over time and gain different experiences on both sides of the software development endeavor. Pratt and White (2019) listed some items in a regular job description. For instance, 'creating a detailed business analysis, outlining problems, opportunities, and solutions for a business; Budgeting and forecasting; Planning and monitoring; Variance analysis; Pricing; Reporting and Defining business requirements and reporting them back to stakeholders' (Pratt and White, 2019, paragraph 5).

A general understanding of IT is required. There is no need for in-depth knowledge, as the BA only functions as a translator. Other responsibilities include 'Oral and written communication skills; Interpersonal and consultative skills; Facilitation skills; Analytical thinking and problem-solving; Being detail-oriented and capable of delivering a high level of accuracy; Organisational skills; Knowledge of business structure;

Stakeholder analysis; Requirements engineering; Costs benefit analysis; Processes modelling and Understanding of networks, databases and other technology' (Pratt and White, 2019, paragraph 11).

Job market requirements

Glassdoor.co.uk (2021) lists the following requirements: 'Identify and resolve project issues; Analyse complex business problems and determine an IT solution; Gather data and analyse business and user needs; Provide recommendations on hardware and software procurement to support client's business goals; Coordinate the development of documentation to enable implementation and turnover of the process of system; Define objectives and scope of business system; Work closely with managers and end-users to determine best IT solution; Conduct post-project evaluation' (Glassdoor.co.uk, 2021).

None of the earlier-mentioned requirements are different from the ones mentioned above. It is, therefore, fair to say that individuals seeking to become a BA need to have a clear understanding of their role.

Salary

The salary levels for BAs are slightly lower in comparison to the other roles (see Table 2). This may be linked to the nature of the role. While a PM or a Software Architect will need to gather experience before becoming excellent in their roles, it is not necessary for the BA to be a senior member of the team.

Table 2. Average annual income — IT Business Analyst (in national currency).

IT business analyst	Min	Average annual salary	Max	Number of recorded salaries
Canada	$50,720	$70,134	$96,980	4,445
France	34,000 €	42,544 €	59,812 €	1,357
Italy	23,852 €	26,641 €	40,000 €	1,312
United States	$54,000	$75,373	$105,000	61,044
United Kingdom	£26,000	£42,426	£70,000	6,546
Germany	43,000 €	54,511 €	80,000 €	1,087
Australia	$65,000	$93,000	$125,000	1,994

2.5. *Subject-Matter Expert*

The Subject-Matter Expert (SME) is an individual with an in-depth understanding of the processes and the industry the client comes from. While the BA links the client and the project team, he may not understand the business altogether. This is where the SME comes into play.

Assuming the project team is a service provider, the role of the SME is only added if the company needs it. This will be the case if the client's industry is unknown and more specific knowledge is needed. In these cases, the BA and the SME will work together. It is advised that the SME should attend meetings early and regularly over the project's life cycle. This ensures that the project is running in the right direction.

Other duties include reviewing test cases, checking and validating requirements, and answering relevant questions linked to the product (Rose, 2017).

2.5.1. *Subject-Matter Expert in agile working environments*

In an agile project, the SME can be a product owner through his expert knowledge. This helps the team to make better products, as the decisions are based on more accurate information. Nevertheless, this additional knowledge of the SME can also become an issue, as other team members may run all problems through the SME. This is likely to generate a bottleneck of decision-making, which may cause delays and ultimately undermine the agile team's very ideas (Schuurman, 2019).

2.6. *Quality Assurance Manager*

Quality assurance or QA is one of the most significant aspects of software development. Suppose the project has reached the point where the previously mentioned roles have created a final product. In that case, it must be tested before it is released. Many of the previous roles are involved in testing throughout the project. A final testing phase is needed to see how the different aspects play together.

In the last few years, the industry has realized that products should be intensely tested before being released to the client.

Some roles in such a team can be the 'QA lead, the Test Architect, QA Analyst, the Automation Tester, the Manual Tester and the UX tester' (Anastasia, 2020). Other sources include a *Software Test Engineer and a Test Manager* (unknown, 2020).

The process is usually divided into different iterations. Every delay during the project cycle is likely to shorten the product's testing and 'repair' phase. Nonetheless, the testers are nowadays part of the project from start to finish, meaning they can make suggestions along the way so that apparent issues can be avoided.

2.6.1. *Quality Assurance Manager in agile working environments*

The QA is the first reference point when the team discovers issues with the product and needs to change elements of it. A solution can be found through a discussion moderated by the QA, and a more efficient product can be created.

Some teams operate without a QA role, which does not necessarily mean that the product quality will worsen. Nevertheless, it has been shown that teams and products benefit from the management skills of a QA (Reichert, 2020).

2.6.2. *Job market requirements and salary perspectives*

The QA manager is another management role learned through experience and less through an educational route. The role is mainly centered on the product and the assurance of quality. This involves the objective judgment of products and likely rejection if the product fails the client's standards.

As an essential requirement, an undergraduate degree is expected in a relevant field. Knowledge and experience in quality assurance and product processing are essential. Other required skills include knowledge about the market and specific trends occurring.

Job market requirements
Glassdoor.co.uk (2021) lists the following responsibilities based on their database: 'Collaborate with the upper management team to set quality

benchmarks; Create standards in accordance with industry standards and customer expectations; Identify quality control processes to ensure criteria are met at all times; Execute tests to check final product adherence to the company standards; Record findings and relay this information to the production team; Make crucial decisions in favour of cost-efficiency without compromising quality and Oversee production to ensure conformity in final product processing.'

The list of standard qualifications over the different job advertisements includes the following: 'Prior experience as a quality manager in a production processing environment; Familiar with company and industry quality standards and processes; Proficient in computer technology and systems; Good understanding of Microsoft Office applications; In-depth knowledge of market trends and conditions; Strong leadership and management skills; Excellent analytical and problem-solving abilities; Able to positively influence others and Great team player with strong interpersonal skills.'

Salary

Table 3 illustrates the salary levels for the role of a QA in the seven different countries. It can be seen that both the number of records of advertisements and the minimum levels are higher than for the previous role. This could indicate a higher demand for QA managers.

Table 3. Average annual income — Quality Assurance Manager (in national currency).

Quality assurance manager	Min	Average annual salary	Max	Number of recorded salaries
Canada	$52,000	$81,000	$125,000	106
France	42,000 €	52,890 €	85,000 €	39
Italy	41,000 €	43,930 €	71,000 €	107
United States	$51,000	$85,000	$142,000	2,177
United Kingdom	£29,000	£44,871	£68,000	276
Germany	41,000 €	62,329 €	102,000 €	84
Australia	$76,000	$115,000	$148,000	84

2.7. *Change control board/Change manager*

This function is usually fulfilled by a group of senior members of the organization. Their main task is to oversee possible changes to the project. These changes can be minor or significant regarding the budget or the entire timeline of the project. As the individuals on the board will not be permanently assigned this task, it is logical to assume that they only meet if needed. Therefore, the change control board is mainly used when multiple functions in the organization are affected (Rose, 2017).

2.7.1. *Change manager in agile working environments*

Change is a concept that does not disappear in an agile work environment. Quite to the contrary, change happens more frequently, which requires the change manager to pay more attention. Therefore, the role remains relevant and requires a higher level of communication with clients and the team (The Change Compass, 2021).

2.8. *Solution team/Software architect*

The Software Architect is also a vital position in the life cycle of a project (Kruchten, 1999). The Software Architect is either an individual or can be part of a team. Similar to the PM, the software architect position has gone through some changes in the last few decades, especially with the introduction of agile work styles.

The position should be understood as an advisory position. They work along with the PM and the programming team. However, software architects do not code any of the software themselves. They are more likely to be visionaries who can create the software using the most efficient and productive methodology. Their main work happens in the analysis and design phases. However, they are constantly consulted throughout the project, especially in the implementation and testing phases.

Software architects utilize a significant number of diagrams and charts to visualize the final product and communicate with the development team and other stakeholders. They dictate needed tools both for the coding and the design phase. More generally speaking, the role includes an understanding and interpretation of the client's software needs in a technically feasible manner. Another area of work is the analysis of an existing system. When a system is already in place, sometimes the software architect will also take an inventory and investigate the current system to identify apparent shortcomings. The software architect makes suggestions to improve the system through standard reporting techniques. Furthermore, the software architect is concerned with software quality and development under the defined technical requirements.

Software architects are usually senior team members of the project, and their responsibilities require a higher level of skill and confidence related to technical related decisions. In many cases, they take over many tasks from the PM. Sherman and Hadar (2015) report that one reason for the change in the role of software architects is that they have become highly skilled technical experts. On the other hand, many tasks are non-technical, such as communication, leadership, and mentoring (Clements *et al.*, 2007).

Berenbach (2008) created a matrix of different areas a software architect needs to be knowledgeable in. These include *interpersonal skills, domain expertise, business knowledge, basic software architecture, and software engineering.*

2.8.1. *Software architects in agile working environments*

Agile work environments have introduced some flexibility, which helps lift some of the substantial responsibilities. Some like Spinellis (2016) hint that Software Architects have become an issue for projects due to their technicality. Their requirements may have become too difficult to implement. However, this may not be universally accepted. Furthermore, the difference between the architecture and the software itself is indistinguishable, which means that the software requirements dictate both the needed architecture and the hardware.

Another development that has influenced the architect's role is the availability of reusing open-source software packages and code. Many people can reuse existing code through source code repositories such as GitHub, SourceForge, and others (Spinellis, 2016).

Marić and Tumbas (2016) highlighted that architecture has become a fluid process that emerges throughout the project. Instead of having one individual being responsible, the task is now divided by the team. Therefore, the role is more formal in comparison to traditional approaches.

Among others, the authors list the following duties (2016, p. 20): 'to identify initial architecturally significant requirements at the beginning of the project, set up (envision) the initial architectural solution for the central part of the software; to have good collaboration with team members, aimed at sharing ideas and resolving problems; to lead technical discussions with other team members.'

2.8.2. *Job market requirements and salary perspectives*

Software architects 'guide team members to determine best practices and requirements for software; oversight and technical approval of all final programs and products before formal launch; Oversee and support the coaching and training of team members to ensure all necessary skills to implement the software application; Actively seek ways to improve business software processes and interactions; Prepare an easy to understand technical report to communicate with subordinates; Use a proactive approach to common challenges and by continually researching best practices in software development; Ensure software security by developing programs to monitor the sharing of private information actively; Try to utilise best practices and software design patterns as much as possible and influence to use by the team as well; Troubleshoot high-level development issues quickly and efficiently to ensure a productive workplace' (Glassdoor.co.uk, 2021).

The requirements seem to consider both aspects of the above-discussed development around the change regarding the role. While many aspects mirror the classical role, the discussion, and the involvement with other team members, illustrates some agile aspects.

According to job recruitment websites, the following categories of qualifications are mentioned frequently:

- *Designing and implementing experience,*
- *Professional certifications,*

- *Project experience, especially in large projects,*
- *Overall project understanding including cutting-edge technical knowledge, cyber security, web and mobile applications development, open-source, and other concepts,*
- *Experience in popular software development languages.*

Salaries

In comparison to the PM, the salary levels seem to be higher (see Table 4). Given the presented duties and responsibilities and that Software Architects are highly skilled individuals, this difference seems reasonable.

2.9. *Quality Assurance Engineer (QAE)*

The role of the QAE, or more commonly the Tester, is critical. Nevertheless, depending on the overall setup of the project, the QAE only participates at different points in the project cycle. More recent methods, such as Scrum or Kanban, rely more on the QAE, as their opinion is already considered at the project's beginning.

The QAE identifies and defines test sequences, which she will later monitor. In a software project, various items need testing, which is not just done before the requirements, but in general when it comes to usability. In the traditional scenario, testing is performed in iterative cycles. The QAE collects data and evaluates the different units in each cycle (Rose, 2017). Modern teams generally work with a continuous delivery model and

Table 4.   Average annual income — Software architect (in national currency).

Software architect	Min	Average annual salary	Max	Number of recorded salaries
Canada	$85,000	$113,000	$151,000	277
France	43,000 €	54,320 €	75,000 €	279
Italy	31,000 €	43,078 €	62,000 €	66
United States	$90,000	$130,185	$189,000	5,666
United Kingdom	£70,371	£70,000	£111,000	488
Germany	60,000 €	77,737 €	99,000 €	177
Australia	$95,000	$136,000	$186,000	126

testing is an integral part of the development pipeline. In general, tests can be run manually or automatically. The overall goal is to reduce the number of bugs in the program, document them, and cycle back to the developers. In many cases, the QAE does provide his own input when it comes to finding a solution for the issues identified.

The primary skills expected are focus and attention to detail, as they evaluate the product before sending it to the client. Their failure would influence the entire project. Coupled with these skills, the QAE should have a detailed understanding of different software languages, which allows her to communicate clearly with the developers.

2.9.1. *QAE in agile working environments*

The role of the QAE has changed significantly from traditional projects. While the Testers used to work mainly toward the end of the project, agile work environments demand them to contribute during the entire project cycle. This brings the advantage that their knowledge can create more efficient sprints but does also require more skill.

One area which demands high levels of knowledge is the technical side. Due to the iterative nature of product developments, testing is ideally done in an automated fashion. Individuals who cannot write scripts to automate the testing may be unable to find jobs or remain relevant, as they lack competitive skills (SmartBearSoftware, 2021).

2.9.2. *Job market requirements and salary perspectives*

The role of the QAE is highly sought after due to the increased demand from the broader economy. As more companies implement software solutions, more QAEs are needed. Nevertheless, generic job descriptions are not published on Glassdoor.co.uk (2021). Other sources, however, specify what kind of responsibilities or skills are needed to land a job as a tester. For instance, TalentLyft.com (2021) describes the following responsibilities as desired by clients: 'analysing users stories and/use cases/requirements for validity and feasibility; collaborate closely with other team members and departments; execute all levels of testing (System, Integration, and Regression); Design and develop automation scripts when needed; Detect and track software defects and inconsistencies; Provide timely solutions; Apply quality engineering principals throughout the Agile product lifecycle and Provide support and documentation.' Regarding the qualifications, the company mainly emphasizes soft inter-personal skills and the ability to work on multiple tasks simultaneously (TalentLyft, 2021).

Salaries
As Table 5 illustrates, there seem to be many job advertisements for the Tester role in the seven countries. Nevertheless, the spread between the minimal and the maximum salary level is relatively low, indicating that high-paid jobs may depend on the project but not necessarily on the candidate's skill level.

2.10. *Database Administrator (DBA)*

The DBA designs and models the database for the product. Depending on where the application is hosted, he works with the team as well as the client. The DBA needs to understand the business requirements and should design a solution that meets the business standards. Therefore, he must have a deeper understanding of different technological aspects, which helps him make an economically sustainable decision. The process includes an overall plan for the solution and minor aspects such as

Table 5. Average annual income — Quality Assurance Engineer (in national currency).

Quality assurance	Min	Average annual salary	Max	Number of recorded salaries
Canada	$40,000	$62,000	$97,000	126
France	28,000 €	41,145 €	56,000 €	8
Italy	22,000 €	27,209 €	43,000 €	31
United States	$44,000	$66,000	$100,000	869
United Kingdom	£20,000	£30,330	£45,000	387
Germany	41,000 €	55,000 €	62,000 €	90
Australia	$49,000	$77,572	$120,000	59

reports, data requirements, programs, and specific components. The overall framework needs to be well documented and is then handed to the developers.

Once the product is completed, the DBA may be responsible for maintaining and managing the databases. These tasks can include security issues, access management, performance checks, and evaluation of errors.

2.10.1. *Database Administrator in agile working environments*

Due to the nature of agile teams, the DBA is involved with different internal and external stakeholders. The DBA works closely with the developers and should, therefore, have a deeper understanding of different development tools (e.g., object orientation, the Unified Modeling Language (UML), encapsulating database access, and mapping objects to RDBs (O/R mapping)).

Many of these tasks (i.e., software testing, release, and maintenance) are handled by a designated DevOps team. Leite *et al.* (2019) referred to DevOps as one of the first positions which emerged from a change toward an agile working style. Dyck *et al.* (2015) defined the role as collaborative and multidisciplinary, focusing on automation and the release of new software versions within a company. The role of DevOps is challenging and offers various perspectives as they need to have a broad understanding of the field. DevOps as a standing position has been widely accepted in the field, and Universities offer courses that prepare young people for their careers. Others see DevOps as the next stage of software development. For instance, the continuous release of new software snippets, as described in the agile literature, is sometimes challenging for agile teams as they have various tasks. Therefore, DevOps is an excellent addition to the structure of the group.

2.10.2. *Job market requirements and salary perspectives*

DBAs are a highly sought after group of professionals. They come with a specific skill set, which allows them to negotiate higher salaries. Indeed (2021) lists the following requirements in their generic job description: 'Identifying who has access to the database; Helping build the structure

Table 6. Average annual income — Database Administrator (in national currency).

Database administrator	Min	Average annual salary	Max	Number of recorded salaries
Canada	$50,000	$78,000	$122,000	295
France	34,000 €	45,666 €	63,000 €	34
Italy	27,000 €	37,066 €	48,000 €	28
United States	$58,000	$82,000	$116,000	16,543
United Kingdom	£19,000	£36,303	£68,000	404
Germany	40,000 €	58,922 €	77,000 €	47
Australia	$60,000	$98,012	$138,000	137

and design of the database; Implementing security measures for the data; Restoring lost data; Building test versions and testing for bugs; Merging databases when necessary; Updating systems when necessary and creating data backups and Continually monitoring database systems.'

Salaries

As the Table 6 illustrates, there seem to be a high number of job advertisements for the role of the DBA in the seven countries. Unlike the previous role, the salary spreads are more comprehensive. They show that depending on the years of experience and the skillset, higher salaries can be negotiated.

2.11. *Software engineer/developer*

Software engineers are the people who create the final product. There is no clear-cut set of requirements and skills, as the tasks and responsibilities vary from project to project. These people are likely assigned various tasks simultaneously.

The reader should consider that many of the above- and below-mentioned roles could be considered Software engineer roles. This, however, depends on the scope of the definition. In a generic job advertisement, many of the previously discussed tasks could be mentioned, such as the interaction with the client, the analysis of software requirements, or the testing of the software product.

2.12. *Design team*

This section discusses the role of the design team. Sometimes, software engineers cover the design part simultaneously, which makes it challenging to clarify specific roles.

Volmer and Sonnentag (2009) define the role of design teams as a specialized task that is goal driven. Software design is a stage between requirements analysis and coding.

TS da Silva *et al.* (2013) clarify that one of the main tasks of the design team is to create a positive user experience. This is mainly supported by the argument that the design is crucial when attracting users, or new potential customers.

There is a range of potential roles that can be part of the software design team: 'Content Strategist, Visual Designer, UX researcher, FrontEnd Developer, Interaction Designer, UX Lead' (Team CourseUX. com, 2021). Bruun *et al.* (2018) expand this list further and include the Usability Tester, the User Researcher, Field Study Specialist, the Data Analyst, the Information architect, and the Technical Writer.

2.12.1. *Designers in agile working environments*

It is interesting to see that the designer's work has changed due to the disruptive nature of the agile work environment. While the project in traditional ways was planned and implemented in a foreseeable way, these new work modes intend to supply new software products in a shorter time frame. Projects may run over a more extended period, and the delivery of software snippets usually does not allow much design work.

TS da Silva *et al.* (2013) investigated the designer's role in an agile project sphere. They criticized previous research, which classified the design job into seven categories, as unrealistic. Bruun *et al.* (2018) illustrated the tasks and responsibilities of UX professionals, based on an extensive literature review. The authors found various disciplines (*Test and evaluation, User research, Design, etc.*) with various tasks and responsibilities. While these roles are all described individually, they can be linked to the field of UX Designers. Next to the obvious design tasks, many duties require the professionals to engage with the customer and client in order to create the best product.

Ratcliff and McNeil (2011) found the following responsibilities of a UX designer: User Interface, Interaction, and Usability Designer; Experience Designer; UI Developers and Front-End Developers; Information Architects; Visual Designers; and Design Researchers. TS da Silva *et al.* (2013) mainly identified three roles: the User Experience Designer, the UI Developer, and the Interaction designer. The authors argue that the designer needs to be a substantial partner in an agile team, as they are responsible for many aspects of the project. This is, however, not always the case. One reason for this is the fear that the designer is underworked when allocated to one project team. As a highly skilled individual, the designer is too expensive when not used for multiple tasks in various projects simultaneously.

2.12.2. *Job market requirements and salary perspectives*

This section concentrates on the UX designer. As presented above, different roles play a significant part in the design team; however, not all roles are always presented.

Job market requirement

The role of a designer is based on many technical aspects. He should be able to operate different tools in order to find solutions. While some aspects can be taught, many of the experiences and skills are learned over time. Similar to other roles, more experience can translate into a higher salary.

Glassdoor.co.uk (2021) describes the requirement for a UX designer as follows: 'Conduct testing of sample applications, websites and software to Assess user experience and ease of design; Use recent studies and findings to establish the best overall design elements to include in UX design experiences; Build storyboards to conceptualise designs to accurately convey project plans to clients and senior management; Create surveys for research through various media platforms to gather feedback on user's ease of use and satisfaction interfacing on company websites and products; Design the aesthetics to be implemented within a website or product, from the layout menus and drop-down options to colors and fonts allowing for interface edits as needed; Analyse customer responses and website data to examine high traffic web pages and determine why certain webpages perform better; Enhance user experience by creating seamless navigation through various digital programs and interfaces within the company; Combine interface design concepts with digital design and establish milestones to encourage cooperation and teamwork' (Glassdoor. co.uk, 2021). It becomes clear that the designer's job is challenging as he actively works on the final product. The input and feedback in the testing phase from the client are essential.

Most recent job advertisements have further required the following qualifications: 'experience in creating and implementing UX design; Proficient with visual design programs such as Adobe Photoshop and others; Ability to work effectively in a collaborative environment to create top-performing interfaces for clients; Experience with coding and ability to troubleshoot using HTML, CSS and comparable languages; Continued education and research into UX trends and current design strategy and technologies; Professional written and interpersonal skills when communicating with customers and clients; Ability to prioritise and manage several milestones and projects efficiently; Account for challenges using problem-solving skills and seek to optimise data for the best possible outcome; Experience creating storyboards and website mapping' (Glassdoor. co.uk, 2021).

These illustrate that a designer needs to be up to date with the most recent developments in the field. Self-studies seem to be an essential element for this role.

Salary
Looking at the different salary levels in the seven countries (see Table 7), higher income levels are possible. However, this again depends on the years of experience and the nature of the project.

Table 7. Average annual income — UX Designer (in national currency).

UX designer	Min	Average annual salary	Max	Number of recorded salaries
Canada	$52,722	$75,705	$108,707	117
France	33,058 €	40,491 €	54,774 €	281
Italy	24,179 €	31,482 €	43,129 €	47
United States	$75,000	$103,000	$140,000	371
United Kingdom	£37,000	£48,128	£62,000	26
Germany	40,000 €	51,987 €	76,000 €	144
Australia	–	$85,000	–	1

3. Summary

This chapter briefly discussed a range of significant roles. While many roles are well known, others may be only known to those more involved in software development. For instance, the UX designer belongs to the design team; however, the team is usually small. People will cover multiple roles simultaneously.

Many of the above-discussed roles have become highly specific, meaning many companies may try to avoid hiring them. For instance, when included in the company, designers will have to work on various projects simultaneously, decreasing quality.

Roles such as the Business Analyst are instrumental and will remain relevant in the following years. More companies have identified the need for software solutions. Business Analysts specializing in a specific sector can be of great value to a company.

In all cases, the roles remain relevant in agile work environments. The Project Manager's job has changed in both the traditional sense and agile projects. While he was responsible for most tasks, his duties have become less technical and more managerial. New roles such as the Business Analyst or the Software Architect support the PM. In an agile work environment, the PM is not expected but still seems to be needed. The Scrum Master and the product owner fulfill similar tasks. However, they are instead focused on the internal team, while the PM can best communicate with external stakeholders.

What may seem surprising is that many of these roles are not learned through an educational path. The PM or the Software Architect is a senior member of a team, who has gained much experience over the years. Due to the changing nature of the roles by introducing agile work environments, more seems to be expected from the educational path. For instance, designers and developers are increasingly involved with the client; this requires soft skills, which universities may need to emphasize.

References

Agiledata.org. (2021). The Skillset of an Agile DBA. Available at: http://agiledata.org/essays/dbaSkills.html. (Accessed 11 July 2021).

Alexander, M. (2019). What is a Project Manager? The Lead Role for Project Success. Available at: https://www.cio.com/article/3224865/what-is-a-project-manager-the-lead-role-for-project-success.html#:~:text=a%20project%20manager%3F-,Project%20managers%20play%20the%20lead%20role%20in%20planning%2C%20executing%2C%20monitoring,or%20failure%20of%20the%20project. (Accessed 21 May 2021).

Anastasia, A. (2020). Roles and Responsibilities Inside a Software Testing Team. Available at: https://testfort.com/blog/qa-team-responsibilities. (Accessed 24 May 2021).

Antonucci, Y. L. and Goeke, R. J. (2011). Identification of appropriate responsibilities and positions for business process management success: Seeking a valid and reliable framework, *Bus. Process Manage. J.*, 17(1), 127–146.

Barber, E. (2004). Benchmarking the management of projects: A review of current thinking, *Int. J. Proj. Manage.*, 22(4), 301–307.

Berenbach, B. (2008, May). The other skills of the software architect. In Proceedings of the First International Workshop on Leadership and Management in Software Architecture (pp. 7–12).

Bruun, A., Larusdottir, M. K., Nielsen, L., Nielsen, P. A. and Persson, J. S. (2018, September). The role of UX professionals in agile development: A case study from industry. In Proceedings of the 10th Nordic Conference on Human-Computer Interaction (pp. 352–363).

Cambridge Dictionary. (2021). Meaning of Role in English. Available at: https://dictionary.cambridge.org/dictionary/english/role (Accessed 20 May 2021).

Carbone, T. A. and Gholston, S. (2004). Project manager skill development: A survey of programs and practitioners, *Eng. Manage. J.*, 16(3), 10–16.

Clements, P., Kazman, R., Klein, M., Devesh, D., Reddy, S. and Verma, P. (2007, January). The duties, skills, and knowledge of software architects. In 2007 Working IEEE/IFIP Conference on Software Architecture (WICSA'07) (pp. 20–20). IEEE.

Cockburn, A. and Highsmith, J. (2001). Agile software development, the people factor, *Computer*, 34(11), 131–133.

Da Silva, T. S., Silveira, M. S., Melo, C. D. O. and Parzianello, L. C. (2013, July). Understanding the UX designer's role within agile teams. In International Conference of Design, User Experience, and Usability (pp. 599–609). Berlin, Heidelberg: Springer.

Drury-Grogan, M. L. and O'Dwyer, O. (2013). An investigation of the decision-making process in agile teams, *Int. J. Inf. Technol. Decis. Making*, 12(06), 1097–1120.

Dyck, A., Penners, R. and Lichter, H. (2015, May). Towards definitions for release engineering and DevOps. In 2015 IEEE/ACM 3rd International Workshop on Release Engineering (pp. 3–3). IEEE.

Edum-Fotwe, F. T. and McCaffer, R. (2000). Developing project management competency: Perspectives from the construction industry, *Int. J. Proj. Manage.*, 18(2), 111–124.

Fowler, M. and Highsmith, J. (2001). The agile manifesto, *Software Dev.*, 9(8), 28–35.

Fryer, B. (2004). *The Practice of Construction Management*, 4th ed., Oxford: Blackwell Publishing.

Gehalt.de. (2021). Available at: https://www.gehalt.de. (Accessed 02 July 2021).

Glassdoor.co.uk. (2021). Glassdoor. Available at: https://www.glassdoor.co.uk. (Accessed 03 August 2021).

Gregorio, D. D. (2012, March). How the Business Analyst supports and encourages collaboration on agile projects. In 2012 IEEE International Systems Conference SysCon 2012 (pp. 1–4). IEEE.

IIBA, n/a. Available at: https://www.iiba.org/professional-development/career-centre/what-is-business-analysis/ (Accessed 24 May 2021).

Indeed. (2021). Database Administrator Duties and Responsibilities. Available at: https://www.indeed.com/hire/job-description/database-administrator. (Accessed 11 July 2021).

Jha, K. N. and Iyer, C. K. (2006). What attributes should a project coordinator possess? *Constr. Manage. Econ.*, 24(9), 977–988.

Kruchten, P. (1999, February). The software architect. In Working Conference on Software Architecture (pp. 565–583). Springer, Boston, MA.

Leite, L., Rocha, C., Kon, F., Milojicic, D. and Meirelles, P. (2019). A survey of DevOps concepts and challenges, *ACM Comput. Surv. (CSUR)*, 52(6), 1–35.

Lung, L.-H. (2019). So, You Want to Be an Agile Functional Manager? 8thlight. com. Available at: https://8thlight.com/blog/lihsuan-lung/2019/01/03/so-you-want-to-be-an-agile-functional-manager.html. (Accessed 02 July 2021).

Marić, M. and Tumbas, P. (2016). The role of the software architect in agile development processes, *Strategic Manage.*, 21(1), 16–22.

Muhoro, N. (2019). Operational Versus Functional Level Strategy. Available at: https://smallbusiness.chron.com/operational-versus-functional-level-strategy-61306.html. (Accessed 30 June 2021).

Pant, I. and Baroudi, B. (2008). Project management education: The human skills imperative, *Int. J. Proj. Manage.*, 26(2), 124–128.

Payscale. (2021). Available at: https://www.payscale.com. (Accessed 24 May 2021).

Pettersen, N. (1991). What do we know about the effective project manager? *Int. J. Proj. Manage.*, 9(2), 99–104.

Pratt, M. and White, S. (2018). What is a business analyst? A key role for business — IT efficiency. CIO FROM IDG.

Ratcliffe, L. and McNeill, M. (2011). Agile experience design: A digital designer's guide to agile, lean, and continuous. New Riders.

Reicher, A. (2020). 3 Reasons Testers Need a QA Manager in Agile. Available at: https://searchsoftwarequality.techtarget.com/tip/3-reasons-testers-need-a-QA-manager-in-Agile. (Accessed 10 July 2021).

Rose, S. (2017). Software Project Team Roles and Responsibilities. Available at: https://medium.com/@SherrieRose/software-project-team-roles-and-responsibilities-152a7d575759. (Accessed 30 June 2021).

Schuurman, R. (2019). The Subject Matter Expert (A Misunderstood Product Owner Stance). Available at: https://medium.com/the-value-maximizers/the-subject-matter-expert-a-misunderstood-product-owner-stance-73e420851365. (Accessed 10 July 2021).

Schwaber, K. and Beedle, M. (2002). *Agile Software Development with Scrum*, Vol. 1. Upper Saddle River: Prentice Hall.

Shastri, Y., Hoda, R. and Amor, R. (2021). The role of the project manager in agile software development projects, *J. Syst. Software*, 173, 110871.

Shehu, Z. and Akintoye, A. (2008). Construction programme management skills and competencies: A deeper insight, *Built Human Environ. Rev.*, 1, 1–17.

Sherman, S. and Hadar, I. (2015, May). Toward defining the role of the software architect. In 2015 IEEE/ACM 8th International Workshop on Cooperative and Human Aspects of Software Engineering (pp. 71–76). IEEE.

SmartBearSoftware. (2021). Testing in an Agile Environment. Available at: https://smartbear.com/blog/testing-in-an-agile-environment/. (Accessed 10 July 2021).

Sommerville, J., Craig, N., & Hendry, J. (2010). The role of the project manager: all things to all people?. *Structural Survey*, 28(2), 132–141.

Sonteya, T. and Seymour, L. F. (2012). Towards an understanding of the business process analyst: An analysis of competencies, *J. Inf. Technol. Educ.*, 11(1), 43–63.

Spinellis, D. (2016). The changing role of the software architect, *IEEE Software*, 33(6), 4–6.

Step Stone. (2021). Available at: https://www.stepstone.de. (Accessed 24 May 2021).

TalentLyft. (2021). Software Tester Job Description Template. Available at: https://www.talentlyft.com/en/resources/software-tester-job-description. (Accessed 11 July 2021).

Team CourseUX.com. (2016). How to Build the Best Design Team: 6 UX Roles. Available at: https://courseux.com/how-build-best-design-team/. (Accessed 24 May 2021).

The Change Compass. (2021). The Ultimate Guide to Agile for Change Managers. Available at: https://thechangecompass.com/the-ultimate-guide-to-agile-for-change-managers/. (Accessed 10 July 2021).

Unknown. (2020). QA Engineering Roles: Skills, Tools, and Responsibilities in a Testing Team. Available at: https://www.altexsoft.com/blog/engineering/qa-engineering-roles-skills-tools-and-responsibilities-within-a-testing-team/. (Accessed 24 May 2021).

Veeraraaghavan, J. (2018). The Role of Functional Managers in an Agile/Scrum Environment. PM-Powerconsulting.com. Available at: https://pm-powerconsulting.com/blog/role-functional-managers-agilescrum-environment/. (Accessed 02 July 2021).

Volmer, J., & Sonnentag, S. (2011). The role of star performers in software design teams. *Journal of Managerial Psychology*, 26(3), 219–234.

Chapter 7

The Role of Project Manager in IT Projects

Omoleye Ojuri

*School of Civil Engineering and Built Environment
Liverpool John Moores University, UK
O.b.ojuri@ljmu.ac.uk*

Information Technology (IT) project management is planning, scheduling, executing, monitoring, and reporting IT projects. The IT project manager's role has become essential in advancing IT-related projects. IT project management is beyond the application of knowledge, utilizing standard tools and procedures, or aligning expertise to handle projects from start to completion. Therefore, the IT project manager is saddled with the responsibilities of dealing with the challenges of linking and consolidating version changes and rapid technology upgrades throughout the IT project life cycle. Consequently, an IT project manager requires more than the standard project management tools and skills. This chapter gives a bit of background to an IT project, including IT project management; however, a section of the chapter discusses the roles/initiatives of the IT project manager in managing IT projects, meaning that the IT project manager oversees its objectives to ensure timely completion of project within budget. Also, the author highlights the six phases of an IT project and explores the team members in a typical IT project organization and their associated responsibilities. There are discussions around IT project manager competencies and Team dedication. Finally, the author identifies the challenges of IT project management. The focus on metrics of key performance indicators (KPIs) of IT projects was how development quality, progress, and planning, including quality of the technical specification, can be measured.

1. Introduction

This chapter covers a wide array of topics associated with information technology (IT) project management. IT project management is part general management, project management, and part technology operations. It is essential to note that various organizations focus entirely on IT projects; meanwhile, IT is unique because several organizations have some level of IT elements. However, IT project management has a broad scope because it involves two distinct subjects: project management and IT. These two disciplines integrate to form an essential subject which includes various IT projects and project management aspects. Several topics from both sides of the subject would be considered. The discussions in this chapter include who an IT project manager is, the role and dynamics in IT project management, and the IT project management life cycle including project team stakeholders. This section also includes the six phases of an IT project and different teams in a typical IT project organization including their associated roles. The latter part of the chapter is highly relevant for IT organizations. It highlights how to manage an IT project and the challenges therein, including skills of the IT project manager in enhancing team commitment. The significance and determination of metrics of KPIs of IT projects are illustrated in the last section of this chapter.

2. What is an IT project?

An IT project is a type of project that deals with computers, IT infrastructure, or information systems. There are numerous types of IT projects which include the following: (1) database management, (2) mobile app development, (3) network system upgrades, (4) software development and application (5) hardware installations, (6) web development, and (7) IT emergency recovery (Koi-Akrofi, 2017).

2.1. *IT project management*

IT project management involves activities which include planning, executing, scheduling, monitoring, and reporting of IT projects (Schwalbe, 2016). Though various organizations attempt to focus wholly on IT projects, IT is unique, because several organizations consist of IT components at one level or the other. Furthermore, IT projects involve interdependent integrations and software updates, thus management of IT projects requires more than standard project management tools and skills to complete.

2.2. *The IT project manager*

IT project manager has a broader range of responsibilities than most other project managers. This is because an IT project manager deals with leadership, scheduling and planning, resource allocation, monitoring, and reporting. Besides, the IT project manager is also responsible for understanding firmware and implementing software integrations. IT managers often build websites and databases and manage these technologies, including building networks and maintaining security for data risks.

Furthermore, the IT project manager's tasks include clear communication, setting realistic goals and adopting the appropriate methodology to achieve them. The triple constraint of any project is also present in IT projects. Therefore, like any other project manager, the IT project manager is concerned with setting a deadline and keeping to a budget.

The IT project manager must possess skills and qualifications that include technical management, ability to analyze data, communication, problem-solving, understanding of technology, data center management, strategic planning, and quality management.

2.3. *Role of project manager in IT projects*

An IT project manager oversees and directs the activities of an organization's IT department and manages teams to execute IT projects within budget and on time. IT projects include managing human resources, directing budgets and schedules, and implementing a project communication plan. An IT project manager plans, coordinates, and incorporates cross-operational IT projects that are significant in scope and impact. In a nutshell, an IT project manager ensures that day-to-day work in a tech department happens as smoothly as possible. Also, the role includes ensuring that personnel and their IT skills are appropriately utilised to drive the timely completion of the project. An IT project manager has the critical obligation of meeting the business or client's requirements.

The following are the roles of an IT project manager:

- Identify the client needs and wants from their IT systems.
- Setting project goals and creating plans to meet them.
- Managing resources in terms of personnel and equipment.
- Maintaining the project schedule and budget.
- Organizing project phases and assessing the business consequences for each one.
- Coordinating the work of the project team, for example, developers.
- Monitoring development and ensuring costs, schedules, and quality requirements of IT projects are achieved.
- Assigning tasks to team members.
- Ensuring a modification from the outdated IT systems to the modern ones.
- Evaluating and approving payments for completed tasks.
- Directing the recruitment of IT employees and mentoring the in-house IT team.
- Ensuring that employees follow the privacy policy, information security, and computer use.
- Providing and reporting of project status to stakeholders.
- Developing a renewal and upgrade schedule for company software programs.

- Ensuring organization's data security by running vendor management process.
- Setting up of timelines to monitor projects.
- Following up the project after completion by devising suitable maintenance and troubleshooting methods.

Based on the roles identified above, the IT project manager is expected to have advanced knowledge of computers, networks, operating systems, and service desk administration. Another essential skill required of an IT project manager is good communication — and clearly explaining complex technical and computer-related issues. Other necessary skills include knowledge of resource planning, budgeting, and scheduling.

3. The IT project management life cycle

This consists of six phases. Just like any other project (Schwalbe, 2016), the IT project will have a start point and an endpoint. However, six stages of project management are utilized in combination with IT stages to manage the project. They are as follows:

To illustrate these phases in managing an IT project, let us look at an organization replacing all sales force laptops with tablets.

(1) **Initiation/Definition**: A sponsor and a governing team are assigned, and they clearly define the project's purpose. Specifically at this stage, there is (a) an appointment of the project manager to oversee the IT project, (b) recruitment of the project team, and (c) a creation of the project charter. For example, the sponsor could be the Leader of IT, and the managing board could consist of the Leader of IT, the Procurement Manager, and the Leader of Sales. The objectives of the project could be to replace all sales force laptops with tablets.

(2) **Planning/Development**: The project team and IT project manager operate jointly to describe all the deliverables or proposed products of the project and then design all of the responsibilities needed to produce each deliverable. The tasks are allocated a start date, end date,

and accountable person(s), and all the responsibilities collectively roll up into the project plan. For example, the project deliverables could be the requirement for the tablets to be procured: the invitation for proposal records to go out to merchants; and the tablets, instruction plans, and instruction manuals to be used to educate the sales force on how to work with their new tablets. The project plan would then be assembled by recording all the duties essential to each of these deliverables, and each of the responsibilities would be allocated a duration, start date, and end date.

(3) **Execution/Implementation**: The project team implements the project plan to generate the deliverables of the project. In the same example, as stated above, the team would commence working on all the tasks listed on the project plan. For instance, as regards the requirement deliverable for tablets to be sourced, the team would begin gathering the requirements for the tablets, then drafting the specifications, then reviewing the specifications, and finally approving the specifications.

(4) **Monitoring and Controlling**: As the project is being implemented by the team, the project manager supervises and directs the team's work for quality, risk, cost, time, scope, and other factors. The project manager consistently reports the project status and any issues and risks to the project sponsor and steering committee. Supervising and directing are continuous procedures throughout the project implementation in ensuring that the project achieves its objectives. For example, if the supplier appointed to supply the tablets suddenly went out of business, this could cause a significant risk to the project. The IT project manager would need to report this to the steering committee immediately to issue a directive.

(5) **Closing**: At the completion of the whole project, project closure confirms that all the project work has been finalized, accepted, and possession of the project deliverables has been passed over from the project team to operations. For instance, when the tablets have been obtained and turned over to the sales force, the sales team has been instructed on how to use their new tablets, and there is an IT team in place to offer ongoing end-user support to the tablet users, then the project can be closed.

(6) **Follow-up**: This phase is after the implementation stage is complete, which comes after the provision of the finished product or project to the client/stakeholder. The follow-up phase involves all the activities that come after the project is delivered. This includes training end users and setting up support systems, among others.

3.1. *Project teams/Stakeholders in IT projects*

There are three types of teams in IT project management:

(1) **Traditional project team**: Even if this team is tasked with an IT project, it is not exclusive to IT but also consists of staff with formal project management expertise.
(2) **Professional service team**: This team delivers technology to external stakeholders/customers, such as software or hardware installation. Although the team is led by a project manager, it can be headed by a director or vice president, and also uses traditional project management forms.
(3) **Internal IT team**: This team manages the delivery and maintenance of the technology in an organization. The team sets up computers and rolls out new systems. It is usually headed by a project manager or director of IT.

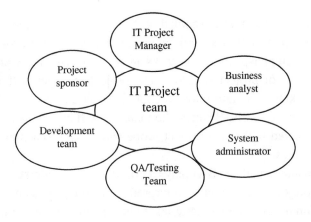

Figure 1.   IT project team members.

The project team in the IT project collectively consists of the project sponsor, project manager, business analyst, developer team, network engineers, UAT, and quality analyst (Maritato, 2013). This team mainly develops the IT projects and executes the projects by delivering the expected outcomes. This is illustrated in Figure 1.

- The developer is the person who designs the tool or platform by understanding the project requirements. Moreover, he/she will ensure that each business requirement is considered and configured to meet client expectations within the project scope.
- The project sponsor mainly helps in providing all the required resources to accomplish the project. The project sponsors are organizational executive board members with a specific vision and goals in executing the plans. The sponsor or client will take care of the budget and resources required to accomplish the project on time and take care of the related regulatory issues.
- The client/business executive team mainly involves providing the business requirements and acting as the linkage between business sponsors and the project management team.

Program management is the team that coordinates with all stakeholders in defining the program policies and procedures and identifying any impacts during the program implementation.

- The project manager is saddled with a crucial role in any IT project for managing vital tasks and understanding the project pros and cons from different aspects. These tasks are achieved by timely preparation and review of project schedule. The project manager will assign the right stakeholders and allocate enough resources for completing the project successfully. Besides, the manager will ensure that the project is completed within the project scope and budget to achieve realistic deliverables.
- The business analyst (BA) plays a crucial role in understanding high-level project requirements, interpreting it and processing technical, functional, and non-functional requirements among others. BA

ensures that enough information is collected and appropriately documented to carry out the project successfully. The BA acts as a linkage between the operations team and the technical team, and gathers the project requirements. In addition, the BA corroborates with each project stakeholder and collects business requirements.

3.2. *How to manage an IT project*

There are some conventional aspects in managing projects, however the management of an IT project might be slightly different which is highlighted in the following section using software project management as an illustration:

(1) **Project requirements**: This stage includes the determination of stakeholder requirements and the creation of a budget. These are documented and attached to an IT project. However, there must be a definition of scope before an IT project can begin.

(2) **Team selection**: After collecting the project's requirements, the IT project manager then can build a team with the appropriate abilities and expertise that match the responsibilities at hand. At this stage, the project manager's communication skill is brought to a place to ensure that all information is well received and processed.

(3) **Project management tool**: The IT project manager can employ project management tools such as the Gantt chart. This supports in organizing and programming projects of all proportions, while it is beneficial for streamlining complicated projects. A project management tool is necessary because it consists of tasks and their timelines, including the link dependencies, setting of milestones, and viewing of the critical path. This tool supports the successful delivery of the project as project data are shared among the whole team.

(4) **Progress monitoring**: The actual progress must match the planned one. This aspect of project tracking is made more accessible and can be achieved using software with a real-time dashboard, which collects

data as it is updated. When processed, it is displayed in charts that indicate costs and tasks, among others.

(5) **Workload management**: The IT project manager needs to ensure that team members are not overtasked or have too few tasks to handle. In avoiding slowing progress in IT projects, the IT manager can reassign tasks based on necessity.

(6) **Making changes**: IT projects are not static, just like every other project. The IT project manager can pivot fast when there are change requests from clients/stakeholders and customers. For instance, the IT project manager can use software to alter these changes by dragging and dropping a particular task to a new deadline on a Gantt chart.

(7) **Reporting**: Since a particular IT project is meant for the client/stakeholder/customer, the IT project manager should keep track and keep stakeholders updated. Several reports can be generated within each milestone achieved in the IT project.

4. Dynamics of IT project manager

In an organization, the IT project managers are usually positioned based on their technological aptitudes rather than their management abilities (Koi-Akrofi, 2017). While the former is essential, the latter cannot be underrated. For IT projects to succeed, project managers must not lack neither technical nor managerial skills. Therefore, an IT project manager must develop competencies that will help effective management and lead the team in a dynamic and challenging organizations such as IT. Acquiring both skills would assist the IT project manager maximize group accomplishment and get the group dedicated to the project's purpose (Araújo *et al.*, 2018).

Commitment is another crucial element in IT project management (Koi-Akrofi, 2017). Specifically, team/group commitment is defined as individuals' recognition and engagement with a particular team/group (Araújo *et al.*, 2018). Research has revealed that team commitment positively impacts the performance and success of IT projects. Meanwhile, it is recognized that team commitment building is challenging to achieve (Thamhain, 2014).

It is essential to state that managerial abilities exclusively are not sufficient to create team/group commitment in any organization (Thamhain, 2013). However, the project manager connects strategy and the team (PMI, 2013, p. 7). Consequently, IT project managers should develop specific competencies and use them to get their team members committed to the purpose. Moreover, team/group performance can be threatened and possible threats neglected, producing significant challenges during project implementation (Araújo *et al.*, 2018).

4.1. *Challenges of IT project management*

There are a variety of issues in IT project management. One of the issues is the interfaces with other aspects of an organization such as finance, human resources, business administration, and other departments within the organization and outside the business (George, 2020). This presents several pressing problems with high stakes because an entire business or organization can be incapacitated if the technology goes wrong (McGrath and Kostalova, 2020).

(1) **Changing technology**: IT is a volatile industry. This presents a challenge because of the rate of change that can be unsteady. Technology is well known for becoming outdated once it rolled out from the manufacturer. Thus, the IT project manager must be prepared to handle this type of inevitable change.

(2) **Communication**: Communication is a vital factor in IT project management. It is a critical challenge specifically when team members in IT projects work remotely in different time zones. This can be an hinderance to effective communication. Therefore, well-designed, transparent, and effective communication channels are essential for the success of IT projects.

(3) **Transparency**: Transparency in IT projects in the form of clear deadlines assists teams in better integrating new technology or responding to change quickly and efficiently.

(4) **Disagreement on methodology**: The type of methodology or process to be used in the IT management of various organizations is a

challenge. This is because projects could go off track and over budget if done without an agreed methodology. This means that an IT project manager should define the process, roles, and tools as the first step in managing any IT project, which should be agreed upon with the professional team members (developer and business analysts, among others). It is necessary because it is the first step to the success of an IT project.

4.2. *Factors essential for successful IT project management*

This section highlights a few of the issues that positively impact the whole execution of successful IT projects.

(1) **Benchmarking**: In plain terms, benchmarking is a procedure that enables organizations to develop upon active viewpoints. The benchmarking procedure promotes organizations to adjust their point of view from internal to external to safeguard that the aims have been established accurately and the steps crucial to accomplish those aims are being taken appropriately. Benchmarking largely comprises establishing guidelines experienced during a previous project or obtained through examination of projects carried out by another organization (Koi-Akrofi, 2017; Barber, 2004). Additionally, it permits the project manager to admit and employ the best systems of project management (Kerzner, 2010, 2013).

(2) **Presence of strategic plan**: Among the highly crucial aspects that influence the efficiency of project management is the existence of a meticulously constructed strategic plan. The organization should have a clear-cut idea as regards its intentions and the objectives it hopes to attain because of the project management activity (The Chartered Institute for IT, 2012; Ibbs and Kwak, 2000). The strategic plan should include a thorough account of the project's aims, the impacts of the project on diverse characteristics of the business, including its competitive situation, and how those intentions would be realized.

(3) **The comprehensiveness of planning**: Every project needs thorough planning to be executed efficiently. The project planning phase

includes establishing the project schedule, breaking down the project in analytically logical stages, apportioning resources to every single phase of the project, and establishing techniques for appraisal of the completed work (Meredith and Mantel, 2011).

(4) **Availability of resources**: The organization must have adequate means to carry out the project for each of the decided targets. If an organization is not economically adequate to carry out a project following the best practices, the procedure of project management is rendered unproductive (Lam *et al.*, 2010).

(5) **Strong leadership and project management skills**: Effective implementation of a project under the greatest systems requires strong leadership and project management competencies. The strategic focal point of the organization requires one to practice regular management of the project to ensure that the work is being implemented under the chosen benchmark. The management should similarly be aware of the adjustments and the reasons for those modifications (The Chartered Institute for IT, 2012).

(6) **Organizational support**: According to Zwikael and Globerson (2006), successful project management is based on focused organizational support. Project managers are supplied with the resources they need to manage the project, and their obligations are highlighted to make sure that the setbacks in the completion of the projects are averted.

4.3. *Project success criteria within the project's life cycle*

The project's success has regularly been linked to the final production and project success principles, however, the correlation between the duo is blurred (Taherdoost and Keshavarzsaleh, 2015). For project management to accomplish the aims, such a project would have gone through harnessing procedures, knowledge, techniques, competencies, and expertise. Koi-Akrofi (2017) identified the following factors for effective project delivery: (1) initial planning and project characterization, (2) central achievement factors for the project time performance, (3) the project cost performance, and (4) project portfolio management. The combination of the four factors should lead to an improved comprehension of strategies in achieving successful IT projects success criteria as illustrated in Table 1. Consequently, in the unpredictable environment of an organizational structure and taking cognizance of work procedures to adjust to market needs, detailed project management becomes highly crucial. (Taherdoost and Keshavarzsaleh, 2016; Taherdoost *et al.*, 2015; Taherdooost and Jalaliyoon, 2014). Table 1 consists of the illustration of project success criteria including the strategies an IT project manager should adopt.

Table 1.   Project success criteria an IT project manager should adopt.

Project criteria	Success strategies
Project definition and planning	• Project's purpose and values must be understood and agreed upon at the earliest time possible. • The desired and expected project outcomes must be agreed upon by project actors. • Development of achievable project plan. • Practical analysis in terms of clear identification and planning of sources of resources and risks should be resolved and agreed upon by projects actors. • Identification of project scope and indication of boundaries. • Appropriate and agreed upon organizational structure and project governance to manage projects actors' skills and the entire project milestones. • Development of effective communication tools for project actors. • Provision of dispute resolution strategies to cater for trust, among other issues.
Project time performance	• Identification of responsibilities of the organization to the project. • Maintaining project schedule using modern and effective tools. • Identification of organization's capacity and maturity to manage project risks — apportioning of ownership of risks among project actors (Supplier, contactors, and professionals among others). • Provision of training on risk management approaches to relevant project actors. • Provision of modern risk management plan.
Project cost performance	• The use of realistic cost management process for budget planning and control. • Using strategies to measure project success for cost performance purpose.

Table 1.   (*Continued*)

Project criteria	Success strategies
	• Provision of project cost appraisal techniques at project milestones to ensure that the budget is not exceeded. • Management of project scope for cost control purposes. • Management and maintenance of project cost performance integrity.
Project Portfolio management	• Maintaining strategies such as prioritizing and managing project programs for project goal achievement. • Analyzing returns on project at each milestone. • Learning on the job based on experience using tacit and explicit knowledge can entrench learning into continuous advancement of project management processes and procedures.
	• The ability of project managers to see 'the big picture' of the organizational and project goals. • Consistent reporting of financial project success as a means of balancing the scorecard. • Determining of metrics to indicate up-to-date project performance.

4.4. *IT project success/failure factors*

It is essential for an IT project manager or information system specialist to possess a checklist for project management. It is essential because success/failure considerations differ across projects. More importantly, the dynamic forces of political and social organizational life surrounding any IT project should be considered substantially (Koi-Akrofi, 2017; Taherdoost and Keshavarzsaleh, 2015; Taherdooost and Jalaliyoon, 2014). Additionally, it is noteworthy that precautionary methods by analyzing the sources of failures become vital as they clarify the occurrence of the failures (Rooney and Heuvel, 2004). It is understandable that any undertaking in the production of a project or service is uncertain; however, IT projects regularly fail when it comes to the complex nature of information technology. This was unearthed in the study conducted by the Standish team between 2004 and 2014, consisting of over 50,000 IT projects where only 29% could be categorized as achievements. Therefore, the following consist of groups in which causes of IT project failures are categorized:

- Lack of achieving the project's purpose.
- Lack of realizing the project's estimate.
- Lack of delivering the expected project capacity

Furthermore, Koi-Akrofi (2017) and Taherdoost and Keshavarzsaleh (2015) explored other failures apart from the ones identified above:

- Communication failure: This is a lack in achieving the specifications and aim of the systems design.
- Procedural failure: This type of failure occurs when the project schedule and estimate are not met.
- Collaborative failure: This type of failure happens when consumers' expectations and frequency product/project usage do not harmonize, meaning that there is a parallel between task performance and consumers' mindset.
- Anticipated failure: This happens when the system does meet the stakeholder requirements, opportunities, or exchanges and values.

Furthermore, Tsun *et al.* (2008) revealed that seven out of ten indicators of a software development project could determine macro faults of misinterpretations, mistakes, and problems in the design.

4.5. *IT project success factors*

An IT project manager plays a significant position in almost every complicated project, particularly to be able to identify project risks and control them. This impacts how an IT project manager evaluates the IT projects risks. Thus, it is pertinent to explore the following questions: 'What are the criteria and strategies that enhance project success?' 'To what extent do the identification and management of project risks avoid project collapse?' Tsun *et al.*'s (2008) investigation revealed that the IT project managers' technical and managerial expertise is significant to project team commitment and ultimately to the project success. The criteria and the strategies in IT project success/failure differ among organizations. Moreover, Tsun *et al.*'s (2008) study findings uncovered inconsistency in considering all success/failure and risk factors. Thus, there is the need for an extensive comprehensive study for clear consistency.

The framework suggested in Figure 2 provides elaborate understanding of success factors to IT projects that should be considered.

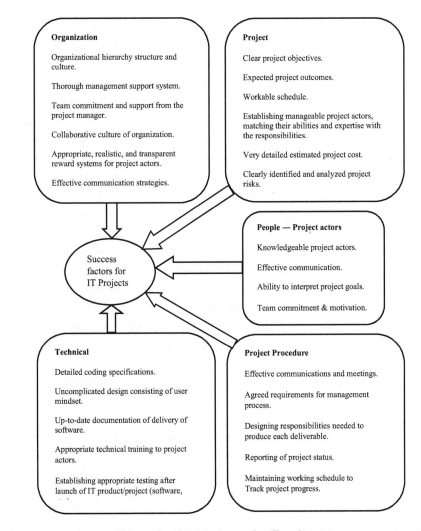

Figure 2.   Success factors for IT project.

5. IT project management Key Performance Indicators (KPIs)

The team in an IT project organization must ensure that all technology-related projects run according to plan, support the organization's overall business strategy, reduce the risk of failure, and are completed on time. Thus, measuring IT project management effectiveness through Key Performance Indicators (KPIs) is an integral part of keeping IT project management operations running smoothly.

To determine how specific IT project management activities are achieved over time, Key Performance Indicators relating to IT project management in metrics and quantitative measurements are used (Ostakhov *et al.*, 2018). Primarily, the project team is guided by the KPI because it reflects where substantial effort and commitment of either the consumer or the project team lie. Thus, it helps if both relevant stakeholders and the IT project manager agree on which system of measurement is to be adopted and how the weights will be calculated, the reporting system, and the interpretation.

In KPIs, metrics exemplify the weight in terms of specific numerical values based on the agreed KPIs. Furthermore, the significance of weights is an indication of the need to measure them during the execution of the project to ensure that timely remedial actions are taken. Thus, it is not important after the completion phase of the project (Ostakhov *et al.*, 2018). This exercise is beneficial because of the following:

- Improves IT performance management and employee productivity.
- Reduces occurrences of viruses found by end users.
- Reduces operational costs for IT projects.
- Improves IT project planning and forecast practices.

The following is a discussion on KPIs that the project manager should measure when implementing or analyzing any IT project.

Approach to measurement: This ratio is one of the indicators of project management KPIs. For instance, the ratio can be calculated as the whole work of the project to the work involved in reducing deficiencies that occur at various phases of the project (testing, productive operation, development, analysis, and during the pilot operation).

The following categories of system of measurement for IT projects (Ostakhov *et al.* 2018) are examined. It should be noted that the system of measurement with weights of the project duration can be calculated monthly or weekly for the entire duration of the project.

(1) **KPI of quality of planning**: This type of KPI is a complex one. Basically, it is used for measuring the actual project completion period in comparison to the planned project completion date or phase. The purpose of using this type of KPI is to provide reliable implementation of IT project work. This is achieved by highlighting significant alterations at the project completion stage. Moreover, the intention of this KPI is to decrease the use of disproportionate allocation of tasks to employees and improper use of budget including extra work to achieve the planned project targets. Thus, the following system of measurement should be used in determining the KPI of quality of planning value: measurement of the timely achievement of project's objectives per milestones including timely commencement of the next project work. For instance, project target is the ratio of actual completion period to the planned period:

$$KPI_{QoP} = \frac{\text{Labor costs}_{planned}}{\text{Labor costs}_{actual}}$$

(2) **KPI of development of quality**: This type of KPI is used to highlight cost reduction of the IT project because cost and quality are relative. The value of this KPI is calculated by highlighting the sources of deficiencies and the removal at the initial stage of the IT project. Thus, the following is recommended as an approach to the measurement of KPI of development quality: The ratio is measured based on the work involved in eliminating defects at various project phases (such as design, development, testing, usage/operation, and feedback) to the total work of the project.

$$KPI_{DQ} = \frac{Manpower\ effort_{defects}}{Manpower\ effort_{project}}$$

The formula above measures the project quality and thus, can be explained in the proceeding section:

- The compliance of the IT Project technological requirements with the customer's requests and perceived value is significant to indicate the IT project quality.

Before the completion of an IT project, it is, however, essential to evaluate the program code not only for functionality but also for the following:

- Conformity with the values of organizational development.
- Acting on customer's requests by promoting project testing and technological specifications before the project development phase.
- Designing project test cases for consumer approval before the start of the technical requirement and testing.

(3) **The KPI of quality of technical requirements**: This type of KPI is highly essential and valuable. It is calculated as % reporting of the quality of the project's technical requirements. For instance, if the value of the KPI of quality of technical requirements is 100% before implementing the project, it thus implies that 20% of the practical aspect delivers 80% of the project's procedure, benefits and service. Then, reducing the design defects in service, process, and the product itself will be more expensive with each successive phase in which the deficiencies are detected.

(4) **The KPI of the process**: This type of KPI highlights how the project group/team is guided by the development process accepted in the IT organization without variations. The importance of quantifying and tracing this type of KPI is when one is examining and influencing the organization execution's process to avert omitting significant development phases planned for the appropriate procedure, service, and the project itself in the appropriate manner.

The KPI of the process is fundamental and reveals an interconnected and all-inclusive method that calculates significant project indicators. This is necessary to sustain the project's financial stability and practicality, and the approach or service for the entire organization.

6. Summary

The chapter focused on understanding the responsibilities of the IT project manager in the project life cycle. Besides giving a bit of background to IT project management, it highlighted how to manage IT projects using software management. The members of the team in a standard IT project organization were identified and their responsibilities explored. Additionally, the factors that cause failures of IT projects and those that support the success of IT projects were examined. The author also discussed the challenges of IT project management. Finally, in measuring KPIs of IT projects, there was a discussion on classes of metrics for IT projects.

References

Araújo, C., Pedron, C. and Quevedo-Silva, F. (2018). IT project manager competencies and team commitment: A new scale proposal, *Revista de Gestão e Projetos — GeP*, 9(1), 39–55.

Barber, E. (2004). Benchmarking the management of projects: A review of current thinking, *Int. J. Proj. Manage.*, 22(4), 301–307. Doi: 10.1016/j.ijproman.2003.08.001.

George, C. (2020). The use of project management skills to overcome organizational challenges, *Int. J. Innovative Sci. Res. Technol.*, 5(3), 340–344.

Hughes, B., Ireland, R., West, B., Smith, N., Shepherd, D. (2012). *Project Management for IT related Projects*. Swindon, UK: BCS, The Chartered Institute for IT.

Ibbs, C. W. and Kwak, Y. H. (2000). Assessing project management maturity, *Proj. Manage. J.*, 31(1), 32–43.

Kerzner, H. R. (2013). *A Systems Approach to Planning, Scheduling, and Controlling*, 8th ed. New York: John Wiley & Sons.

Kerzner, H. R. (2010). *Project Management — Best Practices: Achieving Global Excellence,* New Jersey: John Wiley & Sons.

Koi-Akrofi, G. (2017). Delivering successful IT projects: A literature-based framework, *Texila Int. J. Manage.*, 3(2), 1–14.

Lam, P., Chan, E., Poon, C. S., Chau, C. K. and Chun, K. P. (2001). Factors affecting the implementation of green specifications in construction, *J. Environ. Manage.*, 91(3), 654–661.

Maritato, M. (2013). Mastering project requirements: Assessing how good you are. Paper Presented at PMI® Global Congress 2013 — North America, New Orleans, LA. Newtown Square, PA: Project Management Institute.

McGrath, J. and Kostalova, J. (2020). Project management trends and new challenges 2020+. In Conference Proceedings of Hradec Economic Days 2020 (pp. 1–9).

Meredith, J. R. and Mantel, S. J. (2011). *Project Management: A Managerial Approach*, 8th ed. New York: Wiley.

Ostakhov, V., Artykulna, N. and Morozov, V. (2018). Models of IT projects KPIs and metrics. In Conference: 2018 IEEE Second International Conference on Data Stream Mining & Processing (DSMP).

PMI. (2013). *A Guide to the Project Management Body of Knowledge (PMBOK® Guide),* 5th ed. Pennsylvania: Project Management Institute, Inc.

Schwalbe, K. (2016). *Information Technology Project Management*, 8th ed. United States: Cengage Learning.

Taherdoost, H. and Keshavarzsaleh, A. (2016). Critical factors that lead to projects' success/failure in global marketplace, *Procedia Technol.*, 22, 1066–1075.

Taherdoost, H. and Keshavarzsaleh, A. (2015). How to lead to sustainable and successful IT project management? Propose 5Ps guideline, *Int. J. Adv. Comput. Sci. Inf. Technol.*, 4(1), 14–37.

Taherdoost, H. and Keshavarzsaleh, A. (2015). A theoretical review on IT project success/failure factors and evaluating the associated risks. In 14th International Conference on Telecommunications and Informatics. Sliema, Malta.

Taherdoost, H., Sahibuddin, S. and Jalaliyoon, N. (2015). Security Issues Can Influence onUsage of Electronic Services, *Advances in Information Science and Computer Engineering*, ISSN: 1790–5109, Page: 310–316.

Thamhain, H. J. (2013). Building a collaborative climate for multinational projects, *Procedia Social Behav. Sci.,* 74, 21–33.

Thamhain, H. J. (2014). Managing Technology-Based Projects: Tools, Techniques, People and Business Processes Wiley.

The Chartered Institute for IT. (2012). *Project Management for IT-related Projects,* 2nd ed. Edited by Hughes, B., West, B., Smith, N. and Shepherd, D. I.

Tsun, C. and Cao, D. B. A. (2008). Survey study of critical success factors in agile software projects, *J. Syst. Software*, 81, 961–971.

Xu, X., Zhang, W. and Barkhi, R. (2010). IT infrastructure capabilities and IT project success: A development team perspective, *Inf. Technol. Manage.*, 11(3), 123–142.

Zwikael, O. and Globerson, S. (2006). From critical success factors to critical success processes, *Int. J. Prod. Res.*, 44(17), 3433–3449.

https://doi.org/10.1142/9789811240584_0008

Chapter 8

The IT Project Ecosystem — An Industry Case Study

Peter Tow*, Manmeet Kaur[†], Ian Sharpe[‡] and Monica Almeda[§]

Project Management Office, Western Sydney University, Locked Bag 1797, Penrith NSW 2751, Australia
Freelance Program Director
*peter.tow@gmail.com,
[†]mkaur13@hotmail.com,
[‡]isdsharpe@gmail.com
[§]monica.t.almeda@gmail.com

Projects including today's modern IT Projects do not exist as a discrete unit. Similar to a biological ecosystem, a project team is part of the project ecosystem that includes various internal and external stakeholders. This case study presents the Enterprise Service Management (ESM) Project which was a strategic initiative by Western Sydney University. The ESM Project objective was to optimize student and staff experience through a central and customer-centric enterprise service management platform, in order to drive accountability and service performance. The ESM Project case study provides an example of a modern-day IT Project with an overarching transformation and change purpose. This case study presents a discussion of the challenges and approaches adopted to manage a project through a complex stakeholder landscape and the capabilities required to succeed in delivering transformation and change objectives. The key capabilities identified throughout the case study are the need for the Project Manager to have leadership and stakeholder management skills to navigate a mix of complex organizational ecosystems, people, and technical requirements. The IT project manager must adapt appropriate methodologies, a continuous improvement process and lifelong learning and development to successfully deliver the project.

1. Introduction

Projects including today's modern IT Projects do not exist as a discrete unit. Similar to a biological ecosystem, a project team is part of the project ecosystem that includes various internal and external stakeholders.

Large-scale IT projects are prone to take too long, are usually more expensive than expected, and, crucially, fail to deliver the expected benefits. This need not be the case. Companies can achieve successful outcomes through an approach that helps IT and business join forces in a commitment to deliver value. Despite the disasters, large organizations can engineer IT projects to defy the odds (Bloch, Blumberg and Laartz, 2012).

The planning, design, and building of the project team require a holistic approach and management of the project as a 'Transformation project' rather than an 'IT Project'. Leadership skills are key to ensuring the success of the project and that all the interconnected parts in the ecosystem are able to work successfully together toward a common objective. Successful stakeholder engagement and management are major contributors for successful project delivery.

This case study presents the Enterprise Service Management (ESM) Project which was a strategic initiative by Western Sydney University. The ESM Project objective was to optimize student and staff experience through a central and customer-centric enterprise service management platform, in order to drive accountability and service performance.

The ESM Project case study provides an example of a modern-day IT Project with an overarching transformation and change purpose.

This case study discusses the challenges and approaches adopted to manage a project through a complex stakeholder landscape, and the project management, leadership, and strategic engagement skills and capabilities required to succeed in delivering transformation and change objectives.

2. Overview of the project — Enterprise Service Management (ESM) project

2.1. *Organization — Western Sydney University*

Western Sydney University is located in the city of Sydney in Australia and was formally established in 1989 in order to support the growth and economic development of the Western Sydney region through education and engagement. In 2019, the University had approximately 49,000 students and 3,500 staff. The University is geographically spread over 11 campus locations across the Western Sydney region.

2.2. *Project overview and core objectives*

The Enterprise Service Management (ESM) Project was a strategic initiative undertaken by Western Sydney University. The project comprised the establishment of an enterprise-wide service management system for the University. The project included the design and deployment of a Service Management Platform in conjunction with a broader digital transformation agenda. The project's aim was to provide *Quicker, Simpler, Better* Service via a contemporary, intuitive Portal and underpinned by a comprehensive Knowledge Management system.

In December 2020, the program successfully deployed the 'WesternNow' branded portal platform based on the global leading ServiceNow platform.

The ESM project was approved by the University Executive Committee, based on a Strategic Business Case which was established in 2018. Refer to Figure 1 for the key project milestones.

A governance structure was established and chaired by the Vice President of the Division of Finance and Resources (nominally the Chief Operating Officer) and a representative of the University Executive Committee.

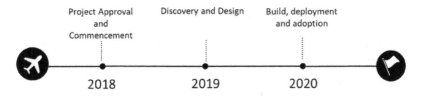

Figure 1. ESM key milestones.

Core Project Objectives

Improved Operational Efficiency
Benefit: reduced workload through automated workflows and central knowledge database

Improved Single Platform Productivity
Benefit: efficiency through improved consistency and simplicity of service engagement and delivery

Productivity

Improved Student Experience
Benefit: increased revenue through student retention and marketing

Improved Staff Experience
Benefit: reduced staff turnover and associated increased productivity

Experience

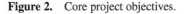

Additional project outcomes

Improved Reporting for Intelligent Analytics
Better data driven decision making, reduced risk and increased trust

Enhanced accountability
Through better controls and transparency ensuring more effective performance management

Improved Resource Planning and Performance
Improved usage of data and analytics, and realignment of productivity benefits into resources

Reduced Complexity and Inconsistency
Through standardised processes and workflows, enabling ongoing continuous improvement

Figure 2. Core project objectives.

The project was primarily owned by the Project Management Office (PMO) which is nominally the organization's transformation office. The system, technical, and architectural ownership was held by IT and Digital Services (IT Department). The ESM project was established to deliver an overarching set of core objectives as described in Figure 2. A selection of the key additional project outcomes is also shown.

2.3. *Core project deliverables*

The project scope comprised core deliverables which were articulated in alignment with the high-level work breakdown structure. The core deliverables are summarized in Figure 3.

The primary visible deliverable of the project was the establishment of centralized digital web portal accessibility (one for students and one for staff), in order to ensure that access to services and knowledge could be funneled through a central point. The illustration of the core staff portal to bring together accessibility for all the streams is shown in Figure 4. The portal was branded as WesternNow, leveraging the naming of the underlying ServiceNow platform.

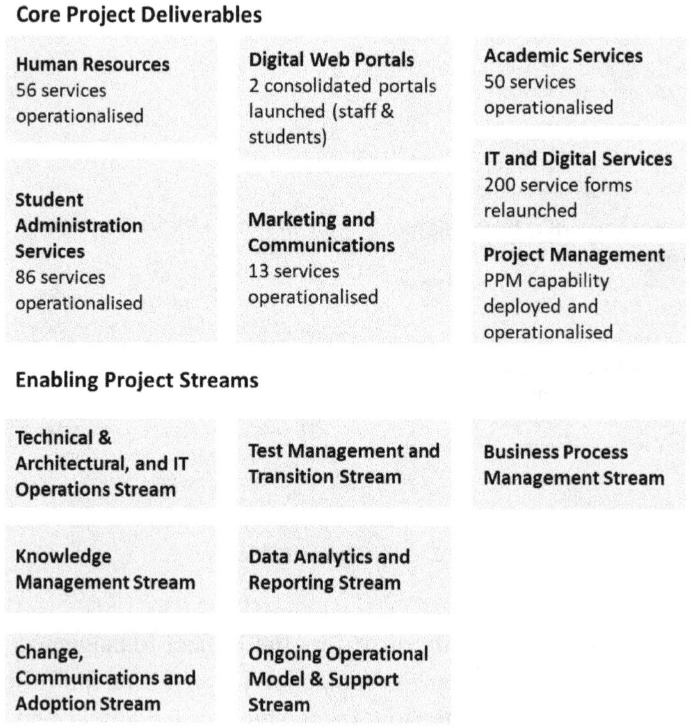

Core Project Deliverables

Human Resources 56 services operationalised	**Digital Web Portals** 2 consolidated portals launched (staff & students)	**Academic Services** 50 services operationalised
		IT and Digital Services 200 service forms relaunched
Student Administration Services 86 services operationalised	**Marketing and Communications** 13 services operationalised	**Project Management** PPM capability deployed and operationalised

Enabling Project Streams

Technical & Architectural, and IT Operations Stream	**Test Management and Transition Stream**	**Business Process Management Stream**
Knowledge Management Stream	**Data Analytics and Reporting Stream**	
Change, Communications and Adoption Stream	**Ongoing Operational Model & Support Stream**	

Figure 3.   Core scope of deliverables.

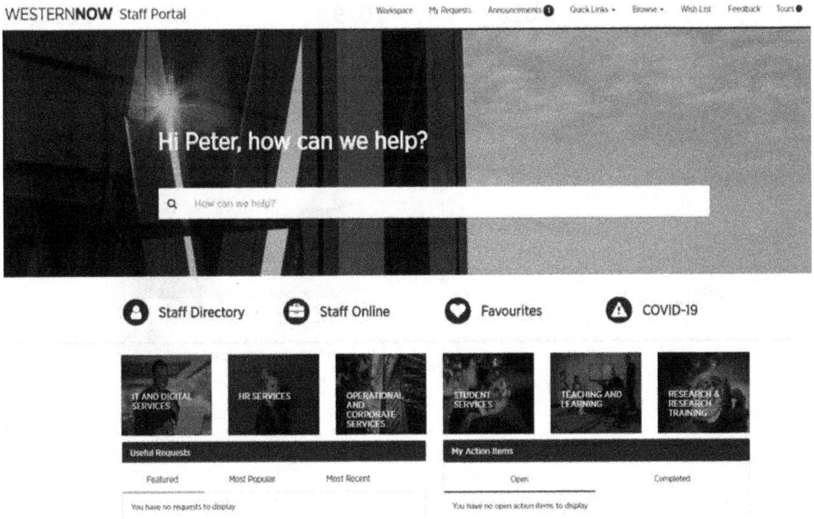

Figure 4.   WesternNow staff portal.

2.4. *Project performance*

The overall project was deemed successful in that the following was achieved:

- Core scope delivered and deployed within budget.
- A majority of the milestones were achieved on schedule, noting that schedule re-baselining was required for a number of project streams, and a slight overall extension of the project closeout was required.
- Key business and process improvement objectives were delivered.
- An ongoing operating model for continuous improvement was established.

A detailed project plan was maintained throughout the project, comprising detailed schedules that fed into a dynamic overarching project roadmap. The overarching program and scope are illustrated in Figure 5.

While all project streams were delivered within the required time frames (i.e., prior to the end of 2020), some of the earlier streams

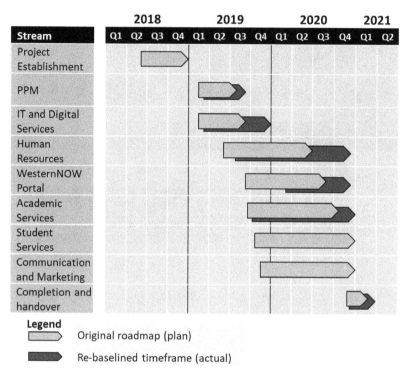

Figure 5. ESM program roadmap.

experienced delays. A key observation was that the earlier streams were behind schedule primarily as a consequence of learning and adapting to the challenges of the project. As the project progressed, the teams' capability expanded significantly through the experience of managing the IT elements of the project, along with complex stakeholder relationships.

3. People and project context

3.1. *Project delivery approach*

The overarching approach to delivering the ESM project was developed and documented in the Project Management Plan (PMP), including the adoption of appropriate project methodologies and principles.

The ESM Project was provided a clear mandate that the primary project purpose be defined as transformational and change, which would be facilitated by the implementation and adoption of the selected IT Platform. The intertwined nature of this purpose necessitated a series of approaches to be adopted to ensure effective performance. The nature of broader areas outside the direct control of the project required consideration of the project's impact on a broader ecosystem, which was addressed by the establishment of a robust governance structure, development of guiding principles, and adoption of an underlying partnership strategy.

A broad set of agile principles was adopted for the project and the development and deployment of software and platform configuration. The incremental approach to development enabled the program to learn and improve within the project, and to better engage with stakeholders in addressing requirements. The adoption of an agile approach also allowed the project to better engage with emerging opportunities and benefits.

With respect to software development, the project adopted an 'off-the-shelf' approach. This was underpinned by a commitment to avoid excessive software development or customization. The adoption of this principle meant in many cases, business processes were required to be changed to reflect the native structure of the platform. The rationale for this approach is based on ensuring long-term sustainability and upgradability for the vendor's product.

3.2. *Roles and context — project team*

The ESM project established a range of core roles and functions within the project structure. These core roles were required throughout the greater part of the project. Resources to fill each role were engaged via a variety of sources, including internal staff secondments, contingent labor hire, and external commercial advisory services. Where necessary, resources from operational segments of the organization were seconded into the project team.

A key principle underpinning the design of the project team was to ensure clarity of responsibility, and in each case a clear delegation of responsibility, accountability, and authority was established.

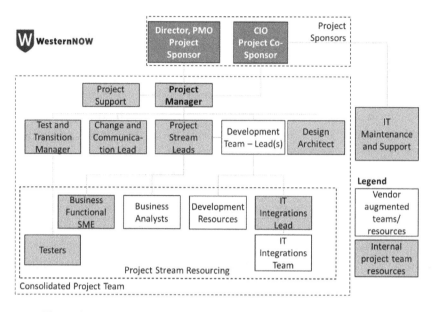

Figure 6.   Enterprise Service Management (ESM) project team structure.

The resourcing plan and project team structure as illustrated in Figure 6 were approved by the Steering Committee.

Key project roles:

- **Project Sponsor** — The project was established with a dual-sponsorship structure, comprising the Chief Information Officer (CIO) and Director of the PMO. This approach was adopted in order to ensure leadership across the broader technical architectural strategy and business transformation objectives. Dual sponsorship has the potential for improved leadership outcomes but has higher-profile risk relating to potential for conflict. In order to mitigate this risk, clear protocols were established at the beginning of the project to ensure decision-making primacy over respective domains and the mix of accountabilities. An underlying theme of partnership was embedded in the project from the start and displayed in action from the top.

- **Project Manager (PM) and Project Stream Leads** — The project manager role was established as the key point of responsibility for the project. It was deemed essential that the PM should be appropriately qualified, with experience in both IT projects and transformation and change. A project support function was established and for each functional project stream, a project stream lead was established across the functional product structure.

- **Business Analyst** — Each functional stream of the project required various forms of business analyst support. The business analyst support was resourced per stream via the relevant vendor partner. Key responsibilities included process mapping, requirements management, and test planning. The business analysis function and resources were supplemented through the vendor partners.

- **Design Architect** — Under the joint leadership of IT and the project management team, an Architectural Committee was established to facilitate the architectural design and decision-making framework. The PM was the Chair of this committee, with a reporting line to the CIO. Each vendor provided technical representation to this committee.

- **Integration Team** — A combined team was established leveraging key representatives from each vendor, under the direction of the IT lead for system integration management. Application leads for legacy systems were also represented.

- **Test and Transition Manager** — An internal and experienced project resource was seconded into the project to provide leadership of test and transition management. Vendor support for test and transition was engaged separately on each stream as required.

- **Business Users/Functional Leads/SMEs** — A number of business unit representatives were invited to join the project team. Each project stream established formal positions to second a business unit subject-matter expert (SME) into the team to provide a stronger link between project, business service owners, and end users. Each project stream established cross-functional governance committees and working groups to ensure appropriate design, decision-making, and stakeholder buy-in. External vendors were closely involved.

- **Business Operations team** — The function ownership was closely engaged through the project. The relationship through the project was multilayered and was underpinned by the Functional SME embedded within each project stream.

- **Development Team** — Development resources were primarily provided by the vendor partners, with an identified team for each steam.
- **IT Maintenance and Support** — The BAU IT operations team was engaged to support the project. The operations team was responsible for coordinating with the PMs for deployment planning, for managing deployment, and for planning the ongoing operational support model.

3.3. *Organizational ecosystem*

No project exists in isolation. The project was delivered within the broader ecosystem of the University, and a deep understanding of the organizational networks and process connection was critical.

Project sponsorship and ownership were unique as it was essentially a jointly owned project by the PMO (transformation office) and IT Department. The transformational aspects of the project were primarily driven by the PMO, while from a technology and IT perspective, assurance and control were provided by the IT department.

An illustrative high-level summary of core elements of the organizational ecosystem is shown in Figure 7.

3.4. *Project governance*

A project governance structure was developed and established. This structure was based on the University's standard project governance model and incorporated a range of working groups as a mechanism to drive the partnerships within the organization and with external service providers (refer to Figure 8).

The ESM Project Steering Committee comprised senior executive members to represent users (or functional business owners) and met formally on a monthly basis. Offline decisions were undertaken if required via circulation of discussion and decision papers. A charter for the steering committee and each of the relevant working groups was documented and included in the PMP.

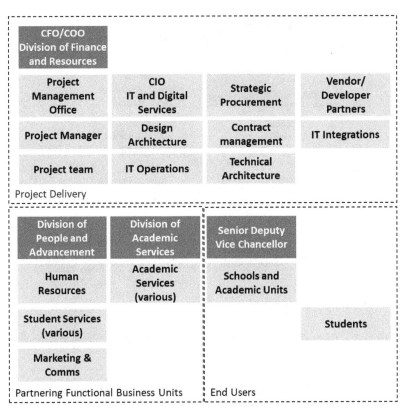

Figure 7. ESM project — Illustrative university ecosystem.

3.5. *Partnering approach*

A strategic approach to partnering was adopted by the project in order to address several key challenges. These challenges were as follows:

- A lack of in-house expertise relating to both capacity and capability.
- An expectation that requirements and opportunities would emerge as the project evolved.
  — The need to transform business operations and ways of working to realize benefits, and
  — The requirement to design the program for long-term ownership of appropriate functions.

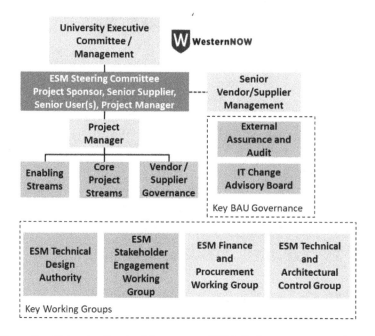

Figure 8.   Enterprise Service Management (ESM) Project governance structure.

In order to address these challenges, a strategic decision was made to adopt a partnership approach.

The key partnerships were structured in the following categories:

- External software provider, vendors, and industry expertise.
- Internal Functional Business Owners and users.

Platform and software provider — The University had a long-standing relationship with ServiceNow, the software platform provider (www. servicenow.com), based on the early adoption by the IT department in 2013. The objectives of the program to establish effective service management across the Enterprise required a singular and core system platform to deliver the necessary benefits at scale, and to enable the desired broader digital transformation outcomes. The strategic review recommended the selection (or continuance) of the ServiceNow platform. This raised concerns around the lack of competition in the market and the potential for commercial impact of the University becoming 'locked in'. As such, it was determined to adopt and pursue a partnership approach to maximize the benefits from the relationship. The partnership approach was based on a negotiated commercial foundation (subject to appropriate procurement processes), leveraging Australian Universities' group agreements to maintain a connection to sector-wide economies of scale and commercial leverage. The University's contributions to the supplier included participation on committees for future product planning, early release and beta testing, presentations at conferences, and case studies. These efforts enabled a deepening of the relationship, and this was able to be leveraged by the project team to enhance technical and business outcomes.

Vendors and industry expertise — A key challenge for the project was around how to identify and secure appropriate resourcing and expertise for the project. The traditional approach is to engage a core technology or vendor partner. This traditional approach had limitations in that there is risk of a single vendor accruing too much commercial leverage. An approach was adopted whereby a dual-vendor partnership was established under an overarching Procurement Strategy.

Leveraging an appropriate procurement process, two core vendors, Deloitte (www2.deloitte.com/au) and CSA (www.csa.com.au.), were selected to provide various levels of expertise.

The presence of dual vendors did create a risk relating to configuration management and concurrent system development. This was addressed through the establishment of processes for governance, oversight, and coordination, in the form of the Technical Design Authority. The partnership approach was underpinned by a structured and robust contract performance management process.

The dual-vendor partnership approach worked effectively, ensuring provision of technical capability and capacity, and maintaining a commercially competitive and high-performance project environment.

Functional Business Owners — The project identified that the transformation of business processes and adoption of new ways of working would require a substantial commitment from functional business units. The contribution of key stakeholders was required for the discovery, design, and testing phases. Furthermore, the realization of productivity benefits was also anticipated as a future challenge that could impact adoption and successful change management outcomes.

- **Genuine relationship-driven partnerships** — to ensure a deep two-way level of engagement with business users and partners.
- **Embedded resources** — positions for key subject-matter experts from each stream's business unit to be embedded within the project.
- **Show not tell, pull not push** — to engage stakeholders through visible demonstration of value, using storytelling to create a compelling narrative, and taking into account stakeholder priorities in design.
- **Involvement in governance committees** — senior and executive leaders were incorporated actively in project governance.
- **Business unit visible leadership** — the business leadership was engaged and committed for ownership of business process decisions.

As time was invested to establish each set of relationships, all streams were eventually delivered and accepted by business owners. The streams with the most engaged stakeholders and leadership delivered higher levels of productivity gains, more improved customer experiences, and faster adoption.

3.6. *Development approach*

The development approach followed by the ESM project was predominantly based on the project life cycle process. A Project Backlog was maintained and the project team selected and prioritized stories for development and deployment.

Due to the rapidly changing environment, a key to success for the University was to ensure the ability to rapidly and effectively develop and roll out new services on the platform.

The intention following project completion is to shift to a 'product delivery' model. To support this shift, a new effective Operating Model was established to further support the ongoing continuous improvement of the platform and to deliver further benefits to the University. The operating model was designed to facilitate new skills, processes, and approaches to be developed. Additional training and development requirements were also considered. It was also identified that stakeholders would need to change to a more collaborative and committed development approach to enable new services and features to be rapidly delivered.

3.7. *Distributed teams and virtual working*

In early 2020, as with most institutions around the globe, the University was impacted by COVID-19 and the subsequent global impact. University physical campuses were closed, and all staff resources were directed to adopt a 'work-from-home' posture. This also impacted vendors and suppliers. This occurred in the middle of the design and build phases for many of the core project streams.

The University being a multi-campus institution was already enabled for virtual and remote working leveraging various virtual tools. The lack of face-to-face capacity meant communications became more difficult and engagement with stakeholders became less frequent.

This new approach to working however had a number of advantages. While design workshop techniques needed to be redesigned, virtual working meant an increase in availability of key resources, with less travel time and shorter, more efficient engagements. At one point, the project team was able to deploy 94 design workshops over a 6-week period.

The University response to COVID-19 also resulted in the termination of some key resources. However, due to the elimination of commuting, resource productivity increased during this time sufficiently to offset the impact of reduced resource levels.

From a business stakeholder perspective, the broader remote working situation also helped drive technology adoption as the concept of remote service provision became more acceptable. This allowed for a better appreciation of the benefits and importance of the project.

The extended period of virtual working created challenges for staff well-being, for both University and vendor partners, which required active management and engagement throughout the project.

4. Key success factors

4.1. *Core project management practices*

The ESM project adopted core project management practices throughout the project team. The project adopted the University project management framework known as Projects @ Western (Western Sydney University, 2020). The following elements are highlighted:

- **Project Management Plan** — The base project plan was documented in the Project Management Plan (PMP). This document was the basis for articulating project management requirements throughout the project. The PMP evolved through the project to address emerging requirements and reflect continuous improvements and learnings.
- **Project Methodology** — The project adopted a hybrid waterfall and agile approach, comprising the University's Projects @ Western project management methodology and underpinned by the adoption of agile principles.
- **Budget Management** — The project budget was approved and funding allocated by the University Executive. Funding was approved as capital expenditure. As such, consideration for the accounting treatment of the investment and subsequent planning for depreciation was determined in conjunction with the University's Finance Office. The total value of the project is confidential; however, the budget was based on a benchmark estimating process informed by a range of experiences and lessons from other projects, and included an appropriate contingency given the high level of design uncertainty and risk. The project scope was delivered under budget, an achievement underpinned by effective management and mitigation of risk.
- **Resource Management** — The core project team was established through internal University resources, including identification of key Business as Usual (BAU) roles to support the project. Contingent labor was engaged when and where required, and technical development resources were engaged via a key set of vendors (including consultants) to ensure appropriate capability and capacity.

- **Risk Management** — The risk management process was documented in the PMP and managed on an active basis. An updated risk register was presented to all governance committees for discussion and acceptance. Mitigation strategies were developed and actions tracked.
- **Commercial Structures** — Commercial elements were established via appropriate procurement processes to ensure relevant value for money, probity, and transparency adherence. All agreements were developed in conjunction with the University's procurement and commercial teams. Overarching vendor contracts were established with agreed rates and negotiated terms and conditions.
- **Change Management** — Change management requirements were embedded into all aspects of the project, including the guiding principles, the design of a partnership approach, engagement strategies, and specifically incorporating this into the role of the project stream leads. This required a capability uplift for many resources and as such formed part of the project on-boarding and induction process.
- **Service Transition** — The IT implementation aspects of the project were required to follow the IT configuration management protocols per the IT Change Advisory Board (CAB) processes.

4.2. *Design principles*

At the initiation of the project, a core set of guiding principles was established. The development of these principles was undertaken on a collaborative basis to ensure broad agreement and buy-in, and to empower the principles to act as a guide to decision-making and performance assessment throughout the project. These principles also provided the basis for engagement with key stakeholders and underpinned the transformation and change outcomes for the project. The visual display of these core principles is in Figure 9.

The benefit of agreeing to a standard set of guiding principles at the start of the project ensured that these became themes throughout the project and strongly influenced the project. For example, the principle of **Adopt and Adapt** provided a clear mandate to standardize work practices and to adopt more 'out-of-the–box' elements from the technology

Figure 9. Enterprise Service Management guiding principles.

platform, which in turn reduces both implementation and ongoing support costs.

4.3. *Establishing people*

The project engaged a range of resources. It was recognized at the beginning of the project that the project team would require time, investment, and experience to create capability to successfully deliver the project. It was recognized that the project was also an opportunity to develop and invest in key staff and therefore to pursue indirect organizational benefits from the project. Most of the project team earned promotions and new roles following the project. The opportunity to establish people also extended to external partners.

System/platform capability — All key project team members were required to learn how to use the platform and system in order to facilitate appropriate decisions, to challenge designs, and to understand the impact on the business units and end users to ensure the design genuinely improves productivity and experience.

IT technical processes — While most of the project management resources had relevant experience in managing IT projects, there was also the need to learn University processes for IT project management and implementation.

Business analysis and process improvement — In order to facilitate transformation and change, an appreciation was required about how digital transformation translates into realizable benefits. Project Managers were therefore enabled to engage with requirements gathering and business process optimization in order to deliver benefits.

Communication and engagement — While the project developed a communications and engagement plan, a strategic decision was taken in that all project team members would be responsible for being involved in communication and engagement. It was recognized that a core element of the project would require the establishment of a project team that could engage and influence the broad number of stakeholders that were impacted by the program.

The program also took advantage of being able to push individuals beyond their initial expectations, and as staff turnover occurred, less experienced staff were elevated to take ownership of project streams, successfully progressing in their development both as IT project managers and as leaders of transformation and change.

4.4. *Adoption and operational sustainability*

The need to consider long-term requirements to support the platform was identified early in the project. Although there are various models related to provision of IT functional administration, there was no established methodology for continuous improvement and engagement with business units for a strategic investment pipeline.

A stream within the project was established to build the long-term operating model in order to ensure the sustainability of the system and platform and to prioritize ongoing investment. The ongoing operating support model was critical to long-term adoption expectations.

4.5. *Communication*

Effective stakeholder management also means communicating with your stakeholders and understanding that not all stakeholders require the same information at the same time (Gifford and Lesser, 2016). The key focus areas that had to operate effectively were internal project communications, technical organizational engagement, and stakeholder engagement.

Internal project communication — A formal and structured approach was adopted initially by the project. The communications plan established a network of regular meetings and stand-ups. Key relationships were identified for regular engagement and to ensure multiple lines of communication were accessible. The project also focused on a culture of communication, which set expectations and included principles such as immediacy, encouraging direct phone calls to discuss and resolve issues as they emerged. It was mandated that hierarchy should be respected (i.e., the formal lines of communication) but not feared, in that no barriers to communication based on hierarchy should prevail. Keeping the broader project team across issues allowed a broader set of minds to be applied.

Technical organizational engagement — The project engaged deeply with the technical sides of the organization, predominantly IT, and also with other functional areas. Formal and informal communication channels were established under the broad guidance of the Technical Architectural Committee and the Committee Design Authority.

Stakeholder engagement — A broad engagement plan was established and implemented. A key challenge was the ability of the team and project to communicate effectively to non-technology stakeholders. A series of 'elevator pitches' were developed to support simple and more effective key messaging.

4.6. *Understanding project complexity*

The success of complex projects in complex project environments and ecosystems requires an understanding of the nature of complexity, the application of relevant tools and techniques, and the underpinning nature of effective leadership.

Most project delivery is rated *complicated* rather than *complex* under the Cynefin framework (Snowden and Boone, 2007). The ESM Project displayed a range of elements of significant complexity. While the individual streams of the project were *complicated*, the overarching remit was clear; there were several factors that shifted the delivery context to *complex* as follows:

- Significant unknowns as to the precise scope required for integrations given a legacy system and process landscape.
- Continual learning experiences with new capabilities and features across system upgrades.
- New needs arising from process optimization which redefined solutions and introduced new challenges.
- Unclear boundaries between ESM and other related major transformations.
- Economic factors (Political and COVID-19) driving major sector disruption and altering prioritization.

Accordingly, a constant *probe, sense, respond* approach at the Governance and Project Delivery level was required to be able to detect and respond to the emergent factors — balancing regular project delivery against schedule and budget, with iterative adjustments at the stream level so that value was the constant compass.

4.7. *Leveraging tools*

The selection and use of appropriate tools and techniques is a key element of successful IT projects. The core concept of the ESM project is about the organization learning to use digital tools and systems to underpin day-to-day ways of working. Consequently, the project was required to lead by example through the use of digital tools where possible.

Project and Portfolio Management (PPM) — The first stream of the ESM project was to establish the ServiceNow PPM tool (ITBM) as a project management tool that could be used for the rest of the project. This tool was then used to provide the following key capabilities:

- Project status and milestone reporting.
- Project financial reporting.
- Test management.
- Agile working.

Schedule management — While high-level roadmaps in a dashboard format (PowerPoint) were developed for executive communications, detailed scheduling utilized Microsoft Project scheduling software for the planning and management of time frames for core streams. The schedules were used to coordinate support planning requirements with operational parts of the business, especially the IT Operations functions.

Financial Management — Oracle Financials as the University's core financial management system was utilized to record and manage project financials.

RACI matrices — An acronym for Responsible, Accountability, Consulted, and Informed, this is a technique that was utilized to plan and drive clarity of responsibilities within the project team and connect to key internal processes. This helped the team gain a common understanding of the various roles and requirements for both project team members and stakeholders.

Teams/Zoom — Virtual collaboration software platforms such as Microsoft Teams and Zoom were a key requirement given the wide physical campus distribution and following the COVID-19 working-from-home environment.

Document control — Microsoft SharePoint was used as the primary function for document control for live documents, collaboration, and distribution. Finalized documentation (e.g., contracts) was stored on the TRIM Content Management System, the formal system of record for the University.

Communication platforms — A range of communications tools were engaged through the course of the project, from project webpages, videos, and Yammer for general updates.

The careful selection of tools as documented in the Project Management Plan was instrumental in setting up standard internal project ways of working that were resilient, taking a systematic approach and reducing key person risks.

4.8. *Testing methodology and acceptance*

The project developed a Test Strategy and Test Plans to provide a set of guiding principles and an overall methodology for how testing, acceptance, and transition were to be conducted for the ESM project.

The aim of the testing was to evaluate the quality of the solution being delivered and to verify that the solution was fit for purpose and met the agreed performance levels. However, it became clear that the testing component of the project was not simply a technical task or gateway, but an engagement function across the project team, business owners, end users, and IT operations teams. The need for effective testing became a core engagement activity across the University and project ecosystem.

There were a number of Testing Principles and approaches that were defined for testing to enable the project's success:

Adaptable approach — The ESM Test Strategy provided the **project-level** test approach and guiding principles. The **Test Plan** for each project stream was defined at the **stream level** and was adapted based on the specific stream context. Testing was conducted according to university's quality standards. The testing was focused on the core criteria for risk and priorities.

ServiceNow PPM Test Management tool — This tool was utilized to facilitate and streamline the management of testing, defect management, and capturing of enhancements.

Agile-Waterfall Hybrid Testing approach — The hybrid testing approach combined the rigor and governance of the waterfall approach while embracing the adaptability and flexibility of agile.

Sufficient Time and Resources — Key roles and responsibilities were defined and testing processes were structured and begun early in the project. The project aimed to allocate resources in sufficient time to participate in testing, develop test cases, and document outcomes and defects.

Test Phases — Testing phases and scope for all project streams were defined in the project Test Plans. Test phases for the streams mainly comprised four (4) phases — Sprint (Unit) Testing, System Integration Testing (SIT), User Acceptance Testing (UAT), and Production Verification Testing (PVT).

5. Insights and observations

5.1. *The person — project manager capabilities*

Modern IT projects are characterized by a broader set of objectives that expand beyond the implementation and deployment of a platform or system. These broader objectives are business transformation and change (Gao and Rusu, 2015).

Through research, PMI has established that project management practitioners require not only technical skills but also leadership and business intelligence skills to support strategic objectives that contribute to their success. This combination of technical, leadership, and strategic, and business management competency is what is now termed as the PMI Talent Triangle (A guide to the project management body of knowledge (PMBOK guide), 2017).

The Western Sydney University ESM project was both an IT project and a broader transformation and change project, requiring a broader range of higher-order leadership capabilities and experience.

With consideration to the transformational and change aspects of the project, the core requirements for project managers were an ability to engage effectively with a range of complex key stakeholders, to understand business improvement imperatives, and to develop and deepen relationships across the enterprise. The leadership ability to communicate and influence was critical.

Outcomes from the case study illustrate these aspects as follows:

- All successful elements of the project were enabled by core project management skills and experience.
- Project managers who had specific IT or technology experience were more effective and efficient. The project managers with a lower level

of technical and technology expertise were eventually able to succeed but needed to progress through a more significant learning experience and required additional support to fast track and guide this learning. The impact of this learning curve was displayed in more effective decision-making, planning, and engaging with technical teams.

- The ability to drive and enable transformation objectives within the complex organizational ecosystem required effective leadership through communication and stakeholder engagement.

5.2. *The people — ecosystem and stakeholders*

The notion of stakeholders was originally introduced to the mainstream general management discussion by Freeman (1984). Two years later, Cleland (1986) brought stakeholder thinking into the project management paradigm (Aaltonen, 2010).

Understanding who your stakeholders are, and why their needs are important to the success of the project, is a key responsibility for any project manager, and a responsibility as well for all the people who are involved in project decisions. Sharing this information with the team, and asking the team to help define the answers, is important if the project is to produce a real solution. For the organization, the overall goal is to capture the value of the challenging opportunity or pressing business need. For the end user of the project's result, the overall goal is to receive the actual product or service and find that it meets their needs (Gifford and Lesser, 2016).

At the commencement of the ESM project, a number of key challenges were identified. Beyond tangible risks, these challenges related to the following:

- Complexities related to integrating Business as Usual (BAU) resources into the project team on an as-required basis, with differing priorities and resource loadings.
- Varying workload expectations across the project and resilience required to adapt to an always-changing organizational context.

- The need to balance competing priorities between IT technology delivery, transformation objectives and the inherent change management challenges with key stakeholders.

The project recognized that while technical resources could be assembled, the project would require effective, visible, and engaged leadership in order to create the high-performance team conditions to address expected challenges, and have the resilience to adapt to new ones. As such, the following approaches were established:

- Establishing and communicating core project principles and values to ensure a commonality of purpose across the broader project. These were used to help reinforce decision rationale throughout the project.
- Ensuring that the Project Manager was selected primarily on leadership capability, rather than just on technical experience, and with a focus on building further technical leadership within the project team.
- The leadership team creating and reinforcing a delivery context that supports high-performance behaviors, such as valuing people, appropriately including others, grounded optimism, clear roles, accountability, and authority evidenced through how people acted.
- Recognizing that failure is a constructive opportunity for the broader team to learn, grow, and to drive stronger future performance. An appropriate allowance to fail needed to be balanced out by a firm focus on active risk management and delivery.
- Investing in the interpersonal relationships within the team and across other teams; ensuring 'people come before technology' was demonstrated.

The project was not delivered without difficulties and setbacks. This broad approach was effective in building a team with the cohesion and resilience to deliver the primary project outcomes successfully, navigating the various challenges, making effective decisions quickly as and as required, and succeeding through the COVID-19 challenges of 2020.

5.2.1. *Stakeholder engagement success*

Stakeholder engagement was one of the key strengths of this project. Integrated business and project teams worked from the beginning of the project to the end. This approach helped to avoid miscommunication, and promoted efficiency gains and fast delivery (Bloch *et al.*, 2012).

A particular insight that emerged from this project is how the effectiveness of stakeholders can be curated through effective and proactive engagement strategies. It was observed through the project that the relationship between the project and stakeholders was dynamic, and that stakeholders could be shifted from a passive and observer state to active promoters of the project and broader objectives.

Over the course of the project, the team was successful in curating stakeholders from business units such that key stakeholders slowly began to become recognized as contributing project team members. This was a direct result of the partnering strategy and reflected by the growing expertise of the various project managers in advanced stakeholder engagement and their ability to influence.

5.2.2. *Effective governance and leadership*

Effective governance is fundamental to all project success. There are three key areas whereby an effective governance structure enabled this project to succeed:

Build and maintain confidence — Despite the ups and downs common to every project, and the expected technical challenges experienced by all IT ventures, the University maintained confidence that the project would deliver a functional platform and drive transformation as expected. This in turn increased the buy-in from all key stakeholders and enabled the continuing provision of appropriate budget and resources.

Appropriate decision making authority — The establishment of standard protocols for decision-making (i.e., ensuring clarity of what level of decision-making was required) enabled difficult, controversial, and strategic decisions to be made, and through collaborative review ensured that these decisions could be enforced and actioned.

Enable broad leadership for change and transformation — Effective governance was based on effective project sponsorship and visible support from leaders involved in the governance committees. This leadership enabled a consistent and engaging message through the organization and built awareness and excitement for the benefits that could be achieved, which in turn led to higher levels of interest and adoption.

It should be noted that effective governance needed to be established and curated by building the appropriate relationships. This was enhanced by demonstrating effective progress, and showcasing technological successes and innovation.

5.3. The process — adopting appropriate methodologies

Modern IT projects that incorporate transformation and change objectives display high levels of complexity, which requires appropriate processes to be adopted. This includes appropriate methodologies incorporating Agile principles and the incorporation of a continuous improvement approach.

The modern IT project manager must incorporate the iterative process for learning and development for all IT and transformation projects that display elements of complexity. In many cases, the relevant skills and expertise are not always available, especially externally, and often must be considered for broader learning requirements. This learning process applies to the Project Manager, the Project Team, suppliers, and to the engagement of key stakeholders, who will develop and evolve over the course of the project.

6. Summary

The ESM Project case study provides an example of a modern-day IT Project with an overarching transformation and change purpose.

This case study presents a discussion of the challenges and approaches adopted to manage a project through a complex stakeholder landscape, and the project management, leadership, and strategic engagement skills and capabilities required to succeed in delivering transformation and change objectives.

The case study project's success can be attributed to a diverse range of factors that are important to the success of any modern IT project with broader transformation and change objectives.

The ESM project was also a significant learning and development opportunity for the project team and project ecosystem.

References

Aaltonen, K. (2010). Stakeholder management in international projects, PhD Thesis, Aalto University, Finland. http://urn.fi/URN:ISBN:978-952-60-3344-0. (Accessed 3 May 2021).

Bloch, M., Blumberg, S. and Laartz, J. (2012). Delivering large-scale IT projects on time, on budget, and on value, *McKinsey Digital,* 1 October. https://www.berendt-partner.de/wp-content/uploads/2014/11/MOBT_27_Delivering_large-scale_IT_projects_on_time_budget_and_value.pdf. (Accessed 3 May 2021).

Brewer, J. L. and Dittman, K. C. (2018). *Methods of IT Project Management,* 3rd ed. Ashland: Purdue University Press, West Lafayette, IN.

Freeman, R. E. (1984). *Strategic Management: A Stakeholder Approach,* Boston: Pitman.

Gao, S. and Rusu, L. (2015). *Modern Techniques for Successful IT Project Management,* 1st ed. Hershey: IGI Global.

Gifford, D. and Lesser, S. (2016). Why Stakeholder Management is Important. https://infoworks.com/why-stakeholder-management-is-important/#:~:text=Stakeholder%20management%20is%20important%20because,lifeblood%20of%20effective%20project%20relationships.&text=These%20needs%20involve%20establishing%20a,to%20successfully%20meeting%20project%20objectives. (Accessed 14 April 2021).

Kloosterman, V. (n.d.). Stakeholder Mapping and Management is Key to Successful Project Management. Continuing Professional Development. https://continuingprofessionaldevelopment.org/stakeholder-mapping-key-to-successful-project-management/. (Accessed 7 April 2021).

Mok, K. Y., Shen, G. Q. and Yang, J. (2015). Stakeholder management studies in mega construction projects: A review and future directions, *Int. J. Proj. Manage.,* 33(2), 446–457.

Mukherjee, S. (2019). How stakeholder engagement affects IT projects, *Int. J. Innovative Res. Sci. Eng. Technol.* (Accessed 14 April 2021). Doi: 10.2139/ssrn.3415959.

Philips, J. (2004). *IT Project Management*, 2nd ed. Emeryville, CA: McGraw-Hill.

Project Management Institute. (2017). *A Guide to the Project Management Body of Knowledge (PMBOK guide)*, 6th ed. Pennsylvania: Newtown Square.

Snowden, D. J. and Boone. M. E. (2007). A leader's framework for decision making, *Harvard Bus. Rev.*, 85(11), 68–76. https://hbr.org/2007/11/a-leaders-framework-for-decision-making. (Accessed 14 April 2021).

Western Sydney University. (2020). Project management framework — Projects @ Western Guide, version 1.

Chapter 9

Project Time and Cost Management

Samson A. Arekete*, Temitope Egbelakin[†] and
Olabode E. Ogunmakinde[‡,§]

*Computer Science Department, Redeemer's University, Ede, Nigeria
[†]School of Architecture and Built Environment, University of Newcastle,
Callaghan, Australia
[‡]Faculty of Society and Design, Bond University, Gold Coast, Australia
[§]bogunmak@bond.edu.au

Whatever may be the purpose of an information technology (IT) project, cost and time management are of particular importance in delivering quality projects. Proper costing and budgeting ensure that IT projects are adequately funded in procurement, development efforts, workforce involvement, and remunerations. Underfunding would not ensure efficient project delivery and lack of proper cost controls would result in overshooting the budget, leading to system-wide disruptions and consequences. It is essential to note that funding for any IT project is almost always scarce and inelastic and should be appropriately allocated and managed. Similarly, most IT projects are time bound. Late project delivery can cause the failure of the entire system. Any quality IT products must take due consideration of timing and budgeting. Various stages of development and procurement must be adequately planned, managed, and controlled. The IT project manager must correctly estimate a whole gamut of factors to achieve a cost-effective and successful IT project implementation. These factors include cost, efforts, scheduling, staffing, work breakdown structure (WBS), budget, milestones, and IT system development and maintenance phases. This chapter shall examine the work breakdown structure, project estimation, effort estimation, cost estimation, and resource estimation. The chapter shall also consider various models related to IT project management. Furthermore, we shall discuss Software Engineering metrics, project schedule development, budget, and earned value management.

1. Introduction

Time and cost management are the most important factors in completing IT projects on time. Most projects delivered behind the scheduled date would be deemed to have failed. The reason is that many things are tied to the delivery time of any project. For instance, a team is called upon to deliver an e-Voting system that would be used in an election holding in eighteen months. The deadline for the project may be fixed for fifteen months. The remaining three months may be left for testing running the system. If the project is delivered on schedule, all other items in the electoral authority's schedule will follow smoothly. However, failure to complete the project on time may spell doom for the entire electoral process.

Time is always a significant constraint in any project. Time is limited and cannot be increased at will. There are only 24 hours in a day, and seven days in a week. Hence, the IT project management team must plan well and develop a realistic schedule that would be acceptable to all parties. Apart from a good time and schedule outlay, it is essential to monitor compliance to the timelines, and quickly address any delays. Regardless of what happens to a project, time ticks away (Schwalbe, 2016).

Finance is usually limited on all projects. A balance in IT project cost is critical to customer satisfaction. A project cost must be well estimated, and the costs well managed to allow for timely delivery and proper execution. Failure to budget adequately for an IT project may spell doom for its delivery on time and to the client's satisfaction.

In this chapter, we examine IT project management in terms of cost and time. Most projects that failed are consequent upon these two factors. We shall look at various factors, tools, and concepts for an IT project's time and cost management.

2. Project time management

2.1. *Work Breakdown Structure (WBS)*

Work breakdown structure (WBS) describes the set of deliverables that is needed in an IT project. It must contain everything that has to do with the project. Since a majority of IT projects involve many people working on different aspects and many phases of deliverables, it is imperative that the project be divided into logical segments that encompass how the entire work should be carried out. Decomposing a project into smaller tasks that are logically related enhances productivity in IT project execution and delivery. WBS uses this technique, which forms one of the essential documents in IT project management. WBS brings together the scope, the cost, and schedule baseline and ensures the alignment of IT project plans (Workbreakdownstructure.com, 2020). PMI defines 'the Work Breakdown Structure as a deliverable oriented hierarchical decomposition of the work to be executed by the project team' (Project Management Institute, 2017). WBS can take one of two approaches: deliverable-based approach or phase-based approach. PMI notes that the former method is usually preferred. The fundamental differences between the two approaches are identified in the first level of the WBS.

The importance of WBS has been underscored by Schwalbe (2016). It provides a tool for planning and managing IT projects in terms of schedules, resources, costs, and changes. It defines the overall project scope. Any item not defined therein should not be undertaken as part of the project. There are five basic input sets in WBS. These are the 'requirements document, project scope management plan, and the scope statement', and the others are 'environmental factors for the enterprise and organizational process assets'. Similar to that, the 'scope baseline and project documents updates' are the outputs of WBS. The former is associated with the WBS dictionary (Schwalbe, 2016).

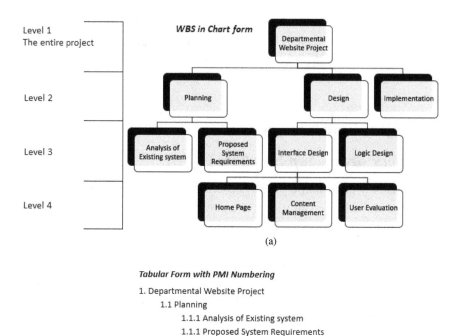

(a)

Tabular Form with PMI Numbering

1. Departmental Website Project
    1.1 Planning
        1.1.1 Analysis of Existing system
        1.1.1 Proposed System Requirements
    1.2 Design
        1.2.1 Interface Design
            1.2.1.1 Home Page
            1.2.1.2 Content Management
            1.2.1.3 User Evaluation
        1.2.2 Logic Design
    1.3 Implementation

(b)

Figure 1.   WBS in chart & tabular forms.

WBS can take the form of a chart or a list. In a chart format, WBS represents an activity tree, like an organizational chart, which shows how tasks are related (Figure 1(a)). An alternative approach is to organize the WBS based on project phases. The numbering style adopts the PMI's Practice Standard for WBS, Second Edition released in 2006. Figures 1 depicts a website development project for a department. Figure 1(b) depicts a sample WBS in a tabular form below the chart, which is popular in project management software tools like MS Project.

WBS can be created using a variety of approaches, including 'guide-lines, analogy, top-down, bottom-up, and mind-mapping'. The US

Department of Defense (DOD) has prescribed forms for WBSs for different projects; contractors must adopt these to prepare their proposals.

2.1.1. *Top-down estimates*

This type of estimate involves breaking down a project through a divide-and-conquer methodology. As the project is decomposed into smaller chunks of activities progressively, resource estimations are also done at each level. For instance, we assume a project will cost $1m. If the project is divided into three sub-systems, we can attach $300,000.00, $500,000.00, and $200,000.00 to each sub-system depending on their complexities. Each of the modules can further be decomposed. This approach can draw inspiration from the cost incurred for a similar project in the past, which can be used as the basis for the current cost estimates and benefit from expert judgment. It is a less costly approach; however, it is also less accurate.

2.1.2. *Bottom-up estimates*

The bottom-up estimate is an activity-based estimating technique wherein the costs of individual activities or works are first estimated and then added up to get a project total. This can emanate from the estimates of the individual work packages of detailed WBS, and then the cost estimates of the individual elements are summed up to obtain the total project cost. Two factors generally determine its accuracy, namely, the size of work items and the estimators' experience. The bottom-up estimate is more time consuming and more expensive to undertake.

2.1.3. *Analogous estimates*

This technique is very useful when we can adapt the actual cost of a previously executed project to a new one that is similar in nature. Expert judgment is required. It is very cost effective and saves time. Estimators look for a similar project and adapt, making adjustments for known differences. When the new project involves significant new components such as a new hardware, programming language, or network component, proper handling is required to avoid a too low estimate.

2.1.4. *Three-point estimate*

Three-point estimates employ a weighted average calculation of the optimistic estimates, the pessimistic estimates, and the most likely estimates as given in Equation (1):

$$TP = \frac{E_{pes} + 4 \times E_{ml} + E_{opt}}{6} \tag{1}$$

where E_{pes} is the pessimistic estimate, E_{ml} is the most likely estimate, and E_{opt} is the optimistic estimate. Let us take an example of estimating the duration of an IT project; we may have an optimistic estimate of 3 weeks, most likely estimate of 4 weeks, and pessimistic estimate of 5 weeks. In this case, our TP would be given as follows:

$$TP = \frac{5 + 4 \times 4 + 3}{6} = \frac{24}{6} = 4 \tag{2}$$

The optimistic estimate presents the best-case scenario and the pessimistic estimate is premised on a worst-case scenario. Expectedly, the most likely estimate is based on the expected scenario.

2.2. *Critical Path Method*

The Critical Path Method (CPM) is used to forecast the total duration of an IT project. It is a network diagramming methodology. It is also known as critical path analysis. CPM helps to guide against project schedule overruns. Several activities (known as critical path) must be done for the project to be completed in the shortest duration of time. This span of time represents the longest path in the network diagram with the minimum slack amount.

In a project, many tasks usually take place in parallel. Besides, most projects enable the navigation of their network diagram through paths. The path with the most crucial functions determines the project's completion date; this is the longest path. The project is considered finished only when all the critical path tasks are completed. Slack, also known as float, is the amount of time that a task can be delayed without causing a disruption in the subsequent project's end date.

We can obtain the critical path by using the WBS activity list to form a network diagram. We then estimate the duration each activity would take. The duration of each activity on each path that can be navigated within the network is added together. The critical path is the path with the longest accumulated duration. Figure 2 is the network diagram for a particular Project 'Z'. We identify four paths in the network diagram all beginning at node (1) and ending at the same terminal node (14). Each path's total duration across the network diagram is obtained by summing up the total activity durations along each path. We identify A-E-J-P-R to be the critical path of Project Z with the longest duration of 23 days.

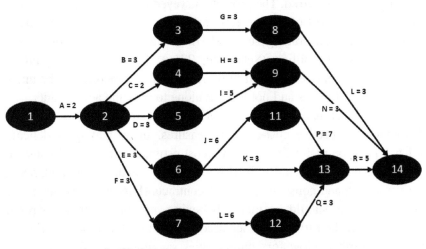

Assumption: All durations are in days

Path 1: A-B-G-L Length = 2+3+3+3 = 11 days
Path 2: A-C-H-N Length = 2+2+3+3 = 10 days
Path 3: A-D-I-N Length = 2+3+5+3 = 13 days
Path 4: A-E-J-P-R Length = 2+3+6+7+5 = 23 days
Path 5: A-E-K-R Length = 2+3+3+5 = 13 days
Path 6: A-F-L-Q-R Length = 2+3+6+3 = 14 days

The critical path is the path with the longest duration through the network, hence Path 4, A-E-J-P-R, is the critical path, of Project Z with 23 days

Figure 2. Activity network diagram.

Critical path analysis enables making trade-off decisions in an IT project. When a critical task is lagging in the schedule, the project manager must respond quickly. He should either renegotiate the deadline with project owners or allocate more resources to subsequent tasks on the critical path to handle that delay or check whether he has the flexibility to complete the project behind schedule. By focusing on the critical path, proactive measures can be taken to manage the project schedule and avoid overruns.

3. Project cost management

3.1. *Project estimation*

Many IT projects have not met budgetary goals and expectation. About 1,500 projects were studied, and findings revealed that an average cost overrun of 27% occurred. The projects surveyed included ERPs, MIS, and CRM systems. Most of the projects surveyed were said to have incurred very huge costs, averaging some $167m, while the worst project cost incurred was $33 billion (Schwalbe, 2016). Cost is usually paid to exchange for a service rendered. It is crucial that IT practitioners be interested in cost estimates and not leave it alone to only the accountants.

In IT project management, estimation is crucial. It serves as the foundation for prospective cost-control measures. In estimating, a delicate balance must be maintained. When a cost estimate is too low, losses are incurred in project execution. Too high estimates, on the other hand, result in overpricing and consequent loss of contracts (Lester, 2017). As a rule of thumb, we should estimate believing nothing will go wrong. Subsequently, the estimate is increased to make up for anticipated problems. We further allow for contingencies ranging from 30–50% in the estimate to take care of unanticipated issues (Sommerville, 2016).

Estimating a project's cost should adopt a structured approach, but determining the appropriate method to adopt requires knowing the rate of precision needed. This is determined by the project's status and the information available. Four popular estimating methods are used. The subjective approach guarantees an accuracy range of ±20%–40%, the parametric method gives the accuracy of ±10%–20%, the comparative approach provides a degree of accuracy of ±10%, while the analytical method guarantees accuracy of ±5%.

3.2. *Effort estimation*

Project size primarily determines the estimation of effort required to execute an IT project. The project's size is measured by the amount of functionality the project provides. On the other hand, project size can be measured in terms of the structural size of artifacts the software processes involved produced. Two software projects that have similar sizes may require efforts which are considerably different in amounts depending on development productivity, which is dependent on the IT project environment. Successful estimation of effort is based on three criteria. The first is a reliable estimate of software size, the second is the knowledge of factors that significantly influence the productivity of development, and the third is having knowledge of how these factors affect productivity (Trendowicz and Jeffery, 2014). Software development is considerably intensive of human involvement, and software development techniques change rapidly. Hence, building a reliable effort model that can be used in several project development environments is a complicated task.

Effort estimation attempts to predict the most realistic amount of effort that is needed to execute an IT Project based on incomplete and uncertain inputs. Effort is quantified by time and cost. Effort is related to productivity by the following formula:

$$PRODUCTIVITY = \frac{SIZE}{EFFORT} \tag{3}$$

Two people may perform at different levels on the same job based on different experiences. With elapsed time, duration is the amount of time required to execute a job item. For instance, a work item may take five working days to perform while the duration estimate is two weeks. To multitask or access external information, extra time may be required. Duration is an estimate based on the calendar time, while effort is the number of man-hours to take on the project.

3.2.1. *LOC-based effort estimation*

A library automation software package is considered to be developed. The software should be installed on workstations that can use various computer graphics peripherals like SVGA, mouse, digitizer, and LaserJet printer. The software scope statement of the application is given as follows: 'The Library automation system should accept data from a user. The user will interact with and control the system through a good human-computer interface. All data and other supporting information will be maintained in a data server. The system will produce outputs on a variety of graphics devices. The software will be designed to control and interact with devices like mouse, digitizer, laser printer, scanner and plotter.'

After refinements, the primary software functions are identified, and an estimation table is developed (Table 1) after applying the decomposition for lines of code (LOC). Based on previous experiences and historical data for systems of this type, we put organization productivity at 600 LOC/pm. The labor rate is estimated at $6000 per month (LRPM), and cost per line of code (CLOC) is given as follows:

$$CLOC = LRPM/LOCPM = 6000/600 = \$10 \qquad (4)$$

where LOCPM is LOC per month.

Table 1.   Lines of code estimates.

Function	Estimated LOC
Biometric Scanners	2,500
Barcode Scanners	3,000
Servers	7,500
DBMS	4,000
Computer graphics display systems	6,000
LAN interfaces	3,500
Design analysis modules	5,500
Lines of code estimates	**32,000**

By line of code (LOC) estimates and history of productivity, total estimated project cost (TEPC) is given as follows:

$$TEPC_{LOC} = LOC \times CLOC = 32000 \times \$10 = \$320,000 \qquad (5)$$

The estimated effort (in person-months) is as follows:

$$Effect_{estimatedLOC} = TEPC_{LOC}/LPM = 320000/6000 \approx 53 \qquad (6)$$

3.2.2. *Function points-based effort estimation*

For function point-based (FP-based) estimation decomposition, we focus on information domain values. For our Library automation system, we would estimate outputs, inputs, external interfaces, files, and inquiries. We assume that the complexity weighting factor is average. This estimate's results are shown in Table 2.

After estimating the complexity weighting factors, the value adjustment factor is estimated. The estimated number of FP is calculated as follows:

$$
\begin{aligned}
FP_{estimate} &= count\ total \times [0.65 + 0.01 \times (\Sigma F_i)] \\
&= 307 \times [0.65 + 0.01 \times 53] \approx 362
\end{aligned} \qquad (7)
$$

We take the organizational productivity for this type of system as 6.5 FP/pm based on historical review. We assume a burdened labor rate of

Table 2.   Values for information domain estimation.

Information domain	Optimistic	Likely	Pessimistic	Estimate count	Weight	FP count
External inputs	19	25	29	24	4	97
External outputs	14	17	27	18	5	76
External inquiries	17	24	32	24	5	97
Internal logical files	5	7	8	4	10	24
External interface files	2	3	6	2	6	13
Count total						307

$6,000 per month, and the cost per FP (CPFP) is approximately given by the following:

$$CPFP = LRPM/FPPM = \$6,000/6.5 = \$923 \qquad (8)$$

From historical productivity data and the FP estimate, the total project cost estimate is put at $320,000, while the estimated effort is 56 person-months, derived as follows:

$$TEPC_{FP} = CPFP \times FP_{estimate} = 930 \times 362 \approx 336,660 \qquad (9)$$

The estimated effort in person-months is as follows:

$$Effort_{estimated} = TEPC_{FP}/LPM = 336,660/6,000 = 56 \qquad (10)$$

3.3. *Cost estimation*

There are always budgetary constraints on IT projects. Therefore, we need serious cost estimates to execute projects within the bounds of budgetary allocation. Following the development of an appropriate resource requirements list, several cost estimates relating to the resources must be developed. Assume that a work item for a project involves performing a specific test in a software project. The specific level of skill the test staff should possess would be stated in the list of activity resource requirements. Similarly, the man-hours and the number of people required to conduct the test are specified. Furthermore, any special software or equipment needs and other requirements are indicated. These pieces of information are required to make a good estimate of costs.

3.3.1. *Types of cost estimates*

In IT projects, various kinds of cost estimates are usually undertaken (Schwalbe, 2016). There are three types of estimates that are commonly used: a 'rough order of magnitude' (ROM) estimate, a 'budgetary estimate' (BE), and a 'definitive estimate' (DE). Table 3 summarizes the three types of cost estimates.

Table 3. Cost estimate types.

Estimate type	Time required	Used for	Accuracy level
ROM	Very early in project 3–5 years to completion	Selection decision	−50% to +100%
BE	Early 1–2 years	Funding budget plan	−10% to +25%
DE	Project at a later stage, less than a year	Purchases, actual costs estimates	−5% to +10%

3.3.2. *Full-Time Equivalent (FTE)*

Labor cost is a very important cost estimate. Since it constitutes a high percentage of the total project costs, we need to estimate how many people are needed and for how many hours they need to work. The skill set of the workforce needed on the project is also considered. We need to determine the full-time equivalent (FTE) of staff to allocate to the project, which may vary depending on the department (Schwalbe, 2016). Table 4 depicts a typical scenario of FTE by department for a five-year project.

It is indeed a challenging task to compute a good cost estimate. However, tools and methods are available to assist. Expert judgment and analogous cost estimates can be used. Top-down and bottom-up estimates are also useful. We can also use three-point estimates, the parametric estimates method, and the cost of quality. Other tools involve using project management estimating software, reserve analysis, and vendor bid analysis (Schwalbe, 2016).

Cost elements in an IT project involve both direct and indirect costs. Cost is direct if incurred when directly associated with the project. Salaries of workers engaged on a full-time basis are an example. Other elements are the cost of procuring software and hardware needed for the project. Indirect costs do not have a direct bearing on the project, but they should also be considered in budgeting. Such costs include rent, insurance, utilities, other administrative expenses, sunk costs, costs associated with a learning curve, and reserves.

Table 4. FTE by department and year.

Department	Year 1	Year 2	Year 3	Year 4	Year 5	Totals
ICT	25	30	35	15	15	120
Marketing	4	3	3	3	3	16
Reservations	15	25	30	10	8	88
Contractors	2	3	1	1	1	8
Totals	46	61	69	29	27	232

3.4. *Resource estimate*

Resources needed for an IT project include people, equipment, and materials. These sets of resources would be assigned to activities. Two main factors that affect resource estimates are the nature of the organization and the project. One also needs to analyze alternatives and have access to estimates data. Pertinent questions to answer when estimating resources for a project or an activity of a project include the following:

- What is the level of difficulty of specific activities of the project?
- How unique is the content project's scope statement, and how may this affect resources?
- Does the organization have experience of handling similar activities? If yes, what level of workforce did the project require and what was their competence?
- Is there a need for the organization to acquire more resources to accomplish the project? Is outsourcing a viable option? Will it help to meet the deadlines?

Resource estimates need inputs from various sources and documents. These include the project's 'schedule management plan, resource calendars, activity list, activity attributes, and risk register'. Resource estimates are foundational to estimate activity durations, project cost estimates, and project human resource management. Similarly, they are also needed in risk management, communications management, and project procurement management.

3.5. *Algorithm models*

Algorithmic cost models employ a 'mathematical expression to predict project costs based on estimates of the project size, the number of software engineers, and other process and product factors. An algorithmic cost model can be developed by analysing the costs and attributes of completed projects and finding the closest fit mathematical expression to actual project' (Sommerville, 2016). The general algorithmic model for software cost estimation is given by the following:

$$E = A \times Size^{B} \times M \tag{11}$$

where E represents effort and A stands for a constant factor, which depends on 'local organizational practices and the type of software being developed'. Size is stated either in lines of code or function points of software or object points. M stands for a multiplier that combines 'process, product, and development attributes'. Others are dependability requirements of the software and team experience in software development. The exponential component, B, is related with the size estimate of the software project and stands for the nonlinearity of costs with project size. It has been observed that extra costs are incurred as the software's size increases. B's value is typically around 1 to 1.5.

3.6. *COCOMO models*

COCOMO stands for COnstructive COst Model. It is an algorithmic cost estimation model and well documented in the literature (Schwalbe, 2016). The Basic COCOMO model relates effort to software size thus:

$$E = b \times KLOC^{c} \tag{12}$$

where *KLOC* denotes the software size in lines of code/1000, E is effort in person-months, while b and c are constants that are determined by kind of project involved. COCOMO distinguishes between three categories of projects, namely, organic, embedded, and semidetached.

Table 5.   COCOMO for three scenarios.

KLOC	**Efforts in person-months**		
	Organic $(E = 2.4KLOC^{1.05})$	**Semidetached** $(E = 3.0KLOC^{1.12})$	**Embedded** $(E = 3.6KLOC^{1.20})$
1	2.4	3.0	3.6
10	26.9	39.5	57.1
50	145.9	239.9	393.6
100	302.1	521.3	904.3
1000	3,390.1	6,872.6	14,331.9

For these categories, the Basic COCOMO model assumes the following values: organic software: $b = 4.4$ while $c = 1.05$; semidetached software: $b = 3.0$ and $c = 1.12$; and embedded software $b = 3.6$ and $c = 1.20$.

Table 5 shows the effort estimates for the three project categories, with different *KLOC* values. We observe that the constant c impacts the estimates significantly. The basic COCOMO model is rather simplistic, basing cost estimates on just three simple project classes.

Two other more sophisticated COCOMO models have been developed. They are the Intermediate COCOMO and Detailed COCOMO. They use fifteen cost drivers (or attributes) which affect costs and productivity. The cost drivers serve as correction factors that modify the nominal effort estimates of a project. They both use b values that are somewhat different from what is used in the Basic COCOMO model. For a nominal project effort estimate of 40 person-months, and low software complexity, for instance, the model applies a correction factor of 0.85 to the estimate, giving 34 person-months. For high complexity, then, the estimate should be corrected to $1.15 \times 40 = 46$ person-months.

A significant upgrade of the COCOMO model yields the COCOMO II model, which is a better reflection of the current and future practices in software development, reflecting the best practices of the 1990s and 2000s on managing software life cycle. It manifests the vast experiences gathered over the years in cost estimation and provides a means of learning about the important changes in software estimation and development over the past few years. The COCOMO II model stipulates three cost estimation models of increased details. The three COCOMO II models are as follows:

- Application composition model: In the early stages of software development, this was a common technique (prototyping, performance, software and system interaction, technology maturity evaluation, and assessment).
- Early design stage model: This is used after the stabilizing requirements, and after the setting out of the basic software architecture.
- Post-architecture stage model: This is applied in the actual software production.

3.7. *Putnam model*

The distribution of manpower with respect to time has been studied in many software developments projects and found to typically approximate the shape of a Rayleigh distribution (van Vliet, 2007). Following this, Putnam developed a model of cost estimation (Putnam, 1978) that suggests that manpower required (*MR*) at time *t* is given as follows:

$$MR(t) = 2Kate^{-at^2} \tag{13}$$

where *a* is a 'speed-up factor represented by the initial slope of the Rayleigh curve' and *K* represents the total required manpower (this also includes manpower required at maintenance phase). *K* is estimated by the volume of the area under the Rayleigh curve. We explain the shape of the curve in the following way. Let $W(t)$ represent a fraction of the problem to which solution has been found at time *t* and $p(t)$ is the capacity to solve problems at time *t*. Then, the progress made at problem-solving at time *t* is directly related to the product of the available capacity to solve problems and the proportion of the problem yet to be solved. Setting the total amount of work remaining to be done to 1, we have the following:

$$\frac{dW}{dt} = p(t)(1 - W(t)) \tag{14}$$

After integration,

$$W(t) = 1 - \exp\left(-\int^t p(\alpha)\,d\alpha\right) \qquad (15)$$

Next, we assume that the capacity of problem-solving is given by $p(t) = at$, i.e., it increases linearly over time. We estimate progress by a Rayleigh distribution as follows:

$$\frac{dW}{dt} = ate^{-(at^2)/2} \qquad (16)$$

The cumulative effort, I, obtained by integrating the equation for $MR(t)$, gives the following:

$$I(t) = K(1 - e^{-at^2}) \qquad (17)$$

Now, we obtain $I(\infty) = K$. The maximum point of the Rayleigh curve is denoted by T, and we obtain $a = 1/(2T^2)$. The point T will be close in time to the point when the software is released to the client. The volume of the area bounded by the Rayleigh curve at the interval 0 to T indicates the initial development effort. Therefore, E is obtained by the following:

$$E = I(T) = 0.3945K \qquad (18)$$

This result validates the rule of thumb that 40% of the total software development effort is expended on actual software development while 60% is expended on maintenance. Putnam's model is, however, more applicable to estimate the cost of 'very large software development projects, which involves more than 15 person-years', and less suitable for small projects (van Vliet, 2007).

4. Function Point Analysis-Based (FPA-Based) methods

FPA is a systematic technique for classifying system components in order to break them down into smaller modules to better understand and analyze them (Farr, 2011). It facilitates cost estimation in software development efforts without taking the path that determines the expected amount of code but depends on counting the constituent data structures featured in the software. FPA is more applicable to projects targeted at business applications where the data structures play a very dominant role and less appropriate for algorithm-based projects (like compilers and real-time applications) (van Vliet, 2007).

According to Grupe and Clevenger (1991), FPA was designed to handle issues of 'estimating and assessing productivity and costs in multi-language, multi-technological, and multi-applications environment. One function point (FP) is one end-user requested business function.'

Function Point Counts are made up of five categories (Farr, 2011):

- External inputs (I): Items that describe distinct application-oriented data, e.g., filenames, menu selections, and a mouse click.
- External outputs (O): Reports, GUI display, and messages are examples of user-provided items that create unique application-oriented data.
- External inquiries (E): Any interactive inputs that require a response, e.g., database query or request an online assistance.
- External files (F): Some interfaces to other systems that are machine-readable.
- Internal files (L): These are the system's logical master files.

According to its functional specification, a software product's size is measured in function points or FPs, which are calculated in three steps:

Step 1: Computation of the unadjusted function point (UFP) using some heuristic expressions.

Step 2: Refinement of UFP to reflect actual complexities of the parameters used in UFP computation of step 1.

Step 3: Computation of FP by further refining UFP to account for the project's peculiar features, which can influence the entire development effort.

The unadjusted function points, *UFP*, are a weighted sum of the five FP categories (van Vliet, 2007) given by the following:

$$UFP = 4I + 5O + 4E + 10L + 7F \tag{19}$$

Further refinement of *UFP* is done through the application of corrections which show the differences in the complexity of the data types. Hence, the constants used in the formula are determined by how complex the data types in question are viewed. Equation (21) refers to UFP of average complexity.

As the wide variety of application characteristics influencing the development effort increases, so does the unadjusted function point. The level of influence exerted by each feature is rated on a scale of six points, going from 0 (no influence/not present) to 5 (strong influence). The cumulative scores for all characteristics define total degree of influence (DI). It yields the technical complexity factor (TCF) given as follows:

$$TCF = 0.65 + 0.01DI \tag{20}$$

The (adjusted) function point measure FP is now obtained as follows:

$$FP = UFP \times TCF \tag{21}$$

FPA measures the system's size and complexity and gives an indication of the effort and cost involved in developing and maintaining a system. It enables carrying out comparative assessments of jobs project by project, application by applications, and organization by organization.

5. Software engineering metrics

A software metric provides a means by which a software system can be measured objectively. It can also be used in relation to a system documentation or development process (Sommerville, 2016). Measurement facilitates understanding of the project and the attendant processes, thereby giving room for objective evaluation. It provides a means of continuous improvement in software process. We use measurement to aid in estimation and productivity appraisal throughout all phases of software project development. It can also be helpful in quality assurance and project control. Measurement can help software developers to assess quality of software, aiding in decision-making as a project moves through phases

(Pressman, 2010). The size of a piece of software measured by the lines of code is an example of software metrics. Another example is the Fog index that measures the readability of narrative text in a code. Others are the 'number of reported faults' after a software product is delivered and man-hours needed to develop a product.

Typically, process metrics are obtained throughout all projects over long periods of time. They provide process indicators, which can assist in long-term improvement of software processes. Project metrics can assist in (1) tracking potential risks, (2) assessing ongoing project status, (3) identifying potential issues before they become 'critical', (4) adjusting tasks or workflow, and (5) evaluating software developers' capacity to ensure software products' quality control. Control metrics and predictor metrics are the two types of software metrics. Control metrics aid in the management of processes, whereas predictor metrics aid in the prediction of software characteristics. As a result, control metrics are related with software processes such as the time and average effort needed to fix reported defects.

Product metrics or predictors are linked to the actual software. We remark that both types of metrics may affect decision-making. Process metrics can guide one to decide if process changes are necessary, while predictor metrics can help in deciding if software changes are needed and whether software is ready for release. Measurements may be used in two ways. One way is by assigning a value to the metrics to measure system quality attributes. The second method is to identify the system components with substandard quality. The former helps to measure system components' characteristics, aggregate these measurements, and use them to assess system quality attributes, perhaps to ascertain maintainability.

Some product metrics are dynamic while others are static. We obtain dynamic metrics by taking measurements during program execution. During system testing or during actual operation, for example, the reported bug numbers or the time it takes to finish a computation can be captured. This is a typical example of dynamic metrics. Static metrics can be collected by taking measurements from representations of the system. These representations may include designs, programs, or documentations. Metrics such as fan-in/fan-out and length of code are examples of static metrics.

6. Developing the project schedule

Each IT project runs over a period. It is essential to develop a project schedule that specifies the start and end dates of an IT project and its allied activities or phases. A realistic project schedule serves as the foundation for tracking project performance during its lifetime. Inputs into the project schedule come from project time management processes, which are usually iterative and often go through a number of cycles before a project schedule is completed. A project schedule and a schedule baseline are the primary outputs of project scheduling development. Project calendars, project documents updates, schedule data, and project management plan updates are other outputs. Computerized models can be obtained using network diagrams, entering resource requirements and availability by time period. These can be adjusted to generate alternative schedules in a fast manner (Schwalbe, 2016). Gantt chart, Critical chain scheduling, PERT analysis, and Critical path analysis are common schedule development tools.

7. Developing the budget

Budget development is critical in IT Project management. It entails allocating a cost estimate of the project to specific material resources or work items, which have been listed on WBS over a period of time. Budgeting enables us to fashion out a cost baseline, which in turn helps to measure project performance and determine project funding requirements. Budgeting enables project document updates, which may involve adding, removing, or modifying in the project schedule or scope statement. Inputs into the budget development include a basis of estimates cost management plan, scope baseline, and activity cost estimates. Other inputs may come from project schedule, risk register, agreements, resource calendars, and organizational process assets.

Imagine a Land Expert project that involves hardware acquisition, software development and testing, training, and so on. A budget for one year may involve items in the WBS depicted in Table 6. The budget is developed on a monthly basis. Organizations typically develop a standard process for preparing budgets. The number of full-time equivalent (FTE) employees for each month is an important part of this process. A full-time employee

Table 6. Land expert cost baseline.

Items in WBS	Month 1	Month 2	Month 3	Month 4	Month 5	Month 6	Month 7	Month 8–11	Month 12	Total
1. Project management										
1.1 Manager	5,000	5,000	5,000	5,000	5,000	5,000	5,000	–	5,000	60,000
1.2 Project developers	15,000	15,000	15,000	15,000	15,000	15,000	15,000	–	15,000	180,000
1.3 Consultants	3,500	3,500	3,500	3,500	3,500	3,500	3,500	–	3,500	38,500
2. Hardware								–		
2.1 Portable devices			20,000	20,000	10,000			–		50,000
2.2 Computer servers			10,000	20,000				–		30,000
3. Software								–		
3.1 Software licensing			10,000	10,000	5,000			–		25,000
3.2 Software development			50,000	50,000	70,000	80,000	60,000	–		314,000
3.2 Software testing				5,000	5,000	5,000	5,000	–		25,000
4. Support and training								–		35,000
4.1 Training costs								–		7,000
4.2 Cost of travels							15,000	–	15,000	90,000
4.3 Support team members					8,000	8,000	8,000	–	8,000	64,000
5. Reserves	20,000	23,500	113,500	128,500	121,500	116,500	111,500	–	46,500	918,500

(FTE) typically works 40 hours per week. A person allocated full-time, or two people given half-time, provides one FTE to a project. FTE offers the yardstick for estimating total cost compensations for each year. Another practice is establishing the amount of money estimated for payment to suppliers for labor costs, purchases, services and goods. Budgeting may also include provisions for other categories such as depreciation, travel, rents and leases, other supplies, and expenses. A full understanding of the budget categories is an essential requisite piece of knowledge before an estimate is developed. It ensures that data are sufficiently collected. This information is useful for tracking costs throughout projects and non-project work, as well as enforcing cost-cutting measures.

Such knowledge is also useful for legal and tax purposes. Besides, budgeting can also provide information on funding requirements for projects. Some IT projects, particularly in government circles, may have all funds provided from the start. Others may depend on recurrent funding to ensure that there are no cash flow constraints. The cost baseline may indicate that more funds are needed in some months than would be expected to be available; accordingly, adjustments should be made to prevent funding issues.

8. Parametric estimating

Parametric estimating uses mathematical models to estimate the cost of projects. Such types of models are built from scratch, but data must be available, especially from previous projects. It can involve statistical models such as regression analysis and other mathematical tools. In a software development project, data such as lines of code cost, project size, project complexity, and level of experience or expertise of programmers could be some of the parameters involved in building the estimates. Parameter estimation is as accurate as the historical information used to create the model.

9. Expert judgment

Expert judgment is a technique in which a decision is made based on a person's knowledge of a subject matter that is relevant to the task at hand.

Anyone with specialized training, skills, or experience can provide this kind of expertise (Project Management Institute, 2017). Individuals or groups can provide the needed expertise in diverse areas such as organizational strategy, technical knowledge of the industry, and benefits management. Other knowledge areas include the project's focus area, the estimation of project duration and budget, and the identification of risks.

Expert judgment is typically obtained from outside the organization where such expertise is not available within. Hence, it is common for an external group or persons with such skills to serve as consultants on a project (Project Management Institute, 2013). Expert judgment can come from units in an organization, stakeholders (e.g., customers or sponsors) or consultants, and technical and professional associations. Other sources of expert judgments are the project management office, industry groups, suppliers, and subject-matter experts.

Expert judgment is useful where it can give a competitive edge. It can furnish advice in planning purchases and acquisitions in IT projects. For instance, if a new software application requires training for effective utilization, expert judgment may suggest that it should be outsourced for users numbering up to 1,000 as it would be a distraction to the IT Department. Expert judgment can be used in estimations to make the organization stand in better stead to win a particular contract, especially winning government contracts. Such expertise may come from within the government department that is going to award the contract.

10. Earned Value Management

Earned value management (EVM) is a strategy for measuring project performance. It works with estimates for scope, cost, and time. With a cost performance baseline in hand, we can assess whether project performance is acceptable by examining how the scope, time, and cost targets were met. To evaluate, we compare actual project figures with the baseline (Schwalbe, 2016). We established the baseline by the approved budget figures in the project plan, and where necessary, any approved changes could be incorporated. The actual information evaluates the following: (1) whether WBS items were completed or not, (2) what percentage of the project was completed, (3) the actual commencement and completion time, and (4) the actual cost expended on the completed project.

EVM was used primarily in evaluating the performance of large government projects, but corporate organizations have now realized the value of using the tool. For each activity or summary activity on the WBS, EVM recommends getting three values. The terms used in EVM are defined as follows:

1. Planned value (PV): 'the portion of the approved total cost estimate planned to be spent on an activity during a given period.' This is known as the budget.
2. Actual cost (AC): 'the total direct and indirect costs expended to accomplish work on an activity in a given period.'
3. Earned value (EV): 'an estimate of the value of the physical work completed.'
4. Rate of performance (RP): 'the ratio of exact work completed to planned work completed at any particular time during the project's life.'

Example of a Web Server Project

We imagine buying and installing a new web server for $5,000.00. The project is expected to take one week. However, the project was completed in two weeks for a total cost of $10,000.00. Suppose we spend $7,500.00 in the first week and $2,500.00 in the second week. If the project was executed half-way by the end of the first week, then the performance rate was 50% by the end of that week. The calculations are given in Equation (22):

$$
\begin{aligned}
EV &= 5,000 \times 50\% = 2,500 \\
CV &= 2,500 - 7,500 = -5,000 \\
SV &= 2,500 - 5,000 = -2,500 \\
CPI &= 2,500 / 7,500 = 33\% \\
SPI &= 2,500 / 5,000 = 50\%
\end{aligned}
\tag{22}
$$

To obtain the variances, we subtract the planned value or actual cost from EV, and to obtain the indexes we divide EV by the planned value or actual cost. Based on previous performance, we can use the CPI and SPI to estimate the cost and time required to finalize the project. Given the same performance, the budget at completion and the allotted time help to determine the estimate at completion (EAC) and estimated completion time.

Cost variance (CV) is determined by deducting the actual cost from the earned value. A negative variance indicates that the project is costing more than anticipated and that the budget is being exceeded. Positive cost variance means execution costs less than planned, which is desirable. Cost variance is zero, which means we have a balanced budget, a perfect estimate. The schedule performance index (SPI) relates planned value to earned value. SPI estimates the project's completion time. An SPI of 1 or 100% means the project is on track. If the SPI is greater than 1 or above 100%, the project is on track, which is better. We note that negative values for cost and schedule variance are calling attention to problems in the areas concerned. It indicates that the project will cost more or take longer than expected.

11. Summary

This chapter focused on time and cost management issues in IT projects. The Work Breakdown Structure has been discussed. Various forms of estimates, including project estimation, effort estimation, and cost estimations, and their tools and techniques, have been outlined. Unique characteristics and complexities involved in IT projects have been highlighted. Estimates enhance budgeting which in turn aids project performance monitoring, and metrics are applied to evaluate how well a project has performed. There are many software tools for IT project management. These have not been discussed in detail because they are outside the purview of this chapter. Interested readers can get trained and readily lay hands on some of these tools. The world today is tending heavily toward IT; hence, it becomes crucial to refine our approach to IT project management.

References

Banker, R., Kauffman, R. and Kumar, R. (1991). An empirical test of object-based output measurement metrics in a Computer Aided Software Engineering (CASE) Environment, *J. Manage. Inf. Syst.*, 8(3), 127–150.

Farr, J. V. (2011). *Systems Life Cycle Costing: Economic Analysis, Estimation, and Management*, (T. G. Kotnour, & W. Karwowski, Eds.) Boca Raton, FL 33487-2742, USA: CRC Press, Taylor & Francis Group.

Grupe, F. H., & Clevenger, D. F. (1991). Using function point analysis as a software development tool. *Journal of Systems Management*, 42(12), 23–26.

Lester, E. I. (2017). *Project Management, Planning and Control Managing Engineering, Construction and Manufacturing Projects to PMI, APM and BSI Standards*, 7th ed. Kidlington, Oxford OX5 1GB, United Kingdom: Butterworth-Heinemann, Elsevier Ltd.

Pressman, R. S. (2010). *Software Engineering: A Practitioner's Approach*, 7th ed. New York, 10020, USA: McGraw-Hill Companies Higher Education.

Project Management Institute. (2013). *A Guide to the Project Management Body of Knowledge (PMBOK®) Guide*, 5th ed. Project Management Institute. Newton Square, PA 19073.

Project Management Institute. (2017). *A Guide to the Project Management Body of Knowledge (PMBOK guide) Software Extension*, 6th ed. Newtown Square, Pennsylvania 19073-3299, USA: Project Management Institute.

Putnam, L. H. (1978). A general empirical solution to the macro software sizing and estimating problem, *IEEE Trans. Software Eng.*, 4(4), 345–361. Doi: 10.1109/TSE.1978.231521.

Schwalbe, K. (2016). *Information Technology Project Management*, 8th ed. Boston, MA 02210, USA: Cengage Learning.

Sommerville, I. (2016). *Software Engineering*, 10th ed. Harlow, Essex CM20 2JE, England: Pearson Education Limited.

Southard, R. (2019). Function Point Analysis. (V. L. Sauter, ed.) University of Missouri–St. Louis. https://www.umsl.edu/~sauterv/analysis/function_point/FPARP488.html.

Trendowicz, A. and Jeffery, R. (2014). *Software Project Effort Estimation*, Heidelberg, New York, USA: Springer. Doi: 10.1007/978-3-319-03629-8.

van Vliet, H. (2007). *Software Engineering: Principles and Practice*, 2nd ed. Chichester, West Sussex, England: John Wiley.

Workbreakdownstructure.com. (2020). Work Breakdown Structure. (R. Duke, Editor) https://www.workbreakdownstructure.com/. (Accessed 31 December 2020).

Chapter 10

Project Quality Management

Samisa Abeysinghe

Technology Consultant, Solution Architect, Seeduwa, Sri Lanka
samisa.abeysinghe@gmail.com

In principle, everyone agrees that project quality management is crucial for project success; it should be forethought and everyone in the project team including all stakeholders should commit to it. However, in practice, based on the project priorities and due to the competing nature of the requirements and constraints, it could become an afterthought and some critical elements concerning quality management could be pushed to the backburner. This is the very reason the project needs to focus on IT project quality management. To achieve great results with project quality management, everyone needs to have a simple but clear understanding of what quality is all about. Ensuring the success of quality management of an IT project is critical for the business success of the project and the organization. The ability to have a sustainable business model depends on the quality of the delivery from the project team to the customers. While there are many measures of quality, the ultimate measure of quality is if the results of the IT projects are working seamlessly in production with the expected level of fit to the purpose of end users and with no downtime. To ensure this, the key pillars of quality management, namely, planning, quality assurance, and quality control, need to be well understood.

1. Introduction

The focus on quality and quality management is one of the key pillars of success for information technology projects. Planning, assurance, and quality control are the key focus areas of information technology project quality management. Not all the outcomes of information technology (IT) projects are tangible, and it is hard to bring visibility to the same. This is because the deliverables are in source code, documentation, and other digital formats. This is a drastic difference compared to other technology and engineering fields such as manufacturing, mechanical engineering, or civil engineering. Hence, there needs to be a systematic and scientific approach to be able to bring about visibility to the quality of the system throughout the project life cycle.

1.1. *Quality*

As per the ISO 9001 definition (ISO, 2000), there are two main dimensions embedded in quality. Those are the requirements of the end users and the characteristics of the project deliverables that are related to the requirements.

The characteristics are used to compare with similar kinds of products or services. In a competitive market environment, there is an associated sentiment of perspective with quality. Products or services might deliver the same features and functions. These features and functions reflect the requirements. Even though the same requirements are being delivered, users might have very different perspectives in association with quality.

The perspective comes from the stakeholders. And, the ultimate stakeholder of an IT system is the end user. If the end user perceives that his or her purpose is met with the IT system, in relation to the characteristics, then they deem that the system is of high quality. Hence, in the delivery of IT projects, quality management needs to focus on the system's ability to fit the end user's perception in relation to characteristics associated with the requirements. From requirements to production, this aspect needs to be kept track of.

Quality is defined as the degree to which a set of inherent characteristics of a system fulfills requirements (ISO, 2000). Quality matters the most to clients, in other words, the end user. The quality of what is being delivered by the project is reflected in the end-user experience and associated satisfaction based on the experience.

2. Understanding project quality management

Project quality management consists of three elements:

(1) Planning quality,
(2) Quality assurance,
(3) Quality control.

2.1. *Planning quality*

Planning quality involves identification of requirements in relation to the quality of the project and the project deliverables. Planning quality also involves documenting the process of meeting the quality requirements. The vision and strategy for achieving high-quality deliverables need to be laid out clearly when planning quality. Then, it goes on to explain the execution and operational models for managing quality throughout the project.

Planning quality needs to focus on quality metrics that are needed to be tracked and monitored throughout the project cycle. Keeping track of stakeholders and their perspectives enable to build a model to trace the requirements from design to implementation. The list of possible risks and the catalog of lessons learned also needs to be modeled in quality planning.

Data play a critical role in an IT project. Quality is directly impacted by the level of understanding the project team has on the data and data sources involved with the project. Data gathering, analysis, representation, and decision-making models in relation to the project quality and project requirements need to be done prudently when planning quality. The outcome of planning quality would be a quality management plan.

2.2. *Eight dimensions of quality management*

David A. Garvin introduced eight dimensions of quality (Garvin, 1990) as follows:

(1) Performance,
(2) Features,
(3) Reliability,
(4) Conformance,
(5) Durability,
(6) Serviceability,
(7) Aesthetics,
(8) Perceived quality.

(1) Performance

Performance refers to a product's primary operating characteristics. This dimension of quality involves measurable attributes. For an IT system, the content provided, functionality of the system, and options provided are part of the operating characteristics. The quality of the user interface provided, time taken to load the system, and time taken to complete end-user use case are some examples of performance characteristics.

(2) Features

Features are additional characteristics that will bring about additional benefits to the users of the product or service. Those additional characteristics supplement their basic functioning. The features could result in tangible or intangible benefits.

Some features will be present in all products or services, but other features will only be found in 'quality' products. For example, not all cars would have heated seats or assisted parking.

(3) Reliability

Reliability is the likelihood that a product or service will not fail within a specific time period. The probability of a product malfunctioning or failing within a specified time should be as low as possible. This also reflects the user's expectation that the IT system would work all the time without failure.

(4) Conformance

Conformance is the precision with which the product or service meets the specified standards.

The degree to which an IT system's design and operating characteristics meet established standards indicates the conformance.

The two most common measures of failure in conformance are defect rates and the post-release production incidents that result in customer service calls.

(5) Durability

Durability measures the length of an IT system's life. When the IT system can be maintained, it has prolonged life and high durability. The IT system will be used until it is no longer economical to operate it due to high support and maintenance costs. This happens when the militance, update and patching rate, and the associated costs increase significantly. The IT system can also see end of life due to evolution of requirements and technology. This results in both economic and technical costs, associated with experiences provided to end users such as the ease of use enabled with new technology, leading to wider adoption and cost savings.

(6) Serviceability

Serviceability is the speed with which the IT system can be put into service when it breaks down, as well as the competence and the behavior of the service personnel. Consumers are concerned not only about a product breaking down but also about the time before service is restored. Serviceability has a major impact on customer satisfaction.

(7) Aesthetics

Aesthetics is a subjective dimension indicating the kind of response a user has toward the IT system. It represents the individual's personal preference. How the system looks, feels, or sounds is clearly a matter of personal judgment and a reflection of individual preference.

(8) Perceived quality
Perceived Quality is the quality attributed to the IT system based on indirect measures. Consumers do not always have complete information about an IT system's attributes, hence indirect measures could be their only basis for comparing the system they are now using and those they have used in the past.

2.3. *Five views of software quality*

David Garvin (1988) described software quality from five different perspectives. The five points are useful for the service to produce a quality product. In other words, these views are about service quality:

(1) Value-based,
(2) User-based,
(3) Process-based,
(4) Product-based,
(5) Transcendent.

(1) Value-based view
Quality depends on the amount the customer is willing to pay for the system. The engineering and quality management rigor would be decided based on the cost plus the margin possible based on the value that the customer is willing to pay. The more bargaining that happens would cause lower resource employment and minimal process enforcement, resulting in poor quality.

(2) User-based view
Quality is fitness for purpose. This view of quality evaluates the IT system in a task context, in terms of how the product meets the user's needs. Hence, it would be a highly personalized view. This view can often be measured through reliability and usability.

(3) Process-based view
Quality is conformance to requirements and specification. It focuses on how well the IT system was constructed to avoid the costs associated with

rework during development and after delivery. Defect counts and rework costs are two characteristics to measure.

(4) Product-based view

Quality is tied to inherent product characteristics. It assumes that measuring and controlling internal product properties (internal quality indicators) will result in improved external product behavior (quality in use). In other words, the quality of the IT system behavior that the customer gets to experience is based on the investment made in project quality management while building the IT system.

(5) Transcendent view

With this view, quality is synonymous with innate excellence. In other words, quality is something that can be recognized but not defined. With this view, quality should only be attributed to those products and services that achieve the highest standards. The line of thinking is 'You will know it when you see it'.

2.4. *Dimensions of quality for services*

Evans and Lindsay (1999) provide a list of eight service dimensions. These dimensions are suitable to be used as metrics for service quality or the consultancy role:

(1) Time,
(2) Timeliness,
(3) Completeness,
(4) Courtesy,
(5) Consistency,
(6) Accessibility and convenience,
(7) Accuracy,
(8) Responsiveness.

Time reflects the customer's waiting time. How long the customer would have to spend before the customer could consume the service reflects both a measurable and a perceived quality of a service. Timeliness is about the completion of the delivery of service on time. Delays in completion of a service reflect lack of quality of a service. Completeness reflects how comprehensive the service offering is, in terms of customers being able to get all they ask for from the service. Courtesy is the treatment of customers by the employees who deliver the service. Consistency reflects the fairness with which each customer is served. In a high-quality service offering, all customers should receive the same level of service. Ease of obtaining the service reflects the accessibility and convenience of the service. A high-quality service is accurate, meaning the service is performed correctly every time for all customers. The ability of the service to react to special circumstances or special requests reflects the responsiveness of the service.

2.5. *Total Quality Management*

Total Quality Management (TQM) is a management approach where all members of an organization participate in achieving and sustaining quality in the long run. This involves improving processes, products, services, and the way the people engage. Samuel (1995) has explored the TQM space in detail.

Customer focus, where the organization is focused on customer success, is a key building block of TQM. All the efforts across the organization on employee training, process improvements, system upgrades, and maintenance must focus on customer success. The progress of all these activities should ideally be determined by the customer.

Engagement of the employees on the quality goals is a must to ensure success of TQM. To enable this, employees must be empowered to self-manage their work in their own teams.

Adhering to the process and enabling thinking in line with the process is an integral part of TQM. To help eliminate variation and deviation from the processes, performance measures must be continuously monitored.

Continual improvement is a large part of TQM. For the organization to be analytical and creative in delivering a high level of quality, a continual improvement model must be in place. This will help the organization to be effective and more competitive in meeting client expectations.

TQM requires that an organization makes informed decisions all the time. For this, it is essential that the organization collect and analyze data on an ongoing basis. This will ensure that the decision accuracy is enhanced and lead to high-quality products and services.

Communication is a key pillar required for TQM. Effective communication is required in planning stages, change management, as well as in day-to-day operations. Effective and timely communication on strategies, timelines, processes, methods, and workflows will ensure TQM success.

2.6. *Quality assurance*

Quality assurance is about executing the quality management plan. Quality assurance ensures that the quality requirements for the project deliverables are fulfilled as the project progresses. Project quality assurance ensures that the project execution is constantly working toward delivering outcomes in accordance with quality requirements.

Some tools used in quality assurance include process checklists, audits, and static and dynamic verifications of interim deliverables. Quality reports and issue logs help keep track of the state of project health in relation to quality requirements. As the project progresses, if the deliverables seem to be drifting from quality requirements, corrective action needs to be taken. The changes to the quality management plan must be tracked. As part of the process, change requests also need to be tracked. The objective of using these tools and techniques in quality assurance is to ensure the avoidance of defects that affect quality of deliverables.

2.7. *Quality control*

Quality control is about quality management process enforcement. While there could be tools, workflows, procedures, and practices defined in the quality management plan and executed though quality assurance process, the rigor with which the process is followed according to the plan needs to be monitored and corrective actions taken when necessary. If project deliverables are not meeting the expected level of quality standard, quality control needs to be able to adjust the deliverables. To be effective, it is not sufficient to do this at the end of the projects; rather, this needs to be done in an agile, iterative manner throughout the project life cycle.

Quality control measures will help track the effectiveness of finding and fixing defects. Metrics such as open vs closed ratio of defects, rate at which defects are found, and rate at which defects are fixed are some examples. These quality control metrics are aimed at monitoring the capability of fixing defects, thereby fulfilling the quality requirements of the project.

2.8. *McCall's quality factors and criteria*

McCall's model classifies all software requirements into 11 software quality factors (McCall, 1977). The 11 factors are clustered into three categories:

(1) Product operation,
(2) Product revision,
(3) Product transition.

Product operation factors reflect how well the system runs. In the production operation of the product, correctness, reliability, efficiency, integrity, and usability factors indicate the quality of the product while in operation.

Product revision factors indicate how easily the product can be changed, tested, and redeployed. Maintainability, flexibility, and testability factors reflect the quality of the product when the products need to be revised to facilitate change.

Product transition factors reflect how well the product can be moved to different platforms and interface with other systems. Portability, reusability, and interoperability indicate the quality of the product with respect to the ability to transition the product to help evolve the system over time.

2.8.1. *Product operation factors*

1. Correctness — functionality matches the specification.
2. Reliability — the extent to which the IT system operates without failure.

3. Efficiency — IT system's ability to enhance the usage of computing resources.
4. Integrity — IT system performs its intended function in an unimpaired manner, free from unauthorized manipulation of the system, whether intentional or accidental.
5. Usability — IT system needs to be easy to use for all end-user categories.

2.8.2. *Product revision factors*

6. Maintainability — ability to find and fix defects in the IT system after release into production.
7. Flexibility — ability to make changes and support change requests in line with business demands.
8. Testability — IT system enables the validation of requirements.

2.8.3. *Product transition factors*

9. Portability — ability to transfer the IT system from one environment to another.
10. Reusability — the components of the IT system can be used in different contexts.
11. Interoperability — the degree to which all the components of the IT system work together seamlessly within the system and across systems.

2.9. *ISO/IEC 25010:2011 quality characteristics*

The ISO/IEC 25010:2011 standard describes a software quality model which categorizes software quality into six characteristics which are sub-divided into sub-criteria (ISO/IEC, 2011).

These characteristics provide a model for indirect measures of the quality of the system. These can be used to build an excellent checklist to monitor and track quality.

2.9.1. *Functionality*

This refers to the existence of a set of functions and their specified properties. The functions are those that satisfy stated or implied needs:

- Suitability,
- Accuracy,
- Interoperability,
- Security,
- Functionality compliance.

2.9.2. *Reliability*

This refers to the capability of software to maintain its level of performance for a period:

- Maturity,
- Fault tolerance,
- Recoverability,
- Reliability compliance.

2.9.3. *Usability*

This refers to the effort needed for use, and for the individual assessment of such use, by a direct or indirect set of users:

- Understandability,
- Learnability,
- Operability,
- Attractiveness,
- Usability compliance.

2.9.4. *Efficiency*

This refers to the relationship between the level of performance of the software and the number of resources used:

- Time behavior,
- Resource utilization,
- Efficiency compliance.

2.9.5. *Maintainability*

This refers to the effort needed to make modifications:

- Analyzability,
- Changeability,
- Stability,
- Testability,
- Maintainability compliance.

2.9.6. *Portability*

This refers to the ability of software to be transferred from one environment to another:

- Adaptability,
- Installability,
- Coexistence,
- Replaceability,
- Portability compliance.

2.10. *ISO 9000:2015 quality management systems*

This International Standard describes fundamentals of quality management systems, which form the subject of the ISO 9000 family, and defines the related terms (ISO, 2015).

This standard provides the fundamental concepts, principles, and vocabulary for quality management systems (QMS) and provides the foundation for other QMS standards. This International Standard is intended to help the user understand the fundamental concepts, principles, and vocabulary of quality management, to be able to implement a QMS effectively and efficiently, and realize value from other QMS standards.

ISO 9001:2015 (ISO, 2015) is an important element of the ISO 9000 family of specifications. ISO 9001:2015 specifies requirements for a quality management system. Organizations can use this specification to demonstrate their ability to consistently provide deliverables that meet customer requirements as well as regulatory requirements. Adherence to this specification can also be used to enhance customer satisfaction. All the requirements of ISO 9001:2015 are generic and are intended to be applicable to any organization.

2.11. *ISO/IEC/IEEE 90003:2019*

This standards document provides guidance on the acquisition, supply, development, operation, and maintenance of computer software and related support services (ISO, 2019).

The guidelines provided in this standards document are not intended to be used as assessment criteria in quality management system registration/certification. However, some organizations can consider it useful to implement the guidelines proposed. It can be used to determine whether the resultant quality management system is compliant or not with the proposed model.

2.12. *ISO/IEC/IEEE 12207-2:2020*

This document provides processes that can be employed for defining, controlling, and improving software life cycle processes within an organization or a project (ISO, 2020).

The processes, activities, and tasks of this standards document can also be applied for quality management process planning.

2.13. *ISO/IEC/IEEE 15289:2019*

This standards document specifies the purpose and content of all identified systems and software life cycle and service management information items (documentation) (ISO, 2019). The information item contents are defined according to generic document types.

This document assumes an organization is performing life cycle processes to manage the software life cycle or system life cycle. Quality management processes become part and parcel of these processes.

2.14. *IEEE 730-2014 — IEEE standard for software quality assurance processes*

This standard specifies requirements for initiating, planning, controlling, and executing the Software Quality Assurance processes of software development or maintenance (IEEE, 2014). This standard is harmonized with the software life cycle process of ISO/IEC/IEEE 12207:2008 and the information content requirements of ISO/IEC/IEEE 15289:2011.

3. Measuring quality

Quality measurements and metrics are needed to help the project team and project stakeholders understand the health of the project and the status of quality of the deliverables. Not only those team members who are directly associated with quality planning, assurance, and control but also those responsible for project management, design, implementation, deployment, and maintenance need to understand how and why quality is measured and the associated metrics.

Note that quality metrics would often be used in communication and collaboration among project team members throughout the project life cycle.

Some of the key areas that need measuring and metrics in IT project quality management include the following:

- Cost incurred on quality management,
- Defects,
- Customer complaints and customer-reported defects,
- Test coverage,
- Product usage across end-user categories,
- Overall system effectiveness,
- User throughput and effectiveness enhancements enabled by the system,

- Delivery metrics,
- Rework rate,
- Schedule realization,
- Audit metrics,
- Maintenance metrics.

The following section will detail these measures and metrics.

3.1. *Defects*

Defects are a primary measure of project quality management. The number of defects is a metric that needs to be tracked with insight into the context of quality efforts. Too many defects could indicate poor quality. Too few defects might indicate good quality if the project team has satisfactory efforts being applied into defect hunting. In case there are process issues in quality assurance, it could lead to fewer defects. Hence, the context of the metric needs to be cross-checked with the situation, project environment, and other metrics.

The defect rate is also an important metric. The number being found over a period indicates the effectiveness of the quality assurance team. The standard of the defects if they are real or serious should also be considered. Over time, as the deliverables take shape and mature, the defect rate should slow down.

The rate at which the defects are fixed is also an important metric to understand the effectiveness of the quality control process. Ideally, over time, the defect fixing rate should be better than the defect finding rate. If not, then there is a problem in relation to the overall approach toward quality management.

3.2. *Customer complaints and customer-reported defects*

The defects found by the customers reflect leakage of defects into project deliverables through quality assurance and quality control procedures executed by the project team. Defect leakage indicates shortcomings in the test review process, missing test cases, misunderstood requirements, poorly designed test cases, incorrect test data, or incorrect production deployment.

The rate and counts of customer complaints could also be reflective of defect leakage. If the requirements were well understood and if quality planning and assurance were done right, the quality management process will be able to minimize customer complaints. Some of the customer complaints are related to lack of system usability. Usability is a non-functional requirement that needs to be planned for testing among other non-functional requirements. Quality control processes need to pay attention to customer complaints and customer-reported defects to get those all fixed. Hence, this metric reflects quality assurance effectiveness on the one hand and quality control efficiency on the other.

3.3. *Test coverage*

Test coverage is the amount of source code executed when test cases are run on a project's software deliverables. The percentage of code executed during testing reflects how much of the implementation is covered in quality assurance. A lower coverage percentage indicates a low confidence level on the amount of quality assurance. Higher coverage indicates higher confidence in quality.

100% test coverage is impossible in most cases. However, the quality planning process needs to include strategies to have provisions to achieve the highest possible coverage. This requires comprehensive understanding of requirements, execution paths, and usage scenarios.

3.4. *Product usage across end user categories*

If the end users perceive the system to be unusable, difficult to use, slow or not meeting their expectations, then they will work around the system rather than use the system. This would be the case for all end users or certain categories of the end users. Quality management needs to have a good understanding of the end-user population, usage statistics, and usage patterns.

4. Business impact of quality management

Quality management needs to pay attention to customer focus. In this, customer means the end users of the project deliverables. Being able to manage a good relationship with customers is a key factor that determines success with achieving quality.

Customer satisfaction made possible through a high-quality system is one of the key business impacts of quality management. Happy and satisfied customers will become system advocates and they will also bring in new business to the system that they are happy with. This connects monetary benefits to customer satisfaction.

Enhanced customer retention and reduction in customer churn are other important business impacts of project quality management. This reduces customer acquisition costs and increases lifetime business value of the customers.

4.1. *Meeting business objectives*

To meet business objectives, project quality management must focus not only on functional requirements but also on non-functional requirements. If there are gaps in functional requirements, end users will immediately back away from the IT system use. Hence, it is a given and a must that the project deliverables fulfill all the must-have and the should-have functional requirements that fit the end-user purpose. In other words, the IT system must be reliable with no bugs. The non-functional requirements will drive end-user perception of the IT system even if the project team fulfills all functional requirements with adequate quality.

System performance makes the user feel that they can use the system effectively. When the system is slow, end users will perceive the IT system to be non-functional. The quality management processes need to ensure that the end users do not perceive the system as slow.

Timeliness of data and information is a key requirement, especially for business users. If business users cannot get data and information through the system in a timely manner, the quality of the system will be seen as poor by them. If the system does not meet timeliness requirements, negative business impacts will result from the system. Timeliness is a top business objective of any IT system. Organizations want to automate and digitize the systems so that they can get timely data and information as well as make timely decisions based on system outputs.

In today's world where businesses are digitally driven and automation is an essential part of business processes, there are wide-ranging business impacts with system downtimes. Stability is a key non-functional requirement from that perspective. The project quality management needs to ensure that there are no incidents once the system is in production. Quality assurance and quality control play a major role in ensuring minimization of the incidents. Availability is a related system attribute in this context and these days 99.9 % uptime is a common expectation.

Functional reliability must augment system usability. Usability is a major business enabler. As it can be seen from the mobile applications and social media platform trends, usability drives application adaptation. The same goes for the project deliverables of an IT project. The organizations sponsoring IT projects would desire a high degree of usability as part of their business objectives. Quality management needs a plan for usability, quality assurance, and control with a high level of rigor.

4.2. *Quality management in relation to customer success*

Customer service must be driven through customer experience and must result in exceptional customer satisfaction. The three domains of customer service, experience, and satisfaction need to be factored into quality planning.

Quality management needs to ensure that the IT project deliverables deliver the highest standards of customer service. It also needs to maintain these standards by continuous evaluation and resolution processes. The processes also need to allow the identification of malfunctions and improve customer service experience and satisfaction.

4.3. *Business sustainability and quality*

Sustainable business models must acquire and retain customers for the long run. The best form of customer acquisition is through word-of-mouth marketing. Quality and experience of the IT system are the main catalysts of word-of-mouth marketing.

Recommendations given by end users to other potential end users are the best form of sales pitch. The IT project quality management needs to focus on quality to the level where the system builds referenceable happy end users.

The reason customers leave a business is because they face issues with the products or services. The customer experience of product and services is driven mostly by the IT systems on which the businesses are based. Hence, for business sustainability, quality management must have a focus on customer retention.

5. Cost of quality management

The cost of quality management has two components: One is the cost spent on quality management activities and the other is the cost resulting from poor quality.

The project management team needs to invest in quality management to prevent massive expenses that could result from poor quality. Note that most IT systems today are impacting human lives directly or indirectly. Hence, the cost of poor quality sometimes would have value beyond monetary value.

The rewards for investing into ensuring a high degree of quality in products and services include positive reputation, sustainability of the business, trust by the customers, customer success, customer satisfaction, and associated socioeconomic benefits.

The potential penalties of not investing into ensuring a high degree of quality would include damage to reputation, project delays, possible project cancellations, frustrated customers, challenges to business continuity, lack of trust in the systems, and loss of income.

5.1. *Budgeting quality management*

In planning the budget, one must consider human costs as well as resource costs. Human and other resource estimates need to be based on functional and non-functional requirements, project scope, project timelines, business objectives of the customer organization, and number and type of stakeholders.

Successful quality management should facilitate communication and collaboration within the team and with the stakeholders. For this, there need to be suitable tools and platforms for communication and collaboration. The quality management budget needs to have a provision for this.

Documentation requires skilled resources, including those needed for illustrations, and proper tools. In the modern business environment, there are tools that help collaborative writing, review, and edit of documentation. The quality management team needs to have access to such tools, and this needs to be budgeted for.

When planning human resources, special attention needs to be paid to the balance of the team. Human resources are the most expensive element in the budget. Being able to put together a team with the right experience and skill set ensures the success of the project deliverables' quality.

Automation of tests suites, deployments, and test execution will save a lot of time and money throughout the project life cycle. However, to gain these benefits out of automation, the project management team needs to be willing to invest in automation tools and allocate time and resources.

5.2. Cost of lack of quality

Poor quality of the project deliverables leads to direct and indirect costs. Poor quality could be reflected in defects reported both by the project team as well as the customer's stakeholders. Defects reflect poor quality against functional requirements for most of the cases.

Poor quality could also be reflected in customer's stakeholder complaints and their negative perceptions toward the project deliverable. These are more reflective of the poor quality against non-functional requirements.

5.2.1. Direct costs

Direct costs of poor quality include additional cycles of rework. Sometimes, the project management team might have to bring in team reinforcements both for development and for quality assurance, causing project budget drains and going beyond the approved budget.

Delay in the deliverables due to time taken to find root causes and fix those will also increase the project budget. The overall project delivery will extend beyond the planned timeline.

Delays in project delivery will in turn cause a delay in production deployments. Production delays would have a direct impact on the revenue streams of the customer organization. Delay in going to market with the systems causes opportunity costs and paves the way for competitors to gain advantage.

5.2.2. *Indirect costs*

Indirect costs include damage to reputation both for the project customer organization and for the project delivery organization. Reputation is hard to quantify in terms of monetary value. However, damage to the reputation would have a negative effect on future revenue potential. For example, customers would back away from the organization's products and services due to poor quality. The project delivery organization would have a considerable reduction in new projects if they cannot guarantee quality of the project deliverables.

Poor quality would cause project team fatigue and frustrations leading to high turnover. Sometimes, it would be hard to track the connection between poor deliverables and associated rework and fatigue. Human resources are an important asset of the project. The mental and physical health of human resources is an indirect cost item that project quality management needs to pay attention to.

5.3. *Quality balanced sheet*

Total cost of quality is the sum of direct and indirect quality. Project quality management needs to maintain an accounting balance sheet to keep track of both direct and indirect cost items. As discussed earlier, cost of quality is an important quality metric. At the same time, keeping track of total cost of quality would help manage the project's cost budget, keep track of delivery timelines, and more importantly the quality of the project deliverables.

Based on the trends and insights revealed by the quality balanced sheet, the quality management leadership would be able to take proactive measures to better manage the quality of the project deliverables and increase the predictability of the quality along the project life cycle.

6. Common issues in quality management

Lack of rigor of quality management procedures can result in poor quality of the project deliverables. The reasons for lack of rigor could be budget concerns, lack of budget allocated, and lack of executive support.

If quality management processes and procedures are not properly factored into the project schedule, then in the rush to meet the project deadlines, the project management could overlook the quality management needs. Quality assurance and quality control need to have streamlined time allocation along the implementation and release cycles. For example, once a release is cut from the development branch, the quality assurance procedures and quality control procedures require cycles for the new release. In addition, time and effort required to find root cause of the defects, fix the defects, verify the fixes and regression testing needs to be taken account. Not only the test team but also the design and implementation teams need to be involved with these activities.

Underallocation of resources can also lead to problems. Resources allocated to multiple projects at the same time might not have enough cycles for quality assurance and quality control. Note that the allocation of a single resource for multiple tasks across projects will cause productivity reduction due to cycles consumed to adjust to context switching.

Testing and verification taking more than one cycle can lead to delay and rework. This means that the project is gradually drifting beyond the initially set deadlines, and in the latter phase of the project there could be cycles of starvation for quality activities.

Lack of understanding of quality standards is a major issue. While the leadership, management, and the planners would have the right ideas, there needs to be emphasis on communicating the rationale and expectations. If the project team lacks understanding of quality standards, that will result in a lack of accountability from the team.

6.1. *Implications of implementation drifting from design*

Deviation of implementation from design causes major issues in quality. Design is done in accordance with requirements. If the design intentions are not met by the implementation, then that could cause problems to quality management. Additional cycles will be required to identify the drift by a quality assurance process and once the drifts are corrected, more cycles would be required to verify the original design intentions. This obviously multiplies the efforts unnecessarily. The best remedy is to identify and fix possible drifts from design intents in the early stage of development and before the artifacts are handed to the quality team for verifications.

Developer testing, code walkthroughs, and architecture and code reviews must be part of the development process. There need to be procedures and protocols used by the developer team to ensure the proper following of standards.

Communication and collaboration are key to helping eliminate problems in this space. Test plans and designs need to be cross-checked and cross-referenced. Project management, development leadership, and quality management leadership need to communicate regularly. There need to be collaboration models to help streamline the quality plan, assurance, and control frameworks with solution design, implementation, and unit testing. That will help minimize the drift and associated problems.

6.2. *Quality traceability*

Being able to trace the flow and connection from requirements to test plans, test suites, and test cases is a must to be able to increase the confidence in quality coverage, ability to get to the root of quality problems, and help communication and collaboration around quality.

Quality assurance and quality control processes would often use traceability to cross check and verify the quality of the deliverables. It also helps to provide visibility to stakeholders to establish the connection between quality processes and requirements. Defects found should be traced back to requirements, which is the initiation point of quality processes and implementation processes, then traced forward toward designs, then to code design intents, and then to code. This will give a 360-degree view across quality, requirements, and implementation.

6.3. *Quality certification*

To ensure that individuals who work for an organization as well as the organization itself can deliver the expected level of quality, quality certifications are used. For example, when an organization is certified for a quality related standard, it means that the organization meets the requirements set in the given standards.

It is ideal that the organization's system of quality management is certified. In the certification process, the certifying body would do an audit against the quality management system. This is not a one-off task. The certification body will do ongoing routine audits of the system to ensure that the organization maintains the quality management system.

6.4. *System design and test plan sync-up*

Quality traceability gives the project team the ability to streamline quality, design, and implementation activities. The sync up is essential to ensure teamwork and facilitate on-time delivery.

Good rapport and understanding between project management, architecture design, code intent design, implementation, and quality management are essential to ensure smooth execution of the test plan, followed up by test results analysis, defect analysis, defect fixing, and reassurance of quality.

7. Tools for quality management

Checklists are a simple yet very powerful tool used in quality management. Ideally, a checklist management system that automates the tracking of execution and facilitates enforcing the practice of a checklist is needed. Such a system would also help with reports and dashboards needed to bring about visibility of the execution of checking gates and verifying lists.

A test plan management system is needed to help design and execute test plans in a timely and effective manner. The system should also cater to stakeholder expectation of visibility and drill down to figure out the state of quality across the overall project.

For vigorous and timely execution of test suites, access to test data must be made systematic. Team members should not have to spend time building and locating datasets each time they want to design or execute test suites. A test data repository with good data organization architecture would be an essential tool.

A test results repository is required to keep track of historic test results and help generate reports quickly. Historic results are useful for quality audits, regression analysis, capturing lessons learned, and evaluating the evolution of quality processes.

Defect management is an essential tool. Many projects design and organize quality management processes and practices around defect management tools. These tools also provide dashboard and reports, often customizable to project needs, to help keep track of the health of project quality management.

Root cause analysis tools are very useful in quality control and problem resolution. The team can get into the practice of using fishbone diagrams, the well-known tool for root cause analysis, using pen and paper. It might help to have an automated system to manage the fishbone diagrams; however, that is not a must. It is ideal to keep all historic root cause analysis artifacts stored in digital format in a repository. That will help with preparing incident reports on past incidents if the need arises later.

Pareto charts help apply the 80–20 rule, where the project team can identify 20% of components or 20% of major factors leading to 80% of problems. Rather than trying to navigate the full defect space, it is much more effective to identify 20% of the components that cause a majority of the defects. When components are identified, then a further drilldown needs to be done to identify major factors. When major factors are addressed, the project team should be able to resolve a majority of the defects quickly. Further, the quality management team would be able to identify the areas of improvement that need to be made in quality assurance processes to prevent such defects in the future.

Quality health visualization dashboards enable stakeholder visibility. Those also enhance the transparency of quality management practices and processes. Around-the-dashboard KPI monitoring, proactive decision-making, risk mitigation, and proactive corrective action can be made to ensure high-quality delivery.

7.1. *Basic testing tools needed*

In today's IT environment, IT systems are able to handle high concurrence, scalability, and handling heavy load. Load testing, stress testing, and metering tools are required to model and mimic the heavy usage scenarios.

Application programming interface (API) testing tools are an essential part of the tool set. IT systems today deliver end-user applications over multiple channels such as mobile applications, web applications, kiosks, desktop applications, and terminals. For a unified experience, business logic consistency, and ease of maintenance, an API-based interfacing model is used. Correctness of functionality mostly depends on the correct functionality of the API layer. For each API, the quality team needs to cover all operations with a range of requests and expected responses. API testing tools enable the easy setup of API tests and help automate the execution of the setup.

Tools that automate the testing of front end user interfaces and back-end functionality are widely available. Spending time and automating tests to cover functionality across the layers of the application stack using a tool kit will save lots of time throughout the project life cycle. Test automation tools also help with regression testing. Automation tools could also be integrated to test data repositories and test results repositories.

7.2. *Emerging tools of cloud and AI era*

Load balancing is a common deployment pattern used in today's API-driven, distributed application with high levels of peak loads. Test tools that can mimic the heavy load, monitor load balancing behavior, and analyze fair distribution of loads across available worker nodes are necessary.

To cater for varying volumes of system usage and the related traffic patterns, scalability test tools are required. These tools need to monitor, analyze, and verify scale-up and scale-down behavior patterns of the system. For this, test tools that can be used to generate peak, steady-state, and low traffic in a varying manner are needed. Testing with constant traffic with few use cases is not useful in this case. Multiple use cases with heavy usage patterns need to be used when designing traffic patterns for testing.

Artificial intelligence-based (AI) and machine learning-based (ML) algorithms and tools can be used to analyze test data repositories and test results repositories to analyze the accuracy and quality of the quality management process itself. Through the project life cycle, the project activities would generate volumes of data in the form of test input data, test output data, and test results. To analyze these beyond the human gut feel, a considerable amount of time and effort would be required. To generate analytical reports and related insights in a quick and effective manner, a quality management process and AI- and ML-based tools and techniques are required.

In addition to quality management process analytics, AI-based tools for automated testing would be handy, especially to help generate traffic patterns, datasets, test scenarios, as well as mimic user behavior patterns.

8. Project team and quality management

The project team plays a crucial part in the success of quality management. The way the project team syncs up with the governance aspects of project management and project quality management determines the level of quality of the project deliverables. The key pillars of governance are people, policies, and processes. The project team represents the people pillar, and they need to understand and adhere to the policies and processes put in place to ensure successful quality management. The team will be composed of a set of roles and each of those roles will have an associated set of responsibilities that they would have to fulfill to help realize success with project quality management.

8.1. *Project roles and associated quality responsibilities*

8.1.1. *Executive roles*

Executive buy-in and support for quality management budget and quality management process rigor is essential for successful delivery of quality. Some of the key considerations of the executives are time to deliver, time to go to market, total cost of the project, and business outcomes enabled through the project deliverables. The communications by the quality management team to executives need to focus on these factors and connect to the business value. When rationalizing the budget, time taken, and rigor needed, these factors must be factored in and one must highlight the criticality of quality in delivering the executive objectives. Executives need to seek the connection between the business objectives and the enablement of achieving those through quality management. Irrespective of how soon the project deliverables can go to market and how low the budget would be in the short run, in the long run, quality will have a lasting impact on total cost of the project, business sustainability, and reputation.

8.1.2. *Project management roles*

Project management mainly focuses on budget, timelines, and customer expectations management. The job role will get increasingly harder with poor quality. To ensure the optimal utilization of resources, rework needs to be eliminated. Poor-quality results in rework as well as pile up of work and backlog lead to possible project delays. Focus on quality from day one in the project management plan is ideal. Project management needs to ensure that quality management processes are provided with needed resources on time within the budget. Project management also needs to give due attention to quality management when tracking and monitoring.

Project management also needs to focus on organizing the team around the quality focus across roles. Quality in all aspects of planning, design, implementation, testing, delivery, and deployment must be coordinated by project management.

8.1.3. *Developer roles*

The contribution by the development team to quality management is immense. The greatest contribution by developers toward quality management comes from timely and methodical developer testing and unit testing. The systematic utilization of unit testing frameworks at the code level and spending time on verifying functional and non-functional aspects then and there during development ensure a high degree of quality. A high coverage percentage at the programming level of unit testing will always lead to high quality.

Following proper techniques to create testable and maintainable software when designing the coding intent and code is another key contribution by developers to quality management.

Collaboration by developing with a quality team in cross-referencing across unit tests, test plans, and requirements is essential. In quality assurance and quality control, developers help with rationalizing test results, help fix defects faster, and contribute to minimizing defect leakage.

8.1.4. *Quality assurance roles*

Quality assurance (QA) roles are the pillars on top of which the project quality management is built. They cover all aspects of quality management including planning, assurance, and control. They are accountable for coordination and collaboration across the team to ensure high-quality deliverables.

The quality team needs to understand the business needs and business objectives of the project at hand. They need to be able to apply empathy toward all stakeholders and especially end users in the quality management process. If the team can meet the quality objectives of the system being fit, the purpose of all end-user roles, the quality team needs to be able to put themselves in the end user's shoes and be able to look at the system deliverables from the end-user perspective.

Collaboration with developers is essential in quality management for the QA team. Being able to understand developer pain points and being able to better relate to them are key skills that the quality team should have to ensure the success of quality assurance and quality control processes.

The quality team needs to aim to earn respect from the development team, build trust, and operate with a good rapport.

The quality team needs to become the champion of quality management across the project team and throughout the project life cycle. They are responsible for playing a quality advocacy role to the whole team.

8.1.5. *Support and maintenance roles*

Support and maintenance teams will engage with the project team from the early stages while maintaining QA and pre-production environments. Some projects would use an agile model and have interim releases in production environments as the project progresses. The support and maintenance teams would have great insight into what the customers think and how the customers use the project delivery artifacts. These insights would be great input into project quality management. The support and maintenance team can act as the customer advocate in reaching quality excellence.

8.2. *Ethics and responsibility toward quality*

The answer to the question 'Who owns quality?' is simple, yet often misunderstood by the team members. The answer is that everyone in the project team must have their own quality. However, it is often misunderstood that the QA team is the one who would own and be responsible for quality.

The responsibilities of each role were explained in the above section. In summary, the quality responsibility of each role and team member is toward the end users and stakeholders.

In today's world, given the widespread use of IT systems for day-to-day use cases and the interconnected use of the systems to run many critical social functions, lives would depend on the IT systems. There are associated physical and mental health implications that stem from the use of IT systems. Due to this, the IT professionals who are involved with the IT projects have a wider social responsibility. They must practice ethics with their full capability and commitment to deliver high-quality IT systems to the society.

8.3. *Process adherence and quality*

The success of process enforcement depends mainly on the engagement by the team. If individuals are engaging and adhering to the processes in place at all levels, then the deliverables will be of very high quality.

To ensure the engagement by the team and the process adherence by all team members, the project quality management must rationalize the processes to the team. Rather than burning cycles in enforcing the process, it is cost and time effective to train, educate, and rationalize the processes in place to the team. That will empower the team to engage to the full.

The mindset of the team members involved should be to follow the process because it helps achieve quality, not because it is there. The 'why' factor addressed in process documentation, communications, and training would help the team better understand why there are such processes in place.

The team must also be educated on the process improvement opportunities and the possibilities of them getting involved. If there are gaps in the process, the protocol must be to first comply with the current process as is and then document the gaps, engage, improve and optimize. Involving team members at all levels for continuous process improvement will ensure better compliance in the future.

9. Agility of quality management

Agile delivery models are very popular in today's project management space. Therefore, project quality management too needs to be able to adopt an agile and iterative delivery model. In agile project management, the whole system requirements specification would not be available when the project is initiated and would be built incrementally as the project progresses. The quality plan, quality assurance model, and quality control model would have to evolve over time to align and fulfill quality expectations and when requirements and deliverables become clearer.

9.1. *Agile iterative models for quality management*

Quality management needs to strive to achieve quality with each sprint and milestone. The rationale of an agile delivery model is to deliver artifacts that can be used in production by the end users. This means that, in an agile delivery model, one needs to focus to ensure that the project deliverables fit the end-user purpose and help realize the delivered use cases.

Continuous integration and continuous delivery would have to be packaged with necessary quality assurance, with integration testing. When you are delivering with a sprint-based model where there will be production-ready milestones every two weeks, there needs to be room in the quality management plan to handle the backlog being identified in every sprint. Managing the backlog in an effective manner is essential for successful quality management; otherwise, defects will get accumulated with every sprint.

9.2. *Incremental test plan building*

In agile delivery, there is incremental buildup of requirements in each iteration. While there could be an overall plan, as the project progresses with iteration of milestones, there will be further clarity on requirements. In sync with the evolution of requirements, test plans need to evolve in each sprint. This also includes expansion and evolution of the UAT plan, OAT plan, and regression test suite.

9.3. *Iterative approach toward quality management*

In the agile iterative approach of delivery, the quality management process needs to ensure that there is no scope creep. There also needs to be room in the plan for the time required to make evolutionary adjustments in quality assurance and quality control.

Agile quality management is as follows:

- Human centric,
- Focused on customer integration,
- Banks on networking among cross-discipline teams,
- Evolutionary,
- Iterative.

10. Project quality management challenges

Challenges faced when implementing project quality management need to be well understood to ensure success. The better the understanding of challenges, the better the project team will be positioned to mitigate the risks, plan better, and overcome the challenges. This section lists some of the key challenges, and how to plan and face those to ensure project success.

10.1. *Budgeting*

For quality management excellence, there needs to be investments in people, tools, certification, and time. Due to budget and time constraints, there could be pressure on quality management rigor. When budgeting, the cost of quality and the cost of poor quality need to be well understood. There needs to be attention on non-monetary costs and long-terms implications.

10.2. *Transparency*

Transparency in quality management processes and progress in relation to quality management of the project is critical. Project stakeholders need to be able to gauge the quality of the deliverables at any given point of time. While stakeholder intervention could be seen as a hindrance to rapid progress, enabling transparency from project inception to project delivery would eliminate many last minute and post-delivery quality problems.

10.3. *Stakeholders buy-in*

Transparency in project quality management would lead to stakeholder buy-in to enable budget investments and time allocations. Quality management needs to keep the stakeholders informed and needs to have a communication plan, provide regular milestone updates, and offer project insights. Engaging stakeholders early and often leads to better relationships and better buy-in from stakeholders.

10.4. *Executive support*

Support from executives for quality management initiatives is critical, as they take key decisions on the budget, timelines, and priorities. Keeping the executives educated is a key responsibility of the project quality management leadership team. Managing executive expectations is also a key part of being able to win executive support. While executives are also part of the stakeholders, they need to be given special attention as their decisions determine the fate of the project and in turn the quality of the deliverables.

10.5. *Communication and collaboration*

Communication within the team and outside the team is a key pillar for project success. Often, there is ample focus on communicating with the external stakeholders outside the team in the form of reports, updates, and progress meetings. However, internal communication within the team and across team disciplines is critical to keep them educated and informed on the quality management initiatives, objectives, and progress. This will help ensure the support from all team members toward the success of quality management throughout the project life cycle.

10.6. *The team — us vs. them*

The term 'team' is often meant to refer to the internal project team. However, the teamwork extends well beyond the project team boundaries. In particular, the team must include the customers, end users, and other relevant customer stakeholders. When it comes to meeting and beating the quality aspirations, the 'us vs. them' viewpoint is a hindrance. The project team as a whole needs to include customer stakeholders into the holistic view of the team, so the communication and collaboration become seamless in clarifying the requirements, meeting the expectations, and thereby ensuring a high degree of project deliverables quality.

11. Summary

Quality consists of the requirements of the end users and the characteristics of the project deliverables that are related to the requirements. To ensure high-quality project deliverables, there need to be focus and commitment both by the project team and by all other stakeholders toward project quality management.

Ensuring quality products and services delivery would require a focus on total quality management. TQM is intended to deliver customer success. A continually improved process where process errors are not repeated will ensure a very high degree of quality.

Quality assurance helps ensure the verification of the product's compliance to requirements and the existence of the associated characteristics. Quality controls ensure that the defects are fixed in a timely manner.

There are multiple standards to help ensure that we meet the quality requirements in a consistent and a repeatable manner. This chapter discussed multiple standards, especially those from ISO, that need to be considered when planning, implementing, and managing project quality management initiatives.

Inspection of the process is as important as inspection of the product. Certifications of quality management systems ensure that the processes, products, and services meet the requirements of the standards through periodic audits.

Cost of quality needs to be given a holistic consideration when planning quality management. The cost of poor quality could end up being much higher than the cost of ensuring high quality. The metrics associated need to be monitored, data collected and analyzed to understand the impact of the quality process and optimize the costs.

Quality is a team effort. The project team needs to collaborate and engage to eliminate communication gaps and work toward the shared objectives of delivering quality products and services. All stakeholders have a role to play in this regard.

References

Garvin, D. A. (1987). Competing on the eight dimensions of quality, *Harvard Bus. Rev.*, November–December. Volume: 87603 Page 101

Garvin, D.A. (1988) *Managing Quality: The Strategic and Competitive Edge.* The Free Press, New York.

Evans, J. and Lindsay, W. (1999). *The Management and Control of Quality*, 4th ed. Cincinnati: South-Western (p. 52).

McCall, J.; Richards, P.; Walters, G., 1977. *Factors in Software Quality*, three volumes, NTIS AD-A049-OI4, AD-A049-OI5, AD-A049-055.

Samuel, H. (1995). Is the ISO 9000 series for total quality management? *Int. J. Phys. Distrib. Logist. Manage.*, 25(1), 51–66.

IEEE. (2014). IEEE 730-2014 — IEEE Standard for Software Quality Assurance Processes.

ISO/IEC. (2011). ISO / IEC 25010:2011 Systems and Software Engineering — Systems and Software Quality Requirements and Evaluation.

ISO. (2015). ISO 9000:2015 Quality Management Systems — Fundamentals and Vocabulary.

ISO. (2015). ISO 9001:2015 Quality Management Systems — Requirements.

ISO. (2019). ISO/IEC/IEEE 90003:2019 Software Engineering.

ISO. (2020). ISO/IEC/IEEE 12207-2:2020 Systems and Software Engineering — Software Life Cycle Processes.

ISO. (2019). ISO/IEC/IEEE 15289:2019 Systems and Software Engineering — Content of Life-Cycle Information Items (documentation).

Chapter 11

IT Risk Management

Ananth Natarajan* and Geetha Gopal[†]

University of Oxford, Oxford, UK
**ananth.natarajan.mmpm18@said.oxford.edu*
[†]*geetha.gopal.mmpm18@said.oxford.edu*

Risk is associated with uncertainty and seen as a threat to the expected outcomes in project management. In Information Technology (IT) projects, the context of risk management goes beyond the common performance measures of scope, time, and cost for the project itself, as these projects may have an ever-larger impact on business performance if they underperform. This chapter reviews the factors that influence and increase risks in projects. It also reviews and reconciles different approaches to IT project risk management. General risk management methodologies, approaches, and tools are reviewed. Complexity in projects and the project portfolio, which can lead to unexpected emergent outcomes, is reviewed. Best practices in identifying, analyzing, mitigating, controlling, and governing risks are considered and discussed. The success approaches in other industries like Energy, Procurement, and Construction (EPC) are considered for use in IT project risk management. Lessons are drawn and recommendations for successful risk management are discussed.

1. Introduction

Risk management is essential to project delivery. It can be viewed as planning for deviations from planned project budget, schedule, and benefits. Projects are increasingly important across all sectors and are central to value creation and to strategic planning for companies, institutions, and governments. The increasing professionalization of project management over the last several decades has led to an exponential growth in tools, techniques, and methods related to risk management. The increasing importance of IT projects, their strong interrelationship with organizational strategy and operations, and track record of under performance makes risk management a critical issue. Several risk management methods and techniques have been adapted to IT project management, which has led to some distinct approaches. This chapter describes a holistic risk management approach that integrates risk management practices into the broader organizational and project context.

This section focuses on the introduction and context for IT project risks, focusing on their importance, track record, and consequently the need for IT project risk management. In the next section, risk management is set in context, starting by deriving a definition of risk and then progressively placing it in the project management and IT project contexts. This chapter proceeds to discuss the practice of risk management by discussing risk identification in Section 3 and risk analysis in Section 4. Risk response development is discussed in Section 5. Proceeding from the planning to project execution phase, risk monitoring and control are discussed in Section 6. Taking a step back to holistically discuss risk governance in Section 7 followed by recommendation for successful IT risk management strategy and practices in Section 8, the conclusion is assessed in Section 9.

1.1. *Introduction to Information Technology (IT) project risks*

Projects are increasingly used for value delivery across several business sectors, making project performance an important concern for business executives (Donk and Molloy, 2008; PMI, 2019). Therefore, project management is increasingly central to organizational strategy (KPMG, 2019). However, IT projects have a severe track record of failure due to insufficient risk management (Moeini and Rivard, 2019). According to the influential 2019 Standish CHAOS report, which reports IT project success rates, about 84% of IT projects failed partially or completely by exhibiting time or cost overruns, benefit shortfalls, or complete abandonment. Therefore, not only are IT projects more critical than generally understood they are also riskier than acknowledged. Some examples include a botched $5 million dollar project that cost Levi Strauss almost $200 million dollars and IT problems at Hong Kong's airport costing the economy about $600 million dollars (Flyvbjerg and Budzier, 2011). Much of these outsized effects come from the broader benefits from these projects which may be tied to wider and deeper strategic and operational issues.

1.2. *IT Project risk management literature overview*

Moeini and Rivard (2019) categorize the streams of IT risk management literature into two dominant groupings of normative and experiential. The discussion of risk management will be in the context of this tension between expert intuition and deliberate analysis. It is now well understood that human judgment uses heuristics and is subject to biases that affect risk assessment. There are broad schools of literature that focus on the adverse or positive effects from heuristics and biases. For instance, the work of Kahneman and Tversky elaborates on the shortfalls of human heuristics and biases (Kahneman, 2012), and Todd and Gigerenzer (2000) discuss their benefits. Biases have been related to project underperformance (Flyvbjerg, 2006), as well as to effective decision-making in complex situations (Klein, 1993). Different risk management approaches can emphasize expert intuition or deliberative methods (Moeini and Rivard, 2019). The appropriate application of risk management methods will depend on the context and the stage of the project.

1.3. *Track record statistics from studies*

Big IT Projects are plagued by significant overruns and benefit shortfalls (Flyvbjerg and Budzier, 2011). Successive Standish CHAOS reports have chronicled the severe performance shortfalls of IT projects. IT projects can consume billions in scarce resources and fail to deliver planned benefits. This is well illustrated in an abandoned five year project to build an integrated electronic health record system for the US Veterans Affairs Department costing $1.1 billion by the time of its cancellation in 2013 (Ehley, 2013). Budzier and Flyvbjerg (2013) report very high average cost overruns of 107% and schedule overruns of 37% for large IT projects. However, the high average cost, schedule overruns, and benefit shortfalls of IT projects are not sufficient to reflect the direness of the situation. A statistical assessment of IT project performance track record revealed an asymmetric, fat-tailed, non-normal distribution significantly weighted toward overrun (Budzier and Flyvbjerg, 2013). This study found that one-sixth of 1,471 IT projects from the data sample were black swan outliers in the fat tail of overrun distributions, with average cost overruns of 200% and schedule overruns of 70%. Black swans are unpredictable outliers with extreme and highly consequential impacts (Taleb, 2008). This significant number of extreme underperformance outliers considerably exceeds the large number of outliers in other project classes such as offshore EPC projects (Natarajan, 2021).

1.4. *Need for risk management in IT projects*

IT projects have unique characteristics compared to projects in other sectors such as EPC. The development team may be continually involved in maintenance and upgradation of the product, unlike in transport and energy projects where there is a handover to entities whose competence is centered on operations. IT projects have an innate potential for change that is absent in physical infrastructure. However, the increasing infusion of IT projects into physical infrastructure, whether transportation or energy infrastructure, has made all projects vulnerable to IT project risks. This is a key reason for the Standish CHAOS report to expand project performance criteria to include value, goals, and satisfaction (Standish, 2016). While these three additional metrics can be related to a broader definition of benefits, it must be noted that risks from IT projects can be significantly greater than planned benefits due to their entrenchment into strategy operations and critical infrastructure.

An equivalent treatment of the three vertices of the triple constraint, namely, cost, time, and scope (benefits), has come in for criticism due to the crucial interconnection of IT projects with either critical business capability or broader project success. The three traditional definitions of success can be made more relevant for projects by determining monetary consequences of delay and benefits underruns, thus providing objective weighting of these factors. In some cases, a significant increase in cost may be outweighed by a timely realization of benefits which can be associated by even higher costs. However, the planned scope may not result in the desired business outcome, and scope in IT projects is subject to change with changing circumstances and continual scope discovery. The broader organizational and project vulnerabilities to IT project risk require a more holistic scenario-planning approach than captured in the cost, benefit, and scope risks directly related to the project itself.

2. Understanding risk management

Risk is an estimate of possible deviation from expectation. For projects, budget, schedule, and benefits are the three key estimates derived during project planning stages. Decisions to commit resources to projects are made based on these estimates or forecasts. Therefore, the potential for deviation from the forecast, or uncertainty, is central to risk management. The definition of uncertainty as the quantifiable probability of possible outcomes and of risk as a subset of uncertainty involving only realization of undesirable outcomes found in Hubbard (2009) is the basis of our discussion of risk. It is to be noted that several definitions of risk relate it to uncertainty, both negative and positive, but this chapter relates risk as undesirable outcomes. Furthermore, another definition is 'strict uncertainty', for when possible outcomes are known but not their probabilities of realization (Hubbard, 2009). Knightian uncertainty or ignorance is popularly called "unknown unknowns" as shown in Figure 1.

Identification and management of emergent risk from strict and Knightian uncertainties is a key concern. Projects are increasingly more complex (Maylor *et al.*, 2013). They are complex systems and have been characterized as Complex Adaptive Systems (CAS) where the dynamics from interactions can engender emergent behavior that is practically

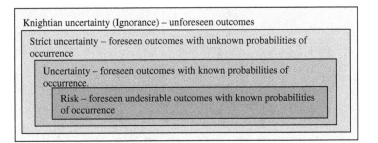

Figure 1.   Risk & uncertainty.

unpredictable (Ellinas *et al.*, 2018; Whyte, 2016; Chang *et al.*, 2013). Knowledge of the characteristics of individual organizations, departments, or project work packs is not sufficient for predicting behavior arising from their interactions (Hitchins, 2007). Complex systems may exhibit 'chaotic' behavior where outcomes are highly sensitive to small changes. The large number of possible outcomes along with their high sensitivity to small changes in prior conditions makes it virtually impossible to predict outcome manifestations even in theoretically deterministic systems (Chan, 2001). Complexity and outcomes can build up rapidly in seemingly simple problems relevant to several real-world operational questions. Complexity results in 'strict uncertainty' and 'unknown unknowns'. Reducing complexity is a key risk management strategy. To avoid individual project failures from having severe strategic or operational impacts, it is recommended to have smaller projects and redundancies in the portfolio for critical projects. Structured complexity assessment and reduction methods such as the complexity assessment tool developed and tested with a global technology firm can be employed for this purpose (Maylor *et al.*, 2013).

2.1. *The context of project risk*

The three basic risk buckets in projects are related to the potential for deviation from the planned budget, schedule, and benefits. For IT projects, risks to critical business systems from deployment issues need to be identified and managed along with the risks to project cost, time and scope delivery. Project risk reduction processes and methods should aim to

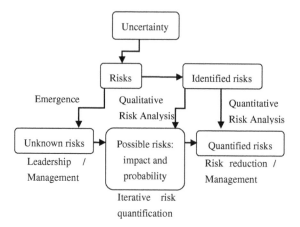

Figure 2.   Risk and risks with probabilities that can be avoided or reduced.

identify unknown unknowns, thus reducing them to strict uncertainty; and reduce strict uncertainty to risk, where the probability of occurrence is known in keeping with Hubbard's (2009) categorization. Risk with known probabilities are quantified to where they can be managed and reduced systematically. This is shown in Figure 2. Residual unknown or uncertain emergent outcomes may have to be identified and managed during project execution emphasizing project management and leadership.

This is related to one definition of the trilemma in project management where it is expressed as cost, time, and scope. Project performance metrics require consistent baselines (Flyvbjerg *et al.*, 2018). The budget, schedule, and benefits planned at project sanction are appropriate metrics as they underlie the financial and corporate commitment to a project. It may be useful to distinguish the risks to the timely delivery of planned benefits within the budgeted costs against the potential risk impacts to business systems affecting a company at an operational and strategic level from deployment issues. As discussed in the introduction, recent representation in the Standish CHAOS report includes metrics related to these broader impacts.

2.2. *Risk management methodology*

Project sanction often occurs after a planning process where the potential benefits, the required budget, and time of delivery are presented to a company's executive leadership for approval. Approval is granted on this basis whereupon a project team led by a project management team is tasked to deliver the project. The tension between experiential knowledge, which emphasizes expert knowledge and experience, and normative knowledge, which emphasizes formal risk management methods, is discussed at length by Moeini and Rivard (2019). Over-prescription of formal risk management processes can be counterproductive by leading to lack of buy-in from project managers. The correct fit depends on the type of project and its phase. It should result in a symbiotic relationship between project management and formal risk management methods and other stakeholders such as the PMO clients.

As illustrated in Figure 3, IT project risk management requires a holistic approach and should occur over the project phases of project selection, planning, and execution. The first phase would require a deeper involvement of executive management and transition to the project management team during the execution phases. The planning phase will need committed involvement from both executive and project leadership. Formal risk management methodologies such as risk identification,

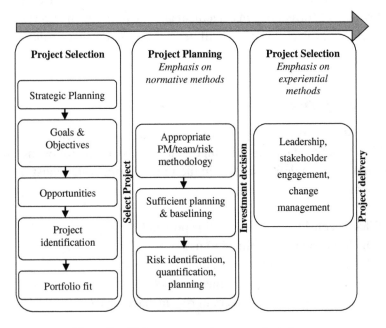

Figure 3.   Risk management across project phases.

qualification, and quantification workshops are best done in the planning stage, and experiential methods which emphasize expert project manager intuition, expertise, and leadership are more crucial during the execution phase. At all stages, it is important to emphasize the cross-organizational, cross-departmental nature of projects highlighting involvement from all stakeholders across boundaries.

2.3. *Risk management tools*

Risk management tools for risk identification are discussed in Section 3, and risk analysis is discussed in Section 4. However, it must be understood that standard or normative risk management methods have been criticized for emphasizing familiar, measurable, and favorable risks over other significant risks and the subjective biases in their assessment, and not being conducive to purposeful action (Moeini and Rivard, 2019; Kutsch *et al.*, 2014). As mentioned earlier, experiential knowledge which accrues from expert knowledge accumulated by project managers and is employed using heuristics and cues can be more effective than normative knowledge employing standard procedures in many situations. The balance between employment of formal risk management and the reliance on expert knowledge held by project managers will depend on the context of the project and the project phase as illustrated in Figure 3.

3. Identify risks

The first step in managing project risks is to define and identify risks. To establish an understanding, it is important to consider the following questions and secure a definition within the project team which must be well documented:

- What is considered as risk in this project?
- Which outcomes are critical to us?
- What are the tolerable thresholds?
- How to measure non-quantifiable risks?
- Who are the key stakeholders in risk management?

The next step would be to identify and list the potential risks along the established definition. It is important to note that risks have the power to manifest in unknown ways. The project definition is a good starting point and is a guideline, but it must not be dealt with as a boundary. It is the project manager's role to align the definition as the project uncovers risks outside the agreed boundaries.

3.1. *General approaches in practice*

There are several popular methods to identify risks in IT projects. The following six methods are commonly used. Risk identification is a collaborative process, and all the approaches discussed below require the participation and insights of multiple stakeholders:

- Brainstorming,
- Structured workshops and interviews,
- Delphi technique,
- Reviewing Previous Projects and gathering insights,
- SWOT analysis,
- Assumptions review.

3.2. *Brainstorming*

Brainstorming is the process of bringing a group of relevant stakeholders into a discussion to gather ideas, insights, and suggestions. Multiple perspectives gathered through brainstorming foster creativity and innovation. In the context of risk management, brainstorming is an effective approach to collect potential risks or topics of concern for the project. Identifying the right set of stakeholders in risk identification brainstorming is an important step. The hindsight in IT project brainstorming is that it is common to note that such sessions revolve around technical risk identification and often neglect non-technical risks. Thus, a diverse set of stakeholders like functional, management, operational, business, and support members must be part of risk identification brainstorming. Brainstorming is a process that adds value to all project phases.

3.3. *Structured workshops*

Structured workshops to gather risks are common in larger projects and programs. In many cases, the results of brainstorming are reviewed further through workshops with relevant stakeholders, often smaller groups, who deep-dive into identified risks. Through specialized workshops, it is possible to identify and structure risks relevant to individual work packages or technical and functional areas. It encourages deeper involvement and fruitful interchanges in specific areas and helps in identifying multiple levels of potential risks. In small-scale projects, structured workshops offer similar insights; the difference often is fewer sessions and smaller groups of stakeholders. These structured workshops are a good fit to the project planning phase. However, care should be taken to avoid overreliance on workshops during project execution when expert intuition and communication become important.

3.4. *Delphi technique*

The Delphi technique commonly used in forecasting is also an effective risk identification approach. Being a structured method, Delphi gathers risks on an Estimate-Talk-Estimate approach from a set of experts who offer insights through a series of questionnaires and an iterative review of results at the end of each round of engagement. When a pre-agreed set of engagement is achieved, the identified risks are weighed based on their scores, a ranking is established, and the results are finalized. As the process of expert engagement is anonymous, this method encourages open communication and reduces the occurrence of cognitive biases in identifying risks. The Delphi technique is useful in all project phases.

3.5. *Reviewing previous projects and gathering insights*

Good project risk documentation is a crucial element in any project for its success. Its impact is not only felt in its own project but also as reference for future projects. They have the potential to serve as reference in different levels such as for similar projects or across a portfolio. Most technological risks in IT projects are repetitive in nature. The environmental and external risks vary depending on factors like resources, partnerships, processes dependencies, security, and data concerns. Reviewing past risk experiences increases the chances of uncovering recurring risks, their behavior, occurrence rates, and potential mitigation measures. Consulting project members who have worked on similar projects is another effective way to identify risks. Reviewing past projects can be helping during the project selection but is particularly useful in the project planning phase.

3.6. *SWOT analysis*

SWOT analysis stands for Strengths, Weaknesses, Opportunities, and Threats, and refers to identifying each of these factors and plotting them into a 2-by-2 matrix which gives a deeper understanding of the risks associated with projects. Not all risks are negative, and the occurrence of some provides new opportunities and growth. The first step in SWOT analysis is to do a thorough brainstorming with a relevant and diverse group of stakeholders and identify the key topics under each area. The next step is to rank, prioritize, and document the topics. The third step is to identify strategies and measures to handle each of the topics together with the relevant stakeholders and secure a consensus. The final one is an iterative step of monitoring, reviewing, aligning, and managing the approaches identified for each topic and category. SWOT is an extremely useful approach in general, but it is best used in innovation and customer-centric IT projects. SWOT is a particularly useful tool in the project selection phase to help the right projects be selected and to align them with overall strategy.

3.7. *Assumptions review*

Assumptions increase complexities in projects and thereby risks. Despite their known negative influences, assumptions cannot be avoided in certain cases and stages, especially early in the planning phase. The assumptions review approach aims to uncover all the assumptions in the project and identify uncertainties, unclarities, and risks in the process. The project team and key stakeholders are required to list down all the assumptions made in the project right from the early stages. These assumptions are reviewed for inaccuracies or discrepancies and the underlying risks are identified. There is always room for new assumptions to creep into a project; hence, this process should be done iteratively throughout the project life cycle to identify and handle them. An assumptions review is best suited for the project planning phase.

3.8. *Pros and cons*

All the six methods discussed above are useful in IT risk identification. Table 1 lists the key pros and cons of these methods in risk identification.

Table 1.   Risk list example.

Approach	Pros	Cons
Brainstorming	• Ability to gather risks. • Congruence of different viewpoints.	• Restrictive to certain early identified risks. • Focus lost in problems rather than solutions.
Structured workshops and interviews	• Multiple reviews of risks. • Quality of identified risks is higher.	• Time and resource intensive. • Loss of interest and participation in subsequent reviews.
Delphi technique	• Anonymity of risk identification. • Individual views are gathered.	• Misunderstanding of risks. • Biases in risk register due to misinterpretation.
Reviewing Previous Projects and gathering insights	• Lessons learnt from past. • Able to gauge the efficiency of risk responses.	• Restrictive solutions as tried and tested methods will be preferred. • Differences in risk setting of past vs present could be easily overlooked.
SWOT analysis	• Identification of strengths, weaknesses, threats, and opportunities. • Handling of positive and negative risks.	• Categorization could be biased. • There is a risk of diverting focus from serious negative project risks.
Assumptions review	• Uncovering the validity of assumptions. • Increases understanding of gaps.	• Tedious and impossible to eliminate or uncover assumptions. • Remedies for assumptions could go out of context as project phases change.

3.9. *Internal and external considerations*

Thorough reviews will help uncover assumptions and underlying known risks early on in a project. This will allow sufficient planning and consideration of multiple mitigation options. As emergent risks surface throughout the different stages of the project, risk identification is best handled as an iterative process. Unknown risks could be from both the internal and external environments. Internal considerations like project governance, resources, slippages, change in direction, and resistance are commonly identified risks. External considerations include market economy, organizational changes, and social and legal implications. Both internal and external factors have the potential to derail projects. Thus, it is important to establish an iterative risk identification and documentation process into the project which must consider both external and internal factors and must be regularly reviewed and aligned.

4. Analyze risks

Risk identification is followed by assessment and analysis to understand the likelihood of the risk's occurrence and its potential impact. The main goal of risk analysis is to increase clarity on project risks, plan for suitable responses or mitigation, make informed decisions, and overall improved risk management. Risks are rampant not only within projects but also across portfolios, and their impact could be felt in different levels. Hence, risk analysis must consider all the levels that the potential risks could impact.

4.1. *Project risk*

Risk assessment of projects is a meticulous and continuous process. The steps involved in risk assessment are listed in Figure 4.

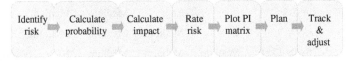

Figure 4.   Risk assessment steps.

Once the risk is identified and documented in the risk register, the next step is to calculate the occurrence or probability of the risk. Categorized based on "low", "medium", and "high", the probability for each risk at that point in time, given the available information, is documented. The same process is followed for the impact, or the potential damage of each risk is established and documented as well. The next step is to rate both probability and impact. The probability scale ranges from "rare" to "most likely", whereas the impact scale ranges from "trivial" to "extreme". The next step involves plotting the risks into a Probability-Impact (PI) matrix. The PI matrix for smaller projects is usually a 3 × 3 matrix, while larger projects and programs tend to use a 5 × 5 matrix or a more granular scale. Table 2 is a 5 × 5 PI matrix.

The PI matrix can be further quantified by assigning numeric values to the risks based on the PI scale. On the probability front, the value starts at 1 for 'rare' and scales up to 5 for 'most likely'. Similarly, the values start at 1 and scale up to 5 for impact as well. The formula for calculating PI value is as follows:

$$\text{PI value} = \text{Probability} * \text{Impact}.$$

The higher the PI value, the greater the risk. An example of PI quantification is given in Table 3 and a complete risk register with PI values is given in Table 4.

4.2. *Portfolio risk*

Project portfolio selection and management can be directly related to strategy (Archer and Ghasemzadeh, 2007). Project portfolios comprise

Table 2. Probability-Impact (PI) matrix.

Probability-Impact matrix		Trivial	Minor	Impact medium	Major	Extreme
Probability	Rare	Low	Low	Low	Medium	Medium
	Unlikely	Low	Low	Medium	Medium	Medium
	Likely	Low	Medium	Medium	Medium	High
	Highly likely	Medium	Medium	Medium	High	High
	Most likely	Medium	Medium	High	High	High

Table 3. Probability-Impact (PI) matrix example.

Probability–Impact matrix		Impact				
		Trivial 0%–19% **(1)**	**Minor** 20%–39% **(2)**	**Medium** 40%–59% **(3)**	**Major** 60%–79% **(4)**	**Extreme** >80% **(5)**
Probability	Rare 0%–19% (1)	Low (1)	Low (2)	Low (3)	Medium (4)	Medium (5)
	Unlikely 20%–39% (2)	Low (2)	Low (4)	Medium (6)	Medium (8)	Medium (10)
	Likely 40%–59% (3)	Low (3)	Medium (6)	Medium (9)	Medium (12)	High (15)
	Highly likely 60%–79% (4)	Medium (4)	Medium (8)	Medium (12)	High (16)	High (20)
	Most likely >80% (5)	Medium (5)	Medium (10)	High (15)	High (20)	High (25)

Table 4. Sample IT project risk register adapted with PI values.

Risk ID	Risk name	Risk owner	Probability	Impact	Risk level (PI category)	Risk score (PI score)
R01	Vulnerabilities from legacy systems	Simon	Highly likely	Major	High	16
R02	Technical incompatibilities	John	Likely	Extreme	High	15
R03	Application testing issues	Teresa	Unlikely	Major	Medium	8
R04	Hardware delivery delays	Mary	Likely	Major	Medium	9

projects and programs. Programs are usually defined as being composed of projects with similar goals, drawing from the same resource pool, and managed together to deliver a "specific package of benefits", such that each project is a portion of a larger program implementation (Maylor *et al.*, 2006). Thus, performance issues in one project can affect all other dependent projects. Organizational strategy and project portfolio selection are related (Lampel and Pushkar, 2007). Quantitative analysis of project portfolio can be based on quantitative inputs such as NPV (Net Present Value) for each project. However, the interrelationship of IT projects with strategy and their potential impact on operations make their impact, and consequently risk, difficult to quantify. In some of the project failures that were recounted earlier, the impact of IT project risk on the wider organization or even broader regional economies was completely unforeseen.

4.3. *Risk analysis shortfalls*

The effectiveness of standard or normative risk analysis procedures has been criticized. In practice, as stated by Kutsch, Browning, and Hall (2014), these procedures are 'focused on the familiar, the measurable, the favorable, the noncommittal, and the controllable while excluding other risks that significantly affected their project performance.' For instance, PI ratings are the most widely used approach for risk assessment in several project-based industries such as the construction industry (Dikmen *et al.*, 2018). However, in practice, probability assessment in IT projects is highly subjective, emphasizes familiar risks, and discounts or excludes those that are difficult to measure (Kutsch *et al.*, 2014). Indeed, this is a common issue across industries, as seen in the discussion on the subjectiveness and bias in risk ratings in the context of the construction industry by Dikmen *et al.* (2018). Even techniques that seem conducive to overcoming these biases such as Brainstorming or the Delphi Technique discussed earlier, which seem conducive to risk exploration, are subject to biases and principal–agent issues. This brings into focus the biases that are present in risk analysis and management and emphasizes the role of prior project track records in analyzing project risks.

4.4. *Planning for emergent risk, correcting forecasting biases*

Optimism bias and underestimation are endemic to IT project estimation (McConnell, 2006). This and the principal–agent problem are a chronic prevalent issue across all project classes, and RCF is a method that has been developed to debias estimates using track records (Flyvbjerg, 2006; Flyvbjerg *et al.*, 2018). Principal–agent issues cause cost and schedule underestimation both within organizations and across contractual boundaries because of the incentives to get projects or contracts approved (Flyvbjerg, B., 2006). Optimism biases in expert project estimation (Natarajan, 2022) based on the demonstrated by the work of Kahneman and Tversky are well understood (Kahneman, 2012; Lovallo and Kahneman, 2003). RCF corrects forecasts that are underestimated due to optimism bias and principal–agent issues (Flyvbjerg, 2006). RCF uses uplifts on within-project estimated costs or schedules using "outside view" track record of similar projects. These comparable projects constitute the reference class. It has been shown that RCF performs better than traditional EVM and Monte Carlo methods (Batselier and Vanhoucke, 2016). A methodology to extend RCF using Machine Learning (ML) to provide project specific forecasts has been demonstrated by Natarajan (2021).

5. Develop risk responses

Risk response development occurs during the project planning phase and is a follow-on to the risk identification and assessment processes described earlier. Risk Response is informed by metrics such as risk ranking and PI matrices and follow the approaches of avoiding, managing, transferring, or mitigating risks. The response phase is subject to the biggest breakdowns in the risk management process (Moeini and Rivard, 2019). A detailed analysis of IT projects identified that about 28% of identified and assessed risks were not actively managed, showing the presence of positivity/optimism biases and principal–agent issues from project management (Kutsch *et al.*, 2014). Additionally, the sense of inadequate empowerment felt by many of the project managers who participated in this study made this merely a checklist or an administrative exercise.

5.1. *Common approaches*

The first response to identified risks in the planning phase is avoiding them by planning or redesigning the project. Risks that cannot be avoided are mitigated by reducing their impact, probability, or both. Risks can also be transferred to other parties that are better at managing them. After all these measures have been adopted, the remaining risks are accepted. Risk response plans are delineated for the remaining risks and for unknown risks that may emerge during project execution.

Developing and implementing a risk response plan increases the chances of project success by not only identifying risk owners and holding them responsible but by also identifying the appropriate response to each risk. The risk management plan is often incorporated into the risk register rather than being considered as additional project documentation. Strategies for handling different types of risks can also be included in a risk response plan. Such consolidation is preferred in smaller projects; however, for major programs and larger projects, it is ideal to have specific documentation for risk strategies, plans, processes, etc. An example of a risk response plan is given in Table 5.

5.2. *Risk appetite*

In the banking industry, the risk appetite framework is a prominent practice. This involves the establishment of processes and regulations to define the level of risks they will be taking in their next ventures. Risk tolerance is more common in IT projects. In IT, systems tend to fail; this is a risk that projects cannot eliminate and are willing to tolerate on certain grounds. Thus, they establish risk tolerance in the form of agreed service levels, planned downtimes, business continuity processes, Recovery Point Objective (RPO), and Recovery Time Objective (RTO) as common practice. Defining and clearly establishing these factors is important in not only managing expectations but also in identifying the responses wherever necessary.

6. Monitor and control risks

A system of check and balance is needed to monitor and control risks effectively. This system is a mix of right direction, processes, people, practices, mindset, and support from the project. Though issues and risks

Table 5. Sample risk response plan.

Risk ID	Risk name	Risk owner	Response type	Risk Response action	Response Trigger event	Contingency plan
R01	Vulnerabilities from legacy systems	Simon	Avoid	Proactive patching on weekly/ monthly schedules	When high or critical vulnerabilities are identified	Document and immediately fix threats which miss proactive efforts
R02	Technical incompatibilities	John	Mitigate	Change control and reviews	Interface issues or breakdowns	Troubleshoot with internal team, seek external vendor help as needed
R03	Application testing issues	Teresa	Transfer	Continuous testing with dedicated testing force and increase user feedback	Issues that are not fixed for more than 2 release cycles	Additional part-time testers
R04	Hardware delivery delays	Mary	Accept	Adjust schedule after thorough understanding and agreement from stakeholders	Confirmed delivery delays from vendors	New orders to be placed

are well identified through extensive reviews and strategized to manage them, it is common to see risks blowing up projects out of their tracks. Regular identification of risks, effective tracking of risk registers, and risk response planning and execution help in managing and controlling risks.

Risk response becomes especially important during project execution when unknown risks and risks with unknown impacts begin to emerge. During execution, timely identification of emerging risks and effective response is important. While this is aided by response plans developed during planning and monitoring/control processes, leadership, transparency, and communication are critical. Some of the other effective practices to make the process easier are discussed as follows.

6.1. *Transparency in risk management*

A culture of open communication encourages timely and efficient identification of risks. To promote a culture of open communication, project teams must facilitate simple processes to identify and report risks, which must be accessible across all levels of the project. Hierarchical or functional boundaries must not be a hindrance in flagging risks. As emergent or unknown unknowns are a real threat to any project and are not possible to identify or predict proactively, such an open culture would empower project managers in identifying and managing risks at the earliest. The risk register and review of potential risks must be a standard agenda in daily or regular project meetings. Risk mitigation options must be evaluated periodically and any changes in the plans or strategy should be communicated across the project organization.

6.2. *Response and mitigation options and practice*

In IT project management, risk controls are broadly classified into two areas and handled differently: technical and non-technical. Technical risks include threats affecting the technological environment, the data layer, security, and outages, to name a few. Non-technical risks include business process continuity, resourcing, cost and schedule slippages, quality issues, changing requirements, and outsourcing issues, to name a few.

Extensive technical controls for change, maintenance, testing, security, process flow, architectural dependencies, auditing, and governance are considered and included. However, with hindsight, they often uncover that greater importance is given to technical risks. Though non-technical risks are identified, their probability and impact are often underestimated or overlooked. This is also a reason why IT projects suffer from massive failures arising from risks which were not handled appropriately. Equal consideration, deliberation, and thorough analysis of non-technical risks and appropriate mitigation options will ensure that this gap is addressed. RCF for accurate estimation, legal emphasis of contractual terms, and clear and fixed requirements are some proven methods to control IT risks.

6.3. *Change management*

Most change initiatives fail; effective change management involves close engagement and monitoring of the process. The reasons for such rampant change failures range from change resistance to ambiguity to unmanaged expectations to changes in requirements. These same factors heavily influence the plans to monitor and control risks. Some risk mitigation measures in projects are met with severe resistance, for example, eliminating legacy systems to avoid potential incompatibility risks or additional investments to expedite testing. Approaching this process through the lens of change management is an effective way to manage resistance to implement risk mitigation measures.

7. Risk governance

The increasing implementation of organizational objectives through projects causes them to be increasingly related to overall organization performance (Fink, 2016). This emphasizes a holistic project governance approach at the organizational capability level which encompasses continuous project identification, assessment, and portfolio management (Fink, 2016; Standish, 2021). Projectization of business activities is causing a paradigm shift in project portfolio management. Traditional positivist or bureaucratic project management, which typically employs well-defined tools and techniques from a positivist viewpoint, is being replaced with less bureaucratic, flexible project-oriented structures (Fink, 2016). The continuous process of software development and its intermeshing into business activities with continuous feedback and inputs are reflected in the emphasis on the Flow process which emphasizes a service-oriented method to reduce friction from traditional projectized software development (Standish, 2021).

Project risk governance is composed of formal mechanisms, structures, as well as relationships and individual expertise. These are interrelated as the mechanisms and structures can play a key role facilitating the cultivation and exercise of relationships and expertise. Project risk governance must be structured so that the interplay between these is symbiotic in nature (Moeini and Rivard, 2019). Appropriate project management methodology selection is important; the 2019 Standish Chaos report mentions significantly higher rates for Agile methods (Standish, 2019). The interconnectedness between IT projects and business capability, as well as the potential for mismatch between IT project scope and evolving business needs, which we had discussed earlier, further emphasizes a risk governance approach.

7.1. *Strategic and portfolio-level considerations*

The project fit to an organizations project portfolio is related to strategic considerations. As stated by Fink, in his book on Project Risk Governance, effective management of the project portfolio and the close alignment of individual project objectives with business strategy are essential to successful outcomes (Fink, 2016). Thus, risk management is related to the project portfolio and organizational strategy, highlighting the need for a holistic approach outlined here. Figure 3 illustrates a high-level flow of activities in the project selection phase which leads to project selection after considering its fit to the project portfolio. Company mission and vision statements are usually articulated for longer multi-year time periods, and strategy planning is typically an annual exercise. The strategy planning exercise informs the identification of goals and opportunities which lead to project identification. Identified projects compete for limited budgets for inclusion in the portfolio. It is useful to view this as an evolutionary exercise in selection where the most fit projects have a better chance of getting included. While project selection often evaluates quantified schedule, budget, and projected benefits, it is helpful to have a project development team to develop a formal business case that holistically evaluates the broader benefits, risks, and strategic fit for executive management. Fink, in his book on Project Risk Governance, discusses how a detailed business case must discuss risks to delivery (cost, schedule) and benefits (value, on-goal, and satisfaction) (Fink, 2016). The business case encapsulates the rationale and costs for the project for the approval process with the participation of senior management. It also serves as a reference for the project manager and team post approval.

7.2. *Taking the right risks*

A project governance approach emphasizes alignment between organizational structures and projects, and between business strategy and projects. The strategic aspect and operational impact of IT projects mean that decisions on taking the right risks begin during the project selection phase with the active participation of executive leadership. Senior Executives should be involved in risk identification and planning processes for projects, programs, and portfolios. Project managers may be more sensitive to project delivery risks while severe outcomes from project failure are often enterprise-wide beyond an individual project. Support and buy-in from senior management signify acceptance of risk and empower the project team. This support fosters beneficial interplay with normative risk management methods employed by project managers and their team, which is important for risk management and project success. Identification and decisions on in-project risks, the "back end" of project risk governance, are best managed by an empowered project team with the appropriate project management leadership as discussed above.

7.3. *Risk governance approaches*

Top management support may be the single biggest factor in IT project success (Young and Jordan, 2008). This is related to the project governance approach where project selection is aligned with organizational strategy as well as the importance of support to individual projects and empowerment of individual project management teams for risk management. The responsibility of senior organizational executives toward project selection and sponsorship is an important incentive for them to be vested in its success by supporting and empowering the project team during the planning and execution phases. Appropriate project management methodology selection is important; the 2019 Standish CHAOS report identifies significantly higher rates for Agile methods (Standish, 2019).

7.4. *Risk governance approaches*

A risk governance approach holistically emphasizes roles both within a project and in the broader organization. A project is a temporary organization that draws on the wider organization for resources (Sydow and Braun, 2018). Furthermore, the project organization is often cross-organizational; it may include several independent entities with contractual relationships, sometimes referred to as a 'metaorganization' (Gulati *et al.*, 2012). In this context, senior executives in organizations are crucial for project sponsorship, and for provisioning project resources especially when required by emergent situations that approach as crises and require engagement with other organizations. Project-specific expertise with the project manager is seen as one of the most important factors for effective risk management (Moeini and Rivard, 2019). This makes the project manager a critical role, and the selection of an appropriate project manager and project management team is an important criterion for successful risk management. Because of the correlation of principal–agent problems with the risk of project performance shortfalls, key responsibilities with both executive and project leadership involve interfacing and maintaining relationships across organizational or contractual boundaries.

8. Success strategies and best practices in managing IT risks

This section discusses some success strategies and best practices for IT risk management that are not specifically covered in the preceding sections.

8.1. *Leadership*

It is pertinent to note the well-known maxim, attributed to the famous Prussian Field Marshal Helmuth von Moltke, paraphrased as "no plan survives first contact with the enemy" (Barnett, 1963). In the project risk context, this can be paraphrased as "no plan survives intact during project execution post project approval". Emergent outcomes emphasize the role of project management expertise and leadership. Experiential knowledge, which is centered on the development of project-specific experience-based knowledge by IT project managers, is seen to have many advantages over normative formal risk assessment by several researchers (Moeini and Rivard, 2019). Prof. Flyvbjerg, an international expert on complex megaprojects, has discussed the importance of project managers who possess a consistent track record of project success, or 'master builders', for successful project delivery (MacNicol, 2016). This makes leadership development and empowerment an important risk governance strategy. Uncertainty and emergence emphasize the ability to recognize issues and mobilize a coherent response to them. Managerial processes are typically control-based, while complex projects necessitate empowering the team, which calls for leadership (Kotter, 1990). Advances in the techniques and measurement of leadership development are important tools for the inculcation of project leadership ability within an organization (Day *et al.*, 2014).

8.2. *Assessing the impact of IT project risk*

Given that the impact of benefit shortfalls from an IT project can cause disproportionately large business impacts, a structured process for identifying causes and impacts is beneficial. As noted earlier, IT project risks can be significantly greater than planned benefits due to their embedment into strategy operations and critical infrastructure. Business risks from product deployment, including effects from transition, potential disruption from transition, emergent issues from the software, and interaction with other business systems, must be managed. High-profile events that have caused the hijacking or destruction of physical infrastructure due to cyber-attacks have underscored software-based vulnerability of critical infrastructure (Shear *et al.*, 2021; Langner, 2011). Furthermore, IT-created products can interact with other emergent situations and result in severe undesirable outcomes without requiring malicious actors. Examples of outsized effects from IT project failures can be found in Enterprise Resource Planning (ERP) implementation projects. ERP implementation constitutes one of the largest classes of investment in IT projects and shows a high failure rate. Failure can jeopardize the core operations of organizations (Huang *et al.*, 2004).

Risk identification and quantification practices related to EPC projects, especially in process and offshore industries, offer learnings for assessing these broader potentially very-high-impact risks. EPC refers to a type of contract used widely in construction projects ranging from infrastructure to refineries. These are often turnkey contracts that encompass design engineering, construction, installation, and commissioning for multi-billion-dollar projects whose delivery and operation are subject to highly consequential risk. EPC projects are complex and are exposed to a wide variety of risks, some of which can result in extreme outcomes, on cost, time, and benefits, leading to project delivery and performance risk post-delivery that could result in catastrophic consequences to people, the environment, and the involved companies.

Risk review and quantification in the process and offshore industries are undertaken using comprehensive, lengthy, painstaking, and detailed exercises conducted by professional third parties and involving all contractors in a spirit of cooperation. Hazard Identification Study (HAZID) is a systematic methodology used in the process and offshore industries for hazard identification by breaking projects into components using detailed analysis. Hazards are related to possible events that result in injury, damage, production losses, or liabilities. Hazard and Operability Study (HAZOP) is a quantitative approach that follows the HAZID at a more mature stage of the project involving multi-disciplinary teams who analyze individual elements of the project design in detail to quantify probabilities of undesirable outcomes. These approaches can be extended to IT projects to identify risks to value, goal achievement, and satisfaction as well as risks to critical business operations.

8.3. *Considerations in project selection*

The right projects are aligned with organizational strategy and business goals and are driven by specific plans toward achieving these goals. In many cases, even the right projects come with big risks which may not be avoidable. However, some of the following considerations help in selecting IT projects whose risks are identifiable and manageable. The first consideration is to make informed decisions following thorough technical and functional assessments. When sufficient time is not spent on critical areas like technical feasibility, functional roadblocks, underlying risks, total cost of operations, and stakeholder sentiments, the impact will be felt too late and may result in failures and delays. The second consideration is that investing in mature technology comes with better costs, advanced support systems, and greater scalability. Though IT projects are driven by a thirst for innovation, being the latest and the best, it is important to take cautious steps with immature technologies. It is to be noted that IT transformation projects that implement mature applications have a higher rate of success as they experience lesser risks in terms of incompatibilities and delays. The third and the most important criterion is consideration in areas like security, privacy, legal, ethical, and social concerns. IT projects suffer from emergent risks in these areas, and hence sufficient consideration must be made in non-technical factors like technological factors.

8.4. *Success approaches and recommendations*

Kutsch, Browning, and Hall, and Mark, state that about 44% of knowable risks in the IT projects they studied were not actively managed (2014). The tension between normative and experiential risk management and ways of making this relationship more symbiotic were discussed in detail in the previous sections. The following approaches for success are recommended to better identify and manage risks:

- Senior Management support and buy-in are the most crucial elements in strengthening projects, which give them additional organizational immunity.
- Scenario-planning exercises help with identifying risks beyond the familiar ones by taking the focus away from individual risks to generating mechanisms and impact (Kutsch *et al.*, 2014).
- Empower project managers to be proactive in risk identification and planning response.
- Institute risk response planning in projects and at portfolio levels.

- Ensure everyone understands the objective of Risk Response Planning, Workshops, Brainstorming, etc.
- Encourage open airing of intuitively identified risks, conduct workshops in a conducive atmosphere that stimulates thinking beyond the familiar, and foster a sense of purposefulness to risk identification, assessment, and response workshops.
- Start identifying project risks as early as possible.
- Get key stakeholders involved in planning.
- Assign risk response actions to risk owners.
- Discuss risks in daily meetings and ensure risks are reviewed, monitored, and controlled on a daily basis.
- Document risks, responses, and status.
- Ensure even in the most agile environment that project risks and the planned responses are documented.

These approaches are beneficial for projects beyond the context in which they are undertaken, and will positively influence the perception of these projects, their leaders, and the members.

9. Summary

The risk management approach that has been discussed employs methods and techniques contingent on the project phase and type, and on the broader organizational context. The prevalence of extreme undesirable performance outliers in IT projects and the potentially outsized nature of IT project risk were discussed. The nature of risk, risk measurement methods, and project phases was outlined; popularly used risk identification and analysis methods in IT projects were elaborated within those frameworks. Processes inspired by practices in other industries that can be employed to identify and quantify broader high-impact risks that can result from IT project deployment issues were reviewed.

The employment of normative and experiential methods along project phases as discussed here is related to the broader debate on the balance between expert inputs versus biases discussed earlier. Looking toward the future, it is also related to the balance between machine learning and expert inputs, which is discussed in the project forecasting context in Natarajan (2022). The balance between different risk management methods, project management expertise, and upcoming AI/ML tools is a dynamic contextually predicated relationship dependent on project type and phase. The relationship between normative and experiential risk management is also related to project governance. The increasing importance of projects to organizational strategy and operations leads us to recommend a project governance approach where organizational risk management encompasses project risk management. Organizational project governance structures and relationships, which emphasize normative risk management, should be designed for a symbiotic relationship with projects and project management, which emphasize experiential risk management.

References

Archer, N. and Ghasemzadeh, F. (2007). Project portfolio selection and management, in Morries, P. and Pinto, J. (eds.) *The Wiley Guide to Project, Program and Portfolio Management,* Hoboken: Wiley (pp. 94–110).

Barnett, C. (1963). *The Swordbearers: Studies in Supreme Command in the First World War,* London: Eyre & Spottiswoode.

Batselier, J. and Vanhoucke, M. (2016). Practical application and empirical evaluation of reference class forecasting for project management, *Proj. Manage. J.,* 47(5), 36–51.

Budzier, A. and Flyvbjerg, B. (2013). *Making-Sense of the Impact and Importance of Outliers in Project Management through the Use of Power Laws,* Oslo: International Research Network on Organizing by Projects.

Chan, S. (2001). Complex Adaptive Systems. [Online]. Available at: http://web.mit.edu/esd.83/www/notebook/Complex%20Adaptive%20Systems.pdf. (Accessed 28 December 2018).

Chang, A., Hatcher, C. and Kim, J. (2013). Temporal boundary objects in megaprojects: Mapping the system with the Integrated Master Schedule, *Int. J. Proj. Manage.,* 31(3), 323–332.

Day, D. V., Fleenor, J. W., Atwater, L. E., Sturm, R. E. and McKee, R. A. (2014). Advances in leader and leadership development: A review of 25 years of research and theory, *Leadersh. Q.,* 25(1), 63–82.

Dikmen, I., Budayam, C., Birgonul, M. T. and Hayat, E. (2018). Effects of risk attitude and controllability assumption on risk ratings: observational study on international construction project risk assessment, *J. Manage. Eng.*, 34(6), 04018037.

Ehley, B. (2013). Another failed gov't tech project cost $1.1 Billion, *The Fiscal Times*.

Ellinas, C., Allan, N. and Johansson, A. (2018). Toward project complexity evaluation: A structural perspective, *IEEE Syst. J.*, 12(1), 228–239.

Fink, D. (2016). *Project Risk Governance: Managing Uncertainty and Creating Organisational Value*, New York: Routledge.

Flyvbjerg, B. (2006). From nobel prize to project management: Getting risks right, *Proj. Manage. J.*, 37(3), 5–15.

Flyvbjerg, B. and Budzier, A. (2011). Why your IT project might be riskier than you think, *Harvard Bus. Rev.*, 89(9), 23–25.

Flyvbjerg, B., Ansar, A., Budzier, A., Buhl, S., Cantarelli, C., Garbuio, M., Glenting, C., Skarmis, M. S., Lovallo, D., Lunn, D., Molin, E., Rønnesti, A., Stewart, A. and Wee, B. V. (2018). Five things you should know about cost overrun, *Transp. Res. Part A*, 118, 174–190.

Gulati, R., Puranam, P. and Tushman, M. L. (2012). Meta-organization design: Rethinking design in interorganizational and community contexts, *Strategic Manage. J.*, 33(6), 571–586.

Hitchins, D. K. (2007). *Systems Engineering: A 21st Century Systems Methodology*, Chichester: Wiley.

Huang, S., Chang, I. and Lin, M. (2004). Assessing risk in ERP projects: Identify and prioritize the factors, *Ind. Manage. Data Syst.*, 104(8), 681–688.

Hubbard, D. (2009). *The Failure of Risk Management: Why It's Broken and How to Fix It*, Hoboken: Wiley.

Kahneman, D. (2012). *Thinking, Fast and Slow*, Penguin. London, UK.

Klein, G. A. (1993). A recognition-primed decision (RPD) model of rapid decision making, in Klein, G. A., Orasanu, J., Calderwood, R. and Zsambok, C. E. (eds.) *Decision Making in Action: Models and Methods*, New York: Ablex Publishing (pp. 138–147).

Kotter, J. (1990). What leaders really do, *Harvard Bus. Rev.*, 90(3), 103–111.

KPMG. (2019). The Future of Project Management: Global Outlook 2019, KPMG, AIPM, IPMA.

Kutsch, E., Browning, T. and Hall, M. A. (2014). Bridging the risk gap: The failure of risk management in information systems projects, *Res. Technol. Manage.*, 57(2), 26–32.

Lampel, J. and Pushkar, P. (2007). Models of project orientation in multi-project organizations, in Morris, P. W. G. and Pinto, J. K. (eds.) *The Wiley Guide to Project Program & Portfolio Management*, New Jersey: John Wiley & Sons Inc.

Langner, R. (2011). Stuxnet: Dissecting a cyberwarfare weapon, *IEEE Secur. Privacy*, 9(3), 49–51.

Lovallo, D. and Kahneman, D. (2003). Delusions of success: How optimism undermines executives' decisions, *Harvard Bus. Rev.*, 56–63. Vol.81(7).

MacNicol, D. (2016). Taking the lead, *Constr. J.*, 1(1), 16–18.

Maylor, H., Brady, T., Cooke-Davies, T. and Hodgson, D. (2006). From projectification to programmification, *Int. J. Proj. Manage.*, 24(8), 663–674.

Maylor, H. R., Turner, N. W. and Murray-Webster, R. (2013). How hard can it be? Actively managing the complexity of technology projects, *Res. Technol. Manage.*, 56(4), 45–51.

McConnell, S. (2006). *Software Estimation: Demystifying the Black Art*, Boston: Addison-Wesley Professional.

Moeini, M. and Rivard, S. (2019). Sublating tensions in the IT project risk management literature: A model of the relative performance of intuition and deliberate analysis for risk assessment, *J. Assoc. Inf. Syst.*, 20. 243–284.

Natarajan, A. (2022). Reference class forecasting and machine learning for improved offshore oil & gas megaproject planning: Methods and application, *Proj. Manage. J.* 53(5), 456–484.

PMI. (2019). *Pulse of the Profession 2019*, Project Management Institute. Newton Square, Pa.

Shear, M. D., Perlroth, N. and Krauss, C. (2021). Colonial Pipeline Paid Roughly $5 Million in Ransom to Hackers, *The New York Times*.

Standish. (2016). *Special CHAOS Report on Digital Transformation Project*, Boston: The Standish Group International, Inc.

Standish. (2019). *The Standish Chaos Report 2019*, Boston: The Standish Group International, Inc.

Standish. (2021). *Infinite Flow*, Boston: The Standish Group International, Inc.

Sydow, J. and Braun, T. (2018). Projects as temporary organizations: An agenda for further theorizing the interorganizational dimension, *Int. J. Proj. Manage.*, 36(1), 4–11.

Taleb, N. (2008). *The Black Swan: The Impact of the Highly Improbable*, Penguin. New York, United States.

Todd, P. M. and Gigerenzer, G. (2000). Précis of simple heuristics that make us smart, *Behav. Brain Sci.*, 23(1), 727–780.

van Donk, D. P. and Molloy, E. (2008). From organizing as projects to projects as organizations, *Int. J. Proj. Manage.*, 26, 129–137.

Whyte, J. (2016). The future of systems integration within civil infrastructure: A review and directions for research, *INCOSE Int. Symp.*, 26(1), 1541–1555.

Young, R. and Jordan, E. (2008). Top management support: Mantra or necessity? *Int. J. Proj. Manage.*, 26(7), 713–725.

Chapter 12

Successfully Delivering Large IT Projects: A Multi-Case Study-Based Analysis

*Indrajit Wijegunaratne and †Kolitha Dassanayake

*(Hons) (Essex), MSc, PhD (London)
Advisor, Blockchain Australia
injiwije@gmail.com
†*DXC Technology. Melbourne, Australia.*
kolithad@gmail.com

Chapters 12 and 13 together comprise an analysis of critical factors that influence the success or failure of large IT projects. A case study-based analysis is undertaken in Chapter 12, and in Chapter 13, these factors are compared and contrasted with construction.

Evidence shows that often large IT projects do not succeed, exceeding their budgets and timelines, and delivering abbreviated scope and value.

The analysis begins by discussing the defining features of a 'large IT project'. Then, through a series of case studies, factors that influence their level of success are initially identified and refined further.

It is recognized that though considerable effort goes into defining the desired 'target state' of a large IT project, typically the capabilities needed to deliver that change are relatively ill defined. Using the techniques of business capability mapping, a reference capability map for large IT projects is constructed and a framework to analyze and identify the required change capabilities is developed.

1. Introduction

Large transformation programs have often failed — either failed to deliver on their original scope, exceeded their budgets and/or timelines, or in many instances failed both. A research study in 2012 of more than 5,400 IT projects by the consulting firm McKinsey and the BT Centre for Major Programme Management at the University of Oxford (Bloch *et al.*, 2012) found that half of all large IT projects (defined as those with an initial budget in excess of $15 million) significantly exceeded their budgets; on average, these projects ran 45% over budget and delivered 56% less value than originally scoped. These IT projects had a combined cost overrun of a massive $66 billion. Sometimes, large IT projects perform so badly that they threatened the very existence of the company: 17% of large IT projects examined (with cost overruns of more than 200%) fell into this category. In Australia, The AGE, a leading newspaper, published a report by the Ombudsman for the State of Victoria on the performance of ten large IT programs in the public sector (Sexton, 2011). This report found that the combined cost of delivering them was AU$1.44 billion more than originally budgeted. A more recent article (Kitani, 2019) states that several very large US companies poured $1.3 trillion into transformation initiatives, of which $900 billion was wasted on failed programs. Sutcliff *et al.* (2019) state that a global survey of 1,350 executives revealed that these businesses spent over $100 billion on digital transformations between 2016 and 2018, but the expected results did not materialize.

Popular Business and IT media publications often prescribe cause and remedy, for instance, unspoken disagreement among top managers about goals, discrepancy between the pilot and scaling it (Sutcliff *et al.*, 2019), lack of focus on the value proposition, communication issues, and not using data to measure and iterate (Kitani, 2019); in a similar vein, McKinsey and Company (2019) propose ten reasons for the failure of large transformations.

Evidence of failure is compelling and accords with observations from the authors' experience. Proposed remedies are usually point prescriptions — 'do X, Y Z for success' — offered without much evidence or reasoning. This chapter takes another approach. Starting with anonymized case studies from the authors' experience, an analysis is conducted on critical factors for success in large transformation programs. A framework is then developed for program planners to identify the capabilities needed to successfully deliver their specific program.

2. Background

It is instructive to pause, clarify, and define the terminology before proceeding further. The subject of analysis of this chapter involves large, complex exercises containing several dependent and interrelated projects collectively aimed at delivering a major business outcome. In the IT industry, this type of endeavor is commonly referred to interchangeably by the labels 'large IT project', 'IT program', 'business transformation program', or 'transformation program', and this terminology is employed in this chapter. Moreover, this chapter's case studies scrutinize this type of large program containing multiple projects, and accordingly this has been referred to as program and program management in the text.

Why large? Why not average sized or small? As described in the foregoing text, there is strong evidence that large IT programs often fail to deliver on their original promise. Moreover, it is evident that the failure of large IT programs has the potential to inflict serious damage to the enterprise. As a practical matter, therefore, an analysis of success factors for large projects holds the promise of most benefit. Hence, the focus of this chapter is directed at large IT programs.

2.1. *What is a large transformation program?*

A definition such as 'number of dependent projects, which, once completed, will change the way that the systems of the enterprise and/or internal and external stakeholders interact with each other in the operation of the businesses' serves as a start.

Unpacking this a little further, notice three axes of complexity:

a. Size and complexity of business transformation — complexity of change to the business model and/or operating model of the enterprise.

b. Size and complexity of the business systems change — complexity of the business rules and functionality, business processes, reporting, etc.

c. Size and complexity of technology change — change to IT systems, integration, and infrastructure.

Usually, these axes are related to each other. For example, a complex business transformation entails complex changes to functionality, rules, and processes of affected business systems, and potentially changes to the underlying IT infrastructure. Equally, there are cases where only a single axis is impacted; for example, a complex network and security infrastructure program where neither the business model nor systems are changed, or suppliers for a milk processing plant change from 'standard' to organic suppliers to reposition the company, altering the business model but not much else.

Additionally, a couple of universal defining characteristics exist:

d. The program comprises multiple individual projects with dependencies and precedence relationships, which need to be managed in concert as a dependent whole.

"Largeness" is a relative measure. A large bank or telco with an annual IT budget of $400 million has a completely different notion of 'largeness' of a program from say a transport/ logistics company with an annual IT budget of $25 million. Accordingly, the final defining characteristic may be expressed as follows:

e. The relative size/ cost of the program compared to their norm.

Therefore, a large complex program will exhibit complexity along one or more of the axes (a), (b), and (c) and conform to (d) and (e). The abbreviated term 'program' is used synonymously in this chapter to refer to programs of this type.

2.2. *Measures of success/failure*

Examining the literature (Bloch, 2012; Sexton, 2011; Sutcliff *et al.*, 2019; Morgan, 2019), these measures of success/failure can be distilled: scope, schedule, budget, quality, and business goals.

Of these, the following may be evaluated and determined as the program progresses, and a final evaluation done at delivery:

a. Was the program completed within the stipulated time?
b. Was the program completed within budget?
c. Did the program deliver the intended business functionality and/or business changes?

The following are measurable in the operation of the transformed enterprise:

d. Does the program deliver the promised value, i.e., benefits, to the enterprise?
e. Are the ongoing (i.e., operational) costs and performance of the delivered program acceptable?

As with the earlier definitions, there are nuances here. For example, given a certain scope, a program may be underestimated in terms of time and budget either due to poor estimation or deliberately, for political reasons (acceptability to the Executives, Board, etc.); if the program is underestimated but delivers to a realistic time frame, would that be a failure? Alternatively, as the program unfolds, the business may want variations, which if unresolved may result in the program not being successful in the stakeholders' eyes despite delivering the original scope.

3. Observations

This section presents examples highlighting key factors that predicate the level of success or failure of a program, based on the authors' experience and anonymized to preclude identification.

3.1. *Case study 1*

3.1.1. *Background*

This case study involves an Australian insurance company early in the decade of the 2000s. The company's IT function had been outsourced sometime prior to the events described below, leaving a skeleton permanent staff in the IT unit. A program was conceived to implement a new customer relationship management system. Peoplesoft CRM (since taken over by Oracle) was selected. The functional scope was customer relationship management and reporting/analytics. The key areas were implementing the PeopleSoft package, integrating with the mainframe (the new system replaced the customer-facing part of the existing mainframe system), implementing required mainframe changes, and delivering the required infrastructure.

Responsibilities for the program were farmed out as follows:

- Peoplesoft implementation: Services team from Peoplesoft.
- Mainframe application changes: Outsourced incumbent Systems Integrator (SI) for applications.
- Infrastructure: Outsourced incumbent SI for infrastructure.

Separate fixed price contracts were struck with each SI. However, there was no single point of accountability for delivery, i.e., no prime contractor or at least a prime program director to whom all contractors were contractually obliged to report. There was a nominal Program Director but without contractual teeth.

3.1.2. *Consequences*

Without a strong central authority, the SIs were not acting in concert to deliver the whole solution; rather, they were focused on performing to the letter of their individual contract. Entreaties by the few permanents to look at the whole picture fell on deaf ears. Predictably, the fixed-price contracts ran out with the solution far from complete — unsurprisingly, integration was a major casualty.

In the end, the SI staff were reengaged on a time and materials basis. The skeleton permanent staff drove the project and it fell over the line about a year late and 50% over the original budget.

3.1.3. *Lesson(s)*

The primary outcome sought from a transformation program is the delivery of the entire solution. In a multi-vendor situation, this fact must be operationalized in the contract/s. Obviously, each vendor must undertake their specific responsibility; in addition, they must work cooperatively in areas where responsibilities overlap (i.e., integration, system, and testing) to deliver the outcome and be held jointly responsible for delivery in these areas. Moreover, a single point of authority for the entire program — a Program Manager/Director — is required.

3.2. *Case study 2*

3.2.1. *Background*

This case study involves an Australian insurance company late in the decade of the 2000s. A very ambitious transformation program was conceived, driven by the Chief Information Officer (CIO), with some support by the business. The scope comprised a major upgrade of the existing CRM system and complete refurbishment of the entire back-end operational processing including product development, premium and claims processing, and replacing the entire analytical environment — data warehouses and data marts and requisite changes to the infrastructure.

The CIO, with hardly any consultation with his senior staff, developed a business case with an implementation time frame of two plus years and a concomitant budget, presented it to the Board, and obtained Board approval. This was introduced as a fait accompli to the senior IT staff.

3.2.2. *Consequences*

The program took nearly 10 years to complete. Well within the two-year time frame, it became quite evident that the estimate was inaccurate. The CIO left the company, and the program went through several rounds of stewardship and eventually wound down almost a decade after commencement.

3.2.3. *Lesson(s)*

This case study underlines the value of accurate estimation. The estimated numbers may not be desirable for the business case. A solid estimate must stand as an objective measure and if the cost or the time frame is not acceptable, then the variable to adjust is the scope. Leaving the scope as is and fudging the estimate to produce an attractive business case constitute a recipe for a delayed and slowly unraveling disaster.

3.3. *Case study 3*

3.3.1. *Background*

This case study involves the same enterprise as in case study 2, and the same program, about three years on. A contract Program Director and his handpicked team have been recruited and have assumed responsibility for the program following the CIO's departure.

The program director instituted a regime of daily risk and issue management, meeting collectively with all individual project managers and senior project staff; the meetings taking about two hours each day.

3.3.2. *Consequences*

The vendor responsible for implementing the back-end operational functionality (product, claims and premium processing) was contracted first to customize their product (which was developed for another geography) for Australia, and then further tailor (i.e., configure) the product for this company/ program.

Quite a way into this program director's stewardship, it transpired that one of the main modules that the above vendor was contracted to deliver by customization and configuration did not exist; it existed only on paper, and they were frantically developing it in their home country. Though minute risks by comparison were given a great deal of attention, this 'elephant in the room' did not come to light in the exhaustive risk and issue management meetings. When the news finally emerged, it shocked all concerned and it was far too late to take any meaningful mitigating action. Unsurprisingly, the program director left along with some of his team, and the stewardship of the program changed hands again.

3.3.3. *Lesson(s)*

Risk and issue management: This is a vital instrument of program control. But, it must be done properly. Individual project managers may attempt to game the system — cover up risks and issues in their own project, deflect attention to parallel projects within the program, etc. This behavior is exacerbated in multi-vendor situations, where the PM not only has to protect one's own reputation but also that of the vendor that he or she represents. This was a typical example, where vendor probably hoped that they would remedy the situation by keeping the customer in the dark and buying some time but were unable to do so.

This is very clearly a situation where the program director, absorbed in the minutiae at the level of leaves, failed to see the problem with the forest. The following are ways in which the situation could have been preempted:

- Not to rely solely on the formal reports produced, but also to sound out informal channels (i.e., walk the floor and talk to people at the coalface).
- Senior managers must possess a level of domain/technical knowledge that enables sifting wheat from the chaff.
- At the outset, instituting processes to ensure authenticity, for example, punishments for gaming the system.

Project reporting: Risk and issue reporting is one aspect of the broader activity of program and project reporting. As a general note of caution, it must be noted that there is a general tendency in reporting upward to magnify good news and gloss over bad news. Reports from the coalface get summarized and increasingly sanitized as they go up the hierarchy, especially at the level of the program director, resulting in bland, sterile reports that airbrush away any incipient problems. Reports of this nature are of absolutely no use for steering the program; exceptions matter far more than hitting the norm for navigating the program.

- Set out measurable criteria to assess progress; do not rely on qualitative assessments. For example, colored dashboards are good if they

can be drilled down to measurable foundational quantities, but qualitative assessments summarized pseudo-quantitatively via a dashboard
(e.g., red, amber, green) are next to useless.

- Be aware that program hierarchy often stands in the way of reporting
authenticity. Even in large and complex programs of work, care must
be taken in establishing the program structure: reduce the hierarchy as
much as practicable.

3.4. *Case study 4*

3.4.1. *Background*

Early in the decade of the 2000s, an Australian Telco initiated a major
transformation program to consolidate and decommission a number of
legacy IT systems supporting their operation by introducing three new
enterprise solutions. Their IT function had been outsourced to a number
of managed service providers and the main objective of the program was
to reduce IT operational cost and minimize the usage of a number of systems. The program was spearheaded by a newly appointed CEO and
backed by the board of directors. The key areas were as follows: (a) implement three new systems to cover ERP, CRM, and Billing and to decommission a number of legacy systems, (b) integrate with certain legacy
systems not planned for decommissioning, (c) deliver the infrastructure
for new systems, and (d) build an Enterprise Data Warehouse to support
reporting and analytic requirements.

Responsibilities for the program were farmed out as follows:

- Implementing new infrastructure for all three new systems and a new
infrastructure platform for the Data Warehouse.
- Integrating the existing legacy system with three new systems.
- Building Extraction Transformation and Load processes to source
data from the three new systems and over 100+ legacy applications to
the new Enterprise Data Warehouse.
- Decommissioning a number of existing legacy systems with similar
functionality to the three new systems.

A number of Program/Project Managers were appointed to support different aspects of the program and a number of outsourced vendors were selected to deliver various areas of the program responsibilities. The whole program was to be delivered within two years and a predefined date set for delivery.

3.4.2. *Consequences*

A majority of the outsourced vendors were unable to deliver expected outcome within time and budget. A number of Program/Project Managers were dismissed, and vendors were threatened with court action. The newly appointed CEO was forced to resign with a multimillion-dollar payout. Finally, the program was abandoned prematurely. The organization was left with the three additional systems and a partially delivered Data Warehouse without decommissioning a single intended system, bringing in added complexity and resulting in increased IT operational costs. It took another five years to clean up the mess from the failed program.

3.4.3. *Lesson(s)*

Program planning was critically insufficient for a transformation of this size. The program should have commenced only after the following:

- Defining the scope adequately for each delivery stream.
- Identifying program complexities, dependencies, and risks.
- Developing realistic estimates for the delivery timelines.
- Reserving sufficient budget allocations based on realistic estimates.
- Reflecting these elements in the delivery contracts with the outsourced vendors.

Without realistic program guide rails reflecting the actual complexity, dependencies, and the concomitant effort, the program was doomed from the start. See also the narrative under 'Lessons' in the next case study.

3.5. Case study 5

3.5.1. Background

This case study involves a large bank. The back-end processing was running on mainframe systems. In the late 2000s, it was mooted, and a program commenced to replace most of the back-end processing with a financials package solution offered by a major global software vendor.

Banking systems are extremely complex, and large banks possess exceptionally complex IT environments. This therefore called for a major program of work, the object of which envisaged a target state that was functionally richer, more user-friendly, and operationally less complex than the then current state, with new a financials solution handling operational processing and the corresponding mainframe systems decommissioned.

3.5.2. Consequences

The program ran into difficulties caused by a combination of the functional and non-functional capabilities of the new package-based solution and the complexity of the IT estate of the bank.

The program was wound down without the original target state being realized, leaving behind a landscape more complex than the original. Most of the original mainframe operational processing was left, plus some modules of the new financials package. Ledgers that need to be maintained had grown in number: ledgers in the new system plus ledgers in the older systems. These ledgers update overlapping information and must be synchronized. Hardly any mainframe systems have been decommissioned.

3.5.3. Lesson(s)

Figure 1 illustrates that this is not an uncommon story in large and complex IT environments, e.g., case study 4 records a similar experience.

The complexity of the IT estate is expected to rise in the interim (which can reflect in the Production environment where interim 'drops' in Production are necessitated). The program encounters difficulties, the

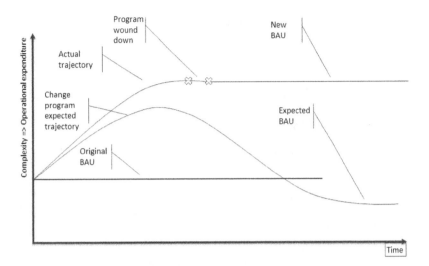

Figure 1.   Expenditure vs time.

program run rate increases, progress is much slower than expected, and eventually a decision is made to wind down the program. Unfortunately, the complexity now, reflective of an interim state in the original scenario, becomes the new business as usual, with the complexity translated into higher operational expenditure.

This is an exceedingly difficult issue to tackle. Better estimation grounded in the actual complexity that needs to be tackled will help. In addition, the program must be designed so that the individual projects are staggered such that the dependencies at any point are manageable. The aim is to flatten the curve — which will stretch it out, but that is the cost of a better prospect of successful delivery.

3.6. *Case study 6*

3.6.1. *Background*

The program is described in case study 1. At the end of the fixed-price period of the program, a financial recalculation was obviously needed. An updated business case was hurriedly prepared justifying the additional expenditure. One of the few permanent members of IT staff was tasked with presenting the new business case incorporating the cost blowout to a very skeptical financial controller of the company and requesting additional funding.

3.6.2. *Progress/Consequences*

The one-on-one meeting did not go well at first. In the middle of the financial discussion, somehow the conversation turned to Rugby (Rugby Union), which in the state of Australia where these events occurred was not a popular sport. However, the financial controller and the IT staffer were both avid followers, and the digression helped to break the financial ice. The financial controller was persuaded, albeit reluctantly, to approve the additional funding and the IT staffer carried the unexpected good news back to the IT division.

3.6.3. *Lesson(s)*

This example illustrates the 'softer' aspects, political and social elements, that influence programs, often having considerable sway over the program's eventual success or failure.

The importance of aspects such as the management of program stakeholders and ensuring that the program team actually works as a team and not as silo-driven and hostile cabals can clear the confounding elements that sometimes beset large programs.

3.7. *Case study 7*

3.7.1. *Background*

This case study involves an Australian insurance company. A customer-focused business transformation program was mooted in the mid-2010s. The main motivations were leveraging the various insurance businesses in which the company operated to explore cross-selling, developing and marketing innovative insurance products, and providing a steep improvement in customer experience in customer relationship management. Claims and premium processing were in scope only to the extent of changes required by the new products. Analytics was another key aspect; integration with the existing back end was also in scope.

At the outset, a small team of internal staff along with a small team from one of the consulting majors developed a high-level architecture, describing current and target states, plus what the interim states look like, and a roadmap. The business case was developed and approved at the Board level — a commendable effort.

The program was instituted under business leadership. The main SI was selected. A separate contract Program Director was recruited. As the program proceeded, however, consulting firms and SIs continued to market themselves and impress the stakeholders, and staff from multiple outfits were hired into the program.

3.7.2. *Progress/Consequences*

Relatively rapidly, the staff size — internal staff from the business and IT as well as contractors/consultants — continued to grow. The original plan — scope and roadmap — was lost to program memory, partly because the new recruits were not aware of the original plans and partly because the consultants and SIs who now walked the corridors had their own barrows to push, and mostly because the program controls were loose.

Unsurprisingly, the program meandered, running through the allocated funds, producing a good deal of make-work, but not delivering much.

Eventually, the scope of the program was severely curtailed, senior external (contract) staff including the program director left, and a very much slimmed down program was absorbed into the IT division.

3.7.3. *Lesson(s)*

There are several lessons here:

- The company (including the chief business stakeholder) had no previous experience with this size of program and hence some significant missteps occurred.
- The initial planning was commendable — a more or less textbook case of a plan and roadmap for a large program.

- The program director had virtually no domain or technical know-how, and clearly the program monitoring and controls were weak.
- Issues discussed previously, such as vendor agendas, sanitation of program, and reporting up the hierarchy with each segment of the program being allowed to run relatively independently, were also at play here.

Important capabilities were lacking in the following:

- Internal competency in the organization with this size program; equally, competency at the Program Director level.
- Program organization and structure.
- Proper guardrails and controls for the program. Though the material — in the form of a well-thought-out roadmap with ancillary detail — was developed that could effectively support a set of program controls, the material was not used.

3.8. Case study 8

3.8.1. Background

Early in the decade of the 2010s, an Australian Government Agency (Agency) initiated a major transformation program to replace their existing .Net-based legacy application suite with a new integrated system to interact with non-government organizations and the Australian public. The new system would enable these non-government agencies to submit their payment requests and digital evidence for services rendered to the Australian public. The new system would validate submitted evidence by interrogating a number of other Government Agency systems prior to every payment. The Agency selected a well-known global IT vendor to deliver this system after a government tendering process. The program was overseen by a newly appointed IT Director and supported by the Agency's senior management.

Key areas in the new system included a web portal, real-time integration with other Government Agency systems, automatic payment reconciliation, and data analytics. Responsibilities included customization of a commercial CRM package, data migration, system development, testing, implementation, and decommissioning of existing legacy systems.

The vendor provided the initial estimation of the cost and delivery time based on the RFQ document. The Agency entered into a fixed-price contract with the vendor, with a delivery timeline of six months as per the initial quote. Although the successful vendor had agreed to deliver the program responding to the RFQ questions to the Agency's satisfaction, they did not have a deep understanding of the current system or the intended system requirement, since the requirements set out in the RFQ were at a very high level (and the details were not provided in the RFQ).

To compound the issue, the Vendor assembled a technical team and assigned a Program Manager to deliver the project, but none of them had been involved in the RFQ Process. A separate vendor bid team did all the work during the RFQ process, and the delivery team was coming into the program entirely afresh.

3.8.2. Consequences

The initial assessment of scope by the Program Manager and the Technical Team unearthed that the business requirements provided were subjective and open to interpretation and articulated at a high level, and hence needed further clarifications from the Agency. They expected to clarify these ambiguous requirements within a couple of sessions. In reality, however, the requirement clarification meetings exceeded 30 sessions, and each one line requirement brought forth hundreds of detailed requirements. The Program Manager informed the Vendor's Senior Management about the scope issue and resigned.

A new Program Manager was appointed to the Program. He immediately stopped the requirement clarification sessions, and instead took a step back and redrew the scope boundaries for the program with much greater clarity (using the knowledge that the project team had accumulated), and then, after many senior-level escalations and negotiations between the Vendor and the Agency, came to a fresh agreement on timeline and cost. The revised estimates took more than twelve months over the original timeline and cost more than two thirds in excess of the original budget. It was agreed between the parties that additional cost is shared between the vendor and the Agency. With this agreement in place, the program was delivered within the revised timeline and budget.

3.8.3. *Lesson(s)*

The major lesson here is the importance of having a well-defined scope, an understanding of existing systems, and addressing delivery ambiguities up front. These are vital planning elements in delivering any large transformation program.

The scope details provided during the RFQ stage were grossly inadequate, and if specifying detailed requirements was not possible for the RFQ, the following steps should have been in place during the RFQ stage and before the commencement of the program:

- The RFQ scope ought to have been more reflective of the intent of the program.
- RFQ should have included assumptions for the requirements that were subjective, and this would have easily highlighted the gaps in the requirements.
- Contract clauses should have been in place to address subjective requirement gaps and delivery shortfalls.
- Inclusion of a prototype phase to mimic the requirements would have been ideal to align Agency expectations with delivery realities.

The following should have been ensured in the initial program planning stage:

- A step to finalize the delivery timeline and program cost should have been included after the clarification and detailing of the requirements, prior to the commencement of the program proper. The initial bid should have committed the vendors to a plus or minus $x\%$ in terms of price and timeline, with the fixed price and timeline negotiation occurring after the details are determined in a discovery phase.
- Subject matter experts from the government agency should have been involved and made the appropriate clarifications prior to the program commencement.

3.9. Case study 9

3.9.1. Background

Both case studies 1 and 7 entailed the replacement of operational systems used by Customer Service staff who were the operational front line for the physical (i.e., the retail outlets) as well as the call center channels, fielding questions on various topics, selling insurance products, and assisting in insurance claims. In both cases, the new systems were replacing green screens, a character-driven interface with a new GUI.

3.9.2. Consequences

Although the GUI screens were designed to capture more of the user task within a single screen, making navigation between related steps easier, the programs faced an enormous degree of resistance from the front line. They had become extremely quick at manipulating the green screens through constant sustained use and were very reluctant to move out of their comfort zones. Another pertinent factor was the incentives that especially the call center staff were given on 'productivity' — often equated to the number of calls they responded to within a given period. They feared that during the transition, and for a period thereafter, they would face adverse financial consequences due to lower turnover. Added to this, there was a fear that 'experts' who enjoyed status and respect because of their familiarity with the system would lose their status among their group.

3.9.3. Lesson(s)

This is unfortunately a tangible issue in many large transformations. Although it may be obvious to senior management, and for that matter to disinterested observers, that the new ways of working will lead to a 'better' work environment, any 'soft' resistance factors at play must be clearly understood and preempted. Good change management becomes invaluable in these situations.

3.10. *Case study 10*

3.10.1. *Background*

Early in the decade of the 2000s, an Australian Government Agency (Agency) decided to build a Data Warehouse to enhance their reporting and data analytics capabilities. Their IT Infrastructure and network needs were supported by outsourced services, while business analysis and application support were provided by in-house staff. Data warehousing concepts were new to Australia at the time and the Agency decided to outsource the development of their Data Warehouse to a well-known Australian IT company, following a tender process. The work commenced, and after the initial requirement design phase the IT Company provided a fixed-cost fee to build and implement the Data Warehouse. The IT Company's team for the project was formed and everything was in readiness to start the development phase. However, the Agency Director was procrastinating, delaying the project contract sign-off. The IT Company's assigned Project Manager was unable to convince the Director to sign on the dotted line. Due to the Project Manager's lack of Data Warehouse development knowledge and experience, he was unable to dispel the misgivings that the Director retained about this forthcoming program of work.

3.10.2. *Progress/Consequences*

Without the Agency Director's sign-off, development work could not commence. The IT Company's assigned Project Manager handed in his resignation: The on-boarded project resource costs were accumulating, and IT Company had to bear the costs. A new, experienced Project Manager with an extensive Data Warehousing background was hired from overseas by the IT Company and given the task of convincing the Agency Director to sign off on the project contract. The new Project Manager had several discussions with the Agency Director and identified that the causes for not signing the contract boiled down to the following:

- The project was supposed to be delivered using the waterfall project methodology and the proposed payment plan only retained 10% of the project cost pending final delivery.

- The Agency Director did not have any prior knowledge of Data Warehouse delivery and could not envisage the achievable benefits for the organization.
- The Agency Director was afraid of project failure as he had an unblemished public service record for 35 years.

The new Project Manager discussed his findings with the IT Company senior executives and presented his plan to address the Agency Director's concerns by proposing the following:

- Sign an agreement to develop a proof of concept for selected business areas to demonstrate Data Warehouse benefits and expected outcomes for very nominal cost.
- Develop and deliver the Data Warehouse in three phases to address concerns related to payment plan retention.

Senior executives endorsed the Project Manager's proposal. The new approach was well received by the Agency Director since it addressed his points of concern; he was further reassured by the new PM's experience and knowledge of the subject area. The Director signed the new agreements to deliver the proof of concept (PoC), and the new Project Manager delivered the PoC and then the Data Warehouse in three phases to achieve a successful outcome for both organizations.

3.10.3. *Lesson(s)*

Success of IT Projects depends on satisfying different needs of multiple stakeholders and tailoring delivery methods to suit these stakeholder expectations. In this case, if the newly appointed Project Manager also followed the rigid waterfall project delivery methodology, this project would have never been delivered, and the IT Company would have made huge losses. Unlike in certain other industries, to deliver successful projects, the IT Project delivery methodology needs to be flexible, tailorable to suit each organizational situation.

Stakeholder confidence and trust are equally important. It is critical that the program manager gains the confidence and trust of the key stakeholders at the outset — and manages to retain and further cement that confidence during program delivery.

4. Analysis

4.1. *Stage 1: Critical success/failure factors (CSFs)*

Drawing upon the groundwork of the foregoing case studies, an analysis with commentary that draws out factors that influence success or failure of large programs is presented as follows.

Table 1.   Analysis of critical success factors.

CSF	Comment
Executive/ Sponsor Support	Any project must have the support of its sponsor/s, the sponsors being the individuals who control funding for the program and who have the ultimate say on its 'life'. Usually, for large programs, the sponsors come from the Executive or Board ranks of the enterprise. A key success factor is the Program Management's ability to keep the sponsors 'onside'. This requires 'hard' skills such as appropriate reporting upward as well as 'soft' skills of stakeholder management. Traceability Case study 10 demonstrates the critical importance of gaining stakeholder confidence and support from the outset. Case studies 4 and 5 are clear examples of program sponsors deciding that 'enough is enough'. Case studies 2 and 7 also show that the program budgets were cut or additional funds not made available as they lost sponsor confidence and support. Case study 8 illustrates that lost sponsor confidence can be restored with good replanning, honest negotiation, and on-time delivery.
Planning	Sufficient time and resources must be spent in planning to get a strong handle on the key parameters of the program and clearly understand its complexities and dependencies. This enables business case and funding allocation to be based on solid groundwork and strong guardrails to be established for the program: o Strategic aims, high-level requirements, business benefits. o High-level architecture.

Table 1. (*Continued*)

CSF	Comment
	o Facets of the program: Individual projects and scope (including business transformation, change management, IT/technical, and communications); their dependencies and precedence: roadmap and Gantt chart representations. o Estimation and resource requirements. o Assumptions (clear, explicit, and realistic). Even for exceptionally large transformation programs, this level of planning can be successfully undertaken using a small, focused, and experienced team of business and IT staff. Planning must happen not only at the commencement of the program, but replanning must be baked into the program's operational process. Traceability Case study 2 is an instance of ego and wishful thinking substituting for careful planning. Case studies 4 and 5 also demonstrate the consequences of less than adequate initial planning. Case study 7 shows the outcomes of good initial planning being turned into shelf-ware. Case study 8 reveals the subsequent pitfalls in not specifying program scope initially in the planning phase.
Program structure and organization	Senior staffing: o There must be a combination of program management, business/domain, and technical skills at the senior-most levels of the program. Moreover, it is imperative that they possess the requisite depth of skills and experience: Program Manager: In our experience, oftentimes, Program Managers with experience and nous in the program's focus areas — domain (e.g., Finance), IT infrastructure, and analytics — are more successful than generic program managers: Domain knowledge and sufficient technical knowledge to separate technical wheat from chaff — especially in multi-vendor situations — are imperative, as are stakeholder management skills. Program Architects must have a keen understanding of the guardrails of the program, also of the 'Why' — the business imperative, ability to herd architects to collaborate and cooperate for the greater good; change and variation management — cutting costs without cutting corners.

Table 1.   (*Continued*)

CSF	Comment
	o The program reporting structure must be as flat as practicable. Furthermore, the depth of the structure must be broadly even across the different areas of the program. For example, change management, business analysis, process design structures three levels deep, and IT development eight levels deep are probably not ideal.
	Vendors and vendor management:
	o A large program is likely to have multiple vendors — in SI, consulting, and delivery roles. Therefore, it is essential to establish, both contractually and in practice, the primacy of vendor responsibilities toward the program.
	o Establish inter-vendor responsibilities and protocols for communication, risk and issue management, and dispute resolution.
	o Tackle potential conflicts of interest, e.g., where the overall Program Director is from an SI who also has responsibilities for areas of delivery.
	Allocation of dedicated business resources:
	o Dedicated business SMEs for the program are crucial for its success. This may be a difficult proposition for most enterprises: their 'best people' will be seen to be essential both for ongoing operational activities and the success of the impending business transformation. These conflicting demands must be successfully resolved.
	Stakeholder identification:
	o Formally identify all stakeholders relevant to the program and explicitly identify their interest in the program, their level of engagement with the program, etc. An analysis helps identify obvious as well as implicit stakeholders.
	o Program management must be careful about having many stakeholders with varied expectations (especially with different and conflicting priorities) to manage — early identification may help obviate this problem.
	Project approach:
	o Methodology: There are popular alternatives to the traditional 'waterfall' approach — many flavors of Agile methods. The program management team must select appropriate approaches for the individual projects of the program.

Table 1. (*Continued*)

CSF	Comment
	It is of the utmost importance that, where selected, Agile methods must operate within the overall framework (described in 'Planning' above) of the program. Agile methods work best within established guide rails.
	The selected approach must be fit for purpose: A state-of-the-art methodology will not have the desired impact unless it is (a) practical and (b) followed by all involved.
	o Tools and processes: Use of appropriate Project Scheduling, Task Management, and Collaboration tools is vital for program success. Ideally, there should be seamless integration from task management through to project scheduling levels.
	o Monitoring and controls: Regular monitoring of project health and project schedule updates are essential to ensure that the project is on the right trajectory where one can take corrective action if required. A key technique to monitor project health is Earned Value Analysis (Chapter 13), which measures project progress from schedule, cost, and value perspectives.
	Governance and control structures:
	o The Governance Board/Steering Committee must have executives with experience in navigating large programs, capable of digesting program reporting and advising the program leadership in steering the program trajectory.
	o Governance reporting must be transparent, clear, and concise, bringing the salient points to the Board's notice.
	o A Project Organization Chart must be in place to manage the project team/ working group and required escalations.
	Communication:
	o A solid communication plan must be in place to address every aspect of the program at each level of the project organization.
	o RACI must be in place to manage the internal/external project communication without any ambiguity.
	Traceability
	Case studies 1 and 7 are poster examples of poor program structure and the consequences.
	Case study 3 highlights a case of willful sanitation of program reports by a vendor and the dire consequences of that behavior.

Table 1.   (*Continued*)

CSF	Comment
	Case studies 1, 3, 4, 5, and 7 all reflect adverse impacts of poor vendor management.
	The above set also demonstrates failures at governance level — the steering committee (or the equivalent instrument of program governance) should have picked up on warning signs such as increasing run rate and delayed delivery.
	Case study 10 describes the ill effects of persisting with an inappropriate delivery approach, even in the face of stakeholder misgivings. Fortunately, this was corrected via timely intervention.
Risk and issue management discipline	o Institute the structure and discipline to identify risks and mitigate them before they become issues.
	o There are some intricacies to be mindful of here, especially in multi-project, multi-vendor situations.
	There is sometimes a tendency to 'game' the risk and issue process — in raising risks against another project/project manager to save one's own project. Vigilance around this is prudent, especially in multi-vendor environments, where risks and issues could degenerate into a buck-passing device between different vendors.
	Also, in multi-vendor situations, a vendor may not report on certain actual risks and issues (with the intention of fixing them internally to the vendor) because of potential contractual penalties to that vendor.
	o The Program Manager and team must not only put in place the structure and the discipline but be vigilant against misuse of this particularly important steering mechanism.
	Traceability
	Most of the failures described have inadequate risk management as a causal factor, which could have alerted the program leadership to troubled waters ahead in time to take corrective action.
	On the other hand, Case study 3 shows the results of a risk and issue management process gone completely awry.
Estimation, realistic timelines, appropriate allocation of funds	Estimation is difficult but critical to the success of the program. One confounding factor in IT-related projects is that estimation is not a mature discipline in comparison with, say, construction (Chapter 13). Optimistic estimation may, on the surface, seem attractive (a) to show the business case in a particularly attractive light or (b) you may be tempted to tweak the costs (without varying the scope) to within what is surmised as acceptable to the program sponsor.

Table 1. (*Continued*)

CSF	Comment
	However, the program leaders as well as the sponsors must be mindful that optimistic estimation (unrealistic timelines and/or insufficient funding), at the outset, sets up the program for a fall, and the program commences with the cards stacked against it.
	Traceability
	Poor estimation is a culprit in most of the failed programs.
	Case study 2 is a clear example. Had the CIO used more of the science of estimation, he would soon have realized that the desired time frame was nowhere near long enough.
	Case studies 4 and 5 indicate that the complex and difficult path ahead was poorly analyzed and its knock-on effects on delivery not incorporated into estimates. They demonstrate that sanitizing estimates almost always backfires on you.
	Case study 8 indicates the misleading estimates derived from poorly clarified and understood scope.
Program operational aspects	Rubber hits the road when planning, estimation, business case, etc., are done and the program proper begins. These preludes are certainly critical in setting up the program for success. Now, it is vital that the follow through is equally diligent and skillful.
	Once the program commences, multiple projects — IT driven, business driven — would have kicked off and at program level must be closely monitored, controlled, and directed.
	Many issues to be mindful of but described below are areas that in the authors' experience often cause programs to come undone.
Program control	Developing the WBS and exercising a finely tuned level of control:
	o Use formal as well as informal levers to gather information.
	o Scope management: be wary of and try to preempt scope changes during the project.
	o Regularly update the project schedule and monitor the project health (e.g., using Earned Value Analysis).
	Stakeholder management:
	o Operationally, the program leadership must engage with the stakeholders; there is no 'one size fits all' here — each stakeholder must be managed individually.
	o One sign to be aware of and preempt if possible is a change of priorities among stakeholders during the program.

(*Continued*)

Table 1.   (*Continued*)

CSF	Comment
Requirements	Especially in very large and complex programs (which could well cover a multi-year timeline), the elicitation of detailed requirements at the outset is not practical. Here, is it important to establish guardrails for the entire program, then under that overall framework split the program into manageable stages and do detailed planning for each stage.
	Also, it is important to note that where the detailed definition of requirements is infeasible at the RFP/RFQ stage, the scope boundary must nevertheless be defined unambiguously so that the detailed definition of requirements can be managed without transgressing the scope boundary.
	Equally, the responding vendors should include compensatory assumptions where requirements are ambiguous.
	Traceability
	Case study 8 is the clearest example of ambiguous scope definition and requirements misleading the initial program planning process, including estimating and quoting, and the downstream consequences that arise.
Change Management & Training	Insufficient attention to organizational change management and training can lead to active resistance to change, although the solution may tick all the functional and non-functional boxes.
	Traceability
	Case study 9 is a good example of the need for change management to smooth out potential resistance to change.
Testing	Testing is the most important 'gate' for the projects of the program. While the best practice described here serves to improve the quality of construction, proper testing is essential to assure everyone that the system works as specified: functional, non-functional (e.g., security, performance, and scalability) tests and regression testing to ensure that there is no adverse impact on existing systems and software.
Managing the interface between BAU operations of the enterprise and program-specific operations	This is an often-neglected area. There is a general understanding that once the program is delivered, the newly delivered parts of the program become part of the business as usual (BAU) functions of the enterprise. However, what is less explicitly recognized is that during the life of the program, the program must interact with parts of the BAU functions of the enterprise, e.g., requirements elicitation, change management, release management, configuration management, and testing.

Table 1. (*Continued*)

CSF	Comment
	At these interfaces, there may be (a) bandwidth/availability and (b) skills and capability mismatches, as well as trust issues between the mostly old-timers managing BAU and the newbies in the program team.

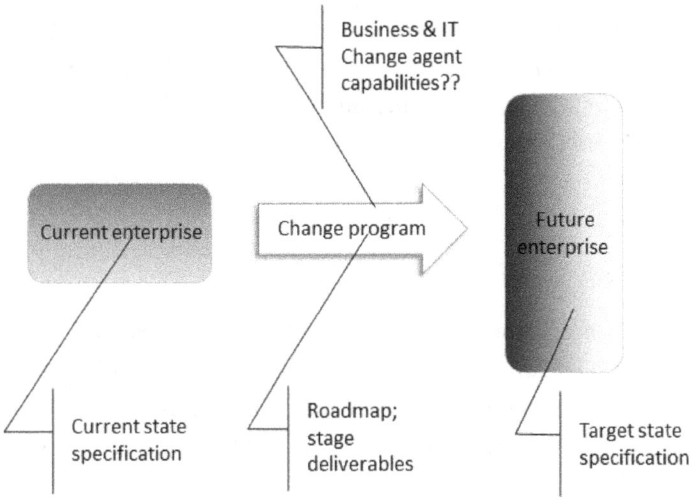

Figure 2. Business transformation initiatives.

4.2. Stage 2: Delivering change: A generalized capability framework for large IT programs

This section takes a step back to place the factors of success and failure in a broader organizational context.

For large IT-driven business transformation initiatives (Figure 2), a substantial effort goes into describing the future state (Wijegunaratne *et al.*, 2014; Wijegunaratne and Madiraju, 2016), addressing its various facets: business/operating model, business capabilities, processes, and IT solutions that support them.

These measures are necessary, but they alone are not sufficient to bring about success. A large transformation involves significant changes on many fronts — business model, organizational structure and culture, and IT systems landscape. It is therefore critically important that the enterprise *actually makes the transition*, that it is successfully reshaped, changed, and evolved. Hence, the 'elephant in the room' is the organization's capability to deliver this change successfully, and the analysis of this chapter has clearly underlined the critical relationship between delivery capability and success/failure. Accordingly, it becomes clear that the essential capabilities required to deliver change, i.e., program delivery capabilities — their current maturity, scale, tooling, etc. — must be subject to a level of scrutiny as stringent as that for the future state. But, the narrative of the previous sections shows that these delivery capabilities are not subjected to a level of scrutiny anywhere near what is necessary.

In this section, a generalized framework is developed to assess a company's readiness to undertake a large transformation program.

4.2.1. *Business capability maps*

A key artifact of enterprise architecture, the business capability map, is a useful way to take forward this analysis. Business capability is a logical structuring of assets — people, knowledge, skills, and systems — of the organization for the purpose of process execution, grouped primarily by skills.

A business capability map is a collection of business capabilities that make up a business domain or an enterprise. These are arranged in a hierarchical fashion, with Level 1 serving as a placeholder for classification (e.g., Planning & governance, Value chain, Enabling, groups of capabilities), Level 2 being the actual capabilities, and Level 3 depicting the subcapabilities within a capability. The sequence of execution between individual capabilities at the same level is not implied.[1]

---

[1] Note that a single business capability map size does not fit all: for example, all insurance companies do not possess the same map. Although at level 1, commonalities will exist among different enterprises engaged in the same business, differences emerge at more detailed levels. These variations represent different levels of emphasis accorded to different business capabilities in different enterprises. Depicting a business capability, say at level 2 or level 3, is an indicator of the importance of that capability to a business: the required (or committed) investment in that capability in resourcing, skills, supporting technology, etc. Therefore, variations are normal, depicting the business areas that an

They have many uses, including assessing the alignment with business objectives. An analysis of business capabilities mapped against business strategic objectives can yield the following:

- Capabilities important to the strategic aims of the business.
- Degree to which the capabilities are currently able to support the strategic objectives of the business (due constraints of current maturity, focus, resource, etc.).

Using these 'heat maps', how to uplift, upscale, or otherwise evolve a capability to support the target state can be determined.

Thus, capability maps are an excellent tool to assess (a) the current capability, (b) desired future capability, and (c) the change needed.

An approach is now developed to use capability maps to similarly assess the organization's capability to effect and deliver change.

4.2.2. *Enterprise's capability to deliver change: Reference business capability map*

Typically, capability maps of a business enterprise depict its steady-state operation, not change agent capabilities. Businesses will argue that deep expertise in them will only be needed when large-scale change is afoot (Wijegunaratne and Madiraju, 2016).

A map of capabilities to effect large-scale transformation has been developed by the authors and is shown in Figure 5. This is a 'reference architecture', representative of large programs in general, which can be customized to develop capability maps for individual programs.

The map contains three groups: Program Planning, Program Delivery and Operations, and Enabling capabilities. The former two are specific to

---

enterprise has chosen to engage and invest in — indicating points of differentiation among similar enterprises.

Therefore, "reference capability maps" can be developed for classes of business domains — general insurance, life insurance, retail banking, etc. The practitioner can then use such a reference map as a start point in developing the business capability map of a particular business.

the program, and the latter capabilities 'interface' with program-specific ones. For example, the program was likely devised (and budgetary parameters indicated) in the organization's business strategy and planning area. The program risk analysis capability must be aligned with the enterprise's risk management capability. Recruitment for the program must go through the enterprise's HR processes; the program's IT components must transition to 'Business as Usual' (BAU) upon delivery, and therefore must conform to the operational standards prescribed by the latter.

4.2.3. CSFs and the capability map: Traceability analysis

First, does this capability map represent all the key success/failure factors discussed in the previous section? A traceability analysis is performed against the CSFs in Table 1, see Table 2.

Thus, the reference capability map of Figure 3 represents all key success/ failure factors and can depict delivery capabilities to work from and customize in program planning.

Table 2.   Capability mapping and traceability to CSFs.

CSF	Capability mapping and traceability to CSFs
Executive /Sponsor Support	Stakeholder communications and relationship management is reflected in the capabilities below: o (Program planning) Key stakeholder analysis o (Program planning) Communications planning o (Program ops and delivery) Stakeholder reporting o (Program ops and delivery) Stakeholder relationship management
Planning	Maps to the capability map as follows: o (Program planning) Strategic objectives & vision o (Program design) Architecture & roadmap o (Program design) Program WBS o (Program design) Program estimation, etc.

Table 2. (*Continued*)

CSF	Capability mapping and traceability to CSFs
Program structure and organization	Maps to the capability map as follows: o (Program structure & org) Organization structure o (Program structure & org) Monitoring, reporting, controls o (Program structure & org) Staffing & other resourcing Vendors and vendor management: o (Program planning) Vendor management processes o (Program ops and delivery) Vendor management Dedicated business resources: o (Program str and org) program staffing Stakeholder identification: o (Program planning) stakeholder analysis o (Program ops and delivery) stakeholder reporting, stakeholder relationship management Program and project approach: o (Program design) program methodology, program tools Program monitoring and controls: o (Program ops and delivery) program management Governance and control structures: o (Program planning) program governance planning o (Program ops & delivery) program governance Communication: o (Program planning) Communications Planning o (Program ops & delivery) Communications management
Risk and issue management discipline	Aspects of risk and issue management that surface: o (Program planning) Program risk analysis: analysis and planning aspects of risk o (Program ops & delivery) risk and issue management: the ongoing management process and discipline of risk and issue management
Estimation, realistic timelines, funds allocation	Estimation management is represented: o (Program planning) Program estimation: initial estimation for costing, business case, etc. o (In program ops & delivery) under variation management, it is expected that reestimation is undertaken where required
Program ops aspects	The 'Program Operations and Delivery' group of capabilities detailed below

(*Continued*)

Table 2.   (*Continued*)

CSF	Capability mapping and traceability to CSFs
Program control	Exercising program control is contained within the capabilities of the level 1 capability set 'program management', covering the gamut of the program.
	Ongoing stakeholder management is taken care of in the level 1 capability set 'stakeholder management'.
Requirements	Business analysis capabilities are represented under individual projects, in the capability set 'projects management'.
Change Management	Change management is shown in the level 1 capability set 'organizational change'.
Testing	Testing capabilities are portrayed under individual projects, in the capability set 'projects management'.
Managing the interface between BAU and program-specific operations	Managing this interface is a critical requisite for program success. The 'soft skills' aspects of managing this interface fall under the stakeholder management capability set.
	It is also necessary that these capabilities within the program and those in the BAU enterprise work together amicably to accommodate each other. That accountability falls within the Program management capability set, specifically within the dependency management capability.

4.2.4. *A framework for program capability assessment*

The change agent capability map is now employed to assess the organization's capability to effect and deliver change.

A hypothetical: The 'Green Unicorn Group' plans a large business transformation exercise. Program planners (internal staff plus a few external consultants) have identified the target state of the business in detail and are now analyzing the capabilities needed for successful program delivery.

They take the reference capability map (Figure 3) and configure it for the program ahead. To simplify things, assume that the reference map was

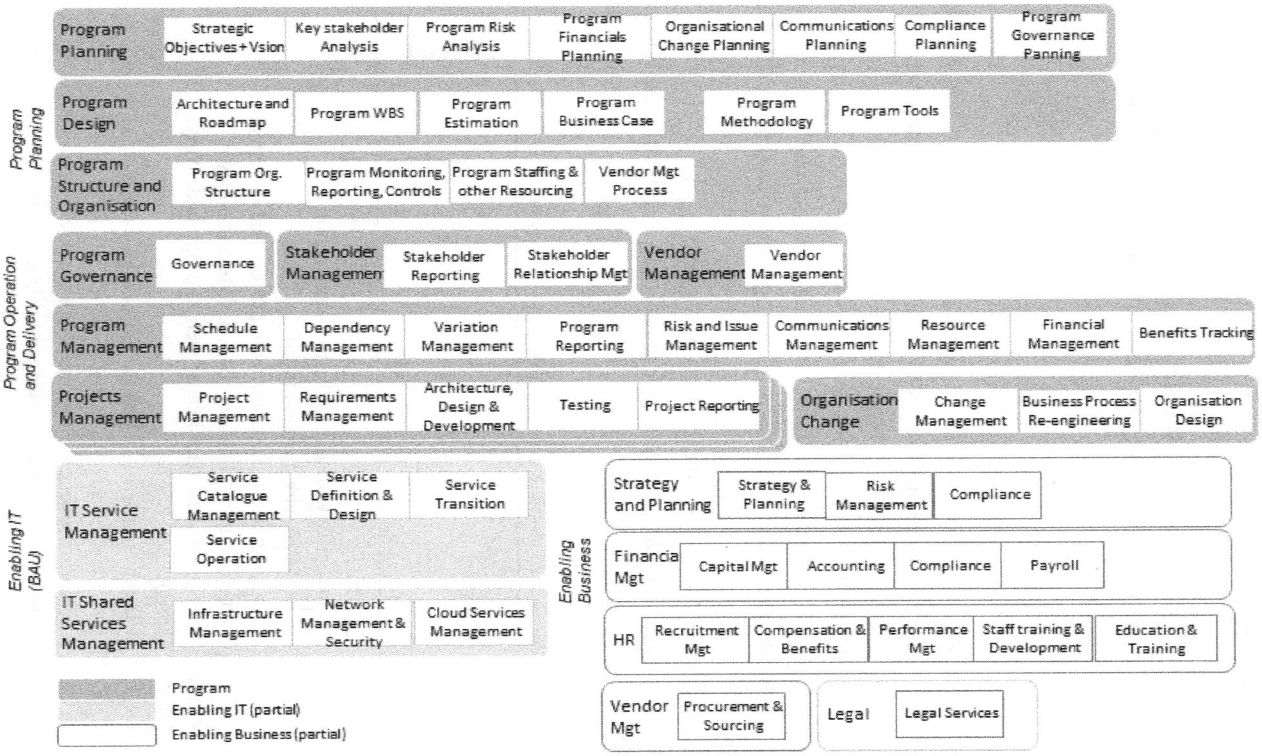

Figure 3. Capability map for business and IT change capabilities.

suitable to use as is. Using workshops, interviews, and prior experience, they determine the following:

- Criticality of a capability for the transformation.
- Desired level of the capability to deliver this transformation and its current maturity level.
- Capability gap.

Some, not all, results are illustrated below in Table 3.

Once the analysis is complete, a comprehensive picture of transformation delivery capabilities — current, desired, and the gap — emerges. This is the best estimate of capability requirements for successful delivery that can be gauged upfront. The planning team has now given the organization not only a detailed picture of the target state and a roadmap (not covered here) but also the gaps that need to be bridged in order to deliver the program safely.

The next step is to determine how to bridge the gaps.

The 2 × 2 grids shown in Figures 4 and 5 help determine the actions to bridge the gaps. In the example, the team is in program planning, and

Table 3. Example capability analysis — green unicorn.

Capability	Level	Criticality	Gap
Program Planning: Program Risk Analysis Program Management: Risk & Issue Management	Desired ○ Familiarity with and ability to assess overall risk associated with business transformation. ○ An integrated risk management process that incorporates business and technology risks, and risks that may arise out of business decisions as well as program delivery. Current ○ The enterprise has a process to assess and manage business risk. ○ IT risk assessment done as technology risk as part of technology life cycle management, and also in the context of individual IT projects. ○ There is no link between the two processes.	H	H

Table 3. (*Continued*)

Capability	Level	Criticality	Gap
Program Design: Program Architecture and Roadmap	<u>Desired</u> o Ability to identify & agree upon key business imperatives; create business, application, technology architectures at business domain/ enterprise level to realize the objectives. o Ability to express the program in program architecture terms, tying outcomes to business, application, technology architecture pieces; obtaining business executive buy-in. o Ability to manage the program architecture model as it evolves. <u>Current</u> o Implemented 'IS/IT'-centric enterprise architecture models. None have been visible to the Business stakeholders. o No experience in tying business strategy and program architecture in representing a program of work in terms of Business, application, and tech architectures.	H	H
Projects Management: Architecture Design (Solution Architecture)	<u>Desired</u> o No experience in tying business strategy and program architecture (of a program of work) to Business, application, technical architectures of pieces of the intended solution o Ability to trace solution components to strategic outcomes/ benefits for the business. <u>Current</u> o Good capability for medium–low-complexity solutions. o Hitherto have not traced solution components to business strategic outcomes.	H	L
Stakeholder Management: Stakeholder Relationship Management	<u>Desired</u> o Understand (and anticipate) explicit and implicit needs, manage expectations, and maintain relationships with key stakeholders. <u>Current</u> o The in-house IT team has virtually no experience of interacting with Business executives who comprise the steering committee.	H	H

(*Continued*)

Table 3.   (*Continued*)

Capability	Level	Criticality	Gap
Program planning: Program WBS and Estimation	<u>Desired</u> o Ability to develop a WBS and accurately estimate the work efforts for large, related sets of work streams comprising multiple individual projects.	H	H
Program Management	o The leadership to manage a complex, interrelated program of work involving in-house and multi-vendor teams.		
Prog Management: Variations	o Ability to tie business benefits to solution components at a granular level. o Assess variations against benefit impact. <u>Current</u> o Project managers with experience of projects of < $10M total spend. o No in-house program management leadership skills. o Currently no benefits management experience (business cases are created at project initiation but not tracked thereafter).	H	H
Organization Change	<u>Desired</u> o Ability to successfully steer the change to the enterprise operating model, structure, and processes that the program delivers. <u>Current</u> o No in-house change management skills.	H	H
IT Service Management Cloud Service Management	<u>Desired</u> o Ability to take a complex Cloud-based system into BAU and manage its operation in BAU. <u>Current</u> o Well-developed in-house expertise in Cloud-based management of their systems — PaaS, SaaS.	H	L

Criticality for
transformation

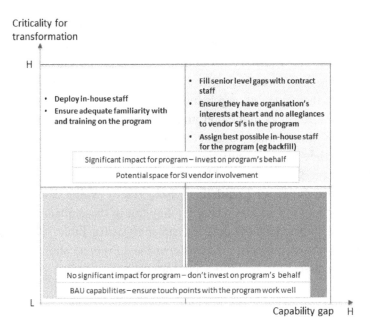

Figure 4. Criticality vs capability framework.

it is too late to think of medium- to long-term staff training, especially for the critical tasks with a high capability gap.

If each quadrant is taken in turn (Figure 4),

- Criticality + capability gap high: Source resources externally recruit contract staff for the senior positions if recruiting permanent staff is not feasible because of the time frame. They would form part of the senior team that directs the program. Accordingly, they must be fully aligned with the interests of the enterprise and have no allegiance to any selected SI vendor. Assign best possible in-house staff to work with the contracted senior staff to ensure continuity. Backfill BAU positions where needed.
- Criticality high, capability gap low: Deploy in-house staff.
  Depending on the particular BAU demands, deploy as many of your best staff to the program team. Source externally, potentially to back-fill the BAU positions where needed.
- These top two (high criticality) quadrants contain the territory that the Green Unicorn Group may look to an SI to cover.

The bottom two quadrants do not impact the program significantly. Therefore, for program purposes, additional investment to develop these capabilities is not necessary. Of course, quite separately to the program, the enterprise may decide to invest to develop these capabilities, especially where the capability gap is high.

Where capabilities in the bottom two quadrants are enabling business or IT capabilities that must interact with the program, the enterprise must ensure that they tick over sufficiently well for the interface with the program to succeed.

These are the general guidelines. But, exactly which capabilities are needed for the program and where do they fall in these quadrants? Green Unicorn Staff have done the detailed gap analysis (in Table 3, capabilities in the bottom two quadrants are not shown) and Figure 5 shows, in a sample, how the assessed capabilities fall into each quadrant.

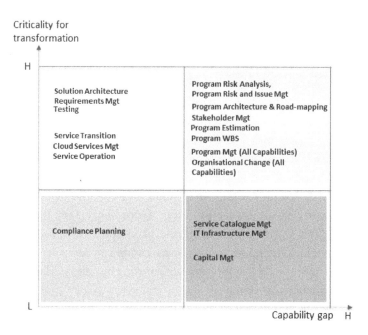

Figure 5. Criticality vs capability example.

These staffing and investment guidelines along with the detailed gap analysis of Table 3 provide the planning team with a granular instrument to take appropriate action. They are now positioned to source the specific skills through contract recruitment, internal training, or if needed focus on the specific skill areas from an SI. The recruitment job descriptions and the SI terms of reference can now be tailored exactly to the skills/ responsibilities sought for this particular program.

5. Summary

This chapter focused on large IT-driven business transformation programs and the key factors that impact their degree of success or failure. The defining attributes of a 'large program' and 'success/failure' were identified at the outset. For the former, the following points are noted:

- Relative size and complexity: the size (budget, schedule) relative to the 'background' profile of work
- Containing multiple dependent projects with precedence relationships needing to be managed as a whole.

For the latter (i.e., success/failure), time, budget, functionality at completion; and in operation, the delivery of promised value (benefits) to the enterprise and the on-going cost were the key traits.

To draw out key lessons, a set of case studies was presented, with most describing failures and a few depicting successful interventions. The dictum that you learn more from failures than successes led the authors to drive the analysis in this fashion. Stepping back from the lesson details and the criteria drawn therefrom, two critical inferences may be drawn:

1. A failure of competence or capability of one form or another: Be it grasping the real complexity of the work at hand, making realistic estimates, assigning proper contractual responsibilities to SI vendors,

allowing scope creep, ignoring original guardrails, faulty risk management, etc.

2. Failure to adhere to best practice: Although best practice in these areas is well known, ad-hoc methods or practices were used in preference to/ignorance of program management best practice.

It is reasonable to posit that one breeds the other, and accordingly, the second part of the chapter is devoted to developing a capability framework for use in program management, especially in program planning. This framework enables, at the program planning stage, to assess the capability gaps (between what the enterprise possesses and what is required) across the range of capabilities needed for the impending program — and then use the most appropriate method to source these capabilities. Given the complexity and situation-specific variables at play in large projects, this contingency-based approach is arguably superior to the 'four things to look out for' type prescriptions found in the popular practitioner literature. A comparative assessment with construction industry practices is done in Chapter 13.

References

Sexton, R. (2011). Bungling in State Public Sector Blamed for IT Blowouts, The Age, Victoria, Australia. Available at: https://www.theage.com.au/national/victoria/bungling-in-state-public-sector-blamed-for-it-blowouts-20111123-1nv3g.html. (Accessed 24 November 2014).

Bloch, M., Blumberg, S. and Laartz, J. (2012). Delivering large-scale IT projects on time, on budget, and on value, *Insights,* 2012, 2–7.

McKinsey and Company. (2019). Why Transformations Fail: A Conversation with Seth Goldstrom. Available at: https://www.mckinsey.com/business-functions/strategy-and-corporate-finance/our-insights/why-transformations-fail-a-conversation-with-seth-goldstrom.

Morgan, B. (2019). Companies that Failed at Digital Transformation and What We Can Learn from Them, *Forbes 2019*. Available at: https://www.forbes.com/sites/blakemorgan/2019/09/30/companies-that-failed-at-digital-transformation-and-what-we-can-learn-from-them/?sh=16fce3d3603c.

Kitani, K. (2019). The $900 Billion Reason GE, Ford and P&G Failed at Digital Transformation, CNBC *Evolve October 2019*. Available at: https://www.

cnbc.com/2019/10/30/heres-why-ge-fords-digital-transformation-programs-failed-last-year.html.

Sutcliff, M., Narsalay, R. and Sen, A. (2019). The two big reasons that digital transformations fail, *Harvard Bus. Rev.* Available at: https://hbr.org/2019/10/the-two-big-reasons-that-digital-transformations-fail.

Wijegunaratne, I. and Madiraju, S. (2016). Addressing enterprise change capability, a constraint in business transformation, *J. Enterp. Archit.,* 12(3).

Wijegunaratne, I., Fernandez, G. and Evans-Greenwood, P. (2014). *Enterprise Architecture for Business Success*, Bentham Books.

Chapter 13

Managing IT Projects: Lessons Learnt from the Construction Sector

Indrajit Wijegunaratne[†], Kolitha Dassanayake[‡] and Robert Eadie*

[†]*(Hons) (Essex), MSc, PhD (London) Advisor, Blockchain Australia*
injiwije@gmail.com
[‡]*DXC Technology. Melbourne, Australia*
kolithad@gmail.com
*Ulster University, School of the Built Environment,
Belfast Campus, Northern Ireland
r.eadie@ulster.ac.uk

The previous chapter discussed, with the help of illustrative examples, the key elements of a large Information Technology (IT) program of work. These elements critically influence its success or failure. This chapter examines these experiences comparing the key factors with comparable programs of work in an older and more mature industry, construction, where the management discipline is expected to be equally advanced in terms of maturity. As the previous chapter discussed large and complex works, this chapter also focuses on similar initiatives.

Construction is taken as the main comparative domain, and here discussion is provided on shared approaches with IT, before defining commonalities and contrasts of a comparable program in construction. Then, as in Chapter 12, through a series of illustrative examples, identification of criteria that influence their level of success is provided. In the main body of analysis, the factors from Chapter 12 are compared and contrasted.

1. Introduction

The key or critical success factors (CSFs) in Project Management (PM) for IT projects identified in Chapter 12 were as follows: 1. Executive/ Sponsor Support, 2. Planning, 3. Program structure and organization, 4. Risk and issue management discipline, 5. Estimation, realistic timelines, and appropriate allocation of funds, 6. Program operational aspects, 7. Program control, 8. Requirements, 9. Change management & Training, 10. Testing, and 11. Managing the interface between business-as-usual (BAU) operations of the enterprise and program-specific operations.

These factors map to the general CSFs discussed in Vrchota *et al.* (2020) which show that if PM is adopted, it ends in a sustainable result by producing a quality product across all industries. As a result, this chapter investigates the construction practice impact in supporting new ways of working in the IT Sector. A majority of the examples in Chapter 12 are private sector, whereas this chapter will use mainly public sector examples.

2. Background

The IT sector is relatively new, having only started to enter the work realm from the 1950s onward. Other disciplines such as construction have been around for millennia. As a result, there are elements of PM that can be adopted from more mature industries that will allow the IT sector to assimilate knowledge. This chapter seeks to use a very mature industry, construction, and compare it to illustrate lessons learned.

2.1. *Definitions*

The terms 'project' and 'program' carry different meanings in IT and construction. Therefore, the terminology needs clarification before proceeding. In Chapter 12, the multi-case study analysis was on large and complex initiatives aimed at implementing transformational change in an enterprise. These were defined and referred to as 'programs' (business transformation programs, transformation programs) in Chapter 12 and contained multiple dependent projects run by project managers reporting to a program manager, who manages the whole. For example, an initiative aimed at transforming customer experience may contain (a) a new CRM system and customer self-service access via the desktop, laptop, mobile, and tablet, (b) Customer analytics, (c) integration with existing 'back office' systems including changes to them, plus decommissioning redundant functionality, (d) network, security, and other infrastructure changes to support the cloud-based CRM implementation, and (e) organizational change management. These may be organized as five dependent projects, but all need to be orchestrated together to achieve the overall business objective. Accordingly, they may be scoped and managed by five PMs reporting to a program manager supported by a small program-level staff contingent.

In construction, however, a 'program' can carry a different connotation. For example, a program manager may manage four construction projects at four separate housing estates. The individual projects have no dependency other than possible staff/resource constraints or overall budgetary constraints.

As a result, the comparison in this chapter is between the type of IT program described above and comparable works in construction; the latter may carry the label 'project'.

Case study analysis in Chapter 12 discussed the relative size and complexity of the three related aspects of the program where they were compared to the norm: business transformation, business systems change, and IT (systems, integration, and infrastructure). Another attribute was also identified: multiple individual projects with dependencies and precedence relationships. While a lot of IT development is ad hoc, construction systemizes PM, and this chapter details these systems and regulations.

Program success/failure can be monitored and assessed during the program's life (with a final assessment at delivery) with time, budget, and functionality (scope) measures. There were two additional measures that came into play post-delivery: ongoing (operational) cost and delivery of promised value. The iron triangle of cost, time, and scope also applies to construction and this is developed within the chapter.

Bröchner and Badenfelt (2011) state that industry comparisons between IT and Construction projects are unusual. Since then, the use of Common Data Environments and Building Information Modeling (BIM) in Construction has produced a crossover between the sectors. In carrying out a comparison between various sectors, Bryde (2010) suggests that while those involved in construction projects considered that their PM performance was better than other sectors, there was little difference in outcomes. However, these papers concluded that comparisons can be completed for PM Practice. While the industry does not matter and the learning is therefore transferable, Turner *et al.* (2009) show that the size of organizations and projects controls matters, with small to medium-sized enterprises (SMEs) requiring less bureaucratic versions of PM and different tool sets. Yet, the main CSFs are still client consultation; planning, monitoring, and control; and resource allocation in all projects. This chapter will compare and investigate CSFs applicable to both large construction and IT projects.

3. Observations and analysis

The Success / Failure Factors in Chapter 12 were dissected and lessons from construction brought to bear on them. This Section follows the sequence of the analysis in Section 4 of Chapter 12.

3.1. *Executive/sponsor support*

The first key success factor identified in the previous chapter is related to Executive / Sponsor Support. The role of the project sponsor was first introduced in Northern Ireland due to issues relating to the Belfast / Bangor railway construction project. The idea was to have a sponsor that oversees the Gateway review process so that the overspend on that project would not reoccur. There have been several public enquiries into this scheme and the information provided is in the public domain.

Translink is the trading name of the Northern Ireland Transport Holding Company (NITHCo) which is a fully government-owned company (NiDirect, 2021) and is funded through government capital. It uses the funding received from the Department for Regional Development DRD (now the Department for Infrastructure DFI) to upkeep and provide public transportation services. Back in January 2001, funding of £14.7 million was provided to complete an upgrade to the Belfast/ Bangor railway line by December 2001. This is one of the busiest railway lines in Northern Ireland, and at that stage, the line transported nearly 2 million passengers a year (NI Audit Office, 2007). The costs doubled to £34 million and the project was delivered 9 months late.

As a result of this scheme going so badly, a review of the process was conducted alongside the Audit report, resulting in the Gateway process being adopted in Northern Ireland (NI Audit Office, 2009). One of the main findings was that 'Procedures for project management and the management of consultants were not sufficiently robust for large scale capital projects' (NI Audit Office, 2007). The Gateway process mandates key review and decision points at defined stages of the program. The Gershon report (1999) identified similar issues in England, Scotland, and Wales in IT Projects. The Gateway process was developed for all projects when published in 2001 and adopted in 2002. Due to COVID-19, the minimum threshold for applying the Gateway process was revised upward to £1 million (Stevenson, 2020).

One is the main elements of the Gateway Process is to ensure that a Senior Responsible Officer (SRO) is appointed for the project. The role of the SRO is to overview the change management process. If the project is large, they ensure the project meets the requirements of the review process at the Gateway stages. The SRO confirms the overall project goal and ensures that the business strategy and objectives are met. Their role includes ensuring that concerns raised at each stage are dealt with before signing off and letting the project progress to the next stage. As a result, they ensure that the brief and business case conditions are met.

The process that the SRO oversees contains strategic gateways and 5 project Gateways: 1. Business Justification, 2. Delivery Strategy, 3. Investment Decision, 4. Readiness for service, and 5. Operational Review and Business Justification. These key decision points act like hurdles that the project must achieve a certain level in. This means that there are 5 points where a failing project can be identified. The two most critical points are before major money is spent: Gateways 1 and 2.

At this stage, value engineering can be applied to elicit savings. Before Gateway 1, a high-level business case is produced. This enables the SRO to ensure that the project is feasible, the brief and high-level aims are achievable, and that the project is likely to provide value for money (VFM). The options are assessed in relation to affordability and achievability. On passing Gateway 1, a project at Gateway 2 has a more detailed Business case assessed, with honed requirements, and a detailed procurement strategy.

At each Gateway, a decision on the viability of the project is taken. A traffic light system is employed: green to red on a 5-point scale.

Green means that all is okay with the project. An assessment indicates that the requirements related to the iron triangle of time, cost, and quality are likely to be met and there will be no large outstanding issues evident.

The second point on the scale is amber/green. Again, an assessment indicates that the requirements related to the iron triangle are likely to be met but attention needs to be paid to risks. This point on the scale, when allocated, means that risks are constantly assessed to ensure that they do not develop into 'show-stoppers'.

The third possible result of the assessment is amber. This is used where it is still feasible to meet the requirements of the iron triangle on the project. However, large issues exist. When Amber is allocated, the SRO needs to resolve these issues urgently. However, it is still possible that issues can be resolved without a major time overrun or cost escalation.

The fourth point on the scale is amber/red. If this result is given, then the requirements of the iron triangle on the project are unlikely to be met as large issues and risks exist that are unlikely to be resolved successfully.

The fifth and last possible result is red. This is the 'stop' result and the project requirements of the iron triangle cannot be achieved.

Using this approach ensures that a successful delivery strategy is in place before large amounts of funding are allocated. One issue in the Translink case study was that the client was kept on the outside and not informed as to how the project was to be managed. The Gateway process ensures that the client is kept informed at all stages of the project and that the project has been thought through prior to money being spent.

3.2. Program planning

Following on from the previous section, based on the same project, the Northern Ireland Government also produced a document called 'Common Minimum Standards for Construction' (IPA, 2012, updated 2017).

This document ensures that the Green Book (Her Majesty's Treasury, 2020) and the Orange Book (HM Government, 2013) are used. The Orange Book defines how risk methodologies should be built into the project and the Green Book allows clear assessment of the financial benefits ensuring VFM. Used jointly, these documents assist in the planning of the process overall, and from a financial and risk standpoint. The issues below were analyzed for IT (Chapter 13) and are compared to construction here.

3.2.1. Strategic objectives and business benefits

Government Strategic objectives have widened because of advice provided by the World Economic Forum (WEF). In addition to the financial elements of the scheme, social value, sometimes called public value, must also be measured (Her Majesty's Treasury, 2020). A holistic approach to the needs of society as well as the client ensues as a move from Maximizing Shareholder Value (making maximum profit) to Stakeholder Capitalism (making organizations assist society in addition to making profit) (WEF, 2020). This philosophy, while reasonably new, is now embedding the ethos that had been applied to construction since 2006. TSO (2015) inserted this in line with EU law as 'respect for Human rights' in the 'fields of Environmental, Social and Labour Law' (Clause 18:2), showing wider aspects of the project that need to be examined.

Case studies of Social Clauses in practice by Eadie and Murphy (2019) show, from a survey of 50 Northern Ireland contractors, that socially responsible practice requires legislation and is implemented due to contractual obligations. The idea that societal change can be fulfilled through government contracts is fleshed out by the WEF (2020) which considers organizations to be organisms rather than machines. From a Government Clients' perspective, IT projects also deliver positive impacts on society and should therefore also be considered in this context.

The Green Book (*Her Majesty's Treasury*, 2020, pp. 75–88) allows for societal benefits to be measured alongside economic market efficiency, meaning all significant costs and non-monetary benefits can be measured. This ensures that sustainability and the sustainable development goals can be built into the process.

All the project goals are assessed and one of the following options are chosen, 1. Business As Usual, with a 90% confidence level, 2. Do Minimum Option, 3. Preferred Option, if not the Do Minimum Option, and 4. More and less ambitious Options 4-to-N as needed, prior to adoption.

All the various benefits are assessed under the following headings: 1. Net Present Social/Public Value for Cost–Benefit Analysis or Net Present Unit Cost, Net Present Unit Cost for Cost Effectiveness Analysis, 2. Relevant present value public sector cost, 3. Appropriate Benefit–Cost Ratio or Net Present Unit Cost, 4. Significant Quantified but unmonetizable benefits, 5. Significant Unquantifiable benefits, and 6. Residual risk and optimism bias allowances. So, using the combination of the options above, all environmental, security, cultural, health, social care, and justice effects are included in the value calculations to taxpayers, ensuring that the population is served by the government. The appraisal should also consider adverse collateral effects and unintended consequences and look at minimizing those.

3.2.2. *High-level architecture*

Simulations are starting to be used in Construction, but are not as widely embedded in IT. Construction Sequencing has been introduced as a result of BIM. The first project in Northern Ireland to use BIM from start to completion was the Dundonald Park and Ride scheme by AMEY Consulting (Eadie *et al.*, 2014).

The use of simulation and clash detection was important as it helped refine the layout for maintenance. This enabled a design where a minimum number of car parking spaces were out of use while servicing the lighting columns. DFI (2015, updated 2019) mandated the use of BIM from Level 2, on 1st April 2016.

BIM promised financial savings at each level of the project life cycle (Eadie *et al.*, 2013). The RICS (2020) report presents an example where using BIM and 'Design for Manufacture and Assembly' at a Holiday Inn in Trafford, Manchester, resulted in a six-month saving on interest loans, and income was generated six months earlier. Overall savings on projects using BIM are well documented. Simulations could be adopted in IT.

3.2.3. *Facets of the program*

One of the reasons the Public Sector adopted the New Engineering Contract (NEC) suite for Government Contracts since May 2006 (DFI, 2018) in Northern Ireland was the need to have conditions of contract (COC) that operated as a toolkit for PM (Department for Communities, 2021). With NEC being proactive and having each of its clauses time bound, the Department for Communities (2021) states the following: 'The main aspect of this transition is moving away from a reactive and hind-sight-based decision-making and management approach to one that is foresight based, encouraging a creative environment with pro-active and collaborative relationships.' This is very different from the litigious nature of the construction industry in Northern Ireland and required a culture change. Eadie (2014) provided three court cases in Northern Ireland that changed European Union (EU) Law, namely, 'Henry Bros Ltd. vs. Department of Education', 'McLaughlin and Harvey vs. Department of Finance and Personnel', and 'Northern Irish Waste Services Ltd vs. Northern Ireland Water Ltd & Ors'. While these cases are related to procurement, it illustrates the adversarial atmosphere in the construction sector, despite the Latham report.

A new and improved way forward was needed, and the first clause in the NEC contract was appealing as it stated that the parties should 'work in a spirit of mutual trust and co-operation'. With the background philosophy in place, the NEC COC set out, through Clause 31.2, the minimum criteria to fulfill the requirements of the program for the job. Producing less than the stipulated information will result in a breach of contract. The following must be submitted for acceptance as part of the Contract (NEC4 Clause 31.2, NEC4 2019):

- *the starting date, access dates, Key Dates and Completion Date,*
- *planned Completion,*
- *the order and timing of the operations which the Contractor plans to do in order to Provide the Works,*
- *the order and timing of the work of the Client and Others as last agreed with them by the Contractor or, if not so agreed, as stated in the Scope,*
- *the dates when the Contractor plans to meet each Condition stated for the Key Dates and to complete other work needed to allow the Client and Others to do their work,*
  - *— provisions for float, time risk allowances, health and safety requirements and the procedures set out in the contract,*
- *the dates when, in order to Provide the Works in accordance with the programme, the Contractor will need*
  - *— access to a part of the Site if later than its access date, acceptances, Plant and Materials and other things to be provided by the Client and information from Others,*
- *for each operation, a statement of how the Contractor plans to do the work identifying the principal Equipment and other resources which will be used and*
- *other information which the Scope requires the Contractor to show on a programme submitted for acceptance.*

This is substantially more detail than what is normally required for an IT Project. Changing the program has a process detailed in NEC4 Clause 31.3, (NEC4, 2019) and the revised program can be refused if the Contractor's plans are not practicable, do not show the information which the contract requires, are not realistic, or do not comply with the Scope. This means that a valid program is submitted at the commencement of the project and amendments are adhered to throughout. An Early Warning (EW) system is included that identifies issues that MIGHT change scope or cost. Program amendments in the NEC4 cannot be ignored.

NEC4 Clause 31.3 (NEC4, 2019) shows that revisions to the program will be deemed accepted if a revised program is ignored. That clause results in amendments submitted by the Contractor coming into force a week after the Contractor notifies the Project Manager of a failure to approve the program. This last element of the clause was only introduced in the NEC4 version of the contract, and from a variety of projects appears to be working well in enforcing adherence to the program and ensuring that changes are not ignored and agreed to at an early stage.

3.2.4. *Individual projects and scope (including business transformation, change management, IT/technical, and communications)*

Scope creep and change management processes have also been built into the NEC4 COC for construction projects. The NEC4 suite (NEC4 2019) is prefaced with the following statement in the UK: 'The Government Construction Board (formerly Construction Clients' Board) recommends that public sector organisations use the NEC contracts and in particular the NEC4 contracts where appropriate, when procuring construction. Standardising use of this comprehensive suite of contracts should help to deliver efficiencies across the public sector and promote behaviours in line with the principles of the Government Construction Strategy.' Using a standard approach means that a similar process of change management is built into all government construction contracts.

The EW system in the NEC4 COC sets the NEC suite apart from other construction contracts. The idea behind this is to get the risk out into the open as early as possible. Changes, risk, and compensation events are then dealt with on an ongoing basis and provide a system of cheaper preventative measures rather than reactionary measures. NEC4 Clause 15.1 (NEC4, 2019) lays the responsibility on both parties to notify the other of any matter which COULD cause changes. A possibility the EW may not change the issues below still exists.

The Contractor and the Project Manager give an early warning by notifying the other as soon as either becomes aware of any matter which could increase the total of the Prices, delay Completion, delay meeting a Key Date or impair the performance of the works in use.

A defined risk management process is used where proposals are discussed to mitigate negative effects of the problems. According to NEC4

Clause 15.3 (NEC4, 2019), the risk reduction meeting's role is to seek solutions, provide a win-win to all parties, decide on the actions to be taken and personnel involved, and lastly, decide what can be removed from the register through a review.

As EWs are cataloged and the Risk Register is updated, the risks are then considered in the decision-making process and cannot be ignored till later in the project. This ensures that, at the earliest possible point within the contract, any warnings on issues like ground conditions not previously envisaged can be dealt with. A similar rigorous change management process could be adopted for IT.

3.2.5. *Dependencies and precedence: Roadmap & Gantt chart representations*

The Critical Path method (CPM) is a project network analysis technique used to predict Total Project Duration (TPD), sometimes called Total Project Time (TPT). This procedure is dealt with in detail within Chapter 9 of this book. Once a Work Breakdown Structure (WBS) is carried out on the project, times for each activity are determined. The critical path (CP) for a project is the series of activities determining the earliest time by which the project can be completed, and it is the longest path through the network diagram and has no slack/float. Activities with zero float on the network diagram are critical as they have no movement flexibility without changing TPT.

This is commonly used for construction projects; however, it is less common in large IT projects. As it determines visually and easily the elements of the package that are critical for delivery of the project on time, and therefore within budget, more use of the method should be made for large IT projects.

Petroutsatou (2019) indicates that construction has moved on from basic CPM to a more supply chain-based approach. However, even the basic CPM method is not widely used within IT projects. This process can be implemented to produce substantial savings within large IT projects.

3.3. *Program structure and organization*

3.3.1. *Program office*

COVID-19 has increased PM risks on projects, as revised requirements were brought in during 2020. These requirements now involve oversight centrally of all SRO activities on Gateway Schemes. Stevenson (2020) states, *A report every six months from CPD to Accounting Officers summarising Gateway™/Assurance Review activity in their Departments and sight of all Gateway™/Assurance Review reports.* This means that the mission and goals of the organization in the delivery of projects are assessed centrally, providing an overview of the various projects being delivered during a period of lockdown. This has been successful in identifying cross-project issues that affect the whole government and it is expected this will continue. Stevenson (2020a) states that on an ongoing basis all the Centres of Procurement Expertise in Northern Ireland need to create a Portfolio, Programme, and Project Office (P3O). These offices provide departmental central visibility on whether the overall delivery will be met and provide support to the individual SROs in relation to project governance and reporting.

The pandemic is a case study and many lessons have been learned in relation to PM due to the variability of the situation on the ground. Northern Ireland has had many different rules throughout the lockdown. Construction was closed on occasions, rules to working practices were amended, and working hours affected.

This has resulted in the PM processes for schemes needing to be more flexible as they needed to react to an ever-evolving situation. Key players in the PM teams being sick led to closures of construction sites in both public and private sectors.

The Ulster University New Belfast Campus is an example (Meredith, 2020) where a worker tested positive leading to the closure of the site for two weeks. On a large project, changes like this are not normal, but during a pandemic the flexibility and planning of the PM team ensuring high-level requirements are met across a central department require centralized assessment.

The formation of P3O sections within the departments allows identification of issues affecting a range of projects and provides a means of disseminating consistent guidance from a central point. This substantially improves the governance of schemes.

3.3.2. *Staffing and resource requirements*

Another result of the Bangor Belfast Railway line case study was that PRINCE2 was implemented for all construction projects in 2002 (DFI, 2010, updated 2019; NI Audit Office, 2016). DFI (2010, updated 2019) recognized that PRINCE2 was originally for IT and reemphasized in Clause 3.2.3 that it should be expanded to construction, stating, *Departments should be aware that it is not acceptable to divorce construction projects from PRINCE2. The specific technical construction or works elements should be taken forward using the Achieving Excellence guidance, but this is only one element of the project. PRINCE2 should be used by Departments to manage the project as a whole.* This confirms that individual issues like procurement are dealt with using Achieving Excellence documentation, but overall PM is provided through a scalable PRINCE2 adoption covering areas like resources.

One of the seven main principles in PRINCE2 is *Defined Roles and Responsibilities.* This means that in construction the Project Initiation Document (PID) identifies people in the various roles at the program management, project board, project manager, and team levels. The organogram ensures that the PM team is in place.

Under the people clauses in the Professional Services contract (PSC) (NEC, 2019a), those working on the contract need to be listed. NEC (2019a) clause 21 states the following:

21.1 The Consultant either provides each key person named to do the job stated in the Contract Data or provides a replacement person who has been accepted by the Service Manager. The Consultant submits the name, relevant qualifications and experience of a proposed replacement person to the Service Manager for acceptance. A reason for not accepting the person is that their relevant qualifications and experience are not as good as those of the person who is to be replaced.

21.2 The Service Manager may, having stated the reasons, instruct the Consultant to remove a person. The Consultant then arranges that, after one day, the person has no further connection with the work included in the contract.

This has both advantages and disadvantages. The client is guaranteed that those with the level of experience named to win the contract are those actually producing the work. They cannot be replaced by those with little experience without the client being willing to accept a lower level of experience or qualification. On the negative side, this causes issues with retirements midway on large jobs. The client can force the consultant to hire someone with identical skills and experience as the retiree. Someone with 40 years' experience and expertise can be difficult to replace, especially on short notice. It stops someone from hiring based on a CV indicating a lot of experience and replacing them with someone just out of university. Smaller organizations should always consider this when naming people during the tender process.

On medium-sized jobs at times, consultants work alone or with a team of draftspersons who are less senior than them. Should a client object to their continued work on a project after 24 hours, they can no longer be part of the team even in an advisory role. To ensure that someone has an in-depth knowledge of the project, consultants should ensure that two members of staff are fully cognizant with a project where possible.

3.4. *Risk and issue management discipline*

In construction, those using the NEC4 COC must have a live risk register as this is part of the contract. This risk register is formed on government contracts using the guidance of the Green Book (Her Majesties Treasury, 2020) and Orange Book (HM Government, 2013). As part of the contract in construction, the NEC4 suite of programs allocates risk between client and contractor and client and consultant in different ways depending on the option taken. There are 6 options in the NEC Engineering and Construction Contract (ECC) suite for contractors as follows:

1. Option A: Priced Contract with Activity Schedule (AS) — Lowest Employer's Risk–Highest Contractor's Risk.

2. Option B: Priced Contract with Bill of Quantities (BOQ) — Next lowest Employer's Risk–Second Highest Contractor's Risk.
3. Option C: Target Contract with AS.
4. Option D: Target Contract with BOQ.

Options C and D balance Employer's and Contractor's risk with the AS having a higher contractors risk than the BOQ.

5. Option E: Cost Reimbursable Contract — Highest Employer's Risk–Lowest Contractor's Risk.
6. Option F: Management Contract — Risk depends on subcontracts.

The different pricing mechanisms will be more completely covered in the next section. However, they bring different allocations of risk and clients choose these for different reasons.

An AS is a series of Lump Sums for activities. As a result, a client would choose Option A above to pass on the complete risk.

If the work is itemized into a BOQ, the risk for omissions to this is still borne by the client as this would have been completed normally by the client's quantity surveyor. The remainder of the risk is passed on to the contractor.

Options C and D are Target Cost contracts. In a Target Cost contract, a Target Cost and a Guaranteed Maximum cost are set. The Guaranteed Maximum Cost is the maximum amount the client will pay for the work. Any additional costs are borne by the contractor. If there are additional costs above the Target Cost but below the Guaranteed Maximum Cost, then these are split between the Client and the Contractor (normally on a 50%/50% basis depending on the percentage split stated in the Contract Data). This is known as pain share. If there are savings and the project is delivered below the Target Cost, then these savings are also split between the client and the contractor on the same basis as pain share but this is known as gain share. These two options share the risk between the contractor and client. Similar to Options A and B, Options C and D have a slight difference in that the risk for omissions to the BOQ is still borne by the client.

The fifth option moves the risk toward the client. The Client is paying the contractor for labor, plant, and materials plus a percentage fee. This type of contract is flexible and allows the client to make changes.

However, the client does not have the financial security of knowing a final price for the work.

The last option F is a Management Contract. To explain this in simple terms, a house extension can be conducted in two ways. The complete work could be given to a builder who prices it. However, the second way is where the foundations are allocated to a contractor, blockwork to another, and so on. This breaks the scheme into small packages of work that the client manages through a management contractor.

For consulting contracts, using the NEC4 PSC, there are only three options but risk is again different for each. These are as follows:

1. Option A: Priced Contract with Activity Schedule — Lowest Employer's Risk–Highest Consultant's Risk.
2. Option C: Target Contract — Balance of Employer's and Consultant's risk.
3. Option E: Cost Reimbursable Contract — Highest Employer's Risk–Lowest Consultant's Risk.

The contract types mirror those for contractors so the risk allocation also mirrors that for contracting options.

Once the overall project risk is allocated through choosing the options, then the project risk is defined in the risk/EW register in Contract Data Part 1 and 2 on both the ECC and PSC contracts. EWs stipulated by the Client in Contract Data Part 1 are further worked up by the consultant or contractor in Contract Data Part 2.

The addition of an EW register in NEC4 has led to many within the industry adding a single column called 'Actions to be taken to avoid or reduce the risk' to the standard Risk Register and combining these into a single register. These revised risk registers now usually have the following columns:

(1) Description of the risk (contains a brief description of the risk),
(2) Time impact in days (normally a percentage value to client and contractor/consultant or a column showing the split),
(3) Cost impact in £ Sterling (normally a percentage value to client and contractor/consultant or a column showing the split),

(4) Responsibility (sometimes called Owner but defines who is responsible for the risk),
(5) Compensation Event (Y or N response and allows the person updating the risk register to state whether it is client's risk under the contract as part of Clause 61),
(6) Cost risk allowance in total of the Prices (this identifies contingency already in the items in the contract),
(7) Probability of the risk occurring, the predicted risk expiry date,
(8) Actual risk expiry date (gets entered and a line through when the risk cannot happen anymore),
(9) To make it compliant with NEC4, actions to be taken to avoid or reduce the risk.

This allows the risks to be monitored and those which have expired ruled out from the risk register on an ongoing basis throughout the project. This means the amount of money allocated to cover risks reduces as the risks get ruled out, resulting in more visibility on the price as the job proceeds.

3.5. *Estimation, realistic timelines, and appropriate fund allocation*

Within construction in the NEC4 suite, there are a range of pricing structures (NEC4, 2019). Additionally, there are pricing documents for ongoing maintenance work. The standard types of pricing documents most commonly used in construction are 1. BOQ, 2. Activity Schedule, 3. Schedule of Rates and Prices, and 4. Quotations for small jobs.

3.5.1. *Bills of Quantities (BOQ)*

When a construction job is broken down into items, a BOQ is prepared. The purpose is to enable bidders to price the work on exactly the same basis so that the one providing the best VFM can be identified in the tender submission. BOQ formation is normally by a quantity surveyor on behalf of a client. In the traditional procurement route, the BOQ is completed by 'Take-off' from a set of drawings completed by the designers.

The priced BOQ has a 'Firm' price or lump sum at the end, a sum of all the items.

Another type of BOQ is called an approximate BOQ. This is used where exact 'Take-off' cannot happen and quantities are estimated. In both types of BOQ, 'remeasure' takes places to ensure that what is actually performed is paid for.

AlAssiry and Mustapha (2020) investigated the use of BOQ in construction projects in Saudi Arabia. They concluded that the *reason for inefficiencies and inaccuracies is due to the lack of standardized methods of costing of construction projects*. Within the United Kingdom, standard methods of measurement (MOM) deal with this issue. These set a standard set of principles that are used to produce the BOQ.

There are three main MOM used in the UK for BOQ formation:

1. New Rules of Measurement (NRM) used for Building Works.
2. Civil Engineering Method of Measurement (CESMM4) used for Civil Engineering Schemes.
3. Manual of Contract Documents for Highway Works (MCHW) Vol. 4 used for Roads Schemes and associated works.

Using a standard MOM removes the standardization of layout issue. Durdyev (2021), currently in press, from an assessment of published literature shows that *design problems, incomplete design, inaccurate estimation, poor planning, weather, poor communication, stakeholder's skill, experience and competence, financial problems/poor financial management, price fluctuations, contract management issues and ground/soil conditions* are the main causes of cost overruns. These issues show the importance of having a set of virtually complete design drawings and specifications before BOQ formation and a reduction in unknowns through investigations, such as environmental and geotechnical. The reduction in unknowns provides final-price certainty to the client.

3.5.2. *Activity Schedule (AS)*

A BOQ is a list of items needed to construct a project, whereas an AS is a list of activities that when completed form the project. If the program is considered, the scheme is broken down into activities with the timeline for each beside it. The AS for NEC ECC options A and C (NEC4, 2019) is easily described as a similar series of activities with costs associated with each. Instead of getting paid after remeasuring from a BOQ, the contractor gets paid when each of the activities is completed. Each activity is priced as a lump sum: the price paid by the client for the completed activity. NEC does not allow part payment. This means that the interim payments on a regular basis that are available when Option B is adopted do not occur as the contractor needs to complete the activities before payment. This effectively increases the risk for the contractor as it in effect makes this option a lump-sum contract.

3.5.3. *Schedule of Rates and Prices (SORP)*

An SORP is similar in layout to a BOQ without a quantities column. It is used where quantities cannot be determined at the Tender stage. It is commonly used for maintenance contracts or responsive works contracts. As the quantity of items is not known beforehand, contractors price to ensure viability of the costs for a period of up to five years (the standard length of some maintenance contracts). Prices increase as a result of the additional flexibility.

3.5.4. *Small jobs*

Eadie and McCavigan (2016) investigated the use of a Random Selection process incorporated in government procurement in Northern Ireland for schemes below £30,000. This method uses a computer-generated random selection process to select six contractors, who have already passed the minimum requirements set, to be invited to tender (DFI, 2016). The study concluded that 42% of respondents considered Random Selection an improvement on the full prequalification process with respondents citing the reduction in bureaucracy as the main driver. This still indicates that there is substantial support for the full quality to be measured in the tender process. Pre-Qualification Questionnaires, Prequalified Select Lists, and the Random Selection process were the three options most favored.

3.5.5. *Quality*

The difficulty in getting the lowest price is that the quality of the final project was not being taken into consideration in construction. The need to assess quality at the tender stage was linked to John Ruskin (1819–1900) in the Washington Post in 1913. The following quotation is credited to him: *It is unwise to pay too much, but it's worse to pay too little. When you pay too little, you sometimes lose everything because the thing you bought was incapable of doing the thing you bought it to do. The common law of business balance prohibits paying a little and getting a lot — it can't be done* (Bergeron and Lacinski, 2000, pp. 66). Assessment of quality alongside price has been adopted by governments across Europe using the restricted procedure. This has been incorporated into UK law through the Public Contract Regulations 2015 (TSO, 2015).

Lack of assessment of quality alongside price led Ramsey *et al.* (2009) to determine that the lowest bidder might not possess the experience, capacity, or expertise to deliver a project when compared to a bid with a slightly higher price. A Greek court case, Lianakis AE v Alexandroupolis (Eur-Lex, 2008), fed into the previous iteration of European Directive 2004/18 (Eur-Lex, 2004) and determined that in a two-stage tender process quality should be assessed differently at each stage.

Quality at the prequalification stage was assessed first, called 'selection criteria', and examined historical aspects of delivery by the organization. In looking back, the theory was that if a good-quality product had been produced in the past by the bidder, the likelihood would be that this could be replicated in the project at hand. After prequalification, bidders are reduced to 5–7 who would proceed to the second stage.

Quality at the second stage was assessed on 'award criteria', issues that were legally obliged to be provided as part of the bid and needed to be attended to for the job at hand. So, selection criteria in the first prequalification stage examine historical delivery from 'the bidder', whereas the second stage award criteria examine what quality the people, plant, and materials will bring as part of 'the bid on the contract in hand'. Lianakis AE v Alexandroupolis (Eur-Lex, 2008) determined that there must be a difference between selection and award criteria and they could not be examined twice. This process, examining historical quality first and the quality being brought to the job second, has proved effective in ensuring the quality of the final product.

3.6. *Program operational aspects — requirements*

The philosophy of Earned Value Management (EVM) was developed by the US military for defense contracts. Network Analysis allows the CP to be determined, and planned work can then be compared with completed work on an ongoing basis throughout the project. Previously in the chapter, it was shown that, initially, a WBS is completed. This can then be programmed and a schedule provided. Linked to this is the pricing of the activities (budget). As elements of time and cost are determined based on estimated values, the 'Earned Value' can be measured.

The term itself comes from the concept that every task 'earns value' on completion. So, as payment occurs on the completion of an activity on the AS, it earns that value. The idea is that this value can be compared to the actual cost and budgeted cost to calculate variance and predict future performance. The process is developed more fully in the Chapter 9.

A Traffic Light status is useful in conveying overall project results with one color. The SPI and CPI ranges are determined, and the following values used to determine the true project color: Green (1.0–.95) — Ok Progress, Acceptable, or Good; Yellow (.94–.85) — Pay Special Attention; or Red (.84, 0) — Stop.

Using these values, the status of the project can be determined and also how much Value Engineering (VE) needs to be carried out to get it back on track. VE is a continuous process where all the components and processes involved in the construction process are critically appraised to determine whether better-value alternatives or solutions are available.

CPM is not widely used within IT. This means the benefits of EVM cannot be accrued. It is proposed that both the CPM and EVM are adopted more widely for IT projects to allow VE to produce benefits.

3.7. *Managing the interface between business-as-usual (BAU) operations and program-specific operations*

There are two documents that are required for government construction projects at their conclusion. These are linked to PRINCE2, but in a slightly different format: Post-Project Review (PPR) and End-Project Report (EPR). When these are put together, they form the Post-Implementation Review (PIR). PPRs have been implemented for Government Construction projects to measure the success of a project and highlight good and poor practices for future projects. PPRs allow analysis of the following:

1. A comparison of proposed benefits (Business Case) with those realized identifies the project effectiveness in meeting its aims.
2. A comparison of planned costs and benefits with actual costs and benefits. EVM is used to carry out a VFM assessment.
3. A list of benefits and how actual circumstances affected these is prepared to create a 'lessons learned' section. The lessons may be positive or negative, so that in the future good practice is adopted and poor practice avoided.
4. An investigation into anything else that could have been done to increase the benefits or positives. This includes a probe into the planned outcomes and the circumstances affecting these during the project. An action plan for future projects is then prepared.

The process is normally completed in five stages:

1. Get individual feedback from Stakeholders (questionnaire);
2. Analyze the data gathered;
3. Organize a meeting to share the findings;
4. Add any amendments that came as a result of the meeting;
5. Summarize the feedback in a written document.

A template for DFI schemes (DFI, 2009) is available online. The EPR is the project manager's report to the project board on completion.

It compares the results to targets in the Project Initiation Document (PID) and examines approved changes / variations and their cause. The client's quality expectations and the requirements (which could be different) should be covered. As PRINCE2 is management by exception, these and the location of Exception Reports are included in the EPR. The PPR benefits examination should be copied into the EPR to prove that the project has met its objectives. In PRINCE2, this forms the formal project closure.

The process is complete when the documents are combined into the single PIR. This process has inputs from all levels of the team. The SRO requests the PIR and guarantees that relevant staff are available to input to the review process. The SRO is responsible for sending the documentation to appropriate stakeholders. The project manager is responsible for compiling the reports and ensuring that the lessons learned are recorded. They are responsible for submitting the completed documentation to the project board. For the process to work, all staff are responsible for informing the project manager of lessons learned, value from variations, and the impact on timescales from activities during the project for inclusion in the documents.

4. Further analysis

The previous section discusses PM practice in Construction corresponding to the topics raised in Chapter 12 (Section 4). This draws from UK Public Sector Construction experience, especially of Northern Ireland, whereas Chapter 12 drew on experience mainly from Australia. It would, however, be fair to posit that these descriptions are broadly representative of construction and IT practice in general. With this caveat, a comparative analysis was done. The convenient abbreviation 'IT' is used to refer to large IT-driven business transformation programs.

Certain practices differ between the two disciplines. These may be partly explained by differences in the nature of the disciplines.

- Construction is physical in that you can touch, feel, and visually inspect what is constructed. In IT, unless you are dealing with hardware, you cannot use any of these senses.

- IT programs can use in-house staff, but in the traditional route in construction, in-house staff and subcontractors are used. In design and build, large construction projects also have staff actively involved in the design and construction. So, construction uses a lot more niche specialists outside own labor than IT.
- In construction, what is delivered is static (i.e., a building, a bridge, and a dam). It may support dynamic things, e.g., cars or trains along a bridge, but does not itself 'run'. IT in contrast (like manufacturing), delivers a 'product' (a system) that runs.
- As a corollary, IT systems need to be tested at the end (as well as at key stages). Testing in the IT sense has no equivalent activity in Construction, other than snagging/inspections of work.
- Arguably, there are a great deal more hard dependencies in a typical Construction project than in IT. It follows that the IT program manager typically has more flexibility to adjust to changing circumstances as the program progresses.

In examining the differences between practices in the two disciplines, the first striking divergence is adherence to standards: In Construction, there are many mandated standards that projects comply with. On the other hand, IT differs: In IT, there are methodologies and 'best practices'. These practices are not mandated in the construction sense but adhered to (or not) at the level of the particular program. The parties involved therefore have no recourse other than the particular contract.

The situation is compounded by the fact that methodologies and best practice in IT change, sometimes relatively rapidly: functional decomposition, data flow diagrams, object-oriented design, Message-oriented middleware, Service-oriented architecture, microservices, etc., and also two major approaches to project organization — waterfall and agile (with various flavors of agile). Under these conditions, standards and best practice do not get sufficient time to establish themselves. In contrast, in construction, materials, equipment, safety, etc., have taken great strides, and construction processes have remained relatively stable, allowing time for these to mature and standards to become established, mandated, and accepted in the community.

Chapter 12 identifies a fluidity of IT standards and best practice and exposes the enterprise in the vagaries of the situation, i.e., the skills of the internal stakeholders, program's senior staff, and the vendor's touted best practice. There is no safety net of industry-mandated common practice upon which to fall back. Some of the details are discussed in Table 1.

Table 1. CSF comparison between IT and construction: summary & findings.

CSF	
Executive/ Sponsor Support	Effective communication with stakeholders is an obvious prerequisite to gaining and maintaining their support. In addition to regular communication, Gateway processes, formal review, and 'go, no-go' decisions at critical stages of a program are excellent methods of open communication. In Construction, Gateway processes are used, especially in the very early stages of the program to very good effect to communicate with stakeholders and take hard decisions. Despite appearing in PM methodologies such as PMBOK and PRINCE2, the level of strict adherence in IT appears variable. Sometimes (see Cp. 13), the activity happens but the quality of data/ evidence presented is dubious. There is room in IT to follow these processes more closely.
Planning	**Strategic objectives and business benefits:** The experience described (of the UK and Northern Ireland Public Sector) shows a sophisticated approach, taking into account not only economic but also the social benefits of a construction project. Moreover, the mandated technique has enshrined an options analysis. In IT, the economic benefits are generally assessed in commercial enterprises, but other benefits may well be taken into account in the public sector, not for profit sector, etc. The main difference however is that in IT a more laissez faire approach is evident, where no uniform standard (other than general accounting practices for quantitative assessments) is adhered to. Options analysis is sometimes done, but not at the level of detail/ rigor in construction.
	High-level Architecture: Use of simulation (as in BIM) is increasingly common in Construction, greatly improving the design process and the cost effectiveness of delivery. In IT, high-level architecture in planning is almost universally employed. However, simulation of the target state, though beneficial, is very uncommon and is perhaps a productive area for research.
	Facets of the program: A formal approach (mandated as a consequence of certain legislative changes) for Construction that encompasses scope, estimation and project planning, and cooperative risk management is described. Such uniformity is not mandated in IT, and again the practices adopted are shaped by the individual enterprises contemplating large business transformations.

(Continued)

Table 1.   (*Continued*)

CSF	
Program structure and org.	Establishing a Portfolio, Programme, and Project Office in Construction is discussed. In IT, too, program offices are typically created for large programs; however, the moot point in IT as articulated in Chapter 12 is the variability in the level of expertise of senior 3PO staff. The requirement to name key people for the program (and contractual obligations on replacement) is common to both disciplines.
Risk and issue management discipline	As in construction, in IT, there are different options for assigning responsibility: from fixed price to time and materials. There are different reward mechanisms for early delivery. The difference is that there is no equivalent granular control mechanism to a BOQ. The ways of granular control (both in Agile and in Waterfall) are based on task completion. There is no equivalent to measurement of quantities, their pricing, and progressive usage. In construction, the type of contract (priced contract with activity schedule to management contract), early warning of variation, cooperative risk/issue resolution, apportioning responsibility, and mature estimation techniques (see below) provide a strong framework for project control and risk mitigation. In comparison with these techniques and processes, it is safe to infer that in IT, risk management is more of an art than a science and is short of maturity.
Estimation, realistic timelines, appropriate allocation of funds	With the maturity of BOQ and AS approaches, estimation is more of a quantitative discipline in Construction than in IT. In fairness to IT, it must be said that there is a great deal of variability in the nature and scope of large IT programs; you will be hard put to find a match elsewhere — the combination of new functionality introduced, systems replaced, systems retired, required integration for the new systems to cohabit in the IT landscape, organizational change management, and preferred delivery approach will be unique to the program. It is difficult therefore to use past data as a basis for estimation. In IT, estimation of time taken for the activities in the project plan (i.e., the equivalent of activity schedules) is the main approach to estimation. Function point analysis is a technique used to understand the complexity of the software to be built and estimate the work. Also, learning from commonalities at the individual project level may be feasible, even though programs may be unique. In IT, estimation remains less of a science. As seen in Chapter 12, one of the root causes of large IT programs going wrong is inaccurate estimation, especially skewed estimates brought about by other agendas such as preconceived delivery dates, program cost ceilings, etc.

Table 1. (*Continued*)

CSF	
Prog. operational aspects — Requirements	The assessment of work completed and therefore the work to complete remains much less of a science in IT — in large programs, each project manager's project reporting is rolled up into program reporting. The PM typically relies on the reporting provided by the in-situ technical staff. There are no 'objective' measures of progress such as BOQ quantities or visual inspections of work completed. This is partly the nature of software development, change management, etc., that are more ephemeral and partly the maturity of the discipline.
Managing the interface between BAU & Prog.	As alluded to at the start of this section, IT needs to deliver a system that *operates* (not only the software component but organizational processes that it is in support of). As such, the new system that the program delivers (which may have ramifications from the operational model of the enterprise down to the software) has to be brought into and socialized with what currently exists. This entails engagement with the business as a usual part of the enterprise along a broad front. There is no equivalence here with Construction. PIRs are common to both disciplines.

5. Summary and conclusions

Chapter 12 concluded that, rising above the specifics, the lack of uniform adherence to best practice and the failure of capability or competence of some form (with the two often feeding each other) were at the root of failures of IT programs.

Comparison with construction in this chapter demonstrates that, while there are unavoidable differences between the two, comparisons are valid in certain areas of practice.

Key points of difference are as follows: Mandated standards and best practice in construction demand adherence and the entrenchment of certain good practices through the maturity of the discipline. IT is much more ad hoc in its observance of best practice and often falls prey to the vagaries of the particular situation.

If asked to identify the key areas for improvement for IT programs, they would be to (a) spend sufficient time and effort in planning, (b) adopt Gateway Review Processes, (c) adopt a well-defined and standardized approach to manage risk, and (d) reintroduce CPM at the program and project levels, the use of which appears to have diminished in IT with the introduction of Agile practices.

There are fruitful areas for further research, for example, the challenges of uniform IT best practice as methodologies, tools, and techniques change relatively rapidly. What could be an IT equivalent of the BOQ of construction? IT Earned Value Analysis?

This chapter will hopefully encourage cross-fertilization of project management best practice so that those working in both fields can avoid pitfalls and adopt successful methodologies.

References

AlAssiry, S. and Mustapha, N. (2020). The impact of quantities accuracy on the final costs of governmental projects in Saudi Arabia, *J. Eng. Sci. Assiut Univ. Fac. Eng.*, 48(2), 186–198.

Bergeron, M. and Lacinski, P. (2000). *Serious Straw Bale: A Home Construction Guide for All Climates*, Chelsea Green Publishing, USA: White River Junction.

Bryde, D. (2010). Is construction different? A comparison of perceptions of project management performance and practices by business sector and project type, *Constr. Manage. Econ.*, 26(3), 315–327.

Bröchner, J. and Badenfelt, U. (2011). Changes and change management in construction and IT projects, *Autom. Constr.*, 20(7), 767–775.

Department for Communities. (2021). Policy Framework for Construction Procurement. Available at: https://www.communities-ni.gov.uk/policy-framework-construction-procurement.

DFI. (2009). Generic PPM Templates. Available at: https://www.finance-ni.gov.uk/sites/default/files/publications/dfp/coe-templates-post-project-review.doc.

DFI. (2010, updated 2019). PGN06/10 Construction Procurement Policy Framework. Available at: https://www.finance-ni.gov.uk/sites/default/files/publications/dfp/PGN-06-10-Construction-Procurement-Policy-Framework_1.pdf.

DFI. (2016). PGN 05/12 Simplified Approach to Procurements Over £30,000 and Under EU Thresholds. Available at: https://www.finance-ni.gov.uk/sites/default/files/publications/dfp/PGN-05-12-Simplified-Approach-to-Procurements-between-%C2%A330k-and-EU-thresholds-%28pdf%20version%29.PDF.

DFI. (2018). PGN 01/15 Standardisation of NEC3 Engineering and Construction Contract Z Clauses. Available at: https://www.finance-ni.gov.uk/sites/default/files/publications/dfp/PGN-01-15-version-May-2018.pdf.

DFI. (2015, updated 2019). PGN 03/15 Building Information Modelling (BIM). Available at: https://www.finance-ni.gov.uk/publications/procurement-guidance-note-0315-building-information-modelling-bim.

Durdyev, S. (2021). Review of construction journals on causes of project cost overruns, engineering, *Constr. Archit. Manage.*, Currently in press.

Eadie, R. and Murphy, M. (2019). Socially responsible procurement: A service innovation for generating employment in construction, *Built Environ. Proj. Asset Manage.*, 9(1), 138–152.

Eadie, R. and McCavigan, M. (2016). Random selection: Winning the lottery in construction contracts, *Int. J. Proc. Manage.*, 9(2), 185–205.

Eadie, R., Heanen, A. and Hall, J. (2014). Civil engineering and the interoperability between Building Information Modelling (BIM) and E-Procurement, in *Proceedings of the 9th International Conference on Civil Engineering Design and Construction (Science and Practice), Varna, Bulgaria*. Available at: https://pure.ulster.ac.uk/en/publications/civil-engineering-and-the-interoperability-between-building-infor-3.

Eadie, R. (2014). Does Europe Need a Specific Prequalification System for Highways Projects. Available at: https://pure.ulster.ac.uk/en/publications/does-europe-need-a-specific-prequalification-system-for-highway-p-3.

Eadie, R., Browne, M., Odeyinka, H., McKeown, C. and McNiff, S. (2013). BIM implementation throughout the UK construction project lifecycle: An analysis, *Autom. Constr.*, 36, 145–151.

Eur-Lex. (2008). Emm. G. Lianakis AE, Sima Anonymi Techniki Etaireia Meleton kai Epivlepseon and Nikolaos Vlachopoulos v Dimos Alexandroupolis and Others, European Court reports 2008 Page I-00251. Available at: https://eur-lex.europa.eu/legal-content/EN/ALL/?uri=CELEX:62006CJ0532.

Gershon, P. (1999). Gershon Report. Available at: https://publications.parliament.uk/pa/cm200304/cmselect/cmworpen/311/31107.htm.

Her Majesty's Treasury. (2020). The Green Book: Appraisal and Evaluation in Central Government. Available at: https://assets.publishing.service.gov.uk/government/uploads/system/uploads/attachment_data/file/938046/The_Green_Book_2020.pdf.

HM Government. (2013). The Orange Book: Management of Risk: Principles and Concepts. Available at: https://assets.publishing.service.gov.uk/government/uploads/system/uploads/attachment_data/file/866117/6.6266_HMT_Orange_Book_Update_v6_WEB.PDF.

IPA. (2012, updated 2017). Common Minimum Standards for Construction: Common Minimum Standards for the Procurement of Built Environments in the Public Sector. Available at: https://assets.publishing.service.gov.uk/government/uploads/system/uploads/attachment_data/file/600885/2017-03-15_Construction_Common__Minimum_Standards__final___1_.pdf.

Meredith, R. (2020). Coronavirus: Work Suspended on £360m UU Campus After Worker Tests Positive. Available at: https://www.bbc.co.uk/news/uk-northern-ireland-54576107.

NEC4. (2019). *Engineering and Construction Contract Option A: Priced Contract with Activity Schedule*, Glasgow, UK: Thomas Telford.

NEC4. (2019a). *Professional Services Contract*, Glasgow, UK: Thomas Telford.

NI Audit Office. (2016). Major Capital Projects. Available at: https://www.niauditoffice.gov.uk/sites/niao/files/226718%20NIAO%20Major%20Capital%20Projects_FINAL%20LW%20RES%20Complete.pdf.

NI Audit Office. (2007). The Upgrade of the Belfast to Bangor Railway Line. Available at: https://www.niauditoffice.gov.uk/publications/upgrade-belfast-bangor-railway-line.

NI Audit Office. (2009). A Review of the Gateway Process & The Management of Personal Injury Claims. Available at: https://www.niauditoffice.gov.uk/publications/upgrade-belfast-bangor-railway-line.

NIDirect. (2021). The Northern Ireland Transport Holding Company. Available at: https://www.infrastructure-ni.gov.uk/articles/northern-ireland-transport-holding-company.

Petroutsatou, K. (2019). A proposal of project management practices in public institutions through a comparative analyses of critical path method and critical chain, *Int. J. Cons. Manage.*, 29, 1–10.

Ramsey, V., Minogue, A., Baster, J., O'Reilly, M. and Lai, H. (2009). Construction Law Handbook 2009 Edition. Available at: https://www.icevirtuallibrary.com/doi/book/10.1680/clh2009.36017.

RICS. (2020). The Future of BIM: Digital Transformation in the UK Construction and Infrastructure Sector. Available at: https://www.rics.org/globalassets/rics-website/media/upholding-professional-standards/sector-standards/construction/future-of-bim_1st-edition.pdf.

Stevenson, S. (2020). Revised Policy and Guidance on Best Practice in Project Delivery and Engagement with the Gateway™/Assurance Review Process. Available at: https://www.finance-ni.gov.uk/sites/default/files/publications/dfp/DAOdof0220.pdf.

Turner, R., Ledwith, A. and Kelly, J. (2009). Project management in small to medium-sized enterprises: A comparison between firms by size and industry, *Int. J. Managing Proj. Bus.*, 2(2), 282–296.

TSO. (2015). Public contracts regulations 2015, The Stationery Office. Available at: http://www.legislation.gov.uk/uksi/2015/102/contents/made.

Vrchota, J., Řehoř, P., Maříková, M. and Pech, M. (2020). Critical success factors of the project management in relation to Industry 4.0 for sustainability of projects, *Sustainability*, 13(1), 281.

WEF. (2020). Measuring Stakeholder Capitalism: Towards Common Metrics and Consistent Reporting of Sustainable Value Creation. Available at: http://www3.weforum.org/docs/WEF_IBC_Measuring_Stakeholder_Capitalism_Report_2020.pdf.

Chapter 14

Software for IT Project Schedule and Cost Management

G. Thilini Weerasuriya[*,§], John Pereira[†,¶], Srinath Perera[*,ǀ]
and Samudaya Nanayakkara[‡,**]

*Centre for Smart Modern Construction, Western Sydney University,
Locked Bag 1797, Penrith, New South Wales 2751, Australia
†Rentman B.V., Drift 17, 3512 BR Utrecht, Netherlands
‡University of Moratuwa, Sri Lanka
§t.weerasuriya@westernsydney.edu.au
¶john@jnx.me
ǀsrinath.perera@westernsydney.edu.au
**samudaya@uom.lk

The management of information technology projects is a challenging process, which requires keeping track of a considerable amount of data. Therefore, project management software is indispensable for project managers, especially for managing the schedule and cost of projects. This chapter explores a selection of prevalently used software applications for schedule management in IT projects. An overview and key features of Asana, Jira, Microsoft Project, Monday.com, and Trello are described. A summary of the features of five other software, Basecamp, GanttPRO, LiquidPlanner, Teamwork, and Zoho Sprints, is also presented. A comparison of these project schedule management software is introduced. The chapter also discusses and compares software applications for cost management, namely, Harvest, Microsoft Project, Paymo, and Zoho Projects.

1. Introduction

The development of computer technology brought about the use of software applications for project management in the 1960s and the 1970s. These software systems were executed on mainframe and minicomputers, and were costly. Project management software decreased in cost and increased in popularity from the 1980s with the increasing use of personal computers. With the invention of the Internet and World Wide Web, project management software with Internet connectivity was introduced, enabling project managers to keep track of projects from any location at any time.

Office productivity software applications such as spreadsheets and word processing software are used by many people for project management activities, including managing project schedule and cost. However, when projects get larger with more variables, using productivity software would take more time and effort to manage. Instead, investing in project management software applications would simplify the task of managing a project. A web search for project management software would unearth hundreds of applications with varying levels of complexity and support for different types of projects and use cases. These software applications come in various forms, such as desktop, web, or mobile applications, and as commercial or free and open-source software. The price of commercial tools varies according to available functions, and frequently a free version with limited functionality or a trial version for a limited time is provided.

Information technology (IT) projects frequently run over time and budget (Sanchez *et al.*, 2017), and selecting the most suitable software for schedule and cost management would contribute towards the success of projects. Therefore, this chapter explores a selection of prevalently used software applications for schedule and cost management in IT projects.

An overview of the features and a comparison of these software is provided to support the selection of a suitable application.

2. Software for schedule management in IT projects

In general terms, schedule management is synonymous with project management. Therefore, 'project management software' predominantly contains schedule management features. This section discusses the major features of popular project management software applications currently used within IT projects.

2.1. *Asana*

2.1.1. *Overview*

Asana (2021) is a software solution for work management and collaboration among team members. It was commercially launched in 2012 by Dustin Moskovitz and Justin Rosenstein. It tracks information related to tasks and helps to identify team members responsible for relevant tasks. Users of Asana can either use predefined templates or flexibly choose unique ways to track project work.

Users on Asana can switch between calendars, timelines, lists, and Kanban boards to view and manage projects. Workspaces are used to group users based on a common aspect, and projects are created within workspaces. Asana's timeline view provides a Gantt chart of the duration, deadline, and dependencies of each task in a project. The project overview helps to identify the status of the project at a given time. Workflows and rules streamline and automate manual steps, thereby saving time. Agile teams can also use Asana by translating Scrum concepts into Asana.

Tasks and subtasks can be created within projects and assigned to users with due dates. Workflows in Asana are constructed from tasks and subtasks. Comments, tags, and attachments can be added to tasks, which provide context and history for each completed task.

Asana can provide users with appropriate permissions an overall assessment of all tasks assigned to an individual. However, this is not a detailed quantification of hours worked by a person which certain other project management software provides.

Asana includes advanced search functionality, with options such as specifying if the search item is a task or conversation, searching by the person assigned, completed tasks, and due date. Custom filters can also be used to drill down further based on people, tags, dependencies, and sub-tasks. These complex searches can be saved as interactive reports which update when new items that match the terms are added. These reports support individuals to monitor their progress over time and for managers to identify employee productivity.

Asana provides a free tier of service, Basic, that offers several features such as unlimited projects, teams, messaging, and multiple project views but limits the number of collaborators in a team to 15. The Premium tier allows unlimited team members and additional features, such as dashboards, pre-set rules, advanced search and reporting, and administrative controls. The Business tier provides all features available in Premium and options to manage portfolios, workload, approvals, custom rules, and so on. The Enterprise tier offers the Business tier features as well as additional security, control, and support.

2.1.2. *Key features*

Reporting: Advanced search functionality exists, and complex searches can be saved as interactive reports.

Dashboards: Provides an overview of tasks assigned to users.

Task management: Provides good task management features with the ability to translate to Scrum concepts as well.

Resource management: Does not provide resource management features.

Support for integrations: Asana provides integrations for over a hundred third-party apps to extend the functionality of the software.

Good fit: Small teams of up to 15 members can make use of the core task management features to handle fewer complex projects.

Not a fit: Large teams that require managing resources and schedules of complex projects may not find Asana suitable for their requirements.

2.2. *Jira*

2.2.1. *Overview*

Jira (Atlassian, 2021) is an issue tracking and project management software created by Atlassian. Initially developed by Mike Cannon-Brookes and Scott Farquhar and released in 2002, Jira began its life as an issue tracking software for developers. In the last two decades, Atlassian has created or acquired different software and integrated them into a set of cohesive tools that complement each other. Jira is available with the following specializations:

- **Jira Core:** Generic project management tools aimed at businesses.
- **Jira Software:** Project management and issue tracking for software teams.
- **Jira Service Management:** Primarily for development and operations teams to manage their engagements.
- **Jira Align:** Connects to multiple Jira instances and provides an enterprise-wide view of projects and services.

Jira Software's capabilities (referred to as Jira for simplicity from now on) cover all aspects of the software development and release lifecycles. Jira offers a high degree of customizability and excels at working within a company's existing workflow. Like Trello, Jira offers boards, columns, and tasks but further incorporates sprints and releases, backlogs, epics, multiple types of issues, and releases.

Jira's focus is on flexibility and being able to customize the software to work with an organization's existing process. To achieve this goal, most aspects of the software can be changed, starting with the type of issues available to create. Issues are the building block of the assignable work in a project and Jira administrators have full control over the types of issues that are available and what type of information they contain. As in other offerings, issues can contain metadata and rich data alike, along with an audit log to track changes to the content. They can also be linked together to create subtasks or if the scope is larger, they can be organized into epics.

Jira also allows you to create workflows that apply to issues. A workflow is a process that is used to ship software, and Jira allows you to create your own organization-specific workflow or select one out of the box. This automates the state changes that an issue transitions through during its lifecycle. Workflows can also limit the actions that a user can carry out on an issue, thus ensuring that everyone follows the organization process as laid out in Jira.

A project manager should always have a clear and up-to-date understanding of a project at any given time. Jira aims to provide this clarity with an extensive reporting and analysis system. Issues can be searched and filtered by dozens of attributes and many different cards are available to get a quick overview or identify upcoming problems.

Atlassian has a separate marketplace for all its product offerings including Jira software. These applications allow deep integration with external services and support incoming as well as outgoing data connections.

Jira's cloud offering comes with multiple price configurations, starting with a free offering for teams of up to 10 users and up to thousands of users on their Enterprise plans.

2.2.2. *Key features*

Reporting: Extensive reporting functionality and analysis via charts.
Dashboards: Has a robust dashboard system that lets you create custom dashboards with many different widgets and charts.
Task management: Excellent task management via the use of issues, epics, and sprints. Basic issues support rich media and highly customizable metadata.
Resource management: Jira offers resource management and time tracking. This functionality can be further extended by apps available in their marketplace.
Support for integrations: Extensive marketplace lists apps across all Atlassian products and allows custom integrations between services by using their API.

Good fit: Great for mature software development teams that can use the extra customizability and all the features on offer. Excellent tools for big-picture project management and analysis.

Not a fit: Smaller teams with simpler software development and release workflows might find it too difficult to use and offer less value.

2.3. *Microsoft Project*

2.3.1. *Overview*

Microsoft Project (2021) is a commonly used project management software worldwide. It is developed and sold by Microsoft and was first commercially available in 1984. Microsoft Project contains robust project planning and scheduling features. Tasks can be created and assigned to team members, and project status can be easily tracked. The software has multiple views to manage tasks, namely, Grid, Board, and Timeline (Gantt chart) views. The Grid view displays tasks as an ordered list. The Board view can be used to understand the status and workflow of tasks using pre-set or custom task boards. The Timeline view provides a visual understanding of tasks and dates along with their assignments and relationships. Customizable templates are also provided to support the planning of projects. Reports and interactive dashboards provide additional insight into managing projects. Team members can collaborate with each other using Microsoft Teams and simultaneously edit project schedules and task lists. Agile methodologies are also supported in newer versions of the software.

Microsoft Project is available as both cloud-based and on-premises solutions. The on-premises solutions are Standard, Professional, and Project Server. The Standard version has project management features such as managing project schedules and costs, and managing tasks, reports, and business intelligence. The Professional edition includes additional features such as team collaboration and connectivity to Microsoft Project Server, which is a scalable solution for project portfolio management, and project and work management. The cloud-based solutions have three pricing plans. The cheapest tier only has features for project planning and scheduling and collaboration. Tools such as reporting, resource management, and timesheet submission are unavailable in the lowest tier but are available in the middle tier. The highest tier contains all the features of the lower tiers as well as project portfolio management and enterprise resource planning and management.

2.3.2. *Key features*

Reporting: Contains pre-installed reports to compare projects and includes graphical reports.

Dashboards: Interactive dashboards can be created to check the overall status of projects and inspect the details of projects.

Task management: Provides strong task management features including the ability to trace task paths for any task. The inactive tasks' feature can be used to perform what-if analyses on project plans.

Resource management: Project teams can be defined, resources for the project can be added, and tasks can be assigned to the resources.

Support for integrations: Project add-ins can be created to extend the functionality of Microsoft Project for scenarios such as project scheduling, resource management, team communication, approvals, and getting reporting data.

Good fit: Medium to large organizations with an established Microsoft ecosystem can make good use of the integration with other Microsoft applications such as Office 365, Skype, Teams, and Sharepoint.

Not a fit: Smaller organizations will find Microsoft Project relatively more expensive, especially since each user requires a license to make use of the team collaboration features of the software. The web version of Project also has certain limitations which may affect users who opt for the lowest cloud-based solution tier.

2.4. *Monday*

2.4.1. *Overview*

Monday.com (2021) is a project management software initially created as an internal tool within the Wix (wix.com) organization in 2010. The product left Wix and became a separate entity in 2012 and was called 'daPulse' in its early years before being rebranded as Monday.com in 2017. Monday focuses on automation and is a very intuitive user interface to improve user's productivity while using the application.

Monday uses boards, workspaces, groups, and items to organize all work. Creating a workspace on Monday prompts you to add a board to it. Boards can be customized so that they follow a template that is optimized for a particular work process. Example templates currently available range from software development, sprint planning, releases & roadmap, and bug queue. Dozens of templates unrelated to the software development process are also available, ranging from human resources to construction, and currently number over 250.

Items are the building blocks for all other features within Monday; they provide the context to build the automation and custom view features. Items can contain rich content and provide additional metadata via status, date, and assignment information. You can also add many other metadata or even connect external services which provide even more attributes to be filled in. The items in Monday seem less structured than more traditional offerings but are very intuitive to the non-technical user. Additionally, you can engage with updates via email and the updates are reflected in the application.

Whatever template you go with, you can always make the board your own by adding or removing views. Views provide additional functionality and insight into the items added on the board. Views can range from tables, Kanban boards, forms, to timelines and use the item information already available to be instantly functional. Additionally, a large list of integrations provide even more extensibility options by integrating with third-party services.

Monday's automation feature is a well-designed tool that provides functionality similar to IFTT/Zapier. It allows you to create rules based on triggers that are predefined and then select actions to be carried out when those triggers fire. These triggers and actions can be chained so you can set up elaborate automated processes to meet your requirements.

Monday is an interesting offering on this list because it is not a product with software development as its primary focus, but it is still quite a good fit for it because of the support for integrations and its customizability. Newly added support for the Gantt view seems to indicate that features specific to software development are actively being worked on and should be expected in newer releases.

Pricing tiers for Monday include a free trial, and paid plans require a minimum of three seats. More expensive plans offer additional views not available on the more basic plans.

2.4.2. *Key features*

Reporting: Reporting and analytics are available only on the Enterprise plans.

Dashboards: Dashboards can be added to the workspace. Users can have multiple dashboards, and dashboards contain widgets that are customized to read from items on the board.

Task management: Provides task management via items added to boards. Items support rich content and can be enhanced via integrations and automation.

Resource management: Does not provide resource management out of the box. Time tracking is available in higher price tiers.

Support for integrations: Extensive integrations' library can be used to add functionality to boards as well as items.

Good fit: Small to large teams that require a lot of integration support and do not mind missing out on some features specifically applicable to software development. Especially well-suited for non-technical users.

Not a fit: Software development teams that have a hard requirement for artifacts generated by their methodologies. Certain charts are only available on higher-tier plans.

2.5. *Trello*

2.5.1. *Overview*

Trello (2021) is a Kanban-style project management and collaboration tool created by Fog Creek Software in September of 2011. Its original authors were Joel Spolsky (of Stack Overflow fame) and Michael Pryor (Co-founder of Glitch). It was spun out as its own company and then later sold to Atlassian to integrate with their suite of project management software.

Trello uses boards, lists, and cards to organize and depict task flow and status. A board in Trello represents the largest collective organization of information and usually maps to a project or sub-project. Each board contains one or more lists that serve to function as a means of organization for cards. A Trello card is the container for a trackable unit of work or collection of sub-tasks. This can be anything from a user story to a bug report to a road map task to be worked on in the future. Metadata related to the task can be stored within it by using texts, images, comments, and checklists. Collaborators can also follow a card for updates, assign themselves or a due date, and use labeling to add further context to a card.

Trello's stand-out feature is its fast and user-friendly user experience. Cards can be dragged and dropped between lists to reflect a change in status. Any changes made to the content are immediately reflected on the screens of anyone currently viewing the board. The intuitive user interface lets people of any experience level collaborate on projects regardless of the size of the project.

Additionally, Trello supports the use of Power-Ups to further extend the base functionality of the application. Power-Ups can be used to customize cards, add automation, or connect external applications and import information stored in those services to gain additional context. The ability to connect to services like Zapier and IFTTT should be highlighted because this opens up many workflow automation possibilities that allow for outward as well as inward flow of information.

On the pricing front, Trello offers multiple plans that suit individual team needs. Starting with a free option that can be used for teams of any size right up to an enterprise-level option that is tailored to meet the requirements of large companies.

2.5.2. *Key features*

Reporting: Does not have native reporting functionality. However, reporting functionality can be added by activating various Power-Ups.

Dashboards: The Trello Business Class plan and above have support for basic dashboards. Dashboards are currently at an early stage in their life-cycle and have rudimentary functionality.

Task management: Provides strong task management capabilities via the use of boards, lists, and cards. Cards support rich content and support for real-time collaboration.

Resource management: Provides basic functionality via filters in boards and calendar view, however, native functionality is lacking. Can be extended by adding Power-Ups and depending on external tools to manage this requirement.

Support for integrations: Extensive list of Power-Ups available in multiple categories. Additionally, Trello offers ways to create private/custom Power-Ups by using their API.

Good fit: Great for small to medium teams that primarily require project and task management. Versatile enough that it can be used in different domains with people of limited technical experience. Promotes fast and light workflows focused on just getting the work done.

Not a fit: Larger teams that require advanced reporting and dashboard capabilities might find Trello's offerings too rudimentary. Additionally, Trello is a little thin on resource management tools out of the box but makes up for it via Power-Ups.

2.6. *Other software for project schedule management*

Many other popular project schedule management software programs are in use in the IT industry. An overview of the software Basecamp, GanttPRO, LiquidPlanner, Teamwork, and Zoho Sprints is given in the following.

2.6.1. *Basecamp*

Basecamp (2021) is a cloud-based software for project management. It has a simple interface which includes tools such as schedules, to-dos, message boards, group chat, file sharing, and automatic check-ins. It also supports third-party integrations for additional customization. Managers can view upcoming milestones, overdue tasks, and tasks assigned to each team member. Individuals can view their tasks, schedules, and project activity. It also provides a feature called Hill Charts that works alongside Basecamp to-do lists. The Hill Charts show a high-level view of project status and progress and are updated by individuals based on their assessment of their progress on to-do lists.

Basecamp provides a free tier with limited features for personal use, free accounts for school and university teachers and students, and a flat monthly subscription rate for businesses with a free 30-day trial.

2.6.2. *GanttPRO*

GanttPRO (2021) is a project management software that is based on Gantt charts. It provides features for time and task management, project planning with auto-scheduling, establishing the project baseline and critical path, project health monitoring, and so on. The drag-and-drop feature in GanttPRO provides an easy method for task rescheduling. It also has options for team and resource management and collaboration, including commenting on tasks, attaching files, and real-time notifications. Projects can be viewed in multiple ways, such as Gantt chart, grid view, board view, and portfolio view. Custom and pre-configured templates save time when creating projects. Project information can be imported and exported in a number of different formats. GanttPRO also has budget tracking and reporting features. API, Google Drive, Jira Cloud, and Slack integrations provide more flexibility in using the software.

GanttPRO pricing tiers include Individual for personal productivity and Team with team collaboration functionality for businesses, which are billed monthly on a per user basis and have a free 14-day trial. An Enterprise tier with advanced management and security features is also available.

2.6.3. *LiquidPlanner*

LiquidPlanner (2021) provides predictive forecasting for when a project will be completed. It is a cloud-based project management software platform that provides a feature called 'planning intelligence'. Its automatic scheduling feature runs simulations to provide schedule forecasts that change in real time. Ranged estimates allow visualization of workload with risk and opportunities. LiquidPlanner organizes work and automatically levels resources. When users log their time, the schedules change accordingly. The software provides multiple views such as schedule, workload, and task board views. Agile teams can also use LiquidPlanner for their schedule management. Dashboards supply quick answers for managers on various aspects of the project.

Pricing for LiquidPlanner begins with a free tier with limited users, projects, tasks, and workspaces. The paid tiers are billed on a per user per month basis. The Essentials tier has a limitation on the number of tasks, projects, and workspaces, while the Professional tier pricing depends on the customizable add-ons selected. The Ultimate tier has no usage limits and includes all add-ons.

2.6.4. *Teamwork*

Teamwork (2021) is a cloud-based project management tool which provides features for task management, time tracking, resource management, and reporting. Tasks can be assigned to team members with due dates and can be viewed as task lists, board views, or Gantt charts. Calendars and milestones allow clear monitoring of project progress. The Workload feature enables resource management by showing the workload of team members based on availability and estimated task completion time. Teamwork also has collaboration options with notebooks, files and versioning, messages, and followers for task progress. Filters can provide custom views of project information which can be saved for future use. Dashboards display project metrics, and project updates can be added to inform stakeholders of project status. Teamwork includes several apps and integrations for additional flexibility.

Teamwork pricing plans include a free plan with basic project and task management features. The second tier provides additional features, such as time tracking and Agile view. The third tier includes resource management features and reports and is suitable for larger teams. The highest tier has enterprise-level features with advanced security and faster speed. Teamwork provides free client user accounts that allow clients to view the project at no additional cost.

2.6.5. *Zoho Sprints*

Zoho Sprints (2021b) is a tool for agile project management. It allows planning of work through estimation points, breaking down of work into user stories, task reminders, and checklists. Releases can be planned by associating work items from the product backlog and tracked through release reports. Scrum Boards display the status of teams and help keep track of progress. Custom fields, layouts, views, and items allow additional flexibility in using the software. Project templates can be used to minimize time spent on recurring projects. Timesheets allow estimation of new sprints using time tracked on preceding sprints. Dashboards and agile reports provide high-level overviews and details on the progress of the project. Individual performance can also be analyzed through user profile dashboards. Zoho Sprints allows easy management of remote work as well. Integration with other Zoho software applications and third-party tools improves the functionality of the software. Hybrid projects can be managed by integrating with Zoho Projects, the project management tool in the Zoho ecosystem.

Zoho Sprints provides a free plan for five users and five projects. The professional version is billed per user with a decreasing price per user with increased numbers of users. Client/vendor user accounts must be purchased separately for the external users to access the portals.

2.7. *Comparison of software for IT project schedule management*

Selecting a suitable software application for project schedule management is a challenging task. The software described in the preceding sub-sections differs in areas such as the available features, usability, and price. A comparison of the project schedule management software is presented in Table 1 according to a set of features necessary for successful project management. Ultimately, selecting a software for schedule management would depend on the preference of the users or organizations, how well

Table 1. Comparison of software for project schedule management.

Features	Asana	Jira	Microsoft Project	Monday	Trello	Basecamp	GanttPRO	LiquidPlanner	Teamwork	Zoho Sprints
					Software tool					
Project planning	✓	✓	✓	✓	✓	✓	✓	✓	✓	✓
Gantt charts	✓	✓	✓	✓	✓	✗	✓	✓	✓	✗
Agile features	✓	✓	✓	✓	✓	✓	✓	✓	✓	✓
Resource management	✗	✓	✓	✗	✗	✗	✓	✓	✓	✓
Collaboration	✓	✓	✓	✓	✓	✓	✓	✓	✓	✓
Reports and dashboards	✓	✓	✓	✓	✗	✓	✓	✓	✓	✓
Support for integrations	✓	✗	✓	✓	✓	✓	✓	✓	✓	✓
Free tier	✓	✓	✗	✗	✓	✓	✗	✓	✓	✓

the software integrates with other existing applications, the cost of the software, and other relevant considerations.

3. Software for cost management in IT projects

Project cost management includes cost estimating, determining budgets, and cost control. Project management software can assist the cost management activities. However, many IT project managers use spreadsheet software for this purpose due to the flexibility provided. On the other end of the spectrum, sophisticated financial accounting software is integrated with project management software to consolidate cost information. Cost management tools provide project managers with the means of creating cost estimates, developing budgets, studying the overall project cost performance, identifying tasks that are over budget, and so on. This section discusses the software tools for cost management in IT projects including Harvest, Microsoft Project, Paymo, and Zoho Projects.

3.1. *Harvest*

Harvest (2021) is an online tool for tracking time and expenses in a project. Time can be tracked by users by starting and stopping timers or by filling daily timesheets through a desktop or mobile apps. Harvest provides visual reports on project progress, team capacity, and individual task details of team members. Invoices can be automatically generated through the tracked time and expense data and emailed to clients. Payments can be kept track of, and online payments are allowed through PayPal and Stripe. Integrations with accounting software are available to streamline company accounting.

Harvest provides a free account for a single user with two projects and a Pro version priced per user per month with unlimited projects.

3.2. *Microsoft Project*

Microsoft Project (2021) is a tool frequently used for IT project cost management. It has features for project budgeting and cost estimation, cost reporting, and earned value management. Resource allocation for complex projects can be determined through cost estimation. Cost-related information is entered as work, material, or costs, and is distinguished as fixed or variable. Human resources and related costs can be defined and assigned to tasks, which enables the calculation of human resource costs. Other resource costs should be calculated by assigning the resources to tasks in the work breakdown structure. A baseline can be set with the budgeted costs and compared with the actual costs. The cost overview report provides information such as forecasted cost, progress versus cost, and a cost status table and chart. Earned value management reporting provides graphs for earned value over time, variance over time, and indices over time. Costs can also be analyzed in depth by exporting cost data to Microsoft Excel. The pricing tiers of Microsoft Project are described in Section 2.3.

3.3. *Paymo*

Paymo (2021) is a project management software application with cost management features. Time tracking can be done in a web browser, desktop, or mobile app, or by clicking and dragging on timesheets. Time tracking data can also be added in bulk for tasks and projects. Project managers can view time entry cards for each team member and customize timesheet settings. Time reports can be updated automatically, and charts display meaningful information at a glance. Paymo also provides leave management features. Managing estimates and expenses, creating invoices, and automating payments are key features available in Paymo. A project plan can be converted into an estimate with tasks, budgets, and costs. Invoices can be generated manually and automatically. Invoices can also be exported as PDF or CSV files or synchronized with accounting tools. Paymo also allows clients to pay online through select payment gateways.

Pricing for Paymo begins with a free plan with a limit on users and features. The middle tier provides additional features such as unlimited tasks, time entries, and invoices, although it does not contain employee scheduling and workloads, Gantt charts, or leave management. The highest tier provides all available features.

3.4. *Zoho Projects*

Zoho Projects (2021a) is a cloud-based project management software. It contains both project scheduling and budgeting features. This provides project managers with the capability of defining and assigning tasks to team members and estimating the costs of the project. The software assists the alignment of organizational expenditure with resources available.

A budget view based on the task level gives the cost of resources for separate tasks, enabling easy identification of areas where overspending may occur. It also allows the integration of invoicing software to facilitate the generation of invoices including Zoho Invoice, the dedicated Zoho application for budgeting and invoices. Zoho Projects contains dashboards and reports which present project managers with relevant cost and performance reports and summaries. For example, the number of hours invoiced per month, total hours invoiced to date, and so on will be displayed on the dashboard

Pricing for Zoho Projects is in three tiers starting with a free tier with two projects and simple task tracking for three users. The Premium tier includes scheduling, resource management, time tracking, and budgeting. The Enterprise tier additionally has features such as portfolio dashboards, workflows, global resource utilization, baselines, and so on.

3.5. *Comparison of software for IT project cost management*

Table 2 presents a comparison of the project cost management software discussed in the preceding sub-sections.

Table 2.   Comparison of software for project cost management.

	Software tool			
Features	**Harvest**	**Microsoft Project**	**Paymo**	**Zoho Projects**
Project budgeting	✗	✓	✓	✓
Time tracking	✓	✓	✓	✓
Cost estimation	✓	✓	✓	✓
Invoice generation	✓	✓	✓	✗
Reports and dashboards	✓	✓	✓	✓
Support for integrations	✓	✓	✓	✓
Free tier	✓	✗	✓	✓

4. Summary

The management of IT projects is a challenging process. Therefore, the use of project management software is indispensable for project managers, especially for managing the schedule and cost of projects. This chapter explored a selection of prevalently used software applications for schedule management in IT projects including Asana, Jira, Microsoft Project, Monday.com, Trello, Basecamp, GanttPRO, LiquidPlanner, Teamwork, and Zoho Sprints. A comparison of the selected project schedule management software was introduced which will support the selection of a suitable software platform. The features of cost management software for IT projects including Harvest, Microsoft Project, Paymo, and Zoho Projects were also presented.

References

Asana. (2021). Manage Your Team's Work, Projects, & Tasks Online Available at: https://asana.com/. (Accessed 20 April 2021).

Atlassian. (2021). Jira: Issue & Project Tracking Software Available at: https://www.atlassian.com/software/jira. (Accessed 15 March 2021).

Basecamp (2021). Project Management & Team Communication Software. Available at: https://basecamp.com/. (Accessed 20 April 2021).

GanttPRO. (2021). Online Gantt Chart Maker for Project Planning. Available at: https://ganttpro.com/. (Accessed 20 April 2021).

Harvest. (2021). Easy Time Tracking Software With Invoicing. Available at: https://www.getharvest.com/. (Accessed 4 June 2021).

LiquidPlanner. (2021). Planning Intelligence For Smart Projects. Available at: https://www.liquidplanner.com/. (Accessed 4 June 2021).

Microsoft Project. (2021). Manage Projects Easily in MS Project. Available at: https://www.microsoft.com/microsoft-365/project/project-management-software. (Accessed 16 April 2021).

Monday.com. (2021). Work Without Limits. Available at: https://www.monday.com/. (Accessed 15 March 2021).

Paymo. (2021). Work and Project Management Software for Teams. Available at: https://www.paymoapp.com/. (Accessed 6 June 2021).

Sanchez, O. P., Terlizzi, M. A. and de Moraes, H. R. d. O. C. (2017). Cost and time project management success factors for information systems development projects, *Int. J. Proj. Manag.*, 35(8), 1608–1626. DOI: https://doi.org/10.1016/j.ijproman.2017.09.007.

Teamwork. (2021). Work & Project Management Software. Available at: https://www.teamwork.com/. (Accessed 16 April 2021).

Trello. (2021). Available at: https://trello.com/. (Accessed 5 March 2021).

Zoho Projects. (2021a). Online project Management Software & Tools. Available at: https://www.zoho.com/projects/. (Accessed 20 April 2021).

Zoho Sprints. (2021b). Online Agile Project Management Software. Available at: https://www.zoho.com/sprints/. (Accessed 4 June 2021).

Chapter 15

Software for IT Project Quality Management

Samudaya Nanayakkara*,¶, Srinath Perera[†],
G. Thilini Weerasuriya[†], Pubudu Gamage[‡]
and Kalani Amarathunga[§]

*University of Moratuwa, Sri Lanka
[†]Centre for Smart Modern Construction, Western Sydney
University, Australia
[‡]Datacom, Auckland, New Zealand
[§]Ministry of Social Development, Auckland, New Zealand
[¶]samudaya@uom.lk

Information Technology (IT) is essential for today's human life, either personal, business, academic, research, military, or any other sector. Therefore, it is essential to ensure the quality of IT products. This chapter contains three key sections: process quality management, structural quality management, and functional quality management. A majority of the process quality management contents are discussed in the chapter on schedule and cost management. However, one of the key quality management processes, namely, test management and related tools, is presented in this chapter. Tools for continuous integration and continuous deployment, performance testing, security testing, integration testing, compatibility testing, accessibility testing, and usability testing are discussed under structural quality management. The next section introduces tools for unit testing, smoke testing, sanity testing, functional testing, system testing, regression testing, acceptance testing, and product verification under functional quality management. Finally, a comparison of quality management tools is presented to provide direction on how to utilize the presently available tools for IT projects. The chapter has studied over 300 quality management tools available presently. This chapter will not be limited to the software for IT project quality management. The objective of this chapter is to provide a complete understanding of IT quality management with necessary theoretical concepts, practical applications, and how it can be applied to IT projects of any scale.

1. Introduction

Today's IT systems are mission critical, and quality is paramount. Therefore, it is essential to handle project quality management properly. All quality aspects can be categorized into three high-level concepts, namely, process quality, structural quality, and functional quality (Chappell, 2013). As shown in Figure 1, project sponsors and the

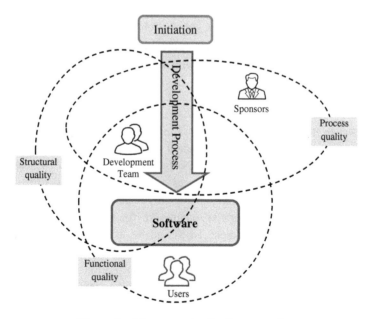

Figure 1.   Three aspects of software quality.

development team are mainly interested in process quality management. It refers to an acceptable level of the total project management, including managing the budget and schedule, the reliability of delivery of the requirements, and managing and resolving risk. The development team is primarily responsible for the structural quality management process. It refers to how the system meets non-functional requirements. Non-functional requirements define system behavior, features, and general characteristics that ultimately affect the user experience. The development team and users are concerned with functional quality management processes, which refer to how the system meets functional requirements. Functional requirements define system behavior and what the system does, or the scope and features of the product.

To successfully deliver a software product, it is essential to properly handle all three quality aspects in each phase of the software life cycle and each small iteration of non-traditional software development as well. However, it is complex and challenging to manage all quality aspects of the entire project. Hence, it is essential to utilize proper software tools to manage quality aspects throughout the software life cycle. Therefore, this chapter introduces presently available software tools that can be used to plan and assure all quality aspects in different phases of the project. This chapter also provides a comparison of commonly available commercial and open-source quality management software products and key parameters on how to select the necessary products to deliver a successful project.

2. Process quality management tools

Process quality management addresses how to manage schedule, budget or cost, and repeatable development processes that reliably deliver quality software products. Schedule and cost management tools such as Microsoft Project, Oracle Primavera, and ProjectLibre, and schedule, cost, communication, and delivery quality management tools such as Asana, Trello, monday.com, and Wrike are utilized to manage the process quality properly. Chapter 14 — Software for time and cost management — has an in-depth discussion on process quality management software tools related to schedule and cost.

Test management is an important quality assurance-related process considered under process quality management. However, the test management process is not usually discussed under schedule management, and it falls within the scope of software quality management. Therefore, this section describes the presently available test management tools. Test management is the process of managing the software testing activities from beginning to end. Test management typically has seven sub-processes under planning and executions phases, as shown in Figure 2.

Test management tools mainly handle storing of requirements, defining test cases, tracking test execution, generating reports, planning test activities, traceability matrix, and bug tracking. The traceability matrix indicates functional coverage during the testing process. Bug tracking is a process of keeping records of reported bugs or defects and tracking the progress of solving these defects in software development projects. Some popular generic bug tracking tools are Bugzilla, Eventum, RedMine, Tra, and Zoho BugTracker. These test management tools facilitate integrating some popular structural and functional quality management tools and automatically execute quality-related tests. Table 1 demonstrates commonly available test process management tools and their features in detail.

Several popular test management tools that are presently available are listed as follows:

- *AWS DevOps*
- *Azure Test Plans*
- *JunoOne*
- *Kualitee*
- *QACoverage*
- *Qase*

- *ReQtest*
- *SonarQube*
- *SpiraTest*
- *Test Collab*
- *TestCaseLab*
- *TestMonitor*

- *Testpad*
- *TestRail*
- *Tricentis qTest*
- *Xqual*
- *Xray*
- *Zephyr*

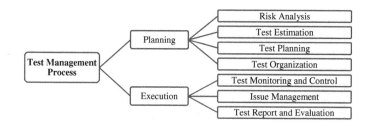

Figure 2.   Test management process.

Table 1.   Test management tools.

JIRA	
Supporting technologies	It is a web-based tool with multi-language support. Jira has REST, SOAP, and XML-RPC interfaces to connect many technology-based services.
Features	Scrum boards, Agile reporting, Kanban boards, and Roadmaps. Developer tool integrations, custom filters, customizable workflows, mobile apps, rich APIs, and can integrate with 3,000+ apps.
Deployment	Software as a Service (SaaS) (free and paid versions).
Limitations	Offline reporting is not supported. There are file size limitations.
Web URL	https://www.atlassian.com/software/jira

IBM Rational Quality Manager	
Supporting technologies	A web-based tool that supports all technologies. Supports agile software teams to manage projects.
Features	Team collaboration, test script construction, test configuration management, execution of test, and reporting.
Deployment	Software as a Service (paid version).
Limitations	Supports limited data models.
Web URL	https://www.ibm.com/docs/en/elm/6.0.4?topic=rational-quality-manager

Micro Focus ALM	
Supporting technologies	A web-based tool supporting all technologies to develop software.
Features	Application life cycle intelligence, functional test, application life cycle management, performance management and test, requirements and release management, quality assurance. Rich analytics graph reports.
Deployment	Software as a Service (paid version).
Limitations	Issues in GUI and user friendliness.
Web URL	https://www.microfocus.com/en-us/products/alm-quality-center

TestManagement.com	
Supporting technologies	Supports all technologies which are used in agile teams with REST and SOAP APIs.
Features	Can deploy applications with CI/CD. Can be integrated with Zephyr, Cucumber Studio, and many necessary apps and services.
Deployment	Software as a Service (paid version).
Limitations	Difficult to integrate non-cloud services.
Web URL	https://www.testmanagement.com/

(Continued)

Table 1.   (*Continued*)

Klaros Test Management	
Supporting technologies	Supports projects written in any technology.
Features	Data management, requirements management, change control, task planning and management. Can provide interfaces to many products.
Deployment	Software as a Service (paid version) and On-premises (free and commercial editions).
Limitations	Lack of inbuilt features
Web URL	https://www.klaros-testmanagement.com/
PractiTest	
Supporting technologies	Supports all technologies used in the industry to develop software.
Features	Traceability of requirements, test management, tracking and tracing bugs. Rich analytical results. Can integrate many automated tools.
Deployment	Software as a Service (paid version).
Limitations	Not available as desktop or mobile versions. Some limitations with user permission management with many projects in different roles.
Web URL	https://www.practitest.com/

3. Structural quality management tools

The structural quality means that the software is well structured in terms of software architecture, database design, and the software code itself. The fundamental objective of structural quality management is to ensure the achievement of non-functional requirements such as accessibility, performance, scalability, security, and stability (Chung *et al.*, 2012). Unlike process quality or functional quality, structural quality is hard to test (Chappell, 2013). Therefore, structural quality management requires experts for proper oversight. For example, design phase quality management, including software architecture design and database design, needs more human inputs to evaluate and maintain quality management aspects. Presently available software tools generally assist in easily, effectively, and neatly drawing diagrams or designs. The main limitation is that these tools do not usually support testing the accuracy of design and improving the structural quality of the software system.

There are many structural quality management software tools for implementation, testing, and integration phases. The following subsections will discuss popular software tools for structural quality management under continuous integration and continuous deployment (CI/CD), performance testing, security testing, integration testing, compatibility testing, accessibility testing, and usability testing.

3.1. *Continuous Integration and Continuous Deployment (CI/CD) tools*

Build automation and continuous integration (CI) were more famous in the software development environment before the introduction of continuous integration and continuous deployment (CI/CD). When the software developer submits or checks the updated source code, the build automation tool will automatically run processes such as compiling source code into binary code, packaging binary code, and running automated tests (Rahman *et al.*, 2017). Apache Ant, Bazel, Maven, Gradle, and Rake are a few popular build automation tools. Continuous integration is an automated process run daily or at specific scheduled times or specific time intervals in the central repository. Continuous integration combines multiple contributors' code changes into a single software project and compiles source code, packages binary code, runs automated tests, and reports success or failure results (Mohammad, 2016). Travis CI, Buildbot, AWS CodeBuild, and Vexor are some popular continuous integration tools.

Modern development methods and cultures such as Agile and DevOps speed up the development process and increase the frequency of releases and the deployment of a large number of new versions. CI/CD focuses on software tools that can automate the complete process, as shown in Figure 3. CI/CD is sometimes called continuous integration and continuous delivery. However, there is a slight difference between continuous

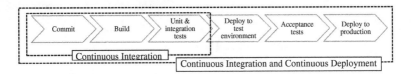

Figure 3.   Continuous integration and Continuous delivery.

deployment and continuous delivery. Continuous delivery sends the software to the client or pre-production server. Continuous deployment goes one step further than continuous delivery. Continuous deployment processes ultimately deploy the software in the production server. There is no human intervention in this process. Only a failure of any test will prevent the deployment of the software. CI/CD provides many benefits in improving structural quality by increasing code quality, ease of debugging and making changes, and mitigating human errors. Additionally, it increases release and delivery speed, reduces cost, and increases flexibility. One of the main limitations is that CI/CD tools are dependent on the tech stack, and each tool usually supports one or only a few development environments.

The CI/CD process uses a headless approach. There are many CI/CD tools in the market today. Some tools are open source, and some tools are proprietary and commercial. Some tools can be deployed on-premises, and some tools are cloud-based software as a service (SaaS). Table 2 lists six presently available popular CI/CD tools and their features.

Table 2.   Continuous integration and continuous deployment tools.

Azure Pipelines	
Supporting technologies	.NET, Android, Anaconda, Node.js, Python, Java, JavaScript, ASP.Net, PHP, Ruby, C#, C++, and Go.
Features	It can be used to develop desktop, web, and mobile apps.
Deployment	Software as a Service (free and paid versions).
Limitations	Requires Azure DevOps and a separate version control system.
Web URL	https://azure.microsoft.com/en-us/services/devops/pipelines
Bamboo	
Supporting technologies	Supports any language. Technologies such as AWS CodeDeploy, Docker, and Amazon S3.
Features	It can be used to develop desktop, web, and mobile apps.
Deployment	Software as a Service (paid version).
Limitations	Needs a code repository such as Git, Mercurial, or SVN repositories.
Web URL	https://www.atlassian.com/software/bamboo

Table 2.   (*Continued*)

Bitrise	
Supporting technologies	iOS, Android, Flutter, React Native, Cordova, and Ionic.
Features	Can manage workflows, codesign, dependency handling, installer, notification management, monitoring, and many other utilities.
Deployment	Software as a Service (paid version) and on a virtual private cloud (commercial).
Limitations	Does not support web or desktop application development.
Web URL	https://www.bitrise.io
BuildMaster	
Supporting technologies	.Net core, WPF, ASP.NET, Java, Java EE, Node.js, PHP, and many others.
Features	Continuously develop and deploy software in any environment.
Deployment	On-premises (free and commercial editions).
Limitations	Limited community and plugins
Web URL	https://inedo.com/buildmaster
Jenkins	
Supporting technologies	Supports any languages and tools such as AccuRev, CVS, Subversion, Git, Mercurial, Perforce, ClearCase, RTC, Apache Maven, Scala projects, Apache Ant, RTC, and Shell scripts.
Features	Extensible automation server support for CI/CD pipeline. Can automate schedule and monitoring projects. Has many plugins.
Deployment	Free and open source (on-premises).
Limitations	Not a cloud-based solution. Has to be updated and maintained manually.
Web URL	https://www.jenkins.io/
TeamCity	
Supporting technologies	Python, C++, C#.NET, VB.NET, PHP, Ruby, Node.js, Java, Apache Maven, Gradle, XAML, etc.
Features	General purpose CI/CD solution. Continuous integration with cloud, Kubernetes, and AWS.
Deployment	Software as a Service (paid version) and on-premises (commercial edition).
Limitations	Needs advanced knowledge to configure.
Web URL	https://www.jetbrains.com/teamcity/

More standard continuous integration and continuous deployment (CI/CD) tools that are currently used are as follows:

- *AppVeyor*
- *Argo CD*
- *Buddy*
- *Codefresh*
- *Codemagic*

- *Codeship*
- *GitHub Actions*
- *GitLab CI/CD*
- *GoCD*
- *Jenkins X*

- *Semaphore*
- *Spinnaker*
- *Visual Studio App Center*

3.2. *Performance testing tools*

Performance testing is a process of testing the software for speed, response time, scalability, reliability, stability, and resource usage. The main objective of performance testing is to identify performance lags (Molyneaux, 2014). Updating the source code and improving the structural quality is the initial and worthwhile solution for performance lags. The most common secondary solution is increasing the resources such as hardware, which is economically unsuitable.

There are several types of performance testing, and each type identifies a particular performance issue. The most common performance tests are load testing, stress testing, endurance or soak testing, spike testing, volume testing, and scalability testing. Load testing checks the software performance under the expected/designed user loads and identifies performance bottlenecks before going live. Stress testing checks what the breaking point is of the software with its system load. Usually, system load is continuously increased to identify how the software handles high traffic or data processing in extreme workloads. Endurance or soak testing is the process of identifying the capability of the software to hold the expected system load for a long period. Spike testing is the mechanism of checking how the system will behave when it suddenly experiences a large system load. Scalability testing is the process of identifying software performance under forecasted future user loads (Molyneaux, 2014). Figure 4 illustrates how the system will be loaded over time in load testing, stress testing, endurance testing, spike testing, and scalability testing methods.

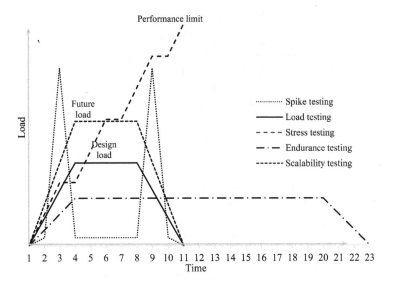

Figure 4.   Different performance testing patterns against the time.

Volume testing, also called flood testing, tests system performance when a large volume of data is populated in the database. Volume testing analyzes system performance by increasing available data in the database. Software usage can be increased over a period. For example, it can be predicted that 50% more users will be present next year. Based on the predictions, scalability testing is used to identify if the system can effectively support the future load. Scalability testing helps to plan additional resource requirements in the future (Tripathi *et al.* 2012).

Usually, performance testing is carried out as headless or without user interfaces or graphical user interfaces. Presently, there are several performance testing tools in the market. Some tools are free and open source, and some tools are proprietary and commercial. Some tools can be deployed on-premises, and some tools are cloud-based software as a service (SaaS). Table 3 demonstrates commonly available performance testing tools and their features.

Table 3.   Performance testing tools.

Apache JMeter	
Supporting technologies	Different applications/server/protocol types: Java, NodeJS, PHP, ASP.NET, etc.
	Web — HTTP, HTTPS, SOAP / REST Webservices, FTP
	Database via JDBC, LDAP, etc.
	Message-oriented middleware (MOM) via JMS, Mail — SMTP(S), POP3(S) and IMAP(S), etc.
	Native commands or shell scripts, TCP, Java Objects.
Features	Supports performance testing including load and stress testing. It can be integrated with Selenium. Available Test IDE that allows fast Test Plan recording. Supports headless mode (non-GUI). Caching and offline analysis are available.
Deployment	Free and open source (on-premises).
Limitations	Does not perform all actions supported by web browsers.
Web URL	https://jmeter.apache.org/

LoadNinja	
Supporting technologies	HTML, Java, Node.js, PHP, ASP.NET, REST, SOAP, JDBC, Mail services, and others.
Features	Can automate load test scripts. Can use real browser impact on testing, real-time analysis, flexibly automate the testing process, and can integrate many tools and services.
Deployment	Software as a Service (paid version).
Limitations	Limitation related to JavaScript codes.
Web URL	https://loadninja.com/

LoadView	
Supporting technologies	System supports to develop all technologies such as HTML, Java, Node.js, PHP, ASP.NET, REST, SOAP, JDBC, Mail services, FTP, AWS, and Azure.
Features	Static Proxy Servers, Load Testing, Monitor Performance, Consultant Directory.
Deployment	Software as a Service (paid version).
Limitations	There are some limitations with concurrent users and load.
Web URL	https://www.loadview-testing.com/

Table 3.   (*Continued*)

NeoLoad	
Supporting technologies	HTTP, GWT, SOAP, Java, REST, .NET, and others. Databases such as Oracle, MySQL, SQL Server, Servers such as Tomcat, IBM, JBOS, LDCS, Apache, and more. Supports all web development technologies.
Features	Codeless performance test design, API testing, advanced correlation, automatic script updates, infrastructure monitoring, APM integrations, functional testing.
Deployment	Software as a Service (paid version) and on-premises (commercial).
Limitations	Performance limited with hosting machine.
Web URL	https://www.neotys.com/

SmartMeter.io	
Supporting technologies	System supports to develop many technologies such as HTML, Java, Node.js, PHP, ASP.NET, REST, SOAP, JDBC, Mail services, etc.
Features	User-friendly performance testing tool with scriptless test recording and reporting, distributed testing, continuous integration, environment monitoring, and supports common applications such as Selenium.
Deployment	On-premises (commercial edition).
Limitations	Not a cloud-based solution. Has to be updated and maintained manually.
Web URL	https://www.smartmeter.io/

WebLOAD	
Supporting technologies	All system development technologies such as HTML, Java, Node.js, PHP, ASP.NET, REST, SOAP, JDBC, Mail services, and others. Supports mobile technologies such as React Native, IONIC, and others.
Features	Performance testing supports JavaScript enabled apps, advanced analytics, complete performance test management. Server-side performance, API load testing, and mobile load testing
Deployment	Software as a Service (paid version) and on-premises (commercial edition).
Limitations	Less user-friendly reports.
Web URL	https://www.radview.com/

Listed as follows are other currently used performance testing tools for load, stress, spike, scalability, endurance, and volume testing:

- *Apica LoadTest*
- *AppLoader*
- *Appvance*
- *Artillery*
- *CloudTest*
- *Fiddler*
- *Flood Element*
- *Fortio*
- *Gatling*
- *JMeter*

- *k6*
- *LoadComplete*
- *Loadero*
- *LoadRunner*
- *Loadster*
- *Loadstorm*
- *LoadUI*
- *Locust*
- *nGrinder*
- *OpenSTA*

- *Predator*
- *Qengine*
- *Siege*
- *Silk Performer*
- *StormForge*
- *StresStimulus*
- *Taurus*
- *The Grinder*
- *Tsung*
- *WAPT*

3.3. *Security testing tools*

Security testing is the process of ensuring confidentiality, integrity, authentication, availability, authorization, and non-repudiation of a software product to examine how it will be secure from unauthorized activities (Islam and Falcarin, 2011). Riley (2020) states that the global losses from IT security-related issues were around $1 trillion in 2020. This emphasizes the importance of security testing in the present context. Security improvement is not a process that should be limited to one phase; it should be started from the system analysis phase. Figure 5 illustrates standard security assessment tests in different phases.

Security architecture review and implementation architecture review are manual assessments by business, development, and security experts. The risk assessment is a combined outcome of test results and expert evaluations based on other environment-related parameters. Table 4 provides details of six popular security testing tools and their main features, supporting technologies, delivery types, and limitations.

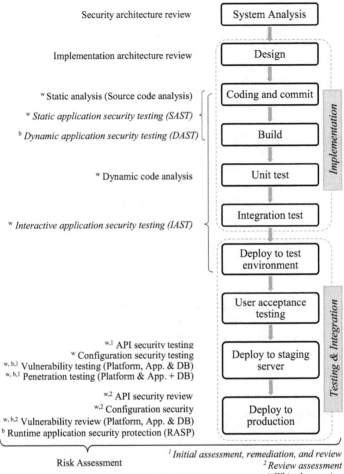

Security architecture review ····· System Analysis

Implementation architecture review ····· Design

^w Static analysis (Source code analysis)
^w *Static application security testing (SAST)*
^b *Dynamic application security testing (DAST)* ····· Coding and commit

····· Build

^w Dynamic code analysis ····· Unit test

^w *Interactive application security testing (IAST)* ····· Integration test

····· Deploy to test environment

····· User acceptance testing

^{w,1} API security testing
^w Configuration security testing
^{w, b,1} Vulnerability testing (Platform, App. & DB)
^{w, b,1} Penetration testing (Platform & App. + DB) ····· Deploy to staging server

^{w,2} API security review
^{w,2} Configuration security
^{w, b,2} Vulnerability review (Platform, App. & DB)
^b Runtime application security protection (RASP) ····· Deploy to production

Implementation

Testing & Integration

Risk Assessment

¹ Initial assessment, remediation, and review
² Review assessment
^w White-box testing
^b Black-box testing

Figure 5.   Common security assessment tests in different phases.

Table 4.   Security testing tools.

Acunetix	
Supporting technologies	HTML5, JavaScript, REST API, SQL, HTTP/HTTPS
Features	Prioritize & control threats, vulnerability assessment, risk management, web scanning, network scanning, in-depth crawl & analysis, authenticated scans, unauthenticated scans.

(Continued)

Table 4. (*Continued*)

Deployment	Software as a Service (paid version) and on-premises (commercial edition).
Limitations	Does not support mobile and desktop applications.
Web URL	https://www.acunetix.com/

Contrast Protect

Supporting technologies	HTTP, GWT, SOAP, Java, REST, .NET, etc., and databases such as Oracle, MySQL, MS SQL Server, Docker, and Kubernetes.
Features	Runtime application self-protection, scalable protection, accurate reports, virtual patching capabilities.
Deployment	Software as a Service (paid version).
Limitations	Identify problems at the production level.
Web URL	https://www.contrastsecurity.com/ runtime-application-self-protection-rasp

DeepSource

Supporting technologies	Go, JavaScript, Ruby, Python
Features	Static analysis, code review, single-file configuration, trace the code metrics, run analysis on pull requests.
Deployment	Software as a Service (paid version) and on-premises (commercial edition).
Limitations	Should integrate with a code repository.
Web URL	https://deepsource.io/

MetaSploit

Supporting technologies	AIX, Android, BSD, BSDi, Cisco, FreeBSD, HP-UX, Irix, Java, JavaScript, Linux, NetBSD, NetWare, Node.JS, OpenBSD, macOS, PHP, Python, R, Ruby, Solaris, Unix, and Windows.
Features	Provides Penetration testing and Dynamic Application Security Testing, Orchestration & automation, An IT operations management solution.
Deployment	On-premises (commercial edition).
Limitations	Fewer reports and analytics outputs.
Web URL	https://www.metasploit.com/

Nessus

Supporting technologies	Web technologies such as Apache Tomcat, OWASP, Databases such as Oracle, SQL Server, MySQL, DB2, PostgreSQL, MongoDB, and Virtualization such as VMware ESX, ESXi, vSphere, vCenter.

Table 4.   (*Continued*)

Features	A platform vulnerability scanner, high-speed asset discovery, configuration auditing, target profiling, malware detection, sensitive data discovery and vulnerability analysis, configuration and compliance audits, SCADA audits, and PCI compliance.
Deployment	On-premises (commercial edition).
Web URL	https://www.tenable.com/products/nessus

Veracode	
Supporting technologies	Supports desktop, web, and mobile technologies. Java, ASP, ASP.NET, Ruby on Rails, JavaScript, Perl, PHP, Python, HTML5, React, Vue.js, REST, iOS, and Android applications.
Features	A dynamic analysis tool, can integrate seamlessly, scan applications, can scan code, binaries, and runtime as well.
Deployment	Software as a Service (paid version) and on-premises (free and commercial editions).
Web URL	https://www.veracode.com/products/dynamic-analysis-dast

Several other security and vulnerability testing tools are presented as follows:

- *Arachni*
- *BeEF*
- *BFBTester*
- *Brakeman*
- *Burp Suite*
- *Coverity Static Analysis*
- *GoLismero*
- *Grabber*
- *Grendel-Scan*
- *Intruder*
- *Iron Wasp*
- *Kali Linux*
- *Kiuwan Security*
- *Knock Subdomain Scan*
- *Metasploit*
- *Netsparker*
- *Nikto*
- *Nikto2*
- *OpenSCAP*
- *OpenVAS*
- *Owasp*
- *Ratproxy*
- *RIPS*
- *Skipfish*
- *SQLMap*
- *Vega*
- *W3af*
- *Wapiti*
- *Watcher*
- *WebScarab*
- *Wfuzz*
- *WireShark*
- *X5S*
- *Zed Attack Proxy*

3.4. *Integration testing tools*

During the software development process, many tests are carried out to ensure the structural quality of the software product. The present systems have a significant number of integrations with other modules or systems (Nanayakkara *et al.*, 2014). When units, modules, or systems are developed separately, integration testing is executed to identify whether the integrated system works as expected after combining them with other modules as a group. There are five common integration testing approaches. These are as follows: (a) big bang integration testing — combines all modules and performs integration test; (b) incremental integration testing — the test starts with a minimum of two modules and subsequent modules are added incrementally when each test is completed; (c) top-down integration testing — tests the top-level units first and then performs step-by-step testing of lower-level units; (d) bottom-up integration testing — tests the bottom-level units first and then perform step-by-step testing of upper-level units; and (e) hybrid or sandwich integration testing — conducts the testing with a combination of top-down and bottom-up approaches (Pressman, 2010). There are a significant number of integration testing tools available presently, and Table 5 shows details of six these tools.

Table 5.   Integration testing tools.

Jmockit	
Supporting technologies	Java, the Java EE APIs, Spring framework.
Features	Provides integration testing for Java EE and Spring-based apps, MockAPIs with recording & verification syntax, using fake API for replacing implementations.
Deployment	Free and open source (on premises).
Limitations	Supports only Java projects.
Web URL	https://jmockit.github.io/
LDRA	
Supporting technologies	Supports most software and web development technologies.
Features	Integration testing tool, with unit test and system-level test, Planning for and executing requirements-based testing. Provides traceability, static analysis, and dynamic analysis.
Deployment	On-premises (commercial edition).
Limitations	Not a CI/CD total process integration tool.
Web URL	https://ldra.com/

Table 5.   (*Continued*)

Mockito	
Supporting technologies	Java, Java EE APIs, Spring boot, MVC.
Features	Behavior-Driven Development (BDD)-style tests with some syntactic aspects.
Deployment	Free and open source (on premises).
Limitations	Supports only Java projects.
Web URL	https://site.mockito.org/

Rational Integration Tester	
Supporting technologies	HTTP, GWT, SOAP, Java, REST. Databases such as Oracle, MySQL, SQL Server. Servers such as tomcat, IBM, JBOS, LDCS.
Features	Server-based web application providing a central repository for virtualized services, Service-oriented architecture (SOA) testing.
Deployment	On-premises (commercial edition).
Limitations	Supports only limited types of architectures.
Web URL	https://www.ibm.com/docs/en/rtw/9.0.0?topic=tester-rational-integration-overview

TESSY	
Supporting technologies	C and C++
Features	Powerful integration testing tool. Can define, link, and trace requirements, design test cases within the Classification Tree Editor. Test results analysis.
Deployment	On-premises (commercial edition).
Limitations	Supports only a very limited technology.
Web URL	https://www.razorcat.com/en/product-tessy.html

VectorCAST	
Supporting technologies	C, C++, and Ada.
Features	Integration testing, requirements-based testing, code coverage analysis, automatic test case creation can integrate compilers. Test execution trace and playback.
Deployment	On-premises (commercial edition).
Limitations	Supports only a very limited technology.
Web URL	https://www.vector.com/int/en/products/products-a-z/software/vectorcast/vectorcast-c/

More integration testing tools presently available are as follows:

- *Buildbot*
- *Citrus Integration Testing*
- *Cucumber*
- *Culerity*
- *DBUnit*
- *Embedded-redis*
- *eZscript*
- *FitNesse*
- *Hamcrest*
- *Hound*
- *Integrated*
- *Jasmine*
- *Pioneerjs*
- *Postman*
- *Protractor*
- *Respawn*
- *Selenium*
- *SoapUI*
- *Spock for JAVA*
- *Spock testing framework*
- *Subliminal*
- *TestDummy*
- *TestNG*
- *TestSwarm*

3.5. *Compatibility testing tools*

Technology has changed intensely over the past decade, and the experts in the industry are trying to adapt to these changes. Computers and mobile devices have become an integral part of our lives, and hardware and software are frequently upgraded. With these changes, it is challenging to ensure that software products can smoothly run on all or specific hardware and software platforms. Compatibility testing is a structural quality management method that is conducted to ensure that the application is compatible with different computing environments such as hardware, operating systems, applications, network environments, browsers, devices, software versions, and mobile devices (Zhang *et al.*, 2015). Backward and forward compatibility tests are another important area in the present culture of rapid software releases. A significant number of compatibility testing tools are available at present, and Table 6 shows details of these tools.

Table 6.   Compatibility testing tools.

BrowseEmAll	
Supporting technologies	Supports most of the web development technologies.
Features	Web compatibility testing, synchronizes data with the different browsers, Selenium integration, full-page screenshots and visuals, supports parallel execution.

Table 6.   (*Continued*)

Deployment	On-premises (commercial edition).
Limitations	Only supports Mac and Windows operating systems.
Web URL	https://www.browseemall.com/

BrowserStack

Supporting technologies	Supports all web development technologies.
Features	Web and mobile compatibility testing platform, display resolutions, geolocation testing. Can test across many browsers, operating systems, and many mobile devices.
Deployment	Software as a Service (paid version).
Limitations	There are issues in compiling reports for multiple parallel tests.
Web URL	https://www.browserstack.com/

Comparium

Supporting technologies	Supports all web development technologies.
Features	Web compatibility testing platform, cross-browser support, reporting and analysis, test recorder, live web testing, parameterized testing, and schedule testing.
Deployment	Free and open source (on-premises and extension to browser).
Limitations	Does not support some older versions of web browsers.
Web URL	https://comparium.app

CrossBrowserTesting

Supporting technologies	Supports most of the web development technologies.
Features	Web compatibility testing platform supports standalone desktop web browsers, mobile browser emulators. Live testing, automated testing, visual testing, and built-in video recorder. Selenium integration. Command-line interface. Can integrate into CI/CD pipeline.
Deployment	Software as a Service (paid).
Limitations	Not available for Linux operating systems other than Ubuntu Desktop. Limited mobile devices.
Web URL	https://www.multibrowser.com/

(*Continued*)

Table 6.   (*Continued*)

LambdaTest	
Supporting technologies	Supports all web development technologies.
Features	Web compatibility testing platform, cross-browser support, issue logging, issue management, live browser testing, automated testing, local testing for a development level, responsiveness testing, multiple concurrent sessions, native browsers. Available for compatibility testing on all Android and iOS mobile browsers.
Deployment	Software as a Service (free and paid versions).
Limitations	Not available for all operating system-based browsers.
Web URL	https://www.lambdatest.com/
MultiBrowser	
Supporting technologies	Supports most of the web development technologies.
Features	Web compatibility testing platform supports standalone desktop web browsers, mobile browser emulators, responsive design screenshots, automated functionality tester, built-in video recorder. Supports manual and automation testing, live testing, browser comparisons, visual testing, responsive testing, page analytics, validating page state, exporting test results. Selenium integration. Command-line interface.
Deployment	On-premises (commercial edition).
Limitations	Have to add new devices manually.
Web URL	https://www.multibrowser.com/

A list of additional integration testing tools is provided as follows:

- *Browser Sandbox*
- *Browserling*
- *Browsershots*
- *Cigniti's Compatibility Testing*
- *Experitest*

- *IE NetRender*
- *mobiReady*
- *QA Wolf*
- *QMetry*
- *Ranorex Studio*
- *Sauce Labs*

- *Selenium Box*
- *Super Preview*
- *TestingBot*
- *Turbo.NET*
- *XBOSoft*

3.6. *Accessibility testing tools*

Accessibility is the practice of making the software usable for as many people as possible. Most often the term accessibility is used to refer to software designed to be used by people with disabilities such as vision disability, physical disability, cognitive disability, literacy disability, and hearing disability. The OAF (Open Accessibility Framework) provides an accessibility-related guideline, and the WCAG (Web Content Accessibility Guidelines) 2.1 provides guidelines for accessibility for web content (Gunderson, 2009). A few common accessibility improving techniques are text-to-speech, closed-captioning, sticky keys, customization of the mouse, predictive text, ToggleKeys, speech recognition, magnification, and keyboard shortcuts. A significant number of accessibility testing tools are available at present, and Table 7 shows details of some of these tools.

Table 7.   Accessibility testing tools.

	Accessibility Insights
Supporting technologies	Supports all web development technologies.
Features	Find out the accessibility of the websites, desktop applications, and mobile applications. Color contrast analyzer.
Deployment	Free and open source (on-premises and extension to browser).
Limitations	Does not support all web browsers.
Web URL	https://accessibilityinsights.io/
	AMP — Level Access
Supporting technologies	Supports all web development technologies.
Features	Comprehensive accessibility testing, Everything Accessibility in One Place, comply with most standards such as WCAG 2.0, CVAA, and regulations. Advanced reporting.
Deployment	On-premises (commercial edition).
Limitations	Supports the latest two versions of web browsers only.
Web URL	https://www.levelaccess.com/solutions/software/amp/
	axe DevTools
Supporting technologies	Supports all web development technologies.

(*Continued*)

Table 7.   (*Continued*)

Features	Comprehensive accessibility testing tools. Several tools for testing are available. Can scan whole sites, scan behind authentication and firewalls, status across drill-down dashboards. Automated testing and intelligent guided testing, CI/CD integrations. Web testing API, Android testing API, and Windows testing API.
Deployment	Free and paid editions (on-premises and extension to browser).
Limitations	Available for Chrome, Firefox and Edge only.
Web URL	https://www.deque.com/axe/

Monsido	
Supporting technologies	Supports all web development technologies.
Features	Accessibility check with broken links, compliance shield, content policies, content quality assurance, data privacy. Automated target and audit functions, checks the color contrast. Complies with most standards and regulations.
Deployment	Software as a Service (paid version).
Limitations	Cannot process the special aspects such as CAPTCHA and modals.
Web URL	https://monsido.com/platform/web-accessibility

Tenon	
Supporting technologies	Supports all web development technologies.
Features	Automated accessibility testing tool. Can integrate with development pipeline, code repositories, issue tracking systems, and integrated development environments.
Deployment	Software as a Service (free and paid versions).
Limitations	Only tests publicly accessible URLs.
Web URL	https://tenon.io/

Wave	
Supporting technologies	Supports all web development technologies.
Features	Accessibility testing tool. Supports WCAG 2.1 standard. Site-wide accessibility scanning and monitoring. Supports advanced API integrations. Available through Firefox and Chrome extensions.
Deployment	Software as a Service and extension to browser (free and paid versions).
Limitations	There is no testing against browsers, operating systems, or devices.
Web URL	https://wave.webaim.org/

The additional accessibility testing tools presently available are as follows:

- *A11Y*
- *AATT*
- *Accessibility Checker*
- *Accessibility Checklist*
- *Accessibility Scanner*
- *Accessibility Valet*
- *Accessibility Viewer*

- *AChecker*
- *aDesigner*
- *Android Studio Project Site*
- *CKEditor 4*
- *Colour Contrast Analyser*
- *Compliance Sheriff*
- *COMPLY First Professional*
- *Cynthia Says*

- *DYNO Mapper*
- *FireEyes*
- *HTML CodeSniffer*
- *Pally*
- *Talk Back for Android*
- *TAW*
- *Web accessibility toolbar*
- *WebAIM*
- *WebAnywhere*

3.7. *Usability testing tools*

Usability is how effectively, efficiently, and satisfactorily a software product can be used with a minimum number of mouse clicks, keyboard, or any other inputs to achieve the user's objective in minimum time and with minimum ambiguity. Usability testing is a user-centered interaction design test for testing software usability by users. Common usability testing methods are A/B testing, tree testing, focus groups, surveys, heat maps, first-click testing, eye-tracking test, and beta testing (Bank and Cao, 2014). All types of usability tests give an opportunity to identify design problems related to user interface (UI) or user experience (UX), find ways to improve it, and learn target user expectations and behaviors. Table 8 demonstrates the presently available usability testing tools and their features.

Table 8.   Usability testing tools.

Clicktale	
Supporting technologies	Supports all web development technologies.
Features	Mouse move heatmaps, click heatmaps, attention heatmaps, scroll reach heat maps, campaign tracking, mouse tracker.
Deployment	Software as a Service (paid version).
Limitations	Weak detailed reports.
Web URL	https://contentsquare.com/clicktale/

heatmap.com	
Supporting technologies	Supports all web development technologies.
Features	Breaking down big data of the websites and tracks most important data on the website, shows real-time statistics, template analysis. Provides instant feedbacks.
Deployment	Software as a Service (free and paid versions).
Limitations	Has to include additional JavaScript tag to web pages.
Web URL	https://heatmap.com/

Crazy Egg	
Supporting technologies	Supports all web development technologies
Features	Provides snapshots, heatmaps, check the usability, visitor analysis, UX/UI audits, A/B testing.
Deployment	Software as a Service (paid version).
Limitations	Funnel tracking and form tracking are not available.
Web URL	https://www.crazyegg.com/

Mobileum — Smartphone Experience	
Supporting technologies	Supports iOS and Android devices' apps.
Features	Tests and monitors the usability and performance of mobile applications. Analysis of smartphone experience. Has powerful reporting tools, easily scripts any testing scenario.
Deployment	Software as a Service (paid version).
Limitations	More emphasis for mobile operators' aspects.
Web URL	https://www.mobileum.com/products/testing-and-monitoring-intelligence/domestic-network-testing/smartphone-experience/

Table 8.   (*Continued*)

Optimal Workshop	
Supporting technologies	Supports all web development technologies.
Features	Provides optimal sorting, first click and tree testing, online surveys, qualitative research, and result analysis.
Deployment	Software as a Service (paid version).
Limitations	Limited integration facilities. No session recording.
Web URL	https://www.optimalworkshop.com/

UXtweak	
Supporting technologies	Supports all web development technologies.
Features	Online usability testing, tree testing, card sorting, session recording, heatmaps, task-driven UX studies, information architecture research, user behavior analytics.
Deployment	Software as a Service (free and paid versions).
Limitations	Need to test with real test users.
Web URL	https://www.uxtweak.com/

The presently available list of popular usability testing tools is as follows:

- *Accelerate*
- *CheckMyColours*
- *ClickHeat*
- *Feng-GUI*
- *HeatMapCo*
- *Hotjar*
- *Koncept*
- *Leanplum*
- *Loop11*
- *Maze*
- *Mixpanel*
- *mouseflow*
- *Optimizely*
- *Qualaroo*
- *SiteSpect*
- *TryMyUI*
- *UsabilityHub*
- *Usabilla*
- *Userbrain*
- *Userfeel*
- *Userlytics*
- *Usersnap*
- *UserZoom*
- *UXCam*

4. Functional quality management tools

Functional quality management is a process, or multiple processes, which helps to achieve the system's functional requirements. Functional requirements describe product features or the system, its components, and functions.

User requirements or business functions are identified during the system analysis phase, and they become the functional requirements or functional specifications. Then, functional requirements become designs and specifications, and the development team will develop the system based on these.

There are many testing mechanisms to make sure developers have correctly developed the functional requirements. Common testing mechanisms are unit testing, smoke testing, functional testing, system testing, regression testing, acceptance testing, and product verification testing. There are many software tools to automate and carry out unit testing, smoke testing, functional testing, system testing, and regression testing. However, acceptance and product verification testing has few software tools available, and most of the time, these tests are carried out manually.

4.1. *Unit testing tools*

Unit testing is an automated testing mechanism to ensure individual components or units correctly operate according to the functional requirements. Unit testing considers only the component itself and executes before integration testing. When a developer commits any piece of software, the CI/CD process automatically builds and runs unit testing, as shown in Figure 3. It can usually check the number of inputs, input types, input values, outputs, values, and types. If any unit test parameter fails, it would notify one to correct it before integration.

Unit testing is the primary functional quality management mechanism, and many tools support writing unit test codes and execute the unit test automatically. Unit testing tools mainly depend on the development programming language or technical stacks. Therefore, many unit testing frameworks support limited programming languages, and Table 9 shows seven unit testing tools and their features.

Table 9.   Unit testing tools.

Cantata	
Supporting technologies	C and C++.
Features	Unit testing, test on the host, extensive platform support, and toolchain integrations, bi-directional requirements traceability.

Table 9. (*Continued*)

Deployment	On-premises (commercial edition).
Limitations	Only available for C and C++.
Web URL	https://nohau.eu/products/cantata-unit-test-coverage/

Embunit

Supporting technologies	C and C++.
Features	Unit testing, integration, regression testing, can test as Whitebox and Blackbox, organizes the test cases, and performs tests.
Deployment	On-premises (commercial edition).
Limitations	Only available for C and C++.
Web URL	https://www.embunit.com/

JUnit

Supporting technologies	Java and Java Virtual Machine.
Features	Unit testing, cross-platform, can integrate with many integrated development environments, can automate testing, can integrate into CI/CD pipeline.
Deployment	Free and open source (on premises).
Limitations	Cannot perform dependency tests.
Web URL	https://junit.org/

NUnit

Supporting technologies	.NET Framework, Mono, Silverlight, Xamarin Mobile, Compact Framework.
Features	Unit testing for .NET. Can test multiple asserts, parallel tests, data-driven tests, several extensions for other languages.
Deployment	.NET-based software.
Limitations	Only available for the .NET-related technologies.
Web URL	https://nunit.org/

PHPUnit

Supporting technologies	PHP programming language and frameworks.
Features	PHP unit testing, works on cross-platform. Results in many formats, including JUnit XML and TestDox.
Deployment	Free and open source (on-premises).

(*Continued*)

Table 9. (*Continued*)

Limitations	Only available for PHP and only has unit testing facility.
Web URL	https://PHPunit.de/

Typemock	
Supporting technologies	C++ and .NET.
Features	Unit testing, supports cross-platforms, can integrate with Visual Studio integrated development environment, supports fake static and private methods, can automate testing.
Deployment	On-premises (free and paid editions).
Limitations	Cross-platform support only for C++ unit testing on Windows and Linux platforms.
Web URL	https://www.typemock.com/

xUnit.net	
Supporting technologies	C#, F#, VB.NET, .NET core, .NET Framework, UWP, ReSharper, CodeRush, Xamarin — Android and iOS apps, Xamarin MonoTouch, TestDriven.NET, Silverlight.
Features	Unit testing for multi-technologies, supports windows desktop application and mobile app development.
Deployment	Free and open source (on-premises).
Limitations	Additional copyrights of The Legion of the Bouncy Castle.
Web URL	https://xunit.NET/

Several additional popular usability testing tools are listed as follows:

- *ABAP Unit*
- *Emma*
- *HtmlUnit*
- *Jasmine*
- *JMockit*
- *JUnit*
- *Karma*
- *LRDA*
- *Microsoft unit testing Framework*
- *Mocha*
- *Parasoft*
- *Quilt HTTP*
- *SimpleTest*
- *TestNG*

4.2. *Integration testing tools*

Integration testing is usually carried out immediately after unit testing. In addition to enhancing the structural quality, integration testing can be used to improve the functional quality aspects. After combining units, modules, or systems that have been developed separately, integration testing can be used to identify if the integrated systems provide the expected functional outcomes as well. Refer to Section 3.4 for more details on integration testing and integration testing tools.

4.3. *Smoke, sanity, functional, system, and regression testing tools*

Smoke testing, sanity testing, functional testing, system testing, and regression testing have different purposes and are executed in different stages of the software development and deployment process. However, there is some similarity in how the test is executed. Therefore, the same list of software tools is used to execute smoke testing, functional testing, system testing, or regression testing. Furthermore, most of these tests are carried out as headful or using user interfaces or graphical user interfaces.

4.3.1. *Smoke testing tools*

Smoke testing is also called build verification testing. It verifies if the build is ready for further testing or not. For verification purposes, smoke testing covers most of the main or critical functions and is not focused on in-depth testing. The smoke test gives quick results; the build is either ready for further testing or is marked as a rejected build.

The smoke test is the gate to enter the domain of quality assurance from the developer's domain. Smoke testing can be executed by the development team or the quality assurance team. If the smoke test is passed, the quality assurance team will process the next steps of the quality assurance process, such as functional testing, system testing, and regression testing. If the smoke test is failed, the build will be rejected, and the development team should rectify the issue. Smoke testing provides early defect identification, minimizing integration issues, saving testing time and effort, improving the effectiveness of the quality assurance team, and needing limited test cases (Chauhan, 2014). There are no separate tools devoted to smoke test. Usually, functional testing tools can perform smoke tests and Table 10 *(refer to Section 4.3.5)* shows famous functional testing tools which can perform smoke tests as well. Table 10 contains features of these tools, and a list of additional tools are listed.

4.3.2. *Sanity testing tools*

Sanity testing is similar to smoke testing, but with two fundamental differences. Smoke testing is executed on unstable builds, and sanity testing is executed in relatively stable builds after multiple rounds of regressions tests. Sanity testing does not focus on the critical or main functionalities of the application; rather, it verifies the new functionalities or previously identified and fixed bugs (Meenakshi and Kumar). Usually, sanity testing is conducted by the quality assurance team. Table 10 *(refer to Section 4.3.5)* shows popular sanity testing tools and their features, and additional tools are listed.

4.3.3. *Functional testing tools*

Functional testing identifies if each component (e.g., text boxes, buttons, radio buttons, checkboxes, dropdowns, menus, toolbars, and outputs) functions properly within the selected module or complete application. The quality assurance team conducts the functional testing internally. Unlike unit testing, functional testing focuses on graphical user interfaces, inputs, processes, and outputs as well. Table 10 *(refer to Section 4.3.5)* illustrates leading functional testing tools and their features, followed by a list of additional tools.

4.3.4. *System testing tools*

System testing is one of the key testing methods carried out by the quality assurance team to identify requirement-related issues on the fully integrated system. The testing will ensure modules are working correctly in the entire integrated system. Unlike integration testing, system testing checks complete end-to-end scenarios. The system is usually developed by using business requirement specifications (BRS), software requirement specifications (SRS), functional specification documents (FSD), and product specification documents (PSD). Designers and developers use one or more of these documents to design and develop the system. The main objective of system testing is to test whether the product complies with the requirements listed in these specification documents. Usually, system testing is carried out by a dedicated testing team from the developer organization and using a similar production environment to check functional and sometimes non-functional requirements as well. Table 10 *(refer to Section 4.3.5)* illustrates major system testing tools and their features and precedes a list of additional tools.

4.3.5. *Regression testing tools*

Regression testing is executed to identify whether previously tested unchanged modules are still performing as usual after another module was added, deleted, updated or bug-fixed. It does not involve testing or retesting of newly added modules or updated modules. There are three types of regression tests based on the scope. These are unit, regional, and full regression testing, also known as unit, partial, and complete regression testing. Unit regression testing is executed on a related changed module, and it is done during the unit testing. The regional regression testing is executed on expected impacts to a set of modules after integration. Usually, impacted modules are decided during the impact analysis meeting. Full or complete regression testing will test the whole system after one or more modules has been changed, added, or deleted. This means that it will test changed features and as well as unchanged features. Table 10 shows popular regression testing tools and their features.

Table 10. Smoke, sanity, system, and regression testing tools.

Applitools	
Supporting technologies	Supports all web development technologies.
Features	Integrates SDK and integrations with platforms, functional testing, visual testing, web testing, mobile testing, cross-browser testing, responsive design testing, and advanced dashboard.
Deployment	Software as a Service (free and paid versions).

(Continued)

Table 10. (*Continued*)

Limitations	Possibility of generating false positive results.
Web URL	https://applitools.com/

Sahi Pro

Supporting technologies	Supports all web development technologies, Windows desktop applications (Java, WPF, Win32, WinForms, .NET, SilverLight, XBAP, UWP), and iOS and Android, Native and Hybrid Applications.
Features	Provides more functions than automation tools, provides more powerful API sets, can test desktop applications, mobile applications, and web applications, and supports CI/CD pipeline operation.
Deployment	Software as a Service (paid version), on-premises, and mobile (commercial edition).
Limitations	Limited debugging capabilities.
Web URL	https://sahipro.com/sahi-pro-much-automation-tool/

TestComplete

Supporting technologies	Supports all web development technologies, desktop and mobile apps and scripting with Python, VBScript, or JavaScript.
Features	Automates functional testing, regression tests, provides object recognizing process with artificial intelligence, automates UI testing for desktop, mobile, and web applications, checks for cross-browser and cross-device compatibility, can integrate with many tools, and supports CI/CD pipeline operation.
Deployment	On-premises (commercial editions).
Limitations	Sophisticated artificial intelligence testing ignores some issues and tries to complete the test process, leading to skipping of some issues.
Web URL	https://smartbear.com/product/testcomplete/

test IO

Supporting technologies	Supports all web development technologies, desktop, and mobile apps, and cloud platforms such as AWS, containerization such as docker, Kubernetes.
Features	Functional regression, user acceptance, usability, sanity, usability, hierarchical presentation, parallel execution of multiple tasks, data export and import, integrate with many tools through APIs, and can execute beta testing as well.
Deployment	Software as a Service (paid version).
Limitations	Limited user story testing, limited bug reproduction capacity, and rapid tests need for several hours.
Web URL	https://test.io/functional-testing/

Table 10. (*Continued*)

Micro Focus Unified Functional Testing	
Supporting technologies	VB script processing technology, AI features.
Features	Automates functional testing for mobile app, web sites and API, provides AI-based test automation system. Creates end-to-end testing with APIs.
Deployment	On-premises (commercial editions).
Limitations	Maintenance cost is very high.
Web URL	https://www.microfocus.com/en-us/products/uft-one/overview

ZapTest	
Supporting technologies	Supports all web development technologies with AI features and integration tools such as JIRA and HP ALM.
Features	Parallel executing scripts, one click documentations and end-to-end functionality testing with functional test scripts, performs cross-disciplined integration.
Deployment	Software as a Service (paid version) and on-premises (free and paid editions).
Limitations	Codeless and provides only system-generated scripts.
Web URL	https://www.zaptest.com/

A list of additional tools for smoke, sanity, functional, system, and regression testing is as follows:

- *AdventNet QEngine*
- *Applitools*
- *Appsurify TestBrain*
- *Capybara*
- *Cerberus Testing*
- *cypress.io*
- *Digivante*
- *IBM Rational Functional Tester*

- *Katalon Studio*
- *Micro Focus LeanFT*
- *Nightwatchman*
- *protractor*
- *Ranorex*
- *Ranorex Studio*
- *Regression Tester*
- *Sauce Labs*
- *Selenium*
- *Subject7*

- *Team Fit*
- *TestDrive*
- *Testimony*
- *TestingWhiz*
- *Testsigma*
- *TimeShiftX*
- *Tricentis Tosca*
- *UFT*
- *Watir*
- *WebKing*
- *Worksoft Certify*

4.4. *Acceptance testing*

Acceptance testing is also known as end-user testing, which is carried out as black box testing. The main objective of acceptance testing is to decide if the system satisfies the specified requirements. The subcategories of acceptance testing are as follows: (a) user acceptance testing (UAT), (b) business acceptance testing (BAT), (c) contract acceptance testing (CAT), (d) regulation acceptance testing (RAT), (e) operational acceptance testing (OAT), (f) alpha testing, and (g) beta testing. The most common acceptance tests are alpha testing, beta testing, and user acceptance testing (Mohd and Shahbodin, 2015; Sawant *et al.*, 2012).

Alpha testing is performed by specialized testers, potential users, or an independent team to ensure that the software functions correctly and achieves the business requirements. Usually, alpha testing is conducted on the developer's site. After alpha testing, beta testing is conducted by a selected team or users called beta testers. The testing version is called a beta version, and some product-based software companies release beta versions to the public to get broader feedback. The beta testing process tries to identify any additional issues after all internal testing processes. User acceptance testing is the final testing method before the new version goes to the production environment. UAT is conducted by actual users to ensure that the software meets the required functions and features. Real-world scenarios are usually used in UAT (Mohd and Shahbodin, 2015; Sarveswaran *et al.*, 2006; Nanayakkara, 2010). There are few exceptional cases where acceptance testing could be automated (Haugset and Hanssen, 2008). Usually, acceptance testing is a manual process done by end users, and there are no common acceptance testing software tools in the market.

4.5. *Production verification testing*

Production verification testing is the final opportunity to identify if the software is completely ready to go live. After user acceptance, the software will be deployed in production servers. Before the software is used, limited test cases will be manually executed to ensure that the software is working correctly in the production environment (Bentley *et al.*, 2005).

There are no standard production verification testing software tools in the market as it is a manual end-user testing method.

5. Comparison of testing during the product life cycle

There are a significant number of operation and testing processes to enhance and ensure software project quality management in three common aspects, namely, process quality management, structural quality management, and functional quality management. Some operations or testing processes primarily require expert inputs and manual human interventions to achieve the quality objectives. However, a majority of processes or tests have a significant number of software tools which can automate, analyze the software itself, simulate and analyze user behaviors, integrate with other process and tools such as CI/CD pipelines, provide reports and feedback, assist to comply with standards and regulations, support planning and design for future requirements, and much more. Figure 6 abstracts the most common processes and tests for quality management in different phases of the software development lifecycle.

6. Chapter summary

The cruciality of present-day IT systems makes it essential to achieve the quality of the final product released to end users. IT project quality management can be classified into three categories: process, structural, and functional. Process quality means proper management of schedule, budget, and resources. Test management is a part of process quality management, and the test manager or quality assurance manager plans it with the project manager and development team lead. Structural quality management mainly focuses on non-functional requirements, and it helps to enhance the overall quality of the final product. There are many software tools to properly handle test management.

Many tools can be utilized to achieve structural quality. CI/CD tools can be used in projects of any scale, and it is an essential tool for

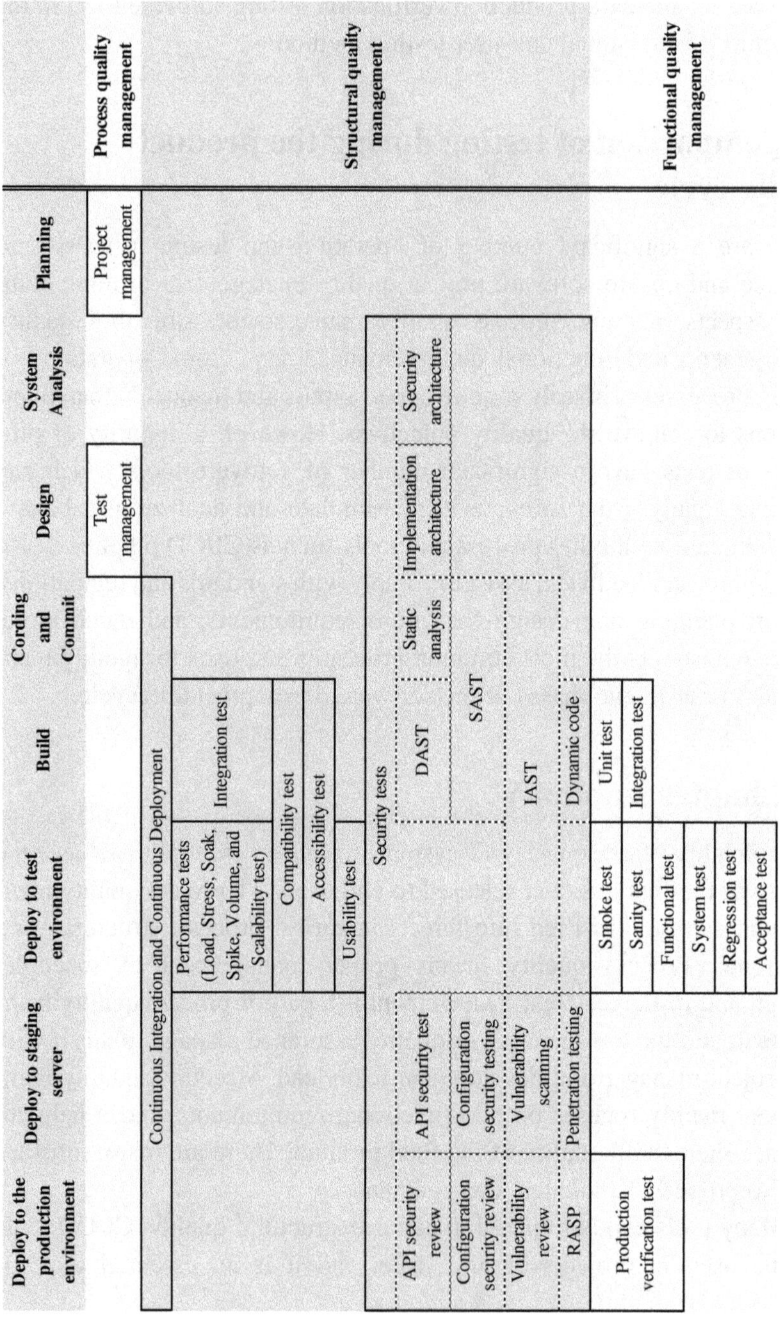

Figure 6.   Project quality management software development life cycle.

large-scale rapid projects. It is recommended to conduct performance testing if the product is mission critical and the user load is high. Security testing is crucial for today's applications, and based on the criticality of the application, asset values, sensitivity of the information, and other parameters, security experts have to decide which security tests should be conducted. Based on the project requirements, compatibility and accessibility testing can be carried out. The project objectives can only be achieved if end users use it satisfactorily. Usability is one of the key parameters of system usage. Therefore, it is essential to improve the usability of the software system. Many software tools support proper handling of different structural quality management aspects.

Functional quality management can be achieved through several types of testing. Unit testing is one of the most common testing mechanisms in any scale projects. Integration testing is another functional quality management process which follows unit testing. Smoke, sanity, functional, system, and regression tests are the next level of functional quality management testing, and there are a significant number of software tools available to manage all of these types of testing. The final two types of testing are acceptance testing and production verification testing, which do not have specific software tools to execute automatically, and end users manually perform these tests prior to launching the live system with minimum issues.

References

Bank, C. and Cao, J. (2014). The guide to usability testing, *Mountain View: UXPin.*

Bentley, J. E., Bank, W. and Charlotte, N. (2005). Software testing fundamentals — concepts, roles, and terminology, in *Proceedings of SAS Conference* (pp. 1–12).

Chappell, D. (2013). The three aspects of software quality: Functional, structural, and process. Retrieved from, Issue. D. C. Associates.

Chauhan, V. K. (2014). Smoke testing, *Int. J. Sci. Res. Publ.*, 4, 2250–3153.

Chung, L., Nixon, B. A., Yu, E. and Mylopoulos, J. (2012). *Non-Functional Requirements in Software Engineering*, Springer Science & Business Media. New York, USA.

Gunderson, J. (2009). Functional accessibility testing using best practices, in *International Conference on Universal Access in Human-Computer Interaction*, Springer (pp. 506–514).

Haugset, B. and Hanssen, G. K. (2008). Automated acceptance testing: A literature review and an industrial case study, in *Agile 2008 Conference*, IEEE (pp. 27–38).

Islam, S. and Falcarin, P. (2011). Measuring security requirements for software security, in *2011 IEEE 10th International Conference on Cybernetic Intelligent Systems (CIS)*, IEEE (pp. 70–75).

Meenakshi, R. P. and Kumar, A. (2015). Different techniques in software testing, *Int. J. Sci. Res. Comput. Sci. Appl. Manage. Stud.*, 4. pp. 1–5.

Mohammad, S. M. (2016). Continuous Integration and automation, *International Journal of Creative Research Thoughts, ISSN*, 2320–2882. Volume.4, Issue 3, pp.938–945.

Mohd, C. K. N. C. K. and Shahbodin, F. (2015). Personalized learning environment: Alpha testing, Beta Testing & user acceptance test, *Procedia-Social Behav. Sci.*, 195, 837–843.

Molyneaux, I. (2014). *The Art of Application Performance Testing: from Strategy to Tools*, O'Reilly Media, Inc. Sebastopol, USA.

Nanayakkara, K. S., Perera, P. & Shantha, F. 2014. Universal Communication Interface through Web Services for Heterogeneous Systems with Dynamic System Life Cycle. *International Journal of Computer Science and Technology*, 5, 48–55.

Nanayakkara, N. 2010. Customizable protocol for information transfer between heterogeneous platforms. MSc in Computer Science, University of Moratuwa.

Pressman, R. S. (2010). A practitioner's approach, *Software Eng.*, 2, 41–42.

Rahman, A., Partho, A., Meder, D. and Williams, L. (2017). Which factors influence practitioners' usage of build automation tools? In *2017 IEEE/ACM 3rd International Workshop on Rapid Continuous Software Engineering (RCoSE)*, IEEE (pp. 20–26).

Riley, T. (2020). The cybersecurity 2020, *The Washington Post*, (Accessed 7 December 2020).

Sarveswaran, K., Nanayakkara, S., Perera, P., Perera, A. & Fernando, S. 2006. Challenges in developing MIS–Case from Government sector. e-Asia Conference. Colombo, Sri Lanka.

Sawant, A. A., Bari, P. H. and Chawan, P. (2012). Software testing techniques and strategies, *IJERA*, 2, 980–986.

Tripathi, M. A. K., Upadhyay, M. S. and Dwivedi, M. S. K. D. Scalability performance of Software Testing by using review technique. *International Journal of Scientific & Engineering Research*, Volume 3, Issue 5, 2012, pp. 1–4, ISSN 2229–5518.

Zhang, T., Gao, J., Cheng, J. and Uehara, T. (2015). Compatibility testing service for mobile applications, in *2015 IEEE Symposium on Service-Oriented System Engineering*, IEEE (pp. 179–186).

https://doi.org/10.1142/9789811240584_0016

Chapter 16

IT Project Management in the Future

Christopher D'Souza*,‡, Roshana Goonewardene†,§ and
Athula Ginige*,¶

*Western Sydney University, Penrith, Australia
†Freelance Project Management Consultant
‡c.d'souza@westernsydney.edu.au
§roshana.goonewardene@gmail.com
¶a.ginige@westernsydney.edu.au

The state of IT project management is at a crossroads. Modern IT projects must satisfy the needs of multiple stakeholders, meet commercially viable outcomes, deliver to global demands, and constantly evolve to meet rapid advances in technology. The advances in IT have led to new tools which in turn demand better and fitting project management processes to support new and complex architectures, skilled global teams, build stakeholder trust, create accurate estimates, manage accountability, and monitor performance. Hence, a modern IT project manager needs new tools, frameworks, processes, skills, and experience to manage such diverse and complex projects. The authors recommend an integrated project management system that consists of several related sub-systems. Some of these should be driven by AI to support the processes related to change management, estimation, resource management, collaboration and decision making. Such an AI based system can enrich building of trust, transparency, accountability and confidence among the stakeholders of the project.

1. Introduction

The nature of IT systems and applications has evolved significantly over the last few decades due to major advances in computer and communication technologies. These IT advances have positively altered the business processes of organizations, both internal and external, as well as the physical and management structures. Evolving organizations have forced the supporting IT systems to continuously evolve in scale and functionality which has forced changes to the process of development and delivery. This in turn has changed how projects need to be managed. The changing approach to IT project management has been further facilitated by the IT tools that were made possible by the new technologies, creating an interesting interdependency. The availability of such tools has enabled new team environments necessitating new leadership, management approaches, processes, and skill sets. Further, to support this, evolving IT project management methodologies, continuous knowledge sharing, and reskilling the project team members have also become a necessity.

The abovementioned changes, project complexities, management approaches, project environments, globalization, and technology are driving projects to be extremely competitive but vulnerable to higher failure rates. This is becoming evident as one undertakes complex, cross-platform, multi-functional, global projects where multiple stakeholders scattered around the globe work remotely to deliver multiple outcomes and business benefits, using existing resources, tools, and bodies of knowledge. As a result, more projects are delivered late and over budget, distorting the facts and figures of successful projects and their outcomes. The measurement of outcomes is distorted because project environments have changed at an alarming rate since the inception of contemporary project management in the 1950s. There is no universally accepted framework to successfully manage the nuances of complex projects, let alone a universally agreed set of Key Performance Indices (KPIs) to assess a project's success. There is a widening gap between the theory (classroom) and practice (industry). Lack of investment, focus on Project Management (PM) as a discipline, and slow maturity of project management discipline, especially IT project management in comparison to others such as engineering and accounting, are possible underlying reasons for the continuing failure rates.

Organizations globally commenced applying formal project management principles to deliver commercial and non-commercial projects around the mid-1950s. Soon, IT projects likewise started to adapt these principles. Before looking at how IT projects will be managed in the future, it will be useful to explore the environment in which an IT project needs to be managed, review the challenges in managing an IT project, and find what measures are required to track the progress of an IT project. The next section 'Journey: IT Project Management Evolution, Past to Present' explores these aspects.

As mentioned at the beginning, it is the rapid evolution of IT systems and IT applications that challenged the existing know-how of IT project management, making the existing PM approaches inadequate for modern day IT projects, leading to the high rate of IT project failures. The section 'Technology Advances: Evolution of IT Systems and Applications' discusses how IT systems have become central to all activities being carried out today. This has few implications; the first is the need to support new functionalities beyond just transaction processing or performing complex calculations. The second is the number of users the new IT systems need to support at any given time which can fluctuate widely. To meet this challenge, new architectures and deployment methods have evolved. Third, the rapidly changing business environment makes it necessary for systems to consciously evolve. These factors have resulted in two key life cycle phases, Development and Operations, merging into a single phase known as DevOps where initial systems now enter a continuous cycle of developments and deployments, whenever new requirements, new stakeholders, new investors, etc., are involved. These continuous cycles challenge project managers to rethink how to assess the success or failure of a project: Can the learnings from a success or failure in one cycle be used in the following cycles? How to manage the learning process within these cycles? What type of managers and teams are needed to deliver these continuous cycles?

The authors conclude the chapter by looking at the future. The section 'Future of IT Project Management' explores possible approaches to manage the challenges and the evolutions taking place. They foresee the project management discipline evolving and providing the frameworks, process, and tools required to deliver the most demanding complex projects by combining knowledge, good practice, process, policies, and proven and adaptable frameworks. This will form an evolving body of knowledge in project management. This knowledge base will lead to creation of AI tools to further enhance management activities. The authors conclude the chapter by emphasizing the need to build human capacity to make best use of these new tools to better manage the projects.

2. Journey: IT project management evolution, past to present

Project Management has been practiced for thousands of years dating back to the Egyptian era. It was in the mid-1950s that organizations globally commenced applying formal project management principles to deliver commercial and non-commercial projects. PM frameworks, principles, and tools used in early projects provided the mechanism to monitor and control the triple constraints, i.e., scope, time, and cost. Performance and quality aspects were a subsequent focal point as the industry advanced and matured through the years since the 1950s.

Projects, project environments, challenges, success criteria, management techniques, frameworks, tools, and processes have all evolved, changed, and adopted to meet the ever-changing demand of project-based organizations (projectized) and functional (matrix) environments. No organizations big or small, commercial or otherwise can avoid the concepts of PM. All organizations in the future will evidently have to embed PM in all their functions, embrace change, and evolve to be successful in a competitive, global environment.

2.1. *Understanding the IT project environment*

Kerzner (2017) states that the growth of PM has come about more through necessity than through desire. As businesses compete with one another to create the next best product or service offering and as technology advances at a phenomenal rate, the changes in policy and politics together with globalization has influenced PM as a discipline to address these truly global challenges, forever changing project environments, thereby changing how projects are scoped, resourced, and delivered.

IT project management environments have evolved and changed since the 1950s due to advancements in technology in contrast to non-IT projects. However, PM as a discipline has lagged in providing advanced and fitting frameworks, policies, and guidance to manage complex IT projects. It has reacted to the changes rather than proactively looking at possible future trends and providing necessary frameworks, tools, policies, and processes. Its slow growth can be attributed mainly to the lack of acceptance of the new and emerging management techniques necessary for successful implementation of truly global, complex, leading-edge technology solutions.

A single project or a single initiative managed by a single project manager at a single location satisfying a single sponsor delivering a single outcome is rarely seen in current project environments, whether large or small. Most typical projects are established and funded to deliver multiple outcomes across complex multi-functional areas by multiple stakeholders. For example, a typical Enterprise Resource Planning (ERP) project could see Enterprise IT, Finance, Supply Chain, Sales and Marketing, Manufacturing, Logistics, PMO, and HR functions working together to deliver multiple outcomes. These projects would typically have multiple streams led by more than one project manager and perhaps even program managers reporting to multiple stakeholders based on their vested interests such as commercial outcomes and business benefits.

Project stakeholders' behaviors can be either passive or active. Active stakeholders are fully engaged and influence the direction and outcomes of the project. They are the ones that are directly impacted by the project or the group most benefited by it. Passive stakeholders have a vested interest in the project and may not always be directly impacted by the project. They may want to know about the project but are not as engaged as active stakeholders. Regardless, it is best to proactively manage both groups of stakeholders equally throughout the life of the project. After all, happy and satisfied stakeholders may provide continued sponsorship, new opportunities, synergies, etc. Responsibility Assignment Matrices (RAM) such as a RACI Matrix can be used to identify whether a key stakeholder should be considered as Responsible (R), Accountable (A), to be Consulted (C), and/or to be Informed (I), against key criteria (Kerzner, 2017). In general, most active stakeholders will be responsible and accountable, while the passive ones are happy when they are 'consulted' and 'informed'. For a project to be successful, stakeholders must be engaged from inception to completion of the project. They need to be educated at times and consulted at other times when key decisions are to be made. Similarly, when decisions are made, they need to be informed, i.e., communicated. A right level of reporting in the right frequency to educate, inform, and communicate the status will provide the project continued support from the stakeholder community.

2.2. *Managing challenges in IT project environments*

Current IT projects are faced with multiple challenges. These challenges will only grow as the technology advances and business needs become further demanding. No two projects are alike. Therefore, all projects will have multiple but unique challenges that impact their success.

Some of the more pressing challenges that are and will influence projects are external factors to projects such as customer and investor demand, pressure on delivering more value, reduced spending, frequent restructures, mergers and acquisitions, and corporate and personal ambitions. While there is no silver bullet to address all these challenges, most organizations mistakenly do not assess these internal and external impacts to projects although they are well understood.

At a macro level, these multifaceted challenges could be broadly attributed to Political, Economic, Social, Technological, Legal, and Environmental (PESTLE) factors. While decomposing each of these factors and analyzing how they influence project environments are beyond the scope of this chapter, at a micro level, some of the common challenges that impact IT project environments are discussed in the next subsection. This is followed by a real-world example of how the challenges were overcome.

2.2.1. *Intangibility and ambiguity*

IT systems cannot be seen, felt, or touched prior to their development. Therefore, models in the form of sketches and wireframes have been used. However, they are not active artifacts, so the client does not get a good understanding of the behavior of the system. A better modeling approach is evolutionary prototyping where an evolving system can be adopted and developed in timeboxed iterations. This iterative development will provide the stakeholders with comfort and confidence on a future system, thus minimizing the intangibility and ambiguity.

2.2.2. *Poorly defined goals and objectives*

Goals and objectives set the project roadmap and act as the blueprint. Clearly defining these goals and objectives for each phase of the project is critical at the start of each phase or iteration of the project. These goals and objectives could be documented by following an evidence-based approach model such as the Specific, Measurable, Achievable, and Timed (SMART) model. Once documented, the set goals and objectives must be assessed periodically and if a project is diverting from these set goals and objectives, corrective actions must be taken to reassess the set goals and objectives or revise the goals and objectives as necessary.

2.2.3. *Managing constraints*

All projects have constraints. Whether it is skilled resources, budget, time, available technology, benefits, quality, or performance, they must be identified and documented and proactively managed not only at the start of projects but throughout the project life cycle. Often, these constraints change from time to time throughout the project life cycle. For example, a project planned with all the required skilled technical resources for a successful project delivery could face resource constraints if one of the critical resources falls ill and is no longer available for a period. Suddenly, this project is at risk of not meeting delivery milestones.

2.2.4. *Unrealistic deadlines*

Deadlines that are unachievable are another PM challenge that can severely affect the quality of the product, impact the morale of the project team and subsequently the future of the project. Hence, making data-driven decisions and educating key decision-makers by engaging them throughout the project life cycle are important.

2.2.5. *Lack of firm requirements and scope*

While it is a challenge to agree on stable requirements and definitive scope upfront, emphasis must be given to at least understand and acknowledge what the project is to deliver. This could be in the form of Statement of Works (SOWs), Epics, a large body of work that will be delivered over a period, Features/Stories in an Agile development arrangement, scope statements in the form of estimated Work Breakdown Structures (WBS), or a mix of such tools (RACI Charts — How-to Guide and Templates, 2021). Loosely written requirements could lead to detrimental outcomes for projects and organizations. Breaking these requirements using the SMART framework could provide the right level of detail and structure required for requirements gathering and documentation.

2.2.6. *Lack of accountability and sponsorship*

A project team performs well when every member feels responsible and tries to fulfill the role assigned to them and the project sponsor is actively engaged. Lack of team accountability or a disengaged sponsor can sink an entire project. A solution to manage this could be to start by mapping a Roles & Responsibility (R&R) matrix and perhaps using an RACI model to assess team and stakeholder responsibilities. Documenting, making the team aware of their roles and responsibilities, enforcing them, and calling out when it is not adhered to result in better accountability.

2.2.7. *Inadequate skills of team members*

A chain is as strong as its weakest link and, in the case of project teams, performance highly depends on their individual skill levels. This is a huge

PM problem that can only be solved with proper experience and foresight. It is important to assess the teams and skill sets required for the project to be delivered successfully against a skills matrix. If there are gaps, seeking viable training opportunities when it does not adversely impact the project outcomes is advisable. Or, the project manager should negotiate or swap skilled resources from another project if possible. Finally, if none of the abovementioned solutions are possible, calling out the skill gaps and documenting possible risks or impacts to project outcomes are necessary.

2.2.8. *Navigating the challenges: A case study*

While there are only seven challenges listed in this chapter, the multitude of the challenge's projects face and the resolutions for each in most cases are unique to each project and the environments they operate in. Hence, to portray the applicability of some of these management approaches against the challenges, the authors focus on a Customer Relationship Management (CRM) project that was delivered where some of the above challenges and proactive management methods were adopted.

The client, a financial services sales and business development function, requested the authors to implement a CRM solution. The client had no previous exposure to a CRM; hence, their requirements and expectations were ambiguous. The client selected Microsoft Dynamics 365 Sales (MS D365 Sales) as a preferred platform with the ambition of integrating MS D365 Sales with the MS Dynamics Enterprise Resource Planning system which was already in production. Agility without limits (2021) contains further details on MS D365 Sales and MS Dynamics. Given the intangible nature of IT systems and the fact that the client had no previous experience, an out-of-the-box MS D365 Sales environment using Azure web services was commissioned for the client to use as a sandbox. Azure is Microsoft's web service provider (Cloud Computing Services | Microsoft Azure, 2021). Next, the client was invited to 'play' in this environment to establish confidence in the product and see what MS D365 Sales had to offer. This provided an opportunity for the client to understand the basic functionality of MS D365 Sales. However, the requirements were still ambiguous. Before moving forward to the next phase, the client was assisted in eliciting the goals and objectives for the project so that it was aligned with the overall goals and objectives of the company. The project was agreed to be delivered by following an Agile SCRUM framework. Further details on Agile SCRUM can be found in Schwaber and Sutherland (2020). Iterations were set to two weeks with demos and retrospectives scheduled on the last day of the Sprint. To get a healthy backlog, a Business Analyst was assigned to the project to work with the client to elicit requirements via agile framework's user stories in Azure DevOps. Once user stories in the backlog were documented following a SMART approach, a workshop was run with all the key stakeholders to prioritize the backlog containing the most valued features which aligned with the goals and objectives set at the outset. The backlog items then were allocated to sprints to create a delivery roadmap for tracking, monitoring, and reporting. Azure DevOps was configured to provide the burnup/burndown/team velocity and other relevant reporting as required. Further details on the agile framework's terminologies such as user stories, backlog, burnup, burndown, and team velocity can be found in Schwaber (2004). To accelerate delivery, the sandbox environment was converted to a development environment. The development and configurations of MS D365 Sales commenced based on the user stories and acceptance criteria elicited in Azure DevOps. Iteration by iteration, this product evolved to be a Prototype to showcase capability and gather feedback from key stakeholders. At every demo, the prototype was enhanced based on client feedback, and any variations to scope were validated against the goals and objectives. Any deviations to these were discussed and agreed upon with the client and the steering committee established as part of the governance structure. Three months into the project, the client requested to expedite the delivery as they needed to launch the fully configured MS D365 Sales into production within two months. Initial estimates indicated that it would take six months to deliver the project end to end. Therefore, this request was deemed unrealistic by the project team and an alternative solution to the client was suggested. An agreement was reached to provide a Minimum Viable Product (MVP) with 70% of the requested functionality within the remaining two months. With the client agreeing to the recommendation, the MVP was released into production for launch on MS D365 Sales.

2.3. *Managing and measuring IT project performance*

Success was measured purely on technical performance in the 1950s with subsequent shifting of that focus to customer acceptance. As project management, complexity, and project environments changed, so did the performance criteria of projects. These could perhaps be broadly categorized as project discipline, project deliverables, and organization related.

For a well-crafted IT platform to work smoothly, many components must come together almost organically. Some of the key components are well-defined and documented requirements, robust design, an enterprise view of the architecture that supports the design, and the IT roadmap. It could also be the availability of skilled resources at the right time. Leadership to support the vision of the project and an organization culture ready to embrace change could also be pivotal for project success. Providing funding to fruition of the vision, supporting the project throughout its life cycle and beyond in operationalizing the products, and services to embed the outcomes could drive the success of most projects.

Delivering on budget, time, and quality to stakeholder satisfaction, are some of the KPIs projects could be measured against. However, IT projects in contrast could also be measured on performance against the legacy systems, adaptability, usability, scalability, modularity, security, end-user satisfaction, Return on Investment (ROI), and Total Cost of Ownership (TCO). Opportunities to reduce the technical debt could also be looked at positively in assessing these measures.

Projects are different from one another in many aspects. Assessing one project against the other or having a set of KPIs that can be applied for all projects is not practical. Project performance success or KPIs hence differ from one project to the other much like project challenges. These depend on many indicators and in most instances are unique to each project and its environment. A common set of KPIs is specified in the following subsections. Defining the KPIs upfront and not only agreeing on these

KPIs but also monitoring and controlling these KPIs and measuring them against project objectives and goals may provide opportunities for projects to be successful. It must be noted that for projects to be successful, not one but many of these KPIs needs to be fulfilled based on the nature of the project and its environment.

2.3.1. *Team performance*

Team performance and growth are as important as meeting all other criteria. A happy, motivated, and performing team could deliver complex features faster. Using burndown/burnup charts, one could measure the throughput of the team during a timeboxed delivery method. This monitoring allows the project manager to closely monitor performance variations and understand the reasons for such variations.

2.3.2. *Customer, team, and stakeholder satisfaction*

A happy customer, satisfied team, and complimentary stakeholder feedback are elements of success for any project. So, engaging these three groups throughout the project, looking for opportunities to improve the engagement, and educating the groups go a long way in achieving success. This can be done by providing demos and invitations during major milestone events and during retrospectives. Such activities provide feedback loops to gauge the level of satisfaction. Other tools such as short and prompt surveys can also be used to gauge the pulse of the group with the objective of keeping them engaged, educated, and satisfied.

2.3.3. *Quality and performance*

Defining, monitoring, and measuring quality and performance and the interpretation of success could be challenging. However, for a project to be successful, especially an IT project, performance could be defined as a key success criterion. With respect to IT, one could measure performance against non-functional requirements (NFRs), comparing the performance from old to the new system or against industry benchmarks. Whichever method or a combination of methods are used, it is a must to agree upon, document, and cost them upfront while tracking and monitoring their progress throughout the project life cycle.

2.3.4. *On budget*

Delivering a project within the agreed budget is always important. If the project runs over budget it could impact cost benefit and lead to unnecessary pressure, administration overheads, loss of confidence, trust and unsatisfied investors. So, budgets must be monitored and controlled. For large projects, a dedicated person who understands financial principles to own the management and reporting of project budget is recommended. If this resource is not available, sound processes, tools, and methods to gather data and to track and monitor budgets should exist. In addition, budget should be assessed at key intervals such as at milestones or end of a deliverable. In agile projects, a monthly or better still sprint burndown from a cost perspective is desirable and a process or a mechanism to report any deviations is important.

2.3.5. *Scope*

Any variations to scope almost always impact time, cost, and related variables/constraints; hence, any changes or revisions to scope must be assessed, monitored, and reported. One must have a scope variation process or sound scope change management process implemented that suits the project and provides the necessary data for decision-making. Changes to scope are inevitable in projects, yet how these changes are managed, monitored, and controlled is critical for project success.

2.3.6. *On schedule*

Projects not delivered on time could only create further complications, loss of confidence, and perhaps may impact trust. Schedule delays could be due to many avoidable or unavoidable reasons. They could be due to external factors or change of scope. It is critical to monitor and control these factors and assess them regularly. On the other hand, a project delivered ahead or on time is hailed as a success story. Schedule is a trade-off between scope, quality, performance, and budget. It could also be traded-off to manage team and stakeholder satisfaction. Monitoring key indicators, assessing the indicators that impact the schedule, and reporting these early via Risks and Issue reporting mechanisms are a must (Pacelli, 2004). Remediation due to schedule changes should be done immediately and plans to avoid further schedule impacts should be put in place.

2.3.7. *Benefits realization*

Projects must deliver benefits to investors. At the time benefits are realized, some projects may no longer be active. However, it is critical to assess and record these to provide opportunities for future growth, deliver tangible value to investors, and opportunities to learn from. A project that has delivered defined benefits to investors is surely a successful project. Therefore, the team should agree, assess, and document project benefits that are both tangible (quantifiable) and intangible (non-quantifiable) at the start of the project. Assessing and revising every time the project deviates from the original goal and communicating with all stakeholders with regard to any deviations and the potential impact on the project benefits and its outcomes are required. A project benefit statement should provide a true reflection of how the projects are monitored, controlled, assessed, and project benefits are accrued. Documentation is important as it becomes an invaluable resource for future projects.

2.3.8. *Organizational and customer adaptability to project outcome*

Project brings about change. These changes could be viewed as a threat by some stakeholders but embraced by others. For a project to be successful, one must monitor and report on organizational adaptability to the new project environment, i.e., the uptake on the product or the service delivered by the project. If the organization or the customer is struggling to adapt to the new product or the service the project has delivered, it could be perceived as an unsuccessful endeavor. This could be due to many factors such as a lack of awareness or communication, lack of engagement or training, and technological challenges. Understanding these potential challenges upfront or as they arise and having mitigation strategies in place to minimize their impact are necessary. Tools such as surveys can be used to assess the adaptability at key intervals.

3. Technology advances: Evolution of IT systems and applications

The goals of IT systems have been constantly evolving. In the late 1950s, IT projects were developed mainly to carry out scientific calculations for military purposes. By the early 1960s, businesses started developing IT projects to perform tasks such as payroll processing and compute what-if scenarios for planning purposes. Most of these were stand-alone applications running on mainframe computers. However, the merger of information with communication technologies opened a wide range of new possibilities bringing in eras of Minicomputers, Personal Computers, and Distributed Computer Systems. Distributed Computer Systems enabled the development of Enterprise Computer applications. Many enterprise applications such as Enterprise Resource Planners, CRM, HR systems, project planning, and management tools were developed to increase the efficiency of business operations.

The types of IT applications have evolved significantly since the advent of the World Wide Web in 1989. Online marketplaces such as Amazon and eBay were developed and then social media applications such as Facebook, Twitter, and LinkedIn emerged. These social media applications evolved to provide two-sided marketplaces such as Facebook Marketplace creating an era of Social Computing (Parameswaran and Whinston, 2007).

To support the shift from enterprise computing to online marketplaces to social computing, Information System applications required the development of new architectures, design methodologies and technologies. Transaction processing was the key functionality provided by enterprise computing. In the era of enterprise computing, system architectures and database technologies evolved to support the processing of complex transactions while maintaining data integrity. These capabilities were provided at the database level. The continuous evolution of technologies, especially communication technologies, and the standardization of communication protocols enabled anyone with a mobile phone, tablet, laptop, or computer to be connected to one another or to backend systems. This, coupled with advances in sensor technology, enabled not only people but also connected devices such as motorcars, refrigerators, light bulbs, rain gauges, temperature sensors, motion detectors etcetera to form a giant communication network, namely, the Internet-of-Things (IOT). By developing inter-operable IT systems, it became possible to better manage buildings and cities; thus, the concepts such as "Smart Building" and "Smart Cities" evolved.

As a result of the evolving needs of business, the types of IT applications required evolved. This in turn made it necessary for the IT systems required for their development to evolve. In this section, the authors discuss the interplay between the expanding functionalities of IT systems and their underlying development strategies from a System Architecture and System Development Methodology perspective as this will have an influence on how IT projects need to be managed in the future.

3.1. *Expanding key functionalities of IT systems*

To support online marketplaces, the IT systems had to implement ways to make payments online. These required a level of security to build trust while interfacing with banks via payment gateways. For example, there was a major growth in the online marketplaces in the late 90s, but it ended with the 'Dot-Com' crash in March 2000. Though many technology platforms were developed for people to buy online, people lacked the trust to use such systems. Building trust is essential for information, material, and money to flow. In an enterprise-wide system, this trust is inherently available within the system. Employees of an organization unreservedly use the system provided by the employer because they trust the system. Similarly, for systems that facilitate business-to-business transactions, the trust is first established outside the system through various contractual arrangements with legal bindings. When IT systems were built for use by the public and became Social Systems, it was necessary to incorporate functionality for building trust and minimizing risk as part of the design. Building trust and minimizing risks associated with exchange of information and transactions had to be incorporated into development and deployment activities. In most existing system development approaches, the relevant development methodologies do not include activities to support trust-building and risk minimization aspects. This necessitated a new set of system architectures and development methodologies to be developed, managed, and distributed across the project life cycle, further increasing the complexity of the project to be managed.

3.2. *Managing complexity through changing system architectures*

The architecture of IT systems defines whether it can support evolving business needs. For example, as businesses move from enterprise-wide operations to Business to Business (B2B) and Business to Consumer (B2C), the IT systems supporting the different aspects of the business need to be integrated for ease of sharing the data. This setup requires people with different competencies to design, develop, and manage the change. The complexity of functionalities and size, along with the need for efficient organization of data, led to new programming languages and database technologies to achieve optimal designs. Traditionally, support for evolving business needs was provided through add-on packages to an existing monolithic system. However, the increasing complexity of applications stretched the efficiency of monolithic architectures to the limit. The runtime performance of monolith systems started degrading as more and more people started using the system. In response to this challenge, a development paradigm based on microservice architecture evolved. Earlier, the applications were running on physical servers but moved to virtual servers to reduce the maintenance cost. Now, the applications are increasingly run as microservices on containerized systems, where each business service is run as an individual microservice on containers that are independent of Operating System (OS) constraints. These newer forms of architecture of IT systems further increased the complexity of PM tasks.

Applications such as one-side or two-sided online marketplaces and social media applications are expected to cater to large numbers of users. The user numbers have increased from a few thousands to tens of thousands, hundreds of thousands, millions, and in a few instances to billions. With such large user numbers, the demand at any given time on the system can greatly fluctuate throughout the day. Running servers to cater to the maximum demand all the time is costly. This has resulted in the development of elastic deployment platforms that can scale up on demand, which are now known as Cloud Native applications (Kratzke and Quint, 2017).

The corresponding development and deployment activities have become another aspect to be managed.

3.3. *Managing evolution through changing development methodology*

Project managers need to be flexible in adopting appropriate development methodologies to manage the challenges of running a project. The popular methodologies being followed are Waterfall, Rapid Action Development (RAD), and Agile (Vijayasarathy and Butler, 2016). The development of large and complex projects requiring fail-safe applications needs documentation-driven approaches, so such projects require more time and budget. So, Waterfall models are adopted in such cases. On the other hand, the RAD approach is suitable when the clients' requirements are not clearly understood, necessitating development of quick and discardable prototypes using Computer-Aided Software Engineering (CASE) tools to elicit clients' responses. The global requirements of B2B and B2C systems have created a new development challenge — changing requirements throughout the project's life cycle. To manage this, the Agile methodology was established. Most business projects are now managed using Agile methodology, where satisfying the flexible needs of multiple stakeholders during the development process is a key concern.

A common theme with regard to the need for modern projects is the 'flexibility to evolve'. The shift from monolithic to microservice architecture enabled new ways to organize the project team to support the evolutionary needs. This decoupling of a system to a set of orchestrated microservices enabled each microservice to be developed by individual teams. The roles of the development teams too changed. Now, each small team can use the Agile approach to satisfy the scope needs of local clients in a global setup, typically in two week scrums. This approach thus provided an effective method to accommodate evolving local requirements. Furthermore, the need to support a continuously evolving system made it necessary for the team that developed the module to manage it during runtime and keep changing it as the requirements evolve. This is because it is inefficient if one team develops and another team manages the application during runtime. Thus, the development and operations or DevOps of each microservice became the responsibility of a single team. Many tools evolved to support this Continuous Integration and either a Continuous Delivery or Continuous Deployment (CI/CD) approach to developing and deploying IT systems (O'Reilly, 2019). Further, as the microservices required for an application increased, the management of these services such as shutting down or restarting was seen as a new challenge which is being managed by newer tools such as Kubernetes.

4. Future of IT project management

A futuristic PM framework needs an integration of several sub-systems to support processes, change management, building trust, estimation, transparency, accountability, resource management, collaborative communication, and confidence building. The future may demand that these frameworks, policies, and procedures be nimble, scalable, adaptable, and be applicable for most projects if not all. As organizations attempt better ways to keep up with technology as they advance, the supporting frameworks to deliver these technological and business advances need to support the greater vision and mission of organizations and commercial viability for their existence.

The authors foresee PM being embedded as a core function in every organization whether large or small, or at least within the IT function, based on the growth and trajectory of the PM discipline. PM as a discipline may evolve and mature as the technology advances across industries, providing frameworks, policies, and procedures. These policies and procedures may need to be reviewed, revised, and reintroduced as the journey continues.

As alluded to in Section 2, the nature of projects differs depending on the project environment, the outcomes it intends to deliver, the benefits it measures against, application of the solution, and the industry it associates with. As projects become more complex, competency areas within PM, such as Risk, Change, Communications, Schedule, Contracts, Budget (Financials), Quality, and Human Resource management, could be considered as separate disciplines or 'sub-systems' on their own, supporting the greater project management 'system'. Further details on systems of systems can be found in Luzeaux *et al.* (2010). Most complex projects are managed as large programs with multiple related projects or streams. In this instance, the program could act as the 'system' and each project or stream under the program could be referred to as a 'sub-system'. The concept of a 'system' connected with 'sub-systems' can be seen at every level in the PM echo system. This view of the project environment provides us the ability to manage inputs and outputs from each sub-system to the other. It also provides us an interrelated view on dependencies, risks, issues, etc., across sub-systems, enabling us to establish, monitor, and control variances. While each sub-system is connected and complements or supports other sub-systems, the overall inputs and outputs of these sub-systems provide the inputs, outputs, structure, framework, and governance to overall project/program benefits, objectives, goals, and outcomes. A well-functioning system is as good as the weakest sub-system. As an example, if a Scope Management sub-system is not functioning well and the monitoring and controlling of the scope is not established nor a sound scope change management framework implemented, then the overall project could suffer. Therefore, is it critical to have a framework and processes to manage all sub-systems within the PM system, and these frameworks and processes must support each sub-system and the overall project environment.

Hybrid frameworks that work for projects and organizations will emerge instead of the existing rigid structures and heavy-handed frameworks laden with administrative workloads associated with managing project teams. This can be seen in requirements gathering by way of User Stories for both functional and non-functional aspects, and moving away from pages of requirements documentation can be seen in the current project environments. In the future, with agile adaptation, refinement and maturity of such frameworks will enable projects to be delivered at speed addressing market demands. Therefore, agile delivery practices may have to be altered to suit appropriate applicable industries.

Projects always bring about a change to achieve a new set objectives or goals. Changes need to be planned, executed, controlled, and managed throughout the project life cycle from inception to completion. Change Management therefore is a critical sub-system within PM. Typically, change is initiated at an organizational level. These change initiatives transition organizations from current to future state, generating projects. Change therefore can be organizational change and scope variations in relation to projects. The organizational change in many cases drive the project scope and result in project outcomes, influencing the direction of the future organizational state. As for scope variations, projects must have a sound process to capture, monitor, control, and manage scope variations throughout the project life cycle. This could be achieved by using tools such as JIRA (Atar, 2020) or Azure DevOps to capture requirements via user stories and tracking variations as the project matures and the scope becomes clearer, or in a more traditional way by version-controlled requirements documentation. Regardless of which process or tools are used for managing scope variations, a sound governance structure must be in place to approve or reject variations. In most cases, this becomes the role and responsibility of the project steering committee or a financially delegated authority. Organizational change management can be a combination of cultural, process, communications, and training aspects of change management that enable the transition from current to future state. For example, a large global organization based in Australia having a majority of their operations in the Asia-Pacific region merging with a large organization based in the United States of America to create a complex large single multinational organization will have multiple organizational change management challenges. At the forefront could be a merging of the two cultures. A strategy to manage this could be to either adopt one or the other or create a new culture altogether. This provides an opportunity for both heritage organizations to leave behind what did not work and move forward to the new norm. This shift in culture will require well-crafted and timely communications to reach the most remote worker in the new organization. The new organization will require variations to processes and workflows or they may need new processes and workflows to replace the old. The process owners and teams that are impacted by the new processes will need to be trained. If the merger results in redundancies, then these will need to be managed skillfully, timely, and tactically. Therefore, organizational change emerges as the most critical part of implementing change or in other words delivering projects. So, Organizational Change Management can be seen to be a discipline on its own, complementing PM and addressing Cultural Change, Communications, Process, and Training aspects of PM. Based on industry trends, Organizational Change is foreseen to be the most challenging and complex of all processes given that it is always centered on human behavior.

Organizations will have to be trained to accept change as a constant to be successful. When technology moves at a faster pace than the pace of maturity of PM teams, will technology bring about innovation to the PM discipline? How can projects be set up to deliver value and outcomes to meet investor ambitions? Based on the historical trends, the authors believe technological advances will drive the maturity of IT project management. For example, continuous integration and continuous deployment principles within DevOps are providing a framework for continuous delivery of products and services that support continuous evolution. This has changed the start–stop delivery approach of traditional projects. In today's IT project environment, there is less start–stop while managing changes but more continuation post-delivery operations.

The future of IT projects cannot be looked at in isolation without considering it in the context of the roles of future project managers and teams. So, the next two subsections will discuss these aspects. This will be followed by a discussion of the future of IT project management. Finally, in the last subsection a summary of the chapter is presented.

4.1. *Future of IT project manager*

According to Cleland and Bidanda (2009), project managers not only have to foresee the future but they must also do it well. Project managers must visualize the roadmap leading to the final project delivery as well as its outcomes, and, in doing so, proactively identify, assess, monitor, and take corrective actions when required. In fact, project managers are now considered as managing a part of the business rather than just managing a project (Kerzner, 2019). Clearly the role of a modern project manager is multifaceted. However, this does not mean that the project manager needs to be an expert in these diverse areas. Rather, the project manager should have teams of subject-matter experts or team leaders with diverse skills to assist and the project manager should entrust them by delegating appropriate responsibilities.

A successful project manager in the future may not only understand and evolve with the PM discipline but should also be knowledgeable about current industry best practices and trends. They may need to understand contemporary business practices, project environments, and be tech savvy at least to the point where they understand commonly used PM tools such as Azure DevOps, JIRA, Confluence, Slack, and scheduling tools (Atar, 2020; Cloud Computing Services | Microsoft Azure, 2021; Kohler, 2013; Slack Features, 2021). Having experience in the industry, particularly in successfully delivering projects in specialized industry domains such as construction, defense, mining, and financial services may help in managing IT projects.

Good team management skills too are necessary for a successful PM. Building consensus is an important tactic for creating an environment for accepting change. This may involve finding members who recognize the problem, especially at different levels of the organization to convince the top management about the impact of changes made by them. Another important trait of a project manager would be to ensure the top management of the organization remains always sold on benefits of the project. Hence, the project manager becomes the glue between top, middle management, and the rest of the organization.

Soft skills, i.e., sound communication, leadership, relationship building, and the ability to manage remote teams virtually, are becoming critical skills required to manage current and future projects. With these expectations, it is a must that the project manager is tech savvy, understands the functional domain, has softs skills, is experienced and perhaps certified, and has aptitude and adaptability to learn as the industry evolves.

4.2. *Future of IT project teams*

Modern projects are managed by interacting with teams. So, team creation and team management are important aspects of a successful PM. Earlier, teams were largely hierarchical in nature with a top-down structure. They were mostly local. However, modern teams are geographically apart, necessitating teams to collaborate virtually. As a result, documenting, tracking, motivating, and providing feedback and reviews happen in a virtual space. Consequently, building trust and empathy is difficult. So, evidence-based approaches need to be used to build trust but without micromanagement. Technology can play a crucial role to glue the teams together. Multi-team systems (MTS) can be used to effectively manage interdependent teams in a large IT project where each team normally works independently on a separate part of the project yet works with other teams in response to changes. The need for change originates from issues such as goal discordance, separation of competency in functional areas, work process dissonance, and information opacity (Wu *et al.*, 2020). Tools such as Slack and MS Teams are already becoming popular in this space. Slack provides the opportunity to work more easily with everyone using features such as Channels, Slack Connect, Messaging, Voice, and video calls similarly to MS Teams. Channels is a dedicated way to help teams follow everything related to individual topics or projects. Slack Connect helps in collaborating with teams at other companies. Text messaging in virtual forums enables teams to search and respond at any time, and video calls and conferencing support face-to-face communication more efficiently (Slack Features, 2021).

4.3. *Where to from here?*

The next leap in PM could lead people to work collaboratively with no boundaries or time zone restrictions. Some areas of PM such as schedule conflict management, resource utilization, risk and issue management, dependency mapping, budget/cost, and time management may be enhanced and managed using AI technology. Project Management AI is a new phrase being used to define such a system that can perform the day-to-day management and administration of projects without requiring human input (Middleton, 2017).

Big data and analytics are already being used in everyday decision-making where quality data are available. Frame and Chen (2018) suggest three categories of uses for data analytics in PM: descriptive, predictive, and prescriptive. Each of these supports project managers in discerning meaningful patterns in data for insights leading to future action. Descriptive analytics can be used to size up the current situation to suggest action. Predictive analytics sizes up the current situation to predict future situations and prescriptive analytics uses structured and unstructured legacy knowledge to guide managers with the optimal course of action. Already, tools such as stratejos which started as AI assistants for estimation and sprint management are now dealing with processing information by machine learning from task descriptions. Stratejos can tie a team member's individual effort with a sprint's history and as a result can alert when a key human resource is pulled away for other projects (Stratejos — Intelligent assistant for tech teams, 2018). A recent survey on the likely impact of AI on PM in the next 10 years indicates that AI will be an integral part of future PM practice, specifically in the management of cost, schedule, and risk (Fridgeirsson *et al.*, 2021). Fridgeirsson *et al.* note that AI can monitor schedules, adjust forecasts, and maintain baselines but will have less impact in knowledge areas and processes that require human leadership skills, such as developing and managing teams and the management of stakeholders.

In addition, project managers are now expected to support the emotional intelligence of the project team since project successes are observed to be based on the emotional quotient of the manager with the teammates and other collaborators (Clarke and Howell, 2009). Burger (2017) notes that while AI lacks the emotional intelligence a human project manager possesses, a robotic project manager can be used to automate chores such as staff evaluation, work assignment, performance monitoring, sanctioning underperformers, and worker grievances. So, perhaps a future human project manager will need to focus more on HR and soft skills.

Another area of future development in PM, though not necessarily in IT Project Management, is the application of blockchain technology. In construction management projects, blockchain is being used to support transparency in contract management of outsourced projects. Dietrich *et al.* (2021) analyzed several publications on ways to improve transparency in supply chain management and found that blockchain is increasingly being recommended as a suitable solution to manage smart contracts. Liu *et al.* (2020) have used a blockchain traceability anti-counterfeiting platform with a criteria-based evaluation sub-system to provide a scientific basis to evaluate suppliers before selecting them at the beginning of PM. Similarly, Meng and Sun (2021) have used blockchain technology to enhance the efficiency and success rate of a scientific research project to cope with traditional problems such as breaches of contracts and confidentiality. Several examples are provided by Hewavitharana *et al.* (2019) to highlight the use of blockchain technology during the life cycle of construction industry projects to support activities such as effectively managing contracts, tracking of inspections of buildings, and improving predictability of project delivery. However, blockchain is not widely used in IT Project Management since the scope of IT projects is more fluid unlike in construction projects, but it could be used in areas of contract and supply chain management in large technology.

In view of the current trends and advancement in technology, it could be a matter of time before AI, analytics, and predictive technologies are used to make decisions within projects. The challenge however could be gathering, storing, and mining quality data that come out of thousands of projects that are done globally.

What if there could be a publicly available knowledge base where one could search lessons learned, KPIs, success, or failure of similar projects in similar industries? What if this could be built on AI technology to learn to predict over time? If the data ingested into these systems are accurate, transparent, and valid, this type of tool or platform could provide much-needed foresight not only to the most experienced but equally to the less experienced. If quality data were available on millions of projects completed across the globe and were readily available for project managers via a single platform at their fingertips, could they make a difference in making future predictions and could they not make educated decisions backed by data and analytics? The answer to that is a resounding yes! The fact that industries are segregated and working in silos and the fact that real transparent data are not available in the public domain mean that the concept of having such a knowledge base could still be a few years away.

However, the authors believe that some organizations are moving toward the correct path at least to build knowledge bases for their own organizations using collaborative tools such as JIRA, Confluence, and Azure DevOps. These tools provide the analytics current-day organizations need to make decisions, such as burnup/burndown trend analysis, team throughput, estimation accuracy, and trend analysis.

4.4. *Summary*

The authors foresee the future of PM to be promising by reflecting on the historical advancement of the PM discipline since its contemporary inception in the 1950s and on the current practices and the advances in technology. The discipline will evolve and provide the frameworks, process, and tools required to deliver the most demanding complex project combining knowledge, good practice, process, policies, and proven, adaptable frameworks. This will form an evolving body of knowledge in PM.

The authors believe technological advances can provide the next big leap in the PM discipline. Due to technological advancements, tools exist where one can map current and future business processes, where these tools then transform processes to business requirements automatically. Modern software enables developers to create applications and database structures with related tables by only providing the structure of the organization's business entities. Technology has further enabled organizations to continuously develop and deploy adopting CI/CD concepts. Automated testing together with defect reporting and resolution tools adds the next layer required to deliver quality outcomes. Artifact life cycle management happens via technology platforms. These artifacts managed via technology platforms present a true dynamic representation of real-time documentation or in other words 'living documentation'. Similarly, code is compiled and stored in code libraries ready to be used/deployed. Collaboration technologies have evolved providing the much-needed boost to ICT, enabling teams across the globe to collaborate across geographies. These tools and platforms have enabled the most remote teams to collaborate, set objectives, monitor progress, clear impediments, and deliver successfully. Reporting produced by current platforms has and will provide the much-needed visibility to projects, enabling a path to build trust and identify issues, risks, and dependencies.

Advancement in technology could provide the necessary tool sets, platforms, and processes to deliver projects successfully. Technology somewhat plays a 'guinea pig' role in the advancement of the PM discipline as technology projects are used to try new ways of delivering projects and improving PM capabilities and bodies of knowledge. A testament to this is Agile development methodologies first used in the IT industry, now equally or widely used in other industries to deliver projects at speed.

The authors believe the next leap in PM is to have an integrated technology platform that combines all if not most of the features and functionalities discussed above, providing the end user a single platform with a single source of truth to manage multidisciplinary, complex projects across industries. Such a future is not far from a technological advancement perspective. However, projects cannot be delivered in isolation purely reliant on technology. There is and always will be the human element to PM that needs focus, dedication, discipline, and development.

The human element of PM is envisaged as a new field of study, body of knowledge, and discipline that complements the PM and delivery of successful projects when coupled with technology.

A summary of this chapter is provided as a table (broken into two as Tables 1(a) and 1(b), to support spanning across 2 pages) of three columns highlighting how PM has changed across various dimensions, from the past to present and how it will possibly be seen in the future.

Table 1. Changing nature of IT project management.

Dimensions	Past	Current	Future
(a)			
Project Environment	Stable business environment.	Changing or transitioning business environments to meet global demands centering on ad-hoc change management projects.	Continuously evolving business environments requiring continuously integrated projects.
Scope	Single project with stable scope satisfying local needs.	Projects within a project, each with fixed or variable scope. Rapid change, unstable requirements.	Projects within a project, each with flexible scope. Steady and rapid changes.
Resources	Dedicated, specialist resources assigned to a single project.	Tech savvy, specialist resources working on distributed environments supporting multiple projects.	AI and Knowledge Management (KM) resources as important assets to automate PM.
Architecture & technology	Monolithic applications running on mainframes or client servers or virtual servers.	Microservice applications running on individual containers to support scalability.	Tools to automate management of hundreds or thousands of microservices. Increasing use of AI for better efficiency, multi-team IS for better management of differences among teams.

Table 1.   (*Continued*)

Dimensions	Past	Current	Future
Organizational structure	Mostly hierarchical or top-down in nature.	Non-hierarchical in nature. PM being increasingly considered as an important part of business.	PM team and business team are considered inseparable.
Stakeholders	Top management has more control than project managers.	Project managers have equal control as top business managers.	Project Manager delegates control to local project leads. Increasingly acts as a liaison officer between business team and project teams.
Management-KPIs	Deliver fully functional system on time and budget.	Deliver scalable system supporting all change.	Deliver usable and scalable system that supports continuously evolving priorities or local priorities even though not all functionalities are expected to be fully met.
(b)			
Operating model	Rapid developments in IT driving business to change.	Changing business uses IT to help it manage the change.	Collaboration between business and IT (both change each other).
Time to market	More time is required because a whole new product is needed.	Grappling to manage time since change requests are ad-hoc in nature.	Most valuable parts of projects are delivered on time.
Perception of PM discipline	A process to manage projects.	A process to manage projects using scientific methods.	A process to manage continuously changing business problems.

References

Agility without limits. (2021). Agility Without Limits. Available at: https://dynamics.microsoft.com/en-au/. (Accessed 16 September 2021).

Atar, A. (2020). Jira 8 Recipes, 1st ed. Packt Publishing. Available at https://learning.oreilly.com/videos/jira-8-recipes/9781838980122/. (Accessed 8 October 2022)

Burger, R. (2017). I, Project Manager: The Rise of Artificial Intelligence in the Workplace. Available at: https://blog.capterra.com/i-project-manager-the-rise-of-artificial-intelligence-in-the-workplace/. (Accessed 15 August 2021).

Clarke, N. and Howell, R. (2009). *Emotional Intelligence and Projects*. Newtown Square, Pa: Project Management Institute.

Cleland, D. I. and Bidanda, B. (2009). Project management circa 2025, *Proj. Manage. J.*, 40(4), 104.

Cloud Computing Services | Microsoft Azure. (2021). Available at: https://azure.microsoft.com/en-au/. (Accessed 16 September 2021).

Dietrich, F., Ge, Y., Turgut, A., Louw, L. and Palm, D. (2021). Review and analysis of blockchain projects in supply chain management, *Procedia Comput. Sci.*, 180, 724–733.

Frame, J. D. and Chen, Y. (2018). Why data analytics in project management? In Spalek S, (ed.), *Data Analytics in Project Management*, 1st ed. Boca Raton, FL: Auerbach Publications.

Fridgeirsson, T. V., Ingason, H. T., Jonasson, H. I. and Jonsdottir, H. (2021). An authoritative study on the near future effect of artificial intelligence on project management knowledge areas, *Sustainability*, 13(4), 2345.

Hewavitharana, T., Nanayakkara S. and Perera S. (2019). Blockchain as a project management platform, in *Proceedings of the 8th World Construction Symposium*, University of Moratuwa (pp. 137–146).

Kerzner, H. (2017). *Project Management: a Systems Approach to Planning, Scheduling, and Controlling*, 12th ed. Hoboken, New Jersey: John Wiley & Sons, Inc.

Kerzner, H. (2019). *Using the Project Management Maturity Model: Strategic Planning for Project Management*, 3rd ed. Newark: John Wiley & Sons, Inc.

Kohler, S. (2013). *Atlassian Confluence 5 Essentials*, 1st ed. Birmingham: Packt Publishing, Limited.

Kratzke, N. and Quint, P. C. (2017). Understanding cloud-native applications after 10 years of cloud computing — A systematic mapping study, *J. Syst. Software*, 126, 1–16.

Liu, A., Liu, T., Mou, J. and Wang, R. (2020). A supplier evaluation model based on customer demand in blockchain tracing anti-counterfeiting platform project management, *J. Manage. Sci. Eng.*, 5(3), 172–194.

Luzeaux, D. and Ruault, J. R. (2010). *Systems of Systems*. London: ISTE.

Meng, Q. and Sun, R. (2021). Towards secure and efficient scientific research project management using consortium blockchain, *J. Sign Process Syst.*, 93(2–3), 323–332.

Middleton, S. (2017). 3 Ways AI will Change Project Management for the Better. Available at: https://www.atlassian.com/blog/software-teams/3-ways-ai-will-change-project-management-better. (Accessed 11 August 2021).

O'Reilly. (2019). *CI/CD in a Cloud Native World*, O'Reilly Media, Inc. Available at https://learning.oreilly.com/videos/jira-8-recipes/9781838980122/. (Accessed 8 October 2022).

Pacelli, L. (2004). Tried and true methods in managing project risks and issues. Paper Presented at *PMI® Global Congress 2004* — North America, Anaheim, CA. Newtown Square, PA: Project Management Institute.

Parameswaran, M. and Whinston, A. B. (2007). Social computing: An overview, *Commun. Assoc. Inf. Syst.*, 19. Doi: 10.17705/1CAIS.01937. pp 762–780.

RACI Charts — How-to Guide and Templates. (2021). Available at: https://racichart.org/. (Accessed 15 September 2021).

Schwaber, K. (2004). *Agile Project Management with Scrum*. Redmond: Microsoft Press.

Schwaber, K. and Sutherland, J. (2020). The 2020 Scrum Guide. Available at: https://scrumguides.org/scrum-guide.html. (Accessed 15 September 2021).

Slack Features. (2021). Available at: https://slack.com/intl/en-au/features. (Accessed 26 July 2021).

Stratejos — Intelligent assistant for tech teams. (2018). Available at: https://stratejos.ai/. (Accessed 11 August 2021).

Vijayasarathy, L. R. and Butler, C. W. (2016). Choice of software development methodologies: Do organizational, project, and team characteristics matter? *IEEE Software*, 33(5), 86–94. Doi: 10.1109/MS.2015.26.

Wu, X. J., Huang, W. W., Chia-An Tsai, J., Klein, G. and Jiang, J. J. (2020). Differentiation and dynamism within the IT development program, *J. Manage. Sci. Eng.*, 5(3), 150–161.

Chapter 17

IT Project Management 4.0: Trends and Future Directions

Srinath Perera*,§, Robert Eadie†,¶, Samudaya Nanayakkara‡,|| and
G. Thilini Weerasuriya*,**

*Centre for Smart Modern Construction, Western Sydney University,
Locked Bag 1797, Penrith, New South Wales 2751, Australia
†Ulster University, School of the Built Environment,
Belfast Campus, Northern Ireland
‡University of Moratuwa, Sri Lanka
§srinath.perera@westernsydney.edu.au
¶r.eadie@ulster.ac.uk
||samudaya@uom.lk
**t.weerasuriya@westernsydney.edu.au

The advancement in technology and greater push toward digitalization brought about by the impact of Industry 4.0 is changing the way IT projects are managed and executed. Consequently, investment in IT is increasing and new software technologies are bringing in new possibilities for project delivery. These changes are impacting the way project stakeholders engage in projects while project management methodologies are evolving. This chapter evaluates and contextualizes these aspects, drawing from the detailed discussion provided in the previous chapters of this book. It then summarizes the future directions of time, cost, quality, and risk management approaches related to IT projects. This chapter concludes by providing a vision toward the next generation of technologies, discussing how these will impact project management.

1. Introduction

The Fourth Industrial Revolution, also known as Industry 4.0, is bringing about extensive changes to the world. The technological advances of Industry 4.0 that merge the physical, digital, and biological worlds are creating scope for vast improvements in nearly all industries globally, as well as related challenges (Schwab, 2016). According to Deloitte Insights (2020), the Industry 4.0 technologies that are most anticipated to impact organizations are the Internet of Things (IoT), Artificial Intelligence (AI), cloud infrastructure, big data/analytics, and nanotechnology. Other Industry 4.0 technologies include advanced robotics, sensors, blockchain, 3D printing, and augmented reality. All of these technologies are disrupting the way industries operate, driving greater innovation and efficiencies. However, a key challenge of Industry 4.0 is the disruption of labor markets, leading to greater inequality (Xu *et al.*, 2018). It is predicted that automation and AI will affect 1.2 billion employees over the next decade, an equivalent of half the world's economy (Eerd and Guo, 2020). Automation is expected to cause employees to upskill in order to adapt to changes within their roles. Jobs in the field of information and communications technology (ICT) would also change, such as the role of computer programmers due to programs being written by AI systems (Peetz, 2020). Nevertheless, the requirement to manage projects will remain in the future, irrespective of the production mechanism. Similarly, managing Information Technology (IT) projects will also still be necessary, even though the human involvement in certain aspects may reduce.

The COVID-19 pandemic caused global disruption in the labor force with a rapid move toward remote work (Buchholz *et al.*, 2021). A hybrid work model is emerging in the post-pandemic economy where some employees continue to work from home and others resume work in the office with the option of flexible remote work (Microsoft, 2021). The IT sector is expected to lead the change in the post-pandemic work model. Consequently, project managers will continue to have the challenge of managing remote project teams to achieve project success.

This chapter will discuss trends in IT investment and resource development in Section 2. Next, Section 3 outlines how project management methodologies will evolve in the future. The latest trends related to project teams and stakeholders are presented in Section 4, while Section 5 provides insight into developments in time, cost, quality, and risk management. Finally, Section 6 conceptualizes project management with next-generation technologies, and the chapter's conclusions are presented in Section 7.

2. IT investment and industry landscape

Everything from Alan Turing's Universal machine to today's quantum computers was a response to the needs of the time, with a transformative influence in the years to come. These innovations have often revolutionized and catalyzed further inventions in the corresponding eras. Investment and resource development are significant in the ICT sector compared with education, construction, logistics, and many other sectors. ICT products and services can be categorized into four subsectors of hardware, software, services, and telecommunication. The IT industry commonly provides services for international businesses, national or local businesses, and self-service providers.

The IT sector can be considered as one of the most successful investments and innovation sectors globally. As an example, the IT sector moved six entrepreneurs from across the world to the top ten billionaires group in 2021. The advent of cloud computing is already contributing to significant market growth. In addition to that, robotics, artificial intelligence, extended reality (XR), blockchain, the IoT, and other novel technologies will be expected to contribute a significant portion to the global economy. The Business Research Company (2021b) has stated that the global ICT market was $8.4 trillion in 2021 and is expected to grow to $11.9 trillion in 2025. The four subsectors of ICT are explored in detail in the forthcoming subsections.

2.1. *Hardware*

Hardware is a generic term for any physical part of the computer system that can be physically touched, picked up, or moved. Hardware equipment is manufactured to facilitate one or more primary operations, including data gathering, data storing, data processing, data outputs, and data communication. However, communication devices are commonly classified under the telecommunication category.

According to The Business Research Company (2021a), the global computer hardware market was $862.93 billion in 2020 and was expected to be $944.09 billion in 2021 and its annual growth rate was 9.4% in 2021. North America leads the industry with 43% market share, and the Asia-Pacific was the second largest region with 29% market share. Africa is identified as the smallest hardware market shareholding region in the world.

The most common hardware category is personal computers (PCs) which include desktop computers, laptops, netbooks, and others. Lenovo and HP cloud acquired nearly half of the market (more than 46%) in 2020. Other top personal computer vendors were Dell, Apple, Asus, and Acer. These six most prominent personal computer vendors held 82.7% market share in 2020. Other notable vendors are IBM, Gigabyte, LG, MSI, Sony, Toshiba, and Huawei.

2.2. *Software*

Any computer system is made up of two segments, namely, hardware and software. Software is a collection of instructions that tell a computer how to work. There is an enormous amount of software, including office suite, communication tools, business management software, games, special-purpose software, design tools, simulations, web browsers, multimedia tools, databases, server software, quality assurance tools, programming environments, utility software, middleware, content management, and scientific and engineering tools.

The operating system (OS) is a special software solution that manages computer hardware and software resources and provides standard services for computer programs. The total market value was $185.23 billion in

2020. Android held more than 70% and iOS owned around 27% of the mobile OS market share in 2020. Including Windows, Linux, KaiOS, PureOS, and reset, mobile OS providers had only around 3% of the market. In 2020, the desktop operating system market was led by Microsoft Windows, which has led for the last two decades. On the other hand, Apple OS X had around 16% share, and Chrome OS and Linux held more than 2% each in 2020. Considering distributions such as Red Hat, Ubuntu, Debian, SUSE, CentOS, Raspbian OS, and others, Linux is the market leader for servers, embedded systems, and IoT-related operating systems. One interesting fact in the OS market is that almost all Top 500 supercomputers use Linux-based operating systems.

According to The Business Research Company (2021c), the global software product market was $930.9 billion in 2020 and was expected to reach $968.2 billion in 2021, and its annual growth rate was 4% in 2021. In 2020, 41% of the software product market was held by the Asia-Pacific followed by North America at 35%. On the other hand, Africa was the smallest region in the global software products market. The topmost software vendors are Microsoft, IBM, Oracle, SAP, and Salesforce. Other notable vendors are Adobe, VMWare, Autodesk, Red Hat Software, Citrix Systems, Canonical, Zoom Video Communications, and others.

2.3. Service

The ICT service sector is one of the key economic contributors in the industry due to millions of employees working worldwide. Common ICT service sectors are consultancy services, IT outsourcing, managed services, security services, and data management, among others. Software as a service (SaaS) is sometimes considered under the IT services sector. Commonly, it is considered under the software sector because it is more than a service — it is a software delivery method.

The leading global IT service sector companies are Accenture, Acumatica, Cognizant, Wipro, Deltek, Unit4, Genpact, Infosys, Concentrix, Teleperformance, ADP, and many others. Their main client sectors are banking, financial services, and insurance (BFSI), IT & Telecom, Manufacturing, Government, Retail, Healthcare, and transport sectors.

The global IT service market size was $389.9 billion in 2020 and $429.6 billion in 2021. According to the Grand View Research (2021), there will be an 11.3% annual growth rate, and in 2028 the industry size will be $911.8 billion.

2.4. *Telecommunication*

All IT industry-related communication infrastructure, as well as its operation and maintenance, is considered under the telecommunication category. During the last few years, telecommunication network usage has become significantly high, popularized by social media, high-quality content creations (e.g., HD and 4K), internet-based streaming services, on-demand video services (e.g., Netflix, Disney+, HBO Max, Paramount+, and Hulu), and many other factors. Further, the COVID-19 pandemic increased online meetings and video conferences, adding to additional network usage.

Communication media, devices, service software, and others facilitate linking of service-providing servers to clients' devices. It will include server-end networks, remote fiber lines, submarine cables, internet service provider's (ISP) links, local fiber links, 4G or 5G networks, and organizational networks (e.g., Ethernet cable, switches, routers, and Wi-Fi routers).

Asia-Pacific and North America have the largest telecommunication market with 34% and 32% portions, respectively. Africa has been identified as the smallest market capital region for telecommunications as well. The most prominent players in the market are AT&T, Verizon Communications, China Mobile, Huawei, Ericsson, Cisco, Arista, and Juniper. The Business Research Company (2021d) stated that the global telecommunication network market was $2555.4 billion in 2020 and was expected to grow up to $2713.5 billion in 2021 with a 6.2% compound annual growth. Experts predict the telecommunication market will be around $3500 billion in 2025.

3. Project management methodologies and how they are going to change in the future

Due to COVID-19, working from home, and the Gig economy, the IT industry has radically changed and is unlikely to revert to the previous normal. As a result, Project Management (PM) methodologies have become vital to successful projects, due to the fragmented nature of these new and future decentralized working arrangements. Chapter 2 (Herath and Perera, 2022) covered seven methodologies that can be used for IT projects. While there are shared characteristics, ideas, and principles, each has an individual focus.

While the scalability of PRINCE2 makes it one of the more widely used methodologies for IT projects (Abdullah *et al.*, 2021), it is often overlooked. The Project Initiation Document (PID) within PRINCE2 defines the client expectations in relation to the project. A PID in place means that all parties can refer to a set of initial targets and have a change management system in place. This means that the clear goals set down in the PID document can be communicated to the team so that they are aware of the desired key success factors.

PRINCE2 is a process-based system into which guidance documents can be incorporated. There are a number of guidance-based systems or standards issued by international bodies, such as the Project Management Institute (PMI) issuing the Project Management Book of Knowledge (PMBOK) and the Association for Project Management (APM) issuing a similar guide known as the Body of Knowledge (APMBOK). These guides allow standards to be set for measuring individual PM competencies from the PMI and APM, as well as the Individual Competence Baseline (ICB) standard from the International Project Management Association (IPMA).

Furthermore, in addition to the project management elements, quality management and social responsibility have come to the fore in recent years, with the development of the United Nations Sustainable Development Goals (UNSDG's). As a result, Chapter 2 (Herath and Perera, 2022) shows that the Project integrating sustainable management (PRiSM) approach is incorporated into PM methodologies, such as PRINCE2 and agile. It was concluded that using this framework, however scaled, while working in an increasingly fragmented industry, was vital for project success.

This has resulted in PRINCE2 being rebranded as PRINCE2 6th Edition in January 2020. While the update did not change the overall structure with its seven principles, themes, and processes, it changed the guidance and restructured the themes to assist in specific examples of 'tailoring' for new working practices and aiding project-specific elements to be covered within the process. PRINCE2 Agile® builds in the ability to speedily adapt through change management alongside the processes within the PRINCE2 system. This combines the traditional system with the Agile flexibility. Islam and Evans (2020) state there are 20 Key Success Factors within PRINCE2, and building in the Agile philosophy ensured that members of the IT team had to recognize some level of uncertainty in the planning phase and validate changes before implementation in the project. However, as pointed out in Chapter 2 (Herath and Perera, 2022), this leads to a significant increase in paperwork to document the change. However, checks and balances are added to the flexibility. This is important as Herath and Perera (2022) point out that one of the major disadvantages of the Agile philosophy is that it may result in poor planning and documentation and lead to unrealistic project goals. However, if combined with PRINCE2 Agile®, the built-in change management process minimizes the impact in relation with the ensuring that the scope remains well defined throughout. What PRINCE2 is not good at, and relies on other documentation forms for, is risk management. In other sectors, such as construction, the NEC4 links variations to risk with well-defined processes. This is currently not as well defined within IT. However, PRINCE2 is one of the generic project management methods used within IT.

Likewise, traditionally, the Critical Path Method (CPM) and Earned Value Management (EVM) were based on a work breakdown structure where elements of the work were linked in a network. The second chapter examines Critical Chain Management (CCM), where in simple terms, the resource constraints are additionally considered as part of schedule delivery. The 'where and how' of resource delivery result in a contingency buffer being developed. The PM maximises the use of this contingency by working closely to the target at the start of the buffer, thereby aiming at delivering at the most optimistic time frame. This approach is little used in IT and should be adopted more widely. On the negative side, while this is mainly for large projects, it requires a clearly defined project to work correctly.

Within IT, the Agile methodology is a commonly used method where scope and delivery can be amended in an incremental and iterative manner to allow movement to meet a changing brief. For most IT projects, getting the scope approved with the client is vital for its success. Scrum is sometimes considered alongside the Agile philosophy and is a framework that allows continuous improvement to occur. Continuous improvement is delivered through previous experience retrospection and allows analysis of team positives and negatives on current or similar projects, while incorporating the previous experience of the team. These iterations known as 'sprints' are valuable as they prioritize the elements which produce the best business value, therefore improving delivery value. The Scrum and Sprint method is only used once the brief has been defined for a particular element of the work through 'grooming' or 'backlog refinement'. Within the Agile philosophy, the Adaptive Project Framework (APF) is used to enforce an agile approach to the frequently altering project conditions. Similar to the just-in-time concept which originated in the car industry, APF allows client changes to be adopted through enhanced engagement and sign-off. However, this excess flexibility given to the client may mean that the original outcome may not be achieved as the scope can be changed on an ongoing basis. The project manager is then limited in what he/she can decide as the client is given the authority to change elements on the iron triangle — cost, quality, and time. This may mean that there is a lack of documentation due to the rapid pace of change. The PRINCE2 method of change management has a process of 'sign-off' which defines the changes made. This is largely missing in APF. However, if these issues are taken into consideration, the conclusion of Chapter 2 is that this should be the 'go-to' method in a rapidly changing environment.

PM processes such as PRINCE2 used to exist largely on paper. However, with the changing workplace over the past few years, digital and electronic systems have been put into place. There has been a move to internet- or cloud-based PM Systems. However, little case law exists in relation to electronic signatures on the contractual elements of these, and the 'gravitas' associated with handwritten signatures still causes issues in many countries, such as Japan (Maeda *et al.*, 2021). In order to overcome the situation, countries worldwide need to refresh laws to accept electronic signatures as equivalent to handwritten ones.

4. Project teams and stakeholders

IT projects exist in an ecosystem which contains internal and external stakeholders, including the project team and clients. Commonly, large-scale IT projects tend to exceed their time and budget, and do not fulfill the expected requirements (Esan-Ojuri, 2022). In Chapter 5, Heinig (2022a) emphasizes that the success of the project is influenced by the proper identification of all internal and external stakeholders at the start of the project. The process of stakeholder management involves analyzing the initial list of stakeholders and their continuous management. Unrealistic expectations of external stakeholders such as customers may stem from their lack of in-depth understanding of IT capabilities. The final product not being in line with clients' expectations would lead to a failure of the project. Therefore, stakeholder management is at the forefront of project management to mitigate project failure. Chapter 8 (Tow *et al.*, 2022) presents a case study of a successful IT project implementation with the boundaries of organizational transformation and change. The project adopted an Agile approach and the project team was designed to establish clear responsibilities for all team roles. This case study is an example of adopting a partnering approach to address shortages of in-house expertise and implementing an off-the-shelf software system. The project highlights the importance of stakeholder engagement by empowering all team members to be involved in communication and engagement to interact with stakeholders broadly. This approach increased efficiency, reduced miscommunication, and sped up project delivery. It also served to increase stakeholder effectiveness and establish stakeholders as active promoters of the project.

Changing environments cause issues in traditional software development methods such as the waterfall model. For example, there is lesser engagement of the client in later stages of a traditional project, and any new customer input provided at the testing stage may be obtained too late to be incorporated into the final product. Therefore, greater involvement of the client at the start of the project in traditional approaches, or continuous client involvement in Agile methods, is necessary to increase the level of fulfillment of the client's requirements.

The fast-changing field of IT influences the composition of project teams. Increased automation and heavy modularization of code have caused the evolution of IT project delivery methodologies, and the roles and responsibilities of project team members have involved. A project team can comprise roles including, but not limited to, project manager, business analyst, software architect, software engineer, quality assurance engineer, database administrator, and DevOps engineer.

At present, many IT projects are based on Agile methodologies such as Scrum or Kanban. Teams in Agile working environments are more flexible, self-organized, and tend to take independent decisions on workload distribution. However, Heinig (2022b) states in Chapter 6 that project managers are frequently found in Agile IT projects, although the role is not envisioned in Agile project approaches. This shows some disconnect between theory and practice. The Scrum Master or Product Owner engages in internal project management tasks, while the project manager can focus on external stakeholder communication. The duties of a business analyst (BA) are distributed among multiple members in agile teams. User stories can be written by the BA and the Scrum Master, and proposed solutions can be verified by the BA acting as a tester to improve the quality of the product. The role of the software architect has also undergone changes in the Agile environment. The architect's responsibilities may be divided among the team rather than relying on a single person. The reuse of software packages and code has also influenced the role of the architect in designing software processes and interactions (Heinig, 2022b). Continuous development product cycles have transformed the role of the quality assurance engineer from being involved at the end of the project to contributing throughout the whole project. The modern practice of CI/CD, which stands for continuous integration and continuous delivery or continuous deployment, requires a new set of skills for building, testing, and deploying software systems. Related to this is the practice of DevOps, which blends software development and IT operations. DevOps also requires a new and multidisciplinary set of skills and knowledge to deliver high-quality software in shorter cycles.

The interaction of project team members is influenced by the advanced technologies available in the world today. The increasing speeds of computer networks facilitate more efficient remote working, communication, and collaboration. Thousands of software applications exist to assist IT teams with their project management activities. Several of these applications such as Asana, Jira, Trello, and Monday.com are discussed in Chapter 14 (Weerasuriya *et al.*, 2022). Compared to teams in other industries, IT project teams had established remote working as a norm many years prior to the COVID-19 pandemic. Therefore, the shift to working from home expedited by the pandemic has had a relatively lower impact on IT project teams. For instance, Tow *et al.* (2022) state that working online increased the availability of resources due to the elimination of the need for commuting. It also drove the acceptance of remote service provision among business stakeholders. However, termination of resources and extended periods of remote working have created challenges for staff well-being. Ensuring the success of the project is paramount regardless of the physical location of the project team. The considerations for project time, cost, quality, and risk are discussed in the next section of this chapter.

5. Time, cost, quality, and risk developments

Chapter 9 (Arekete *et al.*, 2022) and Chapter 10 (Abeysinghe, 2022) deal with the iron triangle of cost, time, and quality management. As each of these is linked, each of the elements needs to be taken into consideration. However, in this book, in the chapters mentioned above, all three are mentioned as sometimes being considered *an afterthought*. However, all three issues are critical to project success as they ensure that the project requirements and constraints are met.

Looking at the financial side first, the lack of use of even a scaled version of PRINCE2 methods has been to the detriment of many IT projects. The Project Initiation Document (PID) and Gateway processes act as hurdles or check points to ensure that proper costing and budgeting occur, and adequate funding is available for all sections of the Design Cycle. It is vital that the brief is defined before the project starts. The business case is essential to ensure that underfunding does not take place. Arekete *et al.* (2022) deal with the three most common types of cost estimates, namely, a 'rough order of magnitude' (ROM) estimate, a 'budgetary estimate'

(BE), and a 'definitive estimate' (DE). These allow the costs to be defined prior to and during the project life cycle with an increasing level of accuracy.

The lack of finances within the project life cycle could result in a reduction in quality or complete failure of the project. In Chapter 9, Arekete *et al.* (2022) provide an overview of four different estimation methods based on the aforementioned categories: Top-down estimates, Bottom-up estimates, Analogous estimates, and three-point estimates. Risk needs to be built into these estimates. The Green and Orange books suggest one way in which this can be done for UK Government projects as seen in Chapter 13 (Wijegunaratne *et al.*, 2022). This is more widely used in other sectors, but IT could supplement the financial assessments with assessments of non-monetary advantages and the impact of risk to further strengthen the predictability of projects, especially large-scale ones.

Nearly all IT projects are time bound and project delivery targets are set. IT projects are notorious for large time overruns. This means effort and money spent in getting adequate planning, management, and governance in place first is money well spent. Governance through PM processes such as PRINCE2 means that issues such as cost, personnel, scheduling, work breakdown structure (WBS), budget, and milestones are in place prior to the IT system development and subsequent maintenance phase.

In relation to Quality Management, Chapter 10 (Abeysinghe, 2022) indicates that the systems are in place with international standards delivering both McCall's Quality Factors and Criteria for software design and Garvin's Factors of service quality. These factors are behind the international standards such as ISO/IEC 25010:2011 Quality Characteristics, ISO/IEC/IEEE 90003:2019, SO/IEC/IEEE 12207-2:2020, and ISO 9000:2015 Quality Management Systems. These standards have produced a move to Total Quality Management from Quality Assurance. Quality assurance deals with the product and looks at whether it is fit for purpose. Total Quality Management concentrates on the process. There is a movement from examining the quality of the final product to ensuring that the process successfully works every time. Rather than dealing with defects, it changes the process incrementally until the defects do not occur.

There is a cost to quality; however, the cost of rework can often reflect the lack of budget for quality allocated or the lack of executive support. Not only does it need to be funded but time for the processes also needs to be built into the program to carry out iterative quality management processes. Testing and verification may mean rework to improve the system in addition to going beyond the delivery milestones initially set. Therefore, lessons coming from this publication are that finance and time for quality must be built in and rationale and expectations correctly communicated. Learning the quality standards is also important to facilitate adequate understanding of when the quality standards need to be applied to ensure processes are put in place for accountability and implementation.

Risk also needs to be built into the project, especially on large IT projects where the risk management process is not as developed as other industries. In Chapter 11, Natarajan and Gopal (2022) outline the description of the risks involved and risk measurement methods through the stages of a contract. They further show how risk identification and analysis are to be used in IT projects. In the future, the balance between machine learning and human expertise will change. As risk forecasting becomes more reliable due to the number of cases available for the artificial intelligence predictor, less human interaction will be needed. This will require a change in project governance to adapt to a more system-based approach to optimizing the estimate of risk. The simplistic versions of risk management can be made redundant and overall governance of the project estimated electronically. This can then link risk management with project management. The overall governance structure which includes time, cost, quality, and risk management is therefore vital to the successful completion of an IT Project.

This is demonstrated through a series of case studies from IT in Chapter 12 (Wijegunaratne and Dassanayake, 2022), and this is followed by a comparison with construction in Chapter 13 (Wijegunaratne *et al.*, 2022). Chapter 12 emphasises that while project management procedures and processes exist, there was an absence of putting these into practice in IT. This was due to lack of skills or expertise as exemplified in many of the case study failures in Australia and the UK. The comparisons with construction show a greater adherence to processes and standards in construction.

The main issue highlighted in these chapters is that there are mandated standards in construction, especially in the public sector. However, with many large projects in IT in the private sector, many of the governance structures put into place in the public sector as a result of failures are not fully applied. The main lesson to be learned from this is that both private and public sectors need to fully use the governance for project management structures as laid out in the international standards and other procedures.

The maturity of the construction discipline is also highlighted against the often ad-hoc nature of IT projects. Chapters 12 and 13 suggest, in support of the previous chapters mentioned, that to resolve these issues that are similar to the more mature industry, the following should be put into place:

(a) The planning process and Critical Path method need to have more prominence in IT projects.
(b) Project management processes including Gateway Review Processes should be adopted to prevent a large overspend, program or scope creep.
(c) Risk management adopted as part of the contract in construction should be more formally adopted within IT.

These three issues correspond to the findings of the earlier chapters through case study examples. This shows synthesis between learning from theory and practice, and steps should be taken to adopt these elements for all IT projects to achieve success.

6. Project management with next-generation technologies

During the last 85 years, the ICT industry has continued to develop from Alan Turing's Universal machine (a concept of computing anything computable) to today's supercomputers. The primary usage of computers evolved from the military and research sectors to include the public, business, industrial, and educational sectors. This subsection discusses several next-generation technologies, their related challenges, and how these technologies will improve the present project management (PM) landscape in IT and other sectors. It extends the discussion provided in the book to the vision of the future, analyzing the impact of next-generation technologies.

6.1. *Next-generation technologies*

The IT landscape is changing rapidly. Several new technologies have emerged and achieved global acceptance during the past decade, including blockchain, cryptocurrency, smart contracts, and deep learning. Furthermore, several older concepts and innovations such as supercomputers, quantum computing, and quantum internet have advanced significantly and achieved successful implementation.

6.1.1. *Blockchain*

Blockchain is one of the cutting-edge technologies that disrupted the landscape of many sectors, including finance, supply chain, state services, entertainment, and food and agriculture (Perera *et al.*, 2020, Perera *et al.*, 2021b). Blockchain is a data storing mechanism that replicates, shares, and synchronizes data across geographical locations such as multiple sites, countries, or organizations through hundreds or thousands of computers (Walport, 2016).

The blockchain concept was developed by utilizing many existing technologies, including timestamping, hashing, public-key cryptography, and peer-to-peer communicating gossip protocols (Nanayakkara *et al.*, 2021b). The blockchain ledger is one of the novel innovations, and a sample is shown in Figure 1. The ledger includes a block index number, created timestamp, a random number called a nonce, a set of transactions or data, the hash value of the previous block, and the hash value of the block. For a given block, the blockchain ledger compares the hash value of the previous block with the hash value of the previous block stored in that block to identify any changes to the data in the previous block (Nanayakkara *et al.*, 2019a). Furthermore, the peer-to-peer network maintains copies of the ledger. These two mechanisms protect against data changes or deletions. Therefore, it is called an immutable ledger.

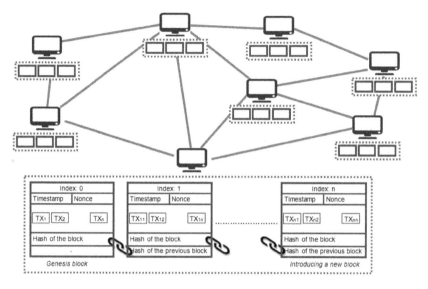

Figure 1.   The basic architecture of blockchain network.

Adapted: Nanayakkara *et al.* (2019b).

Immutable ledger-based blockchain technology provides numerous benefits, including high security, eliminating middlemen, high transparency, fraud resistance, no single point of trust, auditability, and non-physicality (Perera *et al.,* 2020). On the other hand, Nanayakkara *et al.* (2021a) identified 42 quality attributes and categorized them into various aspects. They indicated that developability and maintainability are the key challenges with blockchain technology. It will impact the time, cost, and quality attributes of IT projects. The transactional nature of project management is heavily amenable to the use of blockchain. Therefore, novel blockchain technology will change the IT project management landscape significantly in the near future.

6.1.2. *Cryptocurrency*

Cryptocurrencies can be classified as highly disruptive Fintech movements within the last decade. Blockchain experts categorized cryptocurrencies and other relative finance assets as blockchain 1.0 or first-generation

#	Name	Price	1h %	24h %	7d %	Market Cap	Volume(24h)	Circulating Supply
1	Bitcoin BTC	$30,946.92	0.07%	3.82%	4.91%	$593,514,328,657	$43,968,717,402 1,420,878 BTC	19,179,806 BTC
2	Ethereum ETH	$2,077.14	0.11%	4.49%	6.25%	$255,107,494,983	$15,516,463,413 7,469,454 ETH	122,805,927 ETH
3	Tether USDT	$1.61	0.15%	0.62%	3.25%	$110,408,878,663	$58,954,298,240 36,540,481,065 USDT	68,432,559,807 USDT
4	USD Coin USDC	$1.61	0.16%	0.64%	3.25%	$72,814,664,297	$5,158,176,871 3,197,268,158 USDC	45,009,780,493 USDC
5	BNB BNB	$437.09	0.21%	2.18%	6.76%	$70,556,989,920	$1,006,987,161 2,302,600 BNB	161,337,261 BNB
6	XRP XRP	$0.7838	0.06%	4.61%	9.53%	$39,142,741,098	$2,355,354,757 3,006,518,591 XRP	49,964,184,162 XRP
7	Binance USD BUSD	$1.61	0.15%	0.57%	3.17%	$34,910,237,611	$9,822,593,524 6,085,436,895 BUSD	21,628,100,611 BUSD
8	Cardano ADA	$0.5943	0.03%	4.59%	16.18%	$20,378,521,351	$727,749,805 1,224,261,606 ADA	34,281,893,482 ADA
9	Solana SOL	$48.25	0.33%	6.30%	12.17%	$17,285,255,355	$1,128,415,397 23,363,521 SOL	357,886,307 SOL
10	Dogecoin DOGE	$0.09499	0.12%	3.76%	8.47%	$12,619,210,067	$316,552,378 3,328,040,796 DOGE	132,670,764,300 DOGE

Figure 2. Cryptocurrency market overview.

Source: CoinMarketCap (2022).

blockchain applications (Swan, 2015). Satoshi Nakamoto introduced the first cryptocurrency concept 'Bitcoin' in 2008 through the famous white paper 'Bitcoin: A peer-to-peer electronic cash system'. In 2009, the first blockchain platform 'bitcoin' and the first blockchain application as a cryptocurrency named 'Bitcoin' were launched (Perera *et al.*, 2020). As of October 2021, the market had over 12,600 cryptos worth $2.2 trillion, as shown in Figure 2.

Commonly, cryptocurrencies represent a blockchain-based peer-to-peer transaction mechanism, which leverages a large number of a node-based peer-to-peer networks to verify and approve each transaction (Hewavitharana *et al.*, 2019). Those nodes can be a personal computer, laptop, server, mobile phone, server, or dedicated crypto mining equipment. Other than blockchain, there are a few cryptocurrencies based on Hashgraph, Directed Acyclic Graph (DAG), and Holochain technologies.

However, these technologies are less mature and it is challenging to develop distributed applications.

There are four categories under the generally known label of cryptocurrency: crypto coins, tokens, stablecoins, and non-fungible tokens (NFTs). Crypto coins are the native currency of the blockchain network. Common crypto coins include Bitcoin, Ethereum, EOSIO, Binance, Litecoin, and Cardano. Tokens do not have a native blockchain and are implemented on top of other blockchain networks. Common crypto tokens are Uniswap, Shiba Inu, Chainlink, and others. Usually, crypto tokens provide additional functionality over the currency value. Stablecoins are a specific type of cryptocurrency introduced as a solution to the high volatility of cryptocurrencies. There are four types of stablecoins: fiat-collateralized, crypto-collateralized, commodity-collateralized, and algorithmic. Tether USD, Ethereum USD, Digix Gold, and Ampleforth are examples of different stablecoins. Non-fungible tokens or NFTs are unique identifiers for any type of digital asset. NFTs are commonly used to maintain ownership of collectables, games, art, and other assets (Perera *et al.*, 2020).

Blockchain-based cryptocurrencies provide a credible way to transfer an asset without the involvement of trusted third-party intermediaries or counterparties. Compared to the traditional fiat currencies, cryptocurrencies provide many advantages, such as being irreversible, traceable, decentralized, anonymous or pseudonymous, secure, fast, and having no physical boundaries or legal boundaries. However, performance and power consumption are the main challenges with most cryptocurrencies (Nanayakkara *et al.*, 2019a). Therefore, cryptocurrencies and their applications will shift the development and usage of payment-based software applications into a different phase. It is expected that there will be greater regulation of cryptocurrencies in the future which may bring greater stability to and confidence in its usage.

6.1.3. *Smart contracts and Decentralized Applications (DApps)*

The concept of smart contracts was first introduced by Szabo (1994) as a computerized transaction protocol. A smart contract is a digital contract between two or more parties being directly written into the system and stored across the blockchain network. It removes or mitigates the human factor of decision-making (Perera *et al.*, 2021a). Most of the common contractual conditions can be accomplished by smart contracts. It can be payment terms, compliance requirements, conditions of contracts, and many others without a central authority or external enforcement. This automation process eliminates third-party involvement, minimizing malicious issues and accidental errors.

Smart contracts assist in developing, building, and running various business applications in a distributed manner (Luu *et al.*, 2016). Smart contracts based on these applications are named as DApps (Decentralized Applications). The most significant properties of smart contracts are self-containment, fraud resistance, integrity, non-physicality, and disintermediation. According to many studies, smart contracts and DApps will enhance many business applications in the near future. Further, Hewavitharana *et al.* (2019) stated that smart contracts-based applications would provide appealing solutions to project management-related challenges.

Nanayakkara *et al.* (2021a) reviewed 42 software quality attributes which indicated challenges with respect to developability and maintainability of smart contracts and DApps compared to traditional software solutions. Therefore, the future of the IT project management will be significantly impacted by smart contracts and DApps solutions.

6.1.4. *Supercomputer*

A supercomputer is a computer system with a comparatively higher performance than a general-purpose personal computer or server. However, the first supercomputer was built more than sixty years ago by UNIVAC (Universal Automatic Computer) for the Research and Development Center of the US Navy in 1960. It was called LARC, the shortened form of Livermore Atomic Research Computer. At the same time, the Los Alamos National Laboratory required a computer which had to be 100 times faster than existing computers. As a solution, IBM developed a supercomputer named IBM 7030 Stretch in 1961 (Bevilacqua *et al.*, 2018).

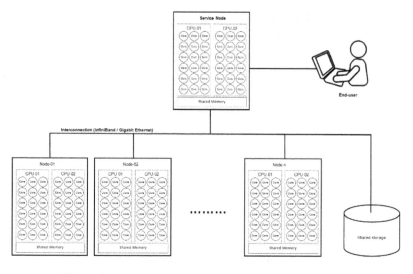

Figure 3.   Typical architecture of a modern supercomputer.

Personal computers or computers or servers have one or more CPUs and are suitable for day-to-day computation requirements. Researchers and computer scientists developed supercomputers in each era to solve computational problems that regular computers could not solve. The basic arrangement of supercomputers has a cluster of a large number of ordinary processors. Usually, these processors are located in a number of nodes. These nodes are connected through a high-speed fiber-optic communication network (Ponce *et al.*, 2019). The most widely used technology is called InfiniBand (IB), and it has very high throughput and very low latency. Some supercomputers use Gigabit Ethernet connections as well (Cano-Cano *et al.*, 2021). From time to time, the supercomputer architecture is changed based on the available technologies. Figure 3 shows the typical architecture of a modern supercomputer.

Supercomputers are expensive and consume a high level of power. Yet, due to its high computational power and the intrinsic value it brings about, there are a significant number of applications already developed for supercomputers. Typical examples are weather forecasting, nuclear power plant analysis, converting seismic data into maps, engineering simulations, chemistry and materials science-related research, military and defense mission-related work, and biological research.

6.1.5. *Deep Learning and beyond*

There are three main terms that are interlinked in the Artificial Intelligence (AI) domain, namely, Artificial Intelligence, Machine Learning (ML) and Deep Learning (DL). Artificial Intelligence is the initial concept that discusses the intelligence demonstrated by machines. Common techniques under Artificial Intelligence are Neural Network, Expert Systems, Genetic Algorithm, Fuzzy Logic, Decision Tree, Case-based reasoning, and others. The Artificial Intelligence concept was introduced around the 1950s, and most of these Artificial Intelligence techniques are being improved and used in many applications.

In the 1980s, a subset of Artificial Intelligence was introduced as Machine Learning, as shown in Figure 4. Machine Learning has the ability to learn without being explicitly programmed. In other words, it can improve automatically through experience and by the use of data. Machine Learning algorithms use training data to build their own model. Typical applications of Machine Learning are computer vision, speech recognition, medicine, email filtering, and others.

Deep Learning is a subset of Machine Learning, as shown in Figure 4 and introduced in the 2010s. The most significant improvement of Deep Learning uses a method to automatically model a hierarchy of data representation that permits software to train itself to perform tasks. Deep Learning utilizes the multilayered neural network model to perform tasks

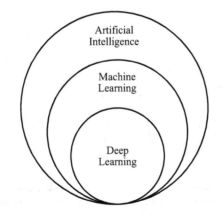

Figure 4.   Artificial Intelligence, Machine Learning, and Deep Learning.

such as computer vision and speech recognition. Learning can be done through supervised, semi-supervised, or unsupervised modes. Compared to other methods, Deep Learning has high self-learning capabilities, can work with unstructured data, is highly effective, highly scalable, supports parallel and distributed algorithms, and supports advanced analytics, minimum performance, and accuracy limitations. However, Deep Learning requires high-performance processing such as GPUs (Graphics Processing Unit) or separate high-performance computers. Due to its self-learning and modeling capabilities, the most controversial thought about Deep Learning and the future of AI is that it will spiral out of human control, similar to some science fiction movies.

6.1.6. *Quantum computing*

Presently, all computer systems, including personal computers, servers, cloud, supercomputers, and blockchain networks, are based on classical computing or binary computing. In this traditional approach, all operations are based on traditional bits. The traditional bit (commonly called bit) represents the status on or off by one or zero values. The important fact is that it can only represent one status at a time. Quantum computing uses Quantum bit or Qubit as the basic unit. It can represent both one and zero states simultaneously with a probability of it, as shown in Figure 5. This is called superposition. Compared to traditional algorithms, quantum

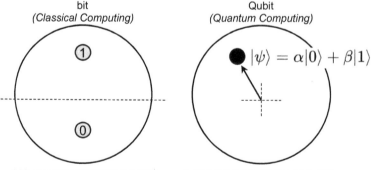

Figure 5.   A bit vs a Qubit.

algorithms could solve certain types of problems at an enormously high speed with these features.

Sarada *et al.* (2021) mentioned that the Google quantum computer is around 158 million times faster than the present fastest supercomputer (some doubt was cast by IBM on the Google quantum supremacy claim). Quantum computing and related applications are still in the research stages, and enormous-power quantum computing can only be used for specific computational operations. There are many challenges with quantum computing, including colossal cost, requiring specific environments (low temperature), needing specific software solutions, and limited applications. Another critical challenge is that classical computers have a low error rate and quantum computers have a high error rate. Researchers state that quantum computing will be a significant challenge to traditional computer security mechanisms.

6.1.7. *Quantum network*

The quantum network is an essential segment of quantum computing and quantum communication systems. The quantum network facilitates data transfer from one Qubit to another physically separated Qubit. Quantum networks operate in a similar manner to the classical computer network. However, similar to quantum computing, a quantum network is also suitable for solving specific problems. For example, communication lines are fiber-optic networks with specific quantum repeaters. One of the vital quantum mechanics in networking is quantum entanglement. This occurs when two physically separated Qubits change their physical properties such as position,

Figure 6. Quantum entanglement.

momentum, spin, and polarisation as shown in Figure 6. The changes in one Qubit are equally replicated in the corresponding physically separated Qubit.

The Quantum network is still at the research level. However, some test implementations proved that the quantum network is a possible solution with ultimate internet communication security.

6.2. Challenges of future IT project management

The next-generation information and communication technologies will change the IT project management landscape in each phase of its life cycle.

6.2.1. Planning

Planning is the foundation for the success of any project. It requires many inputs to make the proper judgment, including requirements, scope, schedule, cost, quality, resources, risk, stakeholders, and environmental factors. There are a number of challenges that will arise with the emerging new technology. The critical challenges in the planning stages are as follows:

- Expert judgment is difficult due to having less experience with new technology (e.g., blockchain, smart contracts, quantum computing, and quantum network related).
- It is difficult to estimate some cost components (e.g., smart contracts, cryptocurrency and blockchain, supercomputer, and quantum computing related).
- Hidden or unknown risks related to technology could be present (e.g., deep learning, smart contracts, and blockchain technology related).
- Environment factors such as government rules and regulations can be introduced in future (e.g., smart contracts, cryptocurrency, and blockchain technology related).
- All stakeholders and their interests are difficult to identify (e.g., cryptocurrency and blockchain technology related).
- It is hard to predict quality attributes and requirements such as performance and security (e.g., cryptocurrency, smart contracts, quantum computing, and quantum network related).

6.2.2. *Analysis*

System analysis is the process of properly identifying end user requirements within the scope. There are fewer impacts from novel technologies in the analysis phase. However, every new technology gives end users additional expectations and creates a grey area most of the time. The uncertainty and additional expectations will make it challenging in the system analysis phase.

6.2.3. *System design*

System design is the major phase of technically planning project outcomes and recording it in design documentation. The phase requires three key inputs such as user requirements, in-depth technology-related details, and experts' inputs:

- The level of uncertainty created by new technologies impacting the analysis phase generates direct consequences on the user requirements.
- Most of these technologies are still emerging, and it is difficult to find in-depth information related to these technologies. Commonly, there is no proper technical documentation, and available versions are not of the production grade (e.g., blockchain and quantum computing).
- Expertise is a crucial requirement of any IT project design, and it is hard to find experts for next-generation technologies (e.g., deep learning, blockchain, and quantum computing).

6.2.4. *Implementation*

Implementation refers to developing the software product. The implementation phase faces many challenges with respect to next-generation technologies including the following:

- Difficulty in finding developers in these technologies (e.g., blockchain).
- Virtually no senior experts in these technologies (e.g., blockchain software architect).
- These technologies have many beta and non-production versions (e.g., blockchain and deep learning).

- The availability of additional tools and libraries is limited (e.g., blockchain).
- Technical documentations are not comprehensive (e.g., blockchain and quantum computing).
- Training programs and resources are limited (e.g., quantum computing and quantum network).
- Hard to find hardware environment (e.g., supercomputer, quantum computing, and quantum network).
- Implementation of proper security is a challenge and creates greater system vulnerability (e.g., quantum computing could break traditional security methods).

6.2.5. *Testing and integration*

After developing the software system, it is necessary to test and integrate it into the production environment properly. There are some challenges raised with next-generation technology product testing:

- It is challenging to simulate the test cases (e.g., time-dependent testing in blockchain, smart contracts, or cryptocurrency applications).
- Test results depend greatly on training samples (e.g., deep learning).
- It is hard to analyze the quality of test results (e.g., cryptocurrencies, blockchain, smart contracts, supercomputer applications, and quantum computing).
- It is not recommended to integrate a new module due to security risks (e.g., cryptocurrencies, blockchain, and smart contracts applications).
- Limited automated test tools are available for these next-generation technologies.

6.2.6. *Operation and maintenance*

Operation and maintenance are the final stages of a software project. After the system is deployed in the production environment, future updates will be considered as a maintenance task. These may arise due to a bug or a new user requirement. The following are some challenges:

- According to research, blockchain, smart contracts, and cryptocurrencies are less maintainable solutions. That means it is challenging to do maintenance with these technologies. However, blockchain- and cryptocurrency-related operations are decentralized and require less effort.
- Supercomputers and quantum computers need a specific environment. Therefore, hardware and environment maintenance costs are high.
- Quantum computing can perform massive calculations, and the technology can adversely impact the security of other IT products. Therefore, even if the project is based on traditional technologies or next-generation technologies, it is necessary to consider these improvements in the IT sector.
- There is a risk related to the lack of management of deep learning and its evolutionary impact on AI solutions. The emergence of self-aware AI aided by technologies such as deep learning could pose a significant threat to humankind. Therefore, it is necessary to manage and regulate the development of these technologies with great care and control. In the absence of a regulatory framework, the impact of these technologies can be catastrophic.

Next-generation technologies will give great benefits. However, there will be some challenges in software and IT projects with regard to their capabilities. Additionally, these technologies can be a threat to traditional ICT solutions (e.g., security). Therefore, it is necessary to assess these risk factors when any project acquires these technologies.

6.3. *Next-generation technologies for project management*

Information and communication technologies significantly strengthen project management in many sectors. Next-generation technologies such as Blockchain, Cryptocurrencies, Smart contracts, Supercomputers, Artificial Intelligence (AI) and Deep Learning, Quantum computing, and Quantum networking may have a considerable positive impact on project management. Furthermore, some presently available modern ICT solutions have already been initiated to assist in project management in many

Table 1. Modern and next-generation technologies for project management.

	AR, VR, and digital twin	Drones, robotics, and 3D printing	Internet of things	Big data and data analytics	AI, Machine learning, and deep learning	Blockchain, cryptocurrency, and smart contracts	Supercomputer	Quantum computing/ networking
Integration Management	Knowledge management Information management		Information management Project monitoring	Expert judgments Information management Data analysis	Expert judgments Knowledge management Data analysis	Knowledge management Information management Project monitoring PM information system	Expert judgments Data analysis	
Scope Management	Data representation Prototypes	Data gathering Prototypes	Data gathering	Expert judgments Decomposition Data analysis	Expert judgments Data gathering Decomposition Data analysis	Data gathering	Expert judgments Prototypes Decomposition Data analysis	
Cost Management	Cost modeling		Supply chain management	Expert judgments Data analysis Performance indexes	Expert judgments Data analysis Performance indexes Estimating techniques	Supply chain management Historical information management PM information system	Expert judgments Data analysis Performance indexes Estimating techniques	

Schedule Management	Dependency management; Precedence Diagram Method	Data gathering	Resource optimization; Information management	Expert judgments; Data analysis; Decomposition; Dependency management; Resource optimization; Information management	Expert judgments; Data analysis; Decomposition; Dependency management; Resource optimization; Estimating techniques	Information management; PM information system	Expert judgments; Data analysis; Decomposition; Dependency management; Resource optimization; Rolling-wave planning; Estimating techniques	Data analysis
Quality Management	Expert judgments; Data representation	Data gathering; Product compliance management and certification		Expert judgments; Data analysis	Expert judgments; Data gathering; Data analysis; Product compliance management and certification	Expert judgments; Data gathering; Audits; Historical information management; Product compliance management and certification	Expert judgments; Data analysis	
Resource Management	Data representation; Training	PM information system		Expert judgments; Training; Data analysis	Expert judgments; Organizational theory; Training; Data analysis; Estimating techniques	PM information system	Expert judgments; Organizational theory; Data analysis; Estimating techniques	

(Continued)

Table 1. (*Continued*)

	AR, VR, and Digital Twin	Drones, Robotics, and 3D Printing	Internet of Things	Big Data and Data Analytics	AI, Machine Learning, and Deep Learning	Blockchain, Cryptocurrency, and Smart Contracts	Supercomputer	Quantum Computing/ Networking
Communications Management	Data representation			Requirement analysis	Communication model Requirement analysis	Information management	Communication model Requirement analysis	
Risk Management	Risk modeling	Data gathering		Expert judgments Data analysis Risk categorization Representation of uncertainty	Expert judgments Data gathering Data analysis Risk categorization Representation of uncertainty	Data gathering	Expert judgments Data analysis Risk categorization Representation of uncertainty	Data analysis Risk categorization Representation of uncertainty
Procurement Management	Compliance management		Data gathering Inspection Compliance management	Expert judgments Data analysis Source selection analysis	Expert judgments Data analysis Source selection analysis	Data gathering Source selection analysis Claim administration Audits Inspection Trust and transparency handling Compliance management	Expert judgments Data analysis	
Stakeholder Management	Data representation			Expert judgments Data analysis	Data analysis	Data gathering Trust and transparency handling	Expert judgments Data analysis	

sectors, especially in construction, energy, healthcare, aerospace, and defense. Modern common ICT innovations are Big data, Data analytics, Virtual reality (VR), Augmented reality (AR), Digital twin, Drones, Robots, Co-bots, and 3D Printing, among others. Table 1 reviews how these modern and next-generation technologies will impact the ten knowledge areas introduced by the Project Management Body of Knowledge.

7. Concluding summary

This book is an attempt to consolidate and develop a body of knowledge in managing Information Technology (IT) projects. This is important because, by nature, IT projects have inherent features that make them relatively unique. IT projects are heavily organizationally oriented, often required to be completed rapidly, have a short life of technology, include a multitude of stakeholders often difficult to identify, have a complex and ill-defined scope, and have numerous linkages to other operations and projects in an organization. The tools and techniques available for managing IT projects are not different from any other project, but the above features make the application significantly different. The onset of Industry 4.0 is exacerbating the differences in managing IT projects.

This body of knowledge in IT project management assimilated knowledge in four key areas. First, it reviewed Project Management Methodologies for IT Projects having a greater focus on agile approaches and compared it with traditional approaches. The second section focused on Project Management Teams and Stakeholders as an essential element of managing IT projects. It is seen as fundamental for IT projects and the role of the IT project manager is crucial. The third section is a critical review of the Time, Cost, and Quality elements of IT projects. The tools and techniques and how these are deployed are evaluated. The fourth and final section analyzes new and innovative technologies and software for improved project management. This chapter extends this knowledge base to provide a vision for the next generation of technologies that will impact and enhance all aspects of managing IT projects.

In essence, PMBOK and APMBOK brought about by PMI and APM, respectively, provide the core methodologies for managing projects with PRINCE2, offering a process-based system. PRINCE2 Agile and other agile-based techniques such as Kanban and Scrum are increasingly useful and popular for fast-paced IT projects and entail most of the features identified before.

The uniqueness of IT projects is recognized in this book in developing a body of knowledge, but at the same time the commonalities of the projects are greater. There are many lessons that can be learned from more mature project-based industry sectors such as construction. IT projects are compared and contrasted and lessons to learn are highlighted throughout this book and in particular in Chapters 12 and 13 (Wijegunaratne and Dassanayake, 2022; Wijegunaratne *et al.*, 2022).

The advancements of Industry 4.0 and the impact of the COVID-19 pandemic have driven the world toward greater remote collaboration. The world has seemingly come to recognize the potential for successful remote project collaborations, and this will no doubt be an important feature in the post-pandemic world of project management. There are many platforms that support managing projects and forming collaborations. These are significantly reviewed in Chapters 14–16 (Weerasuriya *et al.*, 2022; Nanayakkara *et al.*, 2022; D'Souza *et al.*, 2022).

This chapter finally extends the body of knowledge to analyze the impact of the plethora of new technologies that are brought forward in Industry 4.0. IT projects will be central to most organizations and the scale may vary from micro-level IT implementations in organizations to the macro level where multijurisdictional collaborative projects would be commonplace. The proliferation of network-based technologies such as blockchain will no doubt come to the mainstream where business transactions take place. These will naturally span multiple jurisdictions and IT project managers will need to find the capabilities to manage such large-scale projects. These projects will be supported by advanced quantum network infrastructure, communication technologies, and supercomputers supported by AI. The projects of the future will be supported by many technologies that assimilate data (through IoT, sensors, audio and video supported by drones, etc.) and technologies that support, analyze, and predict using data (big data analytics, deep learning, etc.). IT Project Management 4.0 will involve the implementation of these technologies while dealing with the impact on society and the labor markets. The future no doubt will involve IT projects that introduce robots and cobots that assist humans, thus dealing with man and machine simultaneously.

References

Abdullah, A. A., Abdul-Samad, Z., Abdul-Rahman, H. and Salleh, H. (2021). Project management methods, guides and standards: A critical overview, *J. Proj. Manage. Prac.,* 1, 35–51.

Abeysinghe, S. (2022). Project quality management, in Perera, S. and Eadie, R. (eds.), *Managing Information Technology Projects*, Singapore: World Scientific Publishing Co. Pte. Ltd.

Arekete, S. A., Egbelakin, T. and Ogunmakinde, O. E. (2022). Project time and cost management, in Perera, S. and Eadie, R. (eds.), *Managing Information Technology Projects*, Singapore: World Scientific Publishing Co. Pte. Ltd.

Bevilacqua, R., Pataro, G. and Aguilera, G. (2018). Principles of design, something of history and trends, in architectures and operating systems (II. History), in *2018 Congreso Argentino de Ciencias de la Informática y Desarrollos de Investigación (CACIDI)*, IEEE (pp. 1–9).

Buchholz, S., Bechtel, M. and Briggs, B. (2021). Tech Trends 2021.

Cano-Cano, J., Andújar, F. J., Escudero-Sahuquillo, J., Alfaro-Cortés, F. J. and Sánchez, J. L. (2021). A methodology to enable QoS provision on InfiniBand hardware, *J. Supercomputing*, (77)1–13.

CoinMarketCap. (2022). Cryptocurrency Prices, Charts and Market Capitalizations | CoinMarketCap [Online]. Available at: https://coinmarketcap.com//. (Accessed 16 October 2022).

D'Souza, C., Goonewardene, R. and Ginige, A. (2022). IT project management in the future, in Perera, S. and Eadie, R. (eds.), *Managing Information Technology Projects*, Singapore: World Scientific Publishing Co. Pte. Ltd.

Deloitte Insights. (2020). The fourth industrial revolution — At the intersection of readiness and responsibility.

Eerd, R. V. and Guo, J. (2020). Jobs will be Very Different in 10 Years. Here's How to Prepare [Online]. World Economic Forum. Available at: https://www.weforum.org/agenda/2020/01/future-of-work/. (Accessed 15 September 2021).

Esan-Ojuri, O. (2022). The role of project manager in IT projects, in Perera, S. and Eadie, R. (eds.), *Managing Information Technology Projects*, Singapore: World Scientific Publishing Co. Pte. Ltd.

Gopal, G. (2022). Context, priorities, constraints and trends in information technology projects, in Perera, S. and Eadie, R. (eds.), *Managing Information Technology Projects*, Singapore: World Scientific Publishing Co. Pte. Ltd.

Grand View Research. (2021). *Business Software and Services Market Size, Share & Trends Analysis Report*, San Francisco: Grand View Research, Inc.

Heinig, S. (2022a). IT project stakeholders and responsibilities in different software development methodologies, in Perera, S. and Eadie, R. (eds.), *Managing Information Technology Projects*, Singapore: World Scientific Publishing Co. Pte. Ltd.

Heinig, S. (2022b). IT project teams, in Perera, S. and Eadie, R. (eds.), *Managing Information Technology Projects*, Singapore: World Scientific Publishing Co. Pte. Ltd.

Herath, M. and Perera, P. (2022). Overview of generic project management methodologies, frameworks and standards, in Perera, S. and Eadie, R. (eds.), *Managing Information Technology Projects*, Singapore: World Scientific Publishing Co. Pte. Ltd.

Hewavitharana, T., Nanayakkara, S. and Perera, S. (2019). Blockchain as a project management platform, in *World Construction Symposium,* Colombo, Sri Lanka: Ceylon Institute of Builders.

Islam, S. and Evans, N. (2020). Key success factors of PRINCE2 project management method in software development project: KSF of PRINCE2 in SDLC, *Int. J. Eng. Mater. Manuf.,* 5, 76–84.

Luu, L., Chu, D. H., Olickel, H., Saxena, P. and Hobor, A. (2016). Making smart contracts smarter, in *ACM SIGSAC Conference on Computer and Communications Security — CCS'16.*

Maeda, Y., Sugino, S. and Litt, D. G. (2021). Current Status of Electronic Signatures Law and Presumption of Authenticity in Japan: Can a Handwritten Signature or "Hanko" Be Omitted? [Online]. Law Business Research. Available at: https://www.lexology.com/library/detail.aspx?g=d506ebba-daec-448d-8ef7-65fc185b93a0. (Accessed 15 September 2021).

Microsoft. (2021). Current Status of Electronic Signatures Law and Presumption of Authenticity in Japan: Can a Handwritten Signature or "Hanko" Be Omitted? [Online]. Microsoft. Available at: https://ms-worklab.azureedge. net/files/reports/hybridWork/pdf/2021_Microsoft_WTI_Report_March.pdf. (Accessed 10 October 2021).

Nanayakkara, S., Perera, S., Bandara, H. M. N. D., Weerasuriya, G. T. and Ayoub, J. (2019a). Blockchain technology and its potential for the construction industry, in *AUBEA Conference.* Noosa, Australia: Australasian University Building Educators Association.

Nanayakkara, S., Perera, S. and Senaratne, S. (2019b). Stakeholders' perspective on blockchain and smart contracts solutions for construction supply chains, *CIB World Building Congress.* Hong Kong.

Nanayakkara, S., Perera, S., Senaratne, S., Weerasuriya, G. T. and Bandara, H. M. N. D. (2021a). Blockchain and smart contracts: A solution for payment issues in construction supply chains, *Informatics,* 8, 36.

Nanayakkara, S., Perera, S., Weerasuriya, G. T., Gamage, P. and Amarathunga, K. (2022). Software for IT project quality management, in Perera, S. and Eadie, R. (eds.), *Managing Information Technology Projects,* Singapore: World Scientific Publishing Co. Pte. Ltd.

Nanayakkara, S., Rodrigo, M., Perera, S., Weerasuriya, G. and Hijazi, A. A. (2021b). A methodology for selection of a blockchain platform to develop an enterprise system, *J. Ind. Inf. Integr.,* 23, 1–16.

Natarajan, A. and Gopal, G. (2022). IT risk management, in Perera, S. and Eadie, R. (eds.), *Managing Information Technology Projects,* Singapore: World Scientific Publishing Co. Pte. Ltd.

Ng, P. L., Khalfan, M. and Maqsood, T. (2022). Traditional and agile software development project management methodologies, in Perera, S. and Eadie, R. (eds.), *Managing Information Technology Projects,* Singapore: World Scientific Publishing Co. Pte. Ltd.

Peetz, D. (2020). Can Government Actually Predict the Jobs of the Future? [Online]. The Conversation Media Group Ltd. Available at: https://theconversation.com/can-government-actually-predict-the-jobs-of-the-future-141275. (Accessed 16 September 2021).

Perera, S., Hijazi, A. A., Weerasuriya, G. T., Nanayakkara, S. and Rodrigo, M. N. N. (2021a). Blockchain-based trusted property transactions in the built environment: Development of an incubation-ready prototype, *Buildings,* 11, 1–23.

Perera, S., Nanayakkara, S., Rodrigo, M., Senaratne, S. and Weinand, R. (2020). Blockchain technology: Is it hype or real in the construction industry? *J. Ind. Inf. Integr.,* 17, 1–20.

Perera, S., Nanayakkara, S. and Weerasuriya, T. (2021b). Blockchain: The next stage of digital procurement in construction, *Academia Lett.,* 2. pp. 1–2.

Ponce, M., van Zon, R., Northrup, S., Gruner, D., Chen, J., Ertinaz, F., Fedoseev, A., Groer, L., Mao, F. and Mundim, B. C. (2019). Deploying a top-100 supercomputer for large parallel workloads: The Niagara Supercomputer. *Proceedings of the Practice and Experience in Advanced Research Computing on Rise of the Machines (learning).*

Sarada, W., Rajalaxmi, N. and Reddy, G. S. (2021). Quantum computing: Applications and future importance. *Special Issue of First International Conference on Management, Science and Technology.* International Research Journal on Advanced Science Hub.

Schwab, K. (2016). The Fourth Industrial Revolution: What it Means, How to Respond [Online]. World Economic Forum. Available at: https://www.

weforum.org/agenda/2016/01/the-fourth-industrial-revolution-what-it-means-and-how-to-respond/. (Accessed 15 September 2021).

Swan, M. (2015). *Blockchain: Blueprint for a New Economy*, USA: O'Reilly Media Inc.

Szabo, N. (1994). Smart Contracts [Online]. Amsterdam: University of Amsterdam. Available at: http://www.fon.hum.uva.nl/rob/Courses/InformationInSpeech/CDROM/Literature/LOTwinterschool2006/szabo.best.vwh.net/smart.contracts.html. (Accessed 18 July 2018).

The Business Research Company. (2021a). *Computer Hardware Global Market Report 2021: COVID-19 Impact and Recovery to 2030*, London: The Business Research Company.

The Business Research Company. (2021b). *Information Technology Global Market Report 2021: COVID-19 Impact and Recovery to 2030*, London: The Business Research Company.

The Business Research Company. (2021c). *Software Products Global Market Report 2021: COVID-19 Impact and Recovery to 2030*, London: The Business Research Company.

The Business Research Company. (2021d). *Telecom Global Market Report 2021*, London: The Business Research Company.

Tow, P., Kaur, M., Sharpe, I. and Almeda, M. (2022). The IT project ecosystem — an industry case study, in Perera, S. and Eadie, R. (eds.), *Managing Information Technology Projects*, Singapore: World Scientific Publishing Co. Pte. Ltd.

Walport, M. (2016). Distributed ledger technology: Beyond blockchain. *UK Government Office for Science*.

Weerasuriya, G. T., Pereira, J., Perera, S. and Nanayakkara, S. (2022). Software for IT project schedule and cost management, in Perera, S. and Eadie, R. (eds.), *Managing Information Technology Projects*, Singapore: World Scientific Publishing Co. Pte. Ltd.

Wijegunaratne, I. and Dassanayake, K. (2022). Successfully delivering large IT projects: A multi case study based analysis, in Perera, S. and Eadie, R. (eds.), *Managing Information Technology Projects*, Singapore: World Scientific Publishing Co. Pte. Ltd.

Wijegunaratne, I., Dassanayake, K. and Eadie, R. (2022). Managing IT projects: Lessons learnt from the construction sector, in Perera, S. and Eadie, R. (eds.), *Managing Information Technology Projects*, Singapore: World Scientific Publishing Co. Pte. Ltd.

Xu, M., David, J. M. and Kim, S. H. (2018). The fourth industrial revolution: Opportunities and challenges, *Int. J. Financ. Res.*, 9, 90–95.

CPSIA information can be obtained
at www.ICGtesting.com
Printed in the USA
BVHW050459060423
661665BV00002B/44